Negotiating Identities, Language and Migration in Global London

D1824541

ENCOUNTERS

Series Editors: **Ana Deumert**, *University of Cape Town, South Africa*, **Zane Goebel**, *University of Queensland, Australia* and **Anna De Fina**, *Georgetown University, USA*.

The Encounters series sets out to explore diversity in language from a theoretical and an applied perspective. So the focus is both on the linguistic encounters, inequalities and struggles that characterise post-modern societies and on the development, within sociocultural linguistics, of theoretical instruments to explain them. The series welcomes work dealing with such topics as heterogeneity, mixing, creolisation, bricolage, crossover phenomena, polylingual and polycultural practices. Another high-priority area of study is the investigation of processes through which linguistic resources are negotiated, appropriated and controlled, and the mechanisms leading to the creation and maintenance of sociocultural differences. The series welcomes ethnographically oriented work in which contexts of communication are investigated rather than assumed, as well as research that shows a clear commitment to close analysis of local meaning making processes and the semiotic organisation of texts.

All books in this series are externally peer-reviewed.

Full details of all the books in this series and of all our other publications can be found on http://www.multilingual-matters.com, or by writing to Multilingual Matters, St Nicholas House, 31–34 High Street, Bristol, BS1 2AW, UK.

ENCOUNTERS: 24

Negotiating Identities, Language and Migration in Global London

Bridging Borders, Creating Spaces

Edited by
Cangbai Wang and Terry Lamb

MULTILINGUAL MATTERS
Bristol • Jackson

DOI https://doi.org/10.21832/WANG7765

Library of Congress Cataloging in Publication Data

A catalog record for this book is available from the Library of Congress.

Names: Wang, Cangbai, editor. | Lamb, Terry (Terry E.), editor.

Title: Negotiating Identities, Language and Migration in Global London: Bridging
Borders, Creating Spaces/Edited by Cangbai Wang and Terry Lamb.

Description: Bristol; Jackson: Multilingual Matters, [2024] | Series: Encounters: 24 |
Includes bibliographical references and index. | Summary: "This book explores the
transnational practices of migrant groups in global London, illustrating the complex
relations between migrants and the city in the context of globalisation. The chapters
offer a starting point to examine migrants and the city from a comparative perspective
by bringing together case studies of diverse migrant communities"— Provided by
publisher.

Identifiers: LCCN 2023032822 (print) | LCCN 2023032823 (ebook) | ISBN
9781788927758 (paperback) | ISBN 9781788927765 (hardback) | ISBN 9781788927772
(pdf) | ISBN 9781788927789 (epub)

Subjects: LCSH: Cultural pluralism--England—London. | Multiculturalism—England—
London. | Immigrants—England—London—Social conditions. | Group identity—
England—London. | Multilingual communication—England—London.

Classification: LCC HN398.L7 N45 2024 (print) | LCC HN398.L7 (ebook) |
DDC 306.09421--dc23/eng/20230831

LC record available at https://lccn.loc.gov/2023032822

LC ebook record available at https://lccn.loc.gov/2023032823

British Library Cataloguing in Publication Data

A catalogue entry for this book is available from the British Library.

ISBN-13: 978-1-78892-776-5 (hbk)
ISBN-13: 978-1-78892-775-8 (pbk)

Multilingual Matters
UK: St Nicholas House, 31–34 High Street, Bristol, BS1 2AW, UK.
USA: Ingram, Jackson, TN, USA.

Website: https://www.multilingual-matters.com
Twitter: Multi_Ling_Mat
Facebook: https://www.facebook.com/multilingualmatters
Blog: https://www.channelviewpublications.wordpress.com

The policy of Multilingual Matters/Channel View Publications is to use papers that are
natural, renewable and recyclable products, made from wood grown in sustainable
forests. In the manufacturing process of our books, and to further support our policy,
preference is given to printers that have FSC and PEFC Chain of Custody certification.
The FSC and/or PEFC logos will appear on those books where full certification has been
granted to the printer concerned.

Typeset by Nova Techset Private Limited, Bengaluru and Chennai, India.

Contents

Figures

Contributors

Susan L.T. Ashley is Associate Professor in Creative and Cultural Industries at Northumbria University, Newcastle upon Tyne, UK. Her research looks at the democratisation of public culture, with a focus on black and global majority activism in culture and heritage. Her latest book, co-edited with Degna Stone, is *Whose Heritage? Challenging Race and Identity in Stuart Hall's Post-nation Britain* (Routledge, 2023).

Alison Barnes is a Senior Lecturer in Design and a member of the Institute of Culture and Society at Western Sydney University, Australia. Alison is the author of *Creative Representations of Place* (Routledge, 2019) and her research focuses on the differing roles graphic design can play in the mediation, construction and communication of everyday life, belonging and identity. Alison's current research centres on 'graphic heritage', which can be defined as any object through which we experience or are informed about heritage in graphic form, and a particular area of focus is food and conviviality in diverse urban contexts. The analysis of the design of such heritage is able to bring a further nuanced understanding of ways communities reflect their differing heritages in their making of place.

Lucia Brandi is Honorary Research Fellow of the University of Liverpool; she was Research Associate for Impact on 'Memory, Victims, and Representation of the Colombian Conflict' (AHRC); i.e. 'A Museum for Me' (visibilising victims) and 'ArchiCom' (safeguarding grassroots human rights archives; *JCAS* 2021 8, 23). Her background is anti-militarist campaigning and peace-building, and her interest is participatory action research on human and cultural rights; currently Xtachuwin, ELF-funded documentation in Mexico of Totonac culture by young people, following co-creation of Tsikan chu Nipxi' (Mantra Lingua, 2014), the first talking text in Totonac; and the UK public event series 'From Greenham to Nevada' by anti-nuclear activists with academics of the Universities of Kent and Liverpool, memorialising UK nuclear colonialism on the Western

Shoshone Native American Nation. Her monograph *Tutunakú: Language, Power and Youth in Central Mexico* is forthcoming (Legenda, 2023).

Umit Cetin is a Senior Lecturer at the University of Westminster, where he specialises in sociological theory, suicide, religion and transnational migration. He conducted an ethnographic study of suicide among second-generation male Alevi Kurds and since 2010 with Dr Jenkins, he has been working with the Alevi community around religion and identity issues. They are at the forefront of promoting Alevi Studies in the UK and have published a special issue of Kurdish Studies on 'Alevi Kurds: History, Politics and Identity' (Cetin, Jenkins and Aydin (eds), 2020).

Saskia Huc-Hepher is a Reader in Diasporic & Digital French Studies at the University of Westminster. Her 'ethnosemiotic' research focuses on questions of identity, belonging and homemaking among London's French population in both online and offline contexts. She has been involved in several leading digital humanities' projects and is curator of the London French Special Collection in the UK Web Archive (British Library). Huc-Hepher is on the editorial board of the Digital Modern Languages section of *Modern Languages Open* and co-convenes the associated seminar series. She has published in a wide range of journals and her first monograph, *French London: A Blended Ethnography of a Migrant City*, was published by Manchester University Press in 2021.

Celia Jenkins is a Principal Lecturer in Sociology at the University of Westminster where she specialises in sociology of education, religion and research methods. Her research focuses around pedagogic issues in teaching to promote social justice and community educational initiatives to overcome the invisibility and marginalisation of the minoritised Alevi community in the UK and Turkey.

Denise Kwan is a Senior Lecturer at Bristol UWE and is an Associate Lecturer at UAL, London. Her research explores the interdisciplinary crossovers between migration, material culture and social art practice in UK East Asian communities. Working as an artist and researcher, she is interested in the potential of building communities through creative methods and approaches. She is a co-founder of the ESEA artist collective Sunday. In 2018, Denise was awarded the Early Career's Researcher Award from the *British Journal of Chinese Studies*. She co-organised the first academic workshop exploring the subjectivities of British Chinese women at Kings College, London. She has presented her research at a number of national and international contexts including the University of Oxford, Henry Moore Institute, Wakefield and the Wuyi University at Jiangmen, China.

Terry Lamb is Professor of Languages and Interdisciplinary Pedagogy and Co-Director of HOMELandS (Hub On Migration, Exile, Languages and Spaces) at University of Westminster. He has published extensively in the areas of learner/teacher autonomy, multilingualism, and urban studies and is founder editor of the academic journal Innovation in Language Learning and Teaching. He has carried out consultancies in many countries and been involved in numerous research projects, including several at the European Centre for Modern Languages of the Council of Europe. He has been awarded the honour of Chevalier des Palmes Académiques by the French Prime Minister. He is President of FIPLV (Fédération Internationale des Professeurs de Langues Vivantes), an NGO of both UNESCO and the Council of Europe.

Fabrice Lyczba is Senior Lecturer in Cultural Studies at the University of Paris Dauphine in France. His work focuses on transnational constructions of belonging, both in his research and his advocacy work with young refugees in London.

Xiao Ma is currently a Doctoral Researcher at the University of Westminster. Taking an anti-essentialist approach, her research examines the cultural complexities of London's Chinatown through a heritage lens and challenges the homogenising portrait of Chinatown as a bounded urban space defined by fixed ethnic difference. Xiao is also the Cultural Projects Manager and Researcher of China Exchange, a UK registered charity based in London's Chinatown. In the past six years, Xiao has co-produced several heritage-making projects to create diverse and nuanced ways for people to explore the contested history of London's Chinatown.

Julie Marsh is an artist, researcher at CREAM (The Centre for Research and Education in Arts and Media) at the University of Westminster. She is a specialist in interdisciplinary practice, exploring the intersections between film, installation, performance and site-specificity. Through the exploration of real and representational space she investigates how technical machines can perform site, creating critical experiences for audiences that open debate and question social spaces. She has exhibited internationally, most recently as part of the Three British Mosques at Venice Architecture Biennale 2021. Recent exhibitions include, Siting Cinema,

Regents Street Cinema (2022), Venice Architecture Biennale (2021), Assembly at Harrow Mosque (2020), Assembly at Old Kent Road (2020), Brick Lane Mosque, London (2019/8), Black Box Symposium, CAS (Centre for Audiovisual Studies) FAMU, Prague (2019), SCREEN Moving Image Festival, Barcelona (2018). Website: https://site-integrity.com

Benedetta Morsiani is an Assistant Professor in Cultural Anthropology at Northeastern University London, Faculty of Politics and International Relations. She gained her PhD in Cultural Studies from the University of Westminster in 2019. Her research focuses on the understanding of cultural identity performance among young people belonging to diasporic communities and minority groups in Europe. Her work, particularly, investigates sociocultural issues through the study of material culture and forms of symbolic representations, and their intersection with political and economic spheres.

Ailsa Peate is Lecturer in Hispanic and Museum Studies at the University of Westminster. She completed her PhD (2017) in Mexican and Cuban detective fiction. Her previous positions include the role of Research Associate on the AHRC-funded project Memory, Victims and Representation of the Colombian Conflict at the University of Liverpool. She has also lectured in Latin American cultures and international crime narratives at Lancaster University. Her research currently focuses on photographic expressions of Mexico's narcoculture as well as visibilising the stories of women victims of sexual violence through participatory art and gender ethics in museums, galleries and monuments in Colombia and Mexico. Her co-edited volume, *Latin American Crime Scenes* (2019), is available from Peter Lang, and her monograph, *Subverting Sex, Genre and Genre in Cuban and Mexican Detective Fiction* is under contract with Liverpool University Press for publication in 2023.

Giulia Pepe is a researcher and a teacher of Italian as foreign language and as heritage language. She was awarded her PhD by the University of Westminster in 2019. Her doctoral research is published in *New Migrations, New Multilingual Practices, New Identities: The Case of Post-2008 Italian Migrants in London* (Palgrave Macmillan, 2022), in which she investigated the multilingual practices of post-2008 Italian migrants in London. She is currently working on two research projects: one aims at exploring linguistic practices and linguistic challenges of Italian migrants working in Italian hospitality in London in the post-Brexit and post-Covid era; the second one explores migratory trajectories and the use of language of onward Italian-Brazilian migrants living in London.

Cangbai Wang is a Reader and Co-Director of HOMELandS (Hub On Migration, Exile, Languages and Spaces) at the University of Westminster. His research interests fall in the areas of transnational migration, Chinese diaspora and migration-related museum and cultural heritage studies. He has published widely in peer-reviewed international journals including *Asia Pacific Viewpoint, International Journal of Heritage Studies, Asian and Pacific Migration Journal, China Information* and *Modern China*. He is the author of *Museum Representations of Chinese Diasporas: Migration Histories and the Cultural Heritage of the Homeland* (Routledge, 2021) and the co-editor of the book series Routledge Research on Museum and Heritage in Asia. He is currently leading an AHRC-funded research project that is aimed at developing a global network of diasporic Chinese museums.

Acknowledgements

This book is based on a symposium entitled 'Bridging Borders, Creating Spaces: Negotiating Multicultural Identities and Belongings among Migrant Communities in Global London', which was held at the University of Westminster on 28 June 2018. It was hosted by HOMELandS (Hub On Migration, Exile, Languages and Spaces), an interdisciplinary research centre at the University of Westminster that is aimed at exploring the nexus of mobilities, language and space in a global context. As Co-Directors of HOMELandS, we would like to thank all the speakers for their stimulating papers and all the participants for their contribution to the productive discussions. Most chapters in this book are developed from the papers originally presented to the 2018 symposium. We later invited several authors who had not attended the symposium to contribute chapters and are delighted that they agreed to share their research, which, we believe, makes valuable contributions to the interdisciplinary explorations of diverse migrant groups in global London found in this book.

Shortly after we signed the book contract, the Covid-19 pandemic broke out. This caused unexpected interruptions to fieldwork and other research activities, which were essential for the development of several individual chapters, and as a result, the progress of this collective publication was delayed. We would like to express our thanks to Anna Roderick, Editorial Director of Multilingual Matters and the editors of the Encounters series for their understanding and patience, which allowed us to complete our project.

We are very grateful for the support we received from the School of Humanities in the College of Liberal Arts and Sciences at the University of Westminster. We wish to express our special thanks to Andrew Linn for his support of interdisciplinary research into migration, languages and spaces at the University, for his inspirational opening speech at the symposium, and finally for the foreword he wrote to this volume. Finally, we wish to thank sincerely all the contributors for their enthusiasm for the research topic and their sustained commitment to the project during challenging times, without which, this volume would not have been possible.

Foreword

Negotiating Identities, Language and Migration in Global London: Bridging Borders, Creating Spaces is a powerful collection of studies. It is powerful firstly on account of the number of people whose lives and realities are its concern. Out of a city of 9.6 million people, one in three, as the editors note in their introduction, were born abroad. This has resulted in a truly magnificent polyphony of languages being used across the city, but one of the objectives of this book is to demonstrate that this does not mean 300 languages used in isolation from each other but as the soundscape of 'the highly complex and fluid cultural and linguistic landscape of London as a global city'. This book is powerful too in its bold attempt to approach migration and its linguistic and cultural manifestations differently, focusing on *spaces* where new expressions are forged and new cultural meaning is articulated through a variety of mediums, not just linguistic. Its power lies thirdly in seeking to do what sociolinguistic research often advocates but rarely achieves and engages across disciplines so that insights into the expression of cultural identities are not the preserve of a narrow coterie of sociolinguists. In the space which the book constitutes we encounter sociolinguistics in counterpoint with sociology, anthropology, visual arts and heritage & museum studies. Finally, this volume has power because migration is and always has been fundamental to our lives, what we hope for, how we organise and define ourselves.

'Since the earliest times', as the United Nations characterise migration, 'humanity has been on the move' such that, according to the Global Migration Data Portal based on the most recent figures (2023), there are 281 million people in the world who were born abroad. Humans (like other species) have always looked beyond their immediate spaces for a better life for themselves, their families and their communities. That is one of the reasons why political rhetoric about 'ending migration' or 'closing borders' is so toxic: it flies in the face of the most natural behaviour. One of the welcome aspects of *Negotiating Identities, Language and Migration in Global London* is that, while it is rigorous in its methods and sober in its conclusions, it is absolutely a *celebration* of migration. We get to understand how groups from all over the world, from Africa, Asia, Europe and South America, have enriched and continue to enrich and challenge global London through language, food, art, worship, memorialisation and other ways too in what the editors refer to as 'the nexus of migrants, cities and language'. *Negotiating Identities, Language and Migration in Global London* is not just a book for scholars; it is also an exhibition of the colours and flavours of an amazing metropolis.

It is also a glimpse into the future. Global London is being redefined by its immigrant populations who are active across all fronts, translanguaging, performing, art-making, memory-making, negotiating their identities. What we take away perhaps more than anything else is a sense of the dynamism of migrant groups across the capital, changing the complexion of the city. And this will continue as London looks set to become a *megacity* (with a population of over 10 million) within the next 20 years (London Datastore). And, despite the current UK government's expressed desire to bring net migration down, the Office for National Statistics *National Population Projections* anticipate net migration of 2.2 million (based on a projection of 5.6 million immigrants) over the next decade, suggesting a bright future for a city so enriched by its migration past.

In this collection the editors have brought together a team of contributors from the University of Westminster and six further universities from London and beyond, ensuring a palette of perspectives. The array of perspectives doesn't lead to a 'school concert' parade of isolated parts, however, as the contributions are neatly organised into three sections which, respectively, deal with *metrolingual space, performative space* and *heritigisation* space. Migration research is understandably often the preserve of those who themselves are impacted by that migration and typically comprises hermetically sealed 'case studies'. This volume also comprises case studies, but they should be read in the context of the introduction with its ambition to move away from emphasising the exceptional and to draw out common ways in which migrant groups engage with the space and spaces which London provides.

The University of Westminster, which has led this project, is a global institution, embodying the city which is its home, with students from nearly 170 different countries. Our vision is to be 'a place where diversity is celebrated and where everyone is welcome', but we are a *university* community, and that means that diversity and belonging are not just facts of life but properly become objects of scrutiny and analysis, and we seek to learn from our insights and help others be better in response to those insights. For this reason, I'm delighted that the Hub On Migration, Exile, Languages and Spaces (HOMELandS) continues to bring experts together in innovative ways to help us understand and empower our communities, not least those in our own city. The chapters which follow offer so many potential lines of research, and I'm sure that HOMELandS, under the leadership of Cangbai Wang and Terry Lamb, will be responding to them in exciting ways in the years to come.

Andrew Linn
Pro Vice-Chancellor and Professor of Language, History and Society
University of Westminster

1 Introduction: Bridging the Gap between Migration, Cities and Language: An Interdisciplinary Perspective

Cangbai Wang and Terry Lamb

On 22 November 2022, an art exhibition entitled 'Internal Landscapes' was opened in the Horniman Museum and Gardens in Lewisham, Southeast London. The exhibition was curated by the Syrian-born artist Dima Karout based on her year-long encounters with the residents of Lewisham and conversations with the Lewisham Council and local organisations. The prints, sketches and stories on display, made collectively by the artist and people who participated in the art workshops she organised, visualise personal narratives and intimate reflections of local residents' everyday interactions with Lewisham's natural landscape, including Deptford Wharf and Telegraph Hill as well as meaningful places such as the market, allotments and workplaces. The exhibition tells a powerful story of how the place of Lewisham has been shaped by people from diverse cultural, linguistic and ethnic backgrounds and how the arrivals of migrants, old and new, have contributed to the social fabric of this place.

The exhibition is part of 'We Are Lewisham', a cultural programme supported by the Mayor's London Borough of Culture 2022, that celebrates Lewisham's history and diversity and highlights the power of culture to promote diversity and create social changes. One topic that emerged in the informal conversation following the opening ceremony was the number of languages spoken locally every day. One participant who grew up in Lewisham believed that, based on her own experiences, there were probably 100 different languages spoken by people in the Borough, and others came up with some similar figures. People also talked about how the population profile of Lewisham had become increasingly diversified over the past two decades. While the Afro-Caribbean Black communities who first arrived in Britain in the 1950s made up the largest proportion of the local population in the following decades, the Borough has now become the home to Turkish, Italian, Polish, Romanian and many other migrant populations.

The exhibition, and the Borough of Lewisham to which the exhibition was dedicated, epitomises the highly complex and fluid cultural and linguistic landscape of London as a global city. Indeed, London has been a 'honey pot' (Butler, 2003: 2470), a 'magnet' (Kershen, 2015: 11) and a 'hoover' city (Sepulveda *et al.*, 2011: 475) over centuries, pulling in people both nationally and internationally and from a wide range of socio-economic and cultural backgrounds. It was the 'the promised land' (Kershen, 2007) for early entrepreneurs, bankers and merchants from Europe who recognised the potential of an expanding mercantile metropolis, as well as for those, notably the Huguenots, who were denied religious freedom in their countries and came to find sanctuary in the city. 'By the mid-17th century, the capital was a vibrant, cosmopolitan, and increasingly tolerant, city … In the centuries that followed, metaphorically and literally, successive waves of immigrants made their imprint on the London landscape and on the social and political discourse of the nation' (Kershen, 2015: 11–12). London has continued to be a migration hub into the 20th and the 21st centuries. The 1948 British Nationality Act opened the door for an influx of New Commonwealth immigrants from the Caribbean, India, Pakistan, Bangladesh, Hong Kong and many other colonies and former colonies. Members of the post-war immigrant generation as well as their children and grandchildren form a major settled component of London's population (Gidley, 2011: 2). London has also been the country's prime destination for new and increasingly diverse waves of migrants from the 1980s onwards. These include skilled workers, economic migrants as well as refugees coming from places such as Russia, China and Latin America, with no historic connection to the British empire, and migrants from new EU member states who have moved to the UK in large numbers since 2004.[1]

The migration demography of Britain, and of London in particular, has become unprecedentedly dynamic and diverse in the 21st century. According to the Office of National Statistics (ONS), the size of the foreign-born population in England and Wales increased from 7.5 million (13.4%) in 2011 to 10 million (16.8%) in 2021. In 2021, India (920,000), Poland (743,000) and Pakistan (624,000) were the top three countries of birth for the foreign-born in England and Wales, followed by Romania

(538,840), Ireland (324,670), Italy (276,669), Bangladesh (273,042), Nigeria (270,768), Germany (263,368) and South Africa (217,180).[2] Among all regions of the UK, London has the largest number of migrants. Approximately one in three London residents was born abroad. In 2011, 37% of the 'usual resident' population of London (just over 3 million) had been born outside of the UK (Krausova & Vargas-Silva, 2013: 2). Accompanying the growth in the range of countries of origin is an increase in diversity in religious practice and languages spoken. For instance, it has been estimated that about 300 languages are spoken in London (Baker & Mohieldeen, 2000: 475). According to data from 2011, 22% of London's residents above the age of three did not speak English as their main language, and the share is even higher for Inner London, which has the highest percentage of foreign-born residents in the city.[3] The number of plurilingual children in particular is constantly increasing; in 2018, for example, 54.4% of pupils aged 10–11 years in Inner London primary schools were classified as having English as an Additional Language (EAL) (Demie, 2018). The complex composition of London's migration landscape in early 21st-century London, one that is more complex in nature than the capital has previously known, is effectively summarised in the 2005 slogan 'the world in one city' (GLA, 2005), used to win the bid to host the 2012 Olympics.

Why Cities, Why London?

Publications on migration have conventionally focused on a single country or a single region (Anthias, 2022; Çağlar, 2005; Fryer, 1984; Yalçin-Heckmann, 1997). Recently, more and more people have recognised the salience of cities as sites of migration research, calling for 'bringing the city back in' (Bretell, 2003) as the context of the research of transnational migration (Buhr, 2018; Çağlar, 2001; Knowles, 2011; Soysal, 2001; Wang, 2012, 2013; White, 2002; Yeoh & Huang, 2000; among others). The pivotal role of cities in migration research is aptly summarised by geographers Brickell and Datta (2011: 16–17) who argued:

> Situated within the intersections between place and displacement, location and mobility, settlement and return, cities are critical to the construction of migrant landscapes and the ways in which they reflect and influence migratory movements, politics, identities, and narratives ... Under such circumstances, cities, urban spaces, and neighbourhoods have become the sites of powerful and exclusionary politics around multiculturalism, inclusion, belonging, and the construction of history.

Cities of all scales are important locales where migrants settle, encounter those who are different from themselves, and make a living and, for this reason, all cities, big or small, deserve scholarly attention. Global cities are relatively well positioned vis-à-vis other cities in the hierarchies of political power and capital flows (Sassen, 1991, 1992). Owing to this global scale positioning and institutional capacity, global cities deserve particular attention. Moreover, at a time when conventional concepts such as society and nation have become problematic due to accelerated and overlapping forms of movement across national and geographical borders, 'global cities' become an ideal place to study the 'sociology of mobility' (Urry, 2000), built around categories of networks, mobility and fluidity instead of those of nation-states. The crucial role of a global city such as London thus 'provides fertile ground for examining a spectrum of "close" and "strange" encounters between people, the accompanying expressions of emotion and the circulation of embodied affect as they unfold in a culturally diverse world' (Yeoh, 2015: 545). In relation to linguistic diversity, Lamb (2015: 3) has referred to the 'palimpsestic relationships between these diversely plurilingual people' in linguistically superdiverse urban spaces.

Global cities tend to share more similarities with each other in terms of socioeconomic structures, functions and institutional capabilities than with other cities in the same country where they are geographically located (Friedmann, 1986, 1995; King et al., 2011; Knox & Taylor, 1995; Sassen, 1991, 2000). Despite, however, the undeniable resemblance of London to other global cities, such as Paris, New York and Sydney, in terms of scalar positioning and global command capacity, it is embedded in its own historical path and shaped by its specific relationship to global forces. Indeed, London is a distinctive urban space 'where super-diversity is at its most marked' (Vertovec, 2007: 1042) and a migration laboratory for academic research. In this book, we therefore do not treat London as an abstract city. Instead, we examine the particularity of how transnational migrants have contributed to the cultural, material and psychological fabric of London in specific political and social contexts and power relations. In addition, although we take global London as the main site of the fieldwork, we pay constant attention to the 'links between global forces and local life-worlds' (Schuerkens, 2004) in terms of how migrant lives are connected to the host and home countries simultaneously and how they make a living in the intersection of global forces and local social structures.

The analytical focus of our research presented in this book is neither on the migration to cities or the life of migrants in cities. Instead, we examine consistently 'the relationship of migrants *and* (emphasis in original) cities' (Çağlar & Glick Schiller, 2011: 2). We approach 'migrants as residents of cities and actors within them, understanding that to be a resident of a city is to live within, contribute to, and contest globe spanning processes that shape urban economy, politics, and culture' (Çağlar & Glick Schiller, 2011: 19). Here, migrants are seen as urban dwellers who 'dwell in and through being both at home and away, through the dialectic of roots and routes' (Urry, 2000: 132–133), embodying a new kind of dwelling that is inherently linked to diverse forms of mobility in time and space, and, at the same time, interacting with the city as both a context and a structure of opportunities. This perspective enables us, on the one hand, to detect how migrants as embodied subjects have contested social inequality in language and society under conditions of contemporary globalisation (Blommaert, 2010) and, on the other hand, to unveil how migrants have responded to differential incorporation opportunities through varying forms and trajectories of localisation, contributing to the configuration of the city in the process of emplacement.

How Do We Study Migrants and Cities?

London has long been one of the global 'contact zones' (Pratt, 1991) of multiple flows of people, cultures and ideas from around the world. While there are numerous studies of individual migrant groups in London and the UK (e.g. Baumann, 1996; Butler, 2003; Conradson & Latham, 2005; Huc-Hepher, 2021; Knowles, 2013; Nagel, 2002; Ryan, 2018; Wessendorf, 2013; Wilkins, 2019), surprisingly, with notable exceptions (Kershen, 2007, 2015), there have been very few published research publications investigating the nexus between mobility and globality in London from a comparative perspective. As rightly argued by Smith (2017: 172), a limitation of existing knowledge about global cities and transnational networks is 'the dearth of comparative urban studies'. He calls for research into three particularly useful modes of comparison: first, to compare the practices of the same migrant group in different cities; second, to compare and contrast transnational practices undertaken by different migrant groups in the same city; third, to compare the consequences of neoliberal economic policies in different cities where they have been localised (Smith, 2017: 172–173).

This edited volume attempts to address the second mode of comparison by bringing together cutting-edge research on a wide range of London-based migrant communities. Thus, the goal of this book is not merely to document and analyse the social and cultural activities of distinct migrant groups in London, although this is what our research will also do, but in addition, and more importantly, to identify the common issues, challenges, and opportunities that all migrants experience, regardless of differences in ethnic and cultural and linguistic affiliations. We aim to bridge borders, defined here not as physical and legal lines on the map separating nation-states, but instead the more invisible social and cultural boundaries that exist between the representations of different ethnic groups and separate the privileged and the marginalised in global cities structurally. We pay particular attention to the process of bordering 'seen as a form of discursive agency' (Savski, 2023: 1), a process in which migrants endeavour to reconfigure existing discursive categories and power relations in the development of 'together-in-difference' (Ang, 2003: 141), transcending the old Eurocentric homogeneity based on rampant division and fragmentation of migrants based on particularist identities. As shown in the empirical case studies presented in the book, bordering involves social action in which migrants engage with the social and political construction of place, home and communities in mobility and find ways to cross, manage and renegotiate hegemonic language ideology and structural inequality within the global city.

The authors of this edited volume come from diverse academic backgrounds, ranging from sociolinguistics, sociology, anthropology, to visual arts, and heritage and museum studies. The interdisciplinarity is not seen as an obstacle to establishing coherence in our research. Instead, it creates an opportunity for us to 'talk across disciplines' (Brettell & Hollifield, 2007) to engage with key issues crisscrossing migration, cities and language. In the book, we do not see cities simply as geographical environments or abstract physical locations. Neither do we see urban space as the cohesive and glowing cosmopolitan space sometimes celebrated in media and policy documents. Rather, we define cities as contested space fraught with internal tensions between people from different ethnic and linguistic backgrounds and from different sections of the social hierarchy, often characterised by social inequality, racialisation and exclusion (Blommaert, 2010). We concur with Knowles (2004: 80) that urban space 'interacts with people and their activities as an ongoing set of possibilities in which race is fabricated ... (and) space's agency – its meaning, effectiveness and potential uses – is released by the activities of people'. The definition of urban space as a geography of possibilities instead of a static physical environment creates room for conducting nonconventional and interdisciplinary research relating to migrants, cities and language.

In line with this way of thinking, we adopt a broad and flexible approach to defining the notion 'migrants'. For us, 'migrants' refer to people with a migration background or/and associated in different ways with transnational mobilities, including not only the first-generation immigrants to the UK but also their children and families born in Britain, as well as people who are not necessarily physically based in London but related in one way or another to the London migrant landscape. The word 'community' (or its plural form as preferred by some contributors) is used in this book as a descriptive term rather than an analytical one, without implying a bounded conception of any migrant groups. Instead, we keep analytically sensitive to the heterogeneous nature of the social relations and cultural identities both within a migrant group and between different migrant groups and pay constant attention to how migrants negotiate identities and make and remake place across ethnic, cultural, linguistic, social and political boundaries. We also avoid describing migrant identity in terms of binary dichotomies, such as 'minority vs majority', 'immigrants vs local' and 'outsider vs insider', which, 'often come with the logic that there is an antagonistic relationship between the two: the former is (expected to be) victimised by the latter' (Zhu, 2017: 120). Instead, we pay attention to the agentive role of migrants in dealing with different sets of challenges and opportunities to make a living and construct identities in the intersection between local and global contexts. Before putting forward the analytical framework that we use to structure the book, we would like first to introduce the general methodological stance we share in curating this research project.

Beyond Ethnic, Nationalistic and Residential Lenses: The Methodological Stance

Our research into migrants and cities critically addresses three pitfalls in social sciences when applied to migration research. The first pitfall is what is called 'methodological ethnicism' (King, 2001) or problematic 'ethnicity-centred epistemology' (Dahinden, 2016). Earlier literature reporting migration research has been dominated by a triumphal discourse of multiculturalism that many Western countries have adopted since the 1970s as a new social and cultural policy (Bissoondath, 1994; Kymlicka, 2012). While 'multiculturalism' has contributed to an increased recognition and accommodation of non-White immigrant cultures and identities, it has also given rise to an essentialist view of migrant populations that are assumed to exist as bounded groups with a shared identity and associated with a fixed mode of incorporation. Since the late 1990s, there have been growing calls for attention to the constructed nature of ethnic groups, the complex power differentials within ethnic groups, the intense interactions across ethnic boundaries, as well as the diverse relationships of migrants to their places of settlement (Alexander, 2002; Baumann, 1996; Brettell, 2003; Glick Schiller *et al.*, 2006; Vertovec, 1996). In the field of applied linguistics, scholars (Otsuji & Pennycook, 2010; Pennycook & Otsuji, 2015) have also started to question the usefulness of terms such as multiculturalism and multilingualism. Even when these terms are employed to celebrate diversity and provide new possibilities for society and people, the claims are underpinned by European language ideologies, which tend to portray people and their associated practices as composed of multiple discrete languages and cultural practices. In addition, they ignore the fact that difference and diversities are often the result of ongoing interactions between fixed and fluid cultural identities rather than pluralisation of pre-given and essentialist single linguistic and cultural categories.

In the same vein, scholars (notably Alexander *et al.*, 2007; Alleyne, 2002) have problematised the unreflective use of the concept of 'ethnic community' as a self-evident and distinct collectivity of like persons and as the frame through which we understand differences. In the words of Alleyne (2002: 608), the concept of ethnic community presents 'an episte-mological obstacle for the sociologist in the sense of obscuring the social construction which goes into building and sustaining human collectivi-ties, because it may be allowed too easily to become an explanation rather than something to be explained'. It tends to reify an essentialist identifica-tion of a bounded group of people and their particular mode of settle-ment, overlooking the actual degree of heterogeneity in migrants' identities, practices and social ties, which are constructed through their interactions with other migrant groups and with the local society. As sug-gested by Alleyne (2002: 622), one way of rescuing such research from the trap of easy empiricism and unreflective naturalism is to raise the concep-tualisation of community to 'a more abstract level, where we could visu-alise it as a network of agents with ever-changing projects rather than as a tapestry of people with shared roots'.

Research in the first decade of the 21st century witnessed a transition from multicultural identity politics to 'super-diversity' (Meissner & Vertovec, 2015; Vertovec, 2007). This concept does not simply mean the increasing presence of 'more ethnic groups', but to recognise the multi-layered nature of social configurations by calling attention to the interplay of multi-variables, including not only nationality, country of origin and ethnicity, but also variables such as migration channel/legal status and age as well as gender. It suggests a turn from focusing on making group-based claims to focusing on relations (Olwig, 2013: 471) in terms of how diverse social configurations are tied into and shaped by specific constellations of power, politics and policy in which migrants are embedded, and how 'within the same geographical units both nationalistic views and transnational lives may co-exist with different outlooks on residence and belonging' (Grzymala-Kazlowska & Phillimore, 2018: 184). While 'superdiversity' offers the potential to fill the current post-multicultural theoretical void (Fomina, 2010), it has also been criticised by others for a continuing Eurocentric view of demographic diversity underpinning this concept – and thus the social, cultural and linguistic borders between different groups of population in a society governed by the privileged white elites (e.g. Back, 2015; Glick Schiller & Çağlar, 2011; Ndhlovu, 2016).

In global cities such as London, where migrants construct their identities on the basis of everyday urban encounters, what is on the rise, as argued by Maher (2005), is 'metroethnicity'. It refers to 'a reconstruction of ethnicity: a hybridised "street" ethnicity deployed by a cross-section of people with ethnic or mainstream backgrounds who are oriented towards cultural hybridity, cultural/ethnic tolerance and a multicultural lifestyle in friendships, music, the arts, eating and dress' (Maher, 2005: 83). The rise of 'metroethnicity' has been accompanied by the emergence since the early 1980s of Multicultural London English (MLE) in inner London, regarded as an ethnically neutral variable repertoire produced by increasing language contacts between a variety of immigrants from different developing countries (Cheshire et al., 2011). In relation to linguistic diversity, Lamb (2015: 153) has similarly explored the ways in which 'post-multilingual cities' are being conceptualised:

> The presence of 'stylistic agents, tailoring linguistic styles in ongoing and lifelong projects of self-construction and differentiation' and a new 'multilingualism of entanglement' have shifted the discussion towards late modernist explorations of hybridity; constructs such as translanguaging, polylanguaging, transidiomatic practices and metrolingualism, occurring in translocal rather than merely transnational urban spaces. Such research brings rich insights into the ways in which language practices are unravelling in urban contexts.

Each chapter of this book takes the experience of one migrant group in London as the entry point and the empirical foundation for exploring migrants' relationships with the city. Their analysis, however, goes beyond the narrow 'ethnic lens' to explore how migrants make place and negotiate identities in the workplace, schools, streets, neighbourhood, and cultural and religious organisations by interacting with both people from the same ethnic origin and migrants who bear different ethnicities, as well as the ways in which their identity construction is shaped by broader political and social forces nationally and internationally. For instance, Pepe documents and analyses how trans-cultural and trans-linguistic practices in the Italian kitchen have given meanings to the workplace and to migrant lives (Chapter 2). Huc-Hepher and Lyczba discuss how the French university students in London construct and negotiate their emergent identity as young adults through interactions with both local and international students on campus, in student accommodation and associational spaces (Chapter 3). Similarly, Wang unveils how the Chinese New Year Celebration in London has become an annual festival on the city's calendar not only for the ethnic Chinese but also the local and international audiences from diverse ethnic and cultural backgrounds (Chapter 7). Barnes's research shows how the juxtaposition and interactions of the social and economic activities of diverse migrant communities living in Hackney have deeply transformed its streetscapes and generated new life (Chapter 10).

The second pitfall is 'methodological nationalism' in social sciences (Beck, 2007; Smith, 1983; Wimmer & Glick Schiller, 2002), which tends to approach the study of social relations as if they were contained within the borders of individual nation-states. This principle of the 'container society' (Faist, 2000) disregards the fact that societies, both in history and in the present, are embedded in social, economic and political processes and institutions that extend across state borders. Smith (2017: 157) argued that it is more fruitful to study urban space from a transnational perspective, in that 'the "global city" is not an object consisting of key properties that can be identified and measured outside the process of meaning making (but instead) a historical construct forged by an endless interplay of distinctly situated networks, social practices, and power relations'. In this book, we view cities, and London in particular, neither as geographical containers in which migrants live nor as bounded localities where their identities are formed. Instead, cities are seen as open and dynamic spaces of incessant encounters between different people, cultures, languages and ideas in everyday life and in a transnational context.

Instead of seeing migrants in the context of the host country alone or in a territorially bounded urban environment, we ask how the local is made global and the global made local and we explore complex ways in which migrants negotiate identities in the home and host countries in a transnational social field characterised by spatial and temporal 'simultaneity' (Levitt & Glick Schiller, 2004: 1003). For example, Cetin and Jenkins explore the formation of a new ethno-religious identity by the Alevi Kurds in the nexus of local identity politics in Britain and the nationalist movement in Turkey, showing that the construct of the nation-state has continued to impact on the field of transnational migration (Chapter

4). Wang conceptualises the Chinese New Year Celebration in London as a 'double heritagisation process', which is tied into the heritage discourse of both the home and host countries of migrants simultaneously (Chapter 7). Ashley discusses how the heritage practice of the Indian communities in London have been embedded in the colonial past of the British Empire (Chapter 9); Peate and Brandi show us how the museum practices of Latino women in London are shaped by the political movement in Colombia and are shaping gender politics back home (Chapter 12).

The third pitfall in social sciences research into migrant urban practice is the 'residential lens' (Franz, 2018: 310) that tends to overfocus on migrant activities taking place at the meso-level and within highly bounded spatial units such as the neighbourhood. In our research, we see urban space as practiced territory (Crouch, 2001; Hall, 2012; Knowles, 2011) rather than confined physical components, which means that we investigate the multiple and overlapping spatial practices of migrants happening across spaces and places in the city of London and beyond. Hall (2015) made a useful distinction between three interconnected dimensions of urban space. The first one is the city as a 'symbolic space', as perceived in the macro-perspectives of the city; the second one is the city as a 'collective space', as seen in the street (or neighbourhood) perspectives of the city; and the third one is the city as an 'intimate space', as understood from the interior (shop or home) perspectives of the city. Important differences in the visibility, regulation, and practices of migrants in these different spaces of the city are identified. Together, they weave complex and fluid repertoires of migration and city-making. In the same vein, our research examines how migrant urban practices unfold in multi-sited and multi-scalar geographies of space. These include intimate spaces in the form of student accommodation (Chapter 3), the classroom (Chapter 4) and the activity room where the British Chinese women meet and socialise with each other (Chapter 6). They also occur in the collective space of the theatre where the Congolese communities celebrated Black beauty (Chapter 5), the Hackney high street (Chapter 10), and the mosques in Brick Lane and other London locations (Chapter 8). We also see the symbolic space of Trafalgar Square where a traditional festival of migrant communities is celebrated at London's annual public event (Chapter 7). The Memorial of War situated next to London's Wellington Arch is another example of how the complicated and intertwined history of migrant communities and the British Empire has been represented and negotiated in this symbolic city space (Chapter 9). Our research explores how diversity comes from migrants' encounters with various kinds of spaces and through embodied emplacement, rather than from their ethnic origins alone. As Suresh Canagarajah (2017: 22) aptly argues, 'homes and spaces are constructed from within mobility, contact, and diversity – not outside'. At the same time, our research has shown how migrant spatial activities are both embedded in and producing connections with other cities in the UK and places in other parts of the world, as well as how, through these processes, migrants and cities shape each other through everyday encounters.

'Language Spaces': An Analytical Framework

Based on critical engagement with major debates in migration research and in social sciences as discussed above, we develop an analytical frame-work that brings together interdisciplinary research related to migrants and cities through the prism of language. Mobility has significantly changed our understanding of language in the same way as our under-standing and use of language has changed mobility. From the perspective of mobility, the conventional understanding of language as a territori-alised, static and autonomous system of meaning-making belonging to one place or one community has become problematic. As Canagarajah (2017: 3) argued, 'it is not that the forms and functions of language being theorised are new. Mobility has simply made visible new communicative practices'. Scholars have started to see language as unbounded, fluid, unfettered from an imposed structure and embedded in social and mate-rial structures (e.g. Blommaert, 2010, 2013; Canagarajah, 2013; Lamb, 2015, 2020; Lamb & Vodicka, 2018; Li, 2011; Li & Zhu, 2013; Pennycook, 2010, 2012). This requires us to go beyond the structuralist understanding of labelled language as the only way of communicating to explore how people resort creatively to diverse resources available in the 'spatial reper-toires' (Pennycook & Otsuji, 2015) to establish meanings and negotiate relationships. In addition, it also requires 'treating meaning as multimodal and multisensory, by including affective, imaginative, aesthetic, and mate-rial considerations in our analysis' (Canagarajah, 2017: 7).

There has been an emerging trend in applied linguistics that has begun to treat 'space' rather than 'labelled language' as the starting point when analysing social and communicative practices. It moves away from the structuralist tradition, which sees language as an autonomous and supe-rior system for meaning making, to 'a spatial paradigm', which is more sensitive to how language flows across geographical and linguistic bor-ders, and how communication is an activity rather than linguistic forms that produce meanings in relation to the social functions people perform in situated time and space. It compels us to see language not only in terms of structure but also as a practice in terms of doing, emerging and becoming (Pennycook, 2010: 140), a powerful vehicle to generate energy and to create spaces for identity construction and social incorporation through diverse forms of languaging acts. As Canagarajah (2017: 8–9) puts it:

> Mobility requires a qualitatively different orientation to meaning-making and competence in order to explain the paradoxical features of fixity and fluidity, stability and change, order and emergence in communication. It requires a focus on the processes, practices, flows, links, and assemblages involved in meaning-making, beyond a focus on meaning as a product or pre-established norms … It is significant that scholars are now treating social and communicative constructs not as nouns (to index meanings and products), but as verbs, as in grammaring, translanguaging, place making, homing, and meaning-making.

This spatial shift in linguistic theories is also linked up with what Nigel Thrift describes as 'nonrepresentational theory or the theory of practices' (Thrift, 1996, 1997, 1999). While representational thinking focused on meanings represented in written texts or spoken words as end products of highly structured, territorialised, and homogeneous ways of communication, nonrepresentational theory shifts the emphasis away from language and words to the micro-geographies of habitual practices. More specifically, it centres on 'the body-subject, not the body, engaged in joint body-practices of becoming' (Thrift, 1997: 142, cited in Nash, 2000: 655). 'It is concerned with practices through which we become 'subjects' decentred, affective, but embodied, relational, expressive and involved with others and objects in a world continually in process' (Nash, 2000: 655).

Drawing upon the paradigm shift in applied linguistics and the non-representational theory applied in wider social sciences, we define language here in a broad and metaphorical sense, referring to all kinds of material and immaterial practices that give voices to individuals and communities, enabling them to hear and be heard, and to communicate. We argue that language is better understood as a 'verb' related to human action and agency, rather than as a 'noun', involving bodily experiences in the everyday articulation and negotiation of identities, memories and belongings in global London. In other words, we pay attention to different but interrelated acts of 'speaking', referring to the ways in which migrants give meanings and substance to the spaces where they reside and interact with each other and with the local society, through the doing of language, or the act of languaging. While there are multiple ways of doing language, we identify three distinctive but also interrelated types of 'language spaces', namely, the 'metrolingual space', the 'performative space' and the 'heritagisation space', mediated by ethnicity, gender and class and embedded in the transnational histories of people and places. Each space is associated with one specific way of 'speaking' through the medium of urban linguistic practices, cultural performances and heritage-making activities respectively. Our primary concern is migrants' every-day lives, which are negotiated and experienced within and between different 'language spaces'. It stresses the experiential and practical dimensions of language embodied by migrants, and the process of people deploying multiple forms of resources to 'speak' for themselves and to make a difference to the construction of life-worlds. We hope the metaphor of 'speaking' offers an alternative to more static approaches to migration and space, reorientating applied linguistics towards practices rather than representations.

The triad of 'language spaces' acts as an analytical framework for our research and guides the structuring of this book. Each 'language space' is associated with the meaning-making of migrants in a particular realm. The three realms of 'language spaces', and three related ways of 'speaking', are by no means static and mutually exclusive. Neither are they an exhaustive list of all the 'language spaces' where migrants make a voice. Rather, they interact with each other in shaping migrant emplacement and transnational connections, illustrating the complexity and dynamics in migrants' encounters with the city. Together, they produce a 'structure of speaking', referring to the flexible and innovative use of multiple resources by migrants in the making of voices as an embodied political, social and cultural practice.

Metrolingual space

The first section of this book investigates how migrants engage with cultural translation, language ideologies and diasporic identities in what we call the 'metrolingual space'. New conceptualisations of language, such as 'translanguaging' (Creese & Blackledge, 2011; García, 2009; García & Li, 2014) and 'translingual practice' (Canagarajah, 2013), are inspiring for research into language and mobility. Here, we particularly draw on the concept of 'metrolingualism' that was developed by Otsuji and Pennycook (2010) as an extension of the concept of 'metroethnicity' (Maher, 2005). It has a special focus on the creative linguistic practices of migrants across space and the borders of culture, history and politics in the urban context and is, as such, particularly relevant to our research. The value of this term compared to other notions is well explained by Otsuji and Pennycook (2010: 240):

Metrolingualism gives us a way to move beyond current terms such as 'multilingualism' and 'multiculturalism'. It is a product of modern and often urban interaction, describing the ways in which people of different and mixed backgrounds use, play with and negotiate identities through language. ... The notion of metrolingualism gives us ways of moving beyond common frameworks of language, providing insights into contemporary, urban language practices, and accommodating both fixity and fluidity in its approach to language use.

The three chapters in the first section of this book explore from different perspectives and based on different empirical material the process of social changes that are involved in different types of urban encounter. They focus on the translation of cultures both between migrant groups and in migrants' interaction with the city. Migrants pick up diverse forms of practices and strategies for communicating across ethnic, cultural and religious boundaries, enabling cultural translation and enabling them to make sense of who they are in global London. The linguistic practices of migrants as described in the three case studies, be it the young Italian immigrants working in the catering industry (Chapter 2), the French students in London's universities (Chapter 3) or the Alevi Kurd youngsters and students (Chapter 4), have challenged the ascriptions of language and identity based on conventional statist correlations across nation, language and ethnicity. Instead, they seek to 'explore how such relations are produced, resisted, defied or rearranged' (Otsuji & Pennycook, 2010: 246) and how new ways of communication and new cultural, ethnic and religious identities have emerged from contexts of interaction. Together, they show that what matters for migrants is not so much about how to mix or switch distinct codes of language, but how old boundaries and distinctions are managed, and new boundaries or categories are constructed and maintained through the act of languaging.

Performative space

The second section of the book focuses on what we call the 'performative space' where migrants resort to various art forms, rituals and bodily performances to articulate a sense of being and belonging and to search for empowerment. The notion of 'performance' first emerged in linguistic theory (Austin, 1975) and later became an influential theoretical tool through the feminist works of Judith Butler (1990, 1993). Butler used this concept to de-naturalise gender and sexual identities and locate them as a product of regulatory discourses. According to Butler, gender identity and by extension, ethnic and national identities, are embodied, performed and produced passionately through the interaction between personal agency and the determining social structure. 'The performativity rather than fixity of identity at least allows the possibility of challenging and parodying these naturalized codes' (Nash, 2000: 655). In other words, 'Identity is the effect of performance, and not vice versa' (Bell, 1999: 3). We borrow the term 'performance' to de-naturalise ethnicity by looking into the cultural practices of migrants as a political act to perform their identity rather than reifying them as 'typical expressions' of an ethnic identity (Fortier, 1999: 43).

Studies in mainstream applied linguistics tend to give limited attention to non-verbal resources in linguistic interactions. As argued by Canagarajah (2017: 7–8), there is an urgent need to take seriously body features (such as gaze, gesture, posture, proximity and positioning) in the meaning-making process. Performance 'privileges practices over texts' (Larsen & Urry, 2011: 1112). By arguing for the 'performative space', we encourage empirically based research that explores how migrants experience places and speak about identities in multisensuous ways, such as performing black beauty among the Congolese migrants in London (Chapter 5), articulating gendered diasporic identities through visual art (Chapter 6), negotiating diasporic Chinese identity in festivals (Chapter 7) and the construction of religious identity in adapted British mosques (Chapter 8). As seen in these case studies, performativity is not merely about routine but primarily about the 'citationality' of identity, referring to 'the invocation of convention' (Butler, 1993: 226), which 'operates to recall and reconnect with places elsewhere that, through those very movements, are re-membered; at the same time, a site of diasporic belonging is created' (Bell, 1999: 3). Furthermore, performance expresses differences in urban space as a site of constant negotiation. As Mason (1996: 307, cited in Knowles, 2004: 23) argued, 'If social space itself is a field of contention, then social performance becomes a means of urging that contention, of expressing difference, asserting ownership and displaying relationship'. Through performance, migrants are able to contest the dominant discourse on identity, community and place and create a discursive space for the building of a more equal and inclusive society.

Heritagisation space

The third section of the book focuses on what we call the 'heritagisation space' where the diasporic histories of migrants are remembered and negotiated in the present and transmitted to the public and to the next generation, not through outright speaking but the silent 'talking' of things and embodied practices. Chapters in this section bring people's attention to the temporality of place. An important part of place-making for migrants in cities is engaging with the remembering/forgetting of their diasporic (and sometime difficult) migratory past as a way of having them accepted as a valuable part of the city's multiple histories and contested memories. Drawing on critical heritage studies, we see heritage not as static artefacts or historical sites to be professionally preserved but instead fundamentally as an embodied meaning-making process. Here, we draw on the definition of heritage by Smith (2006: 1):

> Heritage wasn't only about the past – though it was that too – it also wasn't just about material things – though it was that as well – heritage was a process of engagement, an act of communication and an act of making meaning in and for the present.

Smith (2006) argued that heritage is used as a discursive tool, or what she called Authorised Heritage Discourse (AHD), by the state-sanctioned cultural institutes and elites to legitimate a nationalising story that ignores or trivialises the historical experience of migrants and their roles in society. The hegemonic heritage discourse of the state not only 'establishes who has the power or "responsibility" to define and "speak for" the past' (Smith, 2006: 42) but also helps to perpetuate social inequality and the political marginalisation of underrepresented migrant groups. In the meantime, heritage is also a resource used by migrant groups to challenge the imposed AHD and redefine received values and identities. Therefore, heritage has the potential to subvert the dominant discourse through the act of interpretation, in terms of having a say on the value and meaning of specific heritage places and the past they represent. Key questions involved in the interpretation of heritage include what heritage is, and by whom and for whom it is acknowledged as heritage (or not) (Tunbridge & Ashworth, 1996: 27).

Chapters in this section present diverse bottom-up cultural practices or actions initiated by different migrant groups, in the form of war commemoration by the Indians in the UK (Chapter 9), the graphic heritage of a streetscape in Hackney (Chapter 10), food heritage experienced by different groups of people in London's Chinatown (Chapter 11) and the museum practice of Colombian women in London as an act both of remembering traumatic experiences during the Colombian armed conflict, and contesting the masculine gender discourse imposed by the state (Chapter 12). These activities show strongly that heritage is 'a moment of action, not something frozen in material form' (Smith, 2006: 83). They give voices to migrants for articulating a sense of place and collective memories, and for investing meaning to the place which they inhabited. The 'heritagisation space' is where multi-vocality of place is engaged through actions. In this way, it makes it possible for the histories and memories of migrant groups to become part of London's heritage landscape, to have been 'organically embedded into the city fabric, have been adapted to a variety of social, physical, and cultural uses and have contributed to model the urban social and spatial morphology' (Giombini, 2020: 54).

'Language Spaces' as Heterotopias

In the final part of this introductory chapter, we would like to go one step further to push for a broader theorisation of 'language spaces' by connecting it to the idea of 'heterotopias' (Foucault, 1973, 1986). What we see in the case studies presented in this book is the creation of new spaces. These are not physical places, even if the 'doing of language' cannot happen without interaction with the real physical environment of the city, be it classroom, restaurant, theatre, street, mosque, museum or public square. 'Language spaces' are a powerful, albeit transitory, time-space, 'a kind of effectively enacted utopia in which the real sites, all the other real sites that can be found within the culture, are simultaneously represented, contested, and inverted' (Foucault, 1986: 24). While the concept of heterotopias has been frequently invoked in geography, architectural theory, and general cultural studies in the discussion of real places, such as bars, fairs, gardens, museums, cemeteries and so on, it has not always necessarily been linked to any specific site in reality. In fact, heterotopias exist 'outside of all places' (Foucault, 1986: 24) as a possibility to undermine language and destabilise 'the order of things' (Foucault, 1973). In this sense, it is equally useful here for the study of language and identities in relation to migrants and cities. As Foucault (1973: xviii) argued:

> Heterotopias are disturbing, probably because they secretly undermine language, because they make it impossible to name this and that, because they shatter or tangle common names, because they destroy 'syntax' in advance, and not only the syntax with which we construct sentences but also that less apparent syntax which causes words and things ... to 'hold together'.

The 'language spaces' we talked about, exercised by the practice of linguistic communication, bodily performance and heritagisation respectively, are not ordinary spaces. Rather, they illustrate different forms of 'heterotopias' in action. What is it that makes 'language spaces' hetero-topias? In our view, they become heterotopias in two senses: spatially, they enable the juxtaposition of seemly discontinuous and incompatible objects, journeys, memories, belongings and world views brought by different people in the urban space of London; temporally, they make it possible for migrants to remember and reinterpret the diasporic pasts critically for the construction of a shared future and to contribute to the city's evolving collective memory-scape. Together, they conjure up a space of difference and a space of negotiation, in which diverse discourses, experiences and pursuits are brought together to be represented, contested and reversed, creating a moment of doing and an opportunity of becoming. By doing this, it undermines the hegemonic language of ethnicity, race, citizenship imposed from above, and destroys the 'syntax' with which the authorised discourses hold things together. In this process, the old language is subverted, and a new language is born. It is a process of liberation and empowerment that gives a voice to migrants who can speak in a new language about identity, place, and heritage as agentive urban subjects.

Conclusion

Most publications on migration in Europe either focus on one single country or Europe as a whole. The role of global cities in migratory circulation, emplacement and encounters is heavily under-studied. This edited volume is aimed at filling this gap by investigating the nexus of migrants, cities and language in global London. Our research suggests strongly that the city where migrants reside is not external to the identities and belongings of migrants in the same way as migrants are not external to the fabric and the ethos of the city. Migrants and cities are mutually constitutive – they produce and reproduce each other through multiple forms of everyday and ongoing negotiations in the city and beyond. What distinguishes our work from others is that we adopt a comparative perspective to study diverse London-based migrant groups through the prism of language. For this purpose, we carefully selected papers that engage with different communities in London, ranging from French, Italian, Kurdish and Latin American, to Chinese, Indian and African diasporas. By going beyond the study of individual migrant groups to identify commonalities in the ways in which different migrant groups interact with each other and with the city, we hope that this book will help bridge the gap between segregated research into different migrant groups; stimulate intellectual dialogues between academic and migrant communities; and lay the groundwork for interdisciplinary and comparative research into migrants in London and beyond.

Rather than offering an abstract and generalised discussion of migrants from a conventional and single-disciplinary perspective, we use 'languaging' as the central concept in linking up relevant research in the literature of applied linguistics, performativity and critical heritage studies, and based on this, we put forward what we call 'language spaces' as a coherent analytical framework to integrate a number of contextualised case studies of migrant communities in London. By developing this innovative and interdisciplinary analytical framework, we are able to bridge the geographic, ethnic and linguistic lacunae in research into migrants and cities. In addition, methodologically, we hope to promote 'language-based' or 'language-sensitive' research, drawing on the plurilingual repertoires and the translanguaging practices of migrant communities, such as those used in Turkish, Italian, Congolese, Chinese, French, Spanish and Hindi communities, and including the many language varieties frequently not acknowledged as 'languages', as a tool for data collection and ethnographic fieldwork. This language approach is needed to generate fresh and in-depth insights into the complex issues of diasporic identities, belonging, and place-making that have broad implications for migration studies in post-Brexit Britain and beyond.

It is not our intention to claim representativeness of the case studies presented in this book for the experiences of all migrant communities in London and Britain. Empirically based and theoretically informed case studies of carefully selected migrant groups in London, as we have presented here, however, do illustrate the complex relations between migrants and the city in the context of globalisation. It is our hope that the research presented in this book will break new ground for interdisciplinary research on identity, language, migration and space in global London and provide insights to support further migration research in other less globally connected but equally diverse cities and regions in the UK and beyond.

Notes

(1) These include the EU-8 accession states joining the enlarged European Union in 2004: the Czech Republic, Estonia, Hungary, Latvia, Lithuania, Poland, Slovakia and Slovenia. In 2007, Romania and Bulgaria (referred to as the EU-2 states) were admitted to the EU. Migrants from the EU-2 initially experienced harsher restrictions on the rights to work than those from the EU-8 states, but these were lifted in 2014. Croatia joined the EU in 2013.

(2) Office for National Statistics, International Migration, England and Wales: Census 2021.

(3) England and Wales Census, 2011, ONS. Usual resident population. Cited from Krausova and Vargas-Silva (2013: 7).

References

Ang, I. (2003) Together-in-difference: Beyond diaspora, into hybridity. *Asian Studies Review* 27 (2), 141–154.

Alexander, C. (2002) Beyond black: Re-thinking the colour/culture divide. *Ethnic and Racial Studies* 25, 552–571.

Alexander, C., Edwards, R. and Temple, B. (2007) Contesting cultural communities: Language, ethnicity and citizenship in Britain. *Journal of Ethnic and Migration Studies* 33 (5), 783–800.

Alleyne, B. (2002) An idea of community and its discontents: Towards a more reflexive sense of belonging in multicultural Britain. *Ethnic and Racial Studies* 25 (4), 607–627.

Anthias, F. (2022) *Ethnicity, Class, Gender and Migration: Greek-Cypriots in Britain.* Abingdon: Routledge.

Austin, J.L. (1975) *How to Do Things with Words.* Cambridge, MA: Harvard University Press.

Back, L. (2015) 'Losing Culture or Finding Super-Diversity?' Discover Society 20. See http://discoversociety.org/2015/05/05/losing-culture-or-finding-superdiversity-2/.

Baker, P. and Mohieldeen, Y. (2000) The languages of London's schoolchildren. In P. Baker and J. Eversley (eds) *Multilingual Capital* (pp. 5–80). London: Battlebridge.

Baumann, G. (1996) *Contesting Culture: Discourses of Identity in Multi-Ethnic London.* Cambridge: Cambridge University Press.

Beck, U. (2007) Beyond class and nation: Reframing social inequalities in a globalizing world. *British Journal of Sociology* 58 (4), 679–705.

Bell, V. (1999) Performativity and belonging. *Theory, Culture and Society: Explorations in Critical Social Science* 16, 1–10.

Bissoondath, N. (1994) *Selling Illusions: The Cult of Multiculturalism in Canada.* Toronto: Penguin.

Blommaert, J. (2010) *The Sociolinguistics of Globalization.* Cambridge: Cambridge University Press.

Blommaert, J. (2013) Complexity, accent, and conviviality: Concluding comments. *Applied Linguistics* 34 (5), 613–622.

Brettell, C. (2003) 'Is the ethnic community inevitable? A comparison of the settlement patterns of Portuguese immigrants in Toronto and Paris'. In C. Bretell (ed.) *Anthropology and Migration: Essays on Transnationalism, Ethnicity, and Identity.* Walnut Creek. CA: AltaMira Press.

Bretell, C. (2003) Bringing the city back in: Cities as contexts for immigrant incorporation. In N. Foner (ed.) *American Arrivals: Anthropology Engages the New Immigration* (pp. 163–195). Santa Fe: School of American Research Press.

Brettell, C.B. and Hollifield, J.F. (eds) (2007) *Migration Theory: Talking Across Disciplines* (2nd edn). New York: Routledge.

Brickell, K. and Datta, A. (2011) *Translocal Geographies: Spaces, Places, Connections.* Abingdon: Routledge.

Buhr, F. (2018) Using the city: Migrant spatial integration as urban practice. *Journal of Ethnic and Migration Studies* 44 (2), 307–320.

Butler, J. (1990) *Gender Trouble: Feminism and The Subversion Of Identity.* London: Routledge.

Butler, J. (1993) *Bodies That Matter: On The Discursive Limits of 'Sex'.* London: Routledge.

Butler, T. (2003) Living in the bubble: Gentrification and its 'Others' in North London. *Urban Studies* 40 (12), 2469–2486.

Çağlar, A. (2001) Constraining metaphors and the transnationalisation of spaces in Berlin. *Journal of Ethnic and Migration Studies* 27 (4), 601–613.

Çağlar, A. (2005) Mediascapes, advertisement industries: Turkish immigrants in Europe and the European Union. *New German Critique* 92, 39–62.

Çağlar, A. and Glick Schiller, N. (2011) Introduction: Migrants and cities. In N. Glick Schiller and A. Çağlar (eds) *Locating Migration: Rescaling Cities and Migrants* (pp. 1–22). Ithaca, NY: Cornell University Press.

Canagarajah, S. (2013) *Translingual Practice: Global Englishes and Cosmopolitan Relations.* New York: Routledge.

Canagarajah, S. (2017) Introduction, The nexus of migration and language: The emergence of a disciplinary space. In S. Canagarajah (ed.) *The Routledge Handbook of Migration and Language.* New York: Routledge.

Cheshire, J., Kerswill, P., Fox, S. and Torgersen, E. (2011) Contact, the feature pool and the speech community: The emergence of Multicultural London English. *Journal of Sociolinguistics* 15 (2), 151–196.

Conradson, D. and Latham, A. (2005) Friendship, networks and transnationality in a world city: Antipodean transmigrants in London. *Journal of Ethnic and Migration Studies* 31 (2), 287–305.

Creese, A. and Blackledge, A. (2011) Separate and flexible bilingualism in complementary schools: Multiple language practices in interrelationship. *Journal of Pragmatics* 43 (5), 1157–1450.

Crouch, D. (2001) Spatialities and the feeling of doing. *Social & Cultural Geography* 2 (1), 61–75.

Dahinden, J. (2016) A plea for the 'de-migranticization' of research on migration and integration. *Ethnic and Racial Studies* 39 (13), 2207–2225.

Demie, F. (2018) English as an additional language and attainment in primary schools in England. *Journal of Multilingual and Multicultural Development* 39 (3), 210–223.

Faist, T. (2000) *The Volume and Dynamics of International Migration and Transnational Social Spaces.* Oxford: Oxford University Press

Fomina, J. (2010) Immigration policy debates and their significance for multiculturalism in Britain. *Polish Sociological Review* 1 (169), 57–86.

Fortier, A. (1999) Re-membering places and the performance of belonging(s). *Theory, Culture and Society: Explorations in Critical Social Science* 16, 41–64.

Foucault, M. (1973) *The Order of Things: An Archaeology of The Human Sciences.* New York: Vintage Books.

Foucault, M. (1986) Of other spaces. *Diacritics* 16 (1), 22–27.

Franz, B. (2018) Using the city: Migrant spatial integration as urban practice. *Journal of Ethnic and Migration Studies* 44 (2), 307–320.

Friedmann, J. (1986) The world city hypothesis. *Development and Change* 77 (1), 69–84.

Friedmann, J. (1995) Where we stand: A decade of world city research. In P.L. Knox and P.J. Taylor (eds) *World Cities in a World-System* (pp. 21–47). Cambridge: Cambridge University Press.

Fryer, P. (1984) *Staying Power: The History of Black People in Britain.* Sterling, VA: Pluto Press.

García, O. (2009) *Bilingual Education in the 21st Century: A Global Perspective.* Oxford: Wiley-Blackwell.

García, O. and Li, W. (2014) *Translanguaging. Language, Bilingualism, and Education.* London: Palgrave.

Gidley, B. (2011) *Migrants in London: Policy Challenges*. The Migration Observatory, 29 March.

Giombini, L. (2020) Everyday heritage and place-making. *ESPES* 9 (2), 50–61.

Glick Schiller, N., Çağlar, A. and Guldbrandsen, T.C. (2006) Beyond the ethnic lens: Locality, globality, and born-again incorporation. *American Ethnologist* 33 (4), 612–633.

Glick Schiller, N. and Çağlar, A. (eds) (2011) *Locating Migration: Rescaling Cities and Migrants*. Ithaca: Cornell University Press.

GLA (Greater London Authority) (2005) *London – The World in a City: An Analysis of the 2001census Results*. Greater London Authority Data Management and Analysis Group.

Grzymala-Kazlowska, A. and Phillimore, J. (2018) Introduction: Rethinking integration. New perspectives on adaptation and settlement in the era of super-diversity. *Journal of Ethnic and Migration Studies* 44 (2), 179–196.

Hall, S. M. (2012) *City, Street and Citizen: The Measure of the Ordinary*. Abingdon: Routledge.

Hall, S.M. (2015) Super-diverse street: A 'trans-ethnography' across migrant localities. *Ethnic and Racial Studies* 38 (1), 22–37.

Huc-Hepher, S. (2021) *French London: A Blended Ethnography of A Migrant City*. Manchester: Manchester University Press.

Kershen, A.J. (2007) *London the Promised Land? The Immigration Experience in a Capital City*. Aldershot: Ashgate.

Kershen, A.J. (2015) *London the Promised Land Revisited: The Changing Face of the London Migrant Landscape in the Early 21st Century*. Abingdon: Routledge.

King, J. (2001) The nationalization of East Central Europe: Ethnicism, ethnicity, and beyond. In N. Wingfield and M. Bucur (eds) *Staging the Past: The Politics of Commemoration in Habsburg Central Europe, 1848 to the Present* (pp. 112–152). West Lafayette: Purdue University Press.

King, L., Byrne, N., Djouadj, I., Lo Bianco, J. and Stoicheva, M. (2011) *Languages in Europe: Towards 2020*. London: The Languages Company.

Knox, P.L. and Taylor, P.J. (eds) (1995) *World Cities in a World-System*. Cambridge: Cambridge University Press.

Knowles, C. (2004) *Race and Social Analysis*. London: SAGE Publications.

Knowles, C. (2011) Cities on the move: Navigating urban life. *City: Analysis of Urban Trends, Culture, Theory, Policy, Action* 15 (2), 135–153.

Knowles, C. (2013) Nigerian London: Re-mapping space and ethnicity in superdiverse cities. *Ethnic and Racial Studies* 36 (4), 651–669.

Krausova, A. and Vargas-Silva, C. (2013) *London: Census Profile*. The Migration Observatory, 20 May.

Kymlicka, W. (2012) *Multiculturalism: Success, Failure, and the Future*. Washington, DC: Migration Policy

Lamb, T.E. (2015) Towards a plurilingual habitus: Engendering interlinguality in urban spaces. *International Journal of Pedagogies and Learning* 10 (1), 151–165.

Lamb, T.E. (2020) Supplementary schools as spaces of hope for a more inclusive world: Challenging exclusion and social injustice in multilingual London. *Journal of Linguistics and Language Teaching*, 10th Anniversary Issue 11 (2), 99–127.

Lamb, T.E. and Vodicka, G. (2018) Collective autonomy and multilingual spaces in super-diverse urban contexts: Interdisciplinary perspectives. In G. Murray and T.E. Lamb (eds) *Space, Place and Autonomy in Language* Learning (pp. 9–28). Abingdon: Routledge.

Larsen, J. and Urry, J. (2011) Gazing and performing. *Environment and Planning D: Society and Space* 29, 1110–1125.

Levitt, P. and Glick Schiller, N. (2004) Conceptualizing simultaneity: A transnational social field perspective on society. *Annual Review of Sociology* 33, 129–156.

Li, W. (2011) Moment analysis and translanguaging space: Discursive construction of identities by multilingual Chinese youth in Britain. *Journal of Pragmatics* 43 (5), 1222–1235.

Li, W. and Zhu, H. (2013) Diaspora: Multilingual and intercultural communication across time and space. *AILA Review* 26, 42–56.

Maher, J. (2005) Metroethnicity, language, and the principle of Cool. *International Journal of the Sociology of Language* 11, 83, 102.

Mason, J. (1996) Street fairs: Social space, social performance. *Theatre Journal* 48, 301–319.

Meissner, F. and Vertovec, S. (2015) Comparing super-diversity. *Ethnic and Racial Studies* 38 (4), 541–555.

Nagel, C. (2002) Constructing difference and sameness: The politics of assimilation in London's Arab communities. *Ethnic and Racial Studies* 25 (2), 258–287.

Nash, C. (2000) Performativity in practice: Some recent work in cultural geography. *Theory Culture and Society* 24 (4), 653–664.

Ndhlovu, F. (2016) A decolonial critique of diaspora identity theories and the notion of super-diversity. *Diaspora Studies* 9 (1), 28–40.

Olwig, K.F. (2013) Notions and practices of difference: An epilogue on the ethnography of diversity. *Identities: Global Studies in Culture and Power* 20 (4), 471–479.

Otsuji, E. and Pennycook, A. (2010) Metrolingualism: Fixity, fluidity and language in flux. *International Journal of Multilingualism* 7 (3), 240–254.

Pennycook, A. (2010) *Language as a Local Practice*. New York: Routledge.

Pennycook, A. (2012) *Language and Mobility: Unexpected Places*. Bristol: Multilingual Matters.

Pennycook, A. and Otsuji, E. (2015) *Metrolingualism. Language in the City*. Abingdon: Routledge.

Pratt, M.L. (1991) Arts of the contact zone. *Profession* 33–40.

Ryan, L. (2018) Differentiated embedding: Polish migrants in London negotiating belonging over time. *Journal of Ethnic and Migration Studies* 44 (2), 233–251.

Sassen, S. (1991) *The Global City: New York, London, Tokyo*. Princeton, NJ: Princeton University Press.

Sassen, S. (1992) *Global Cities*. Princeton: Princeton University Press.

Sassen, S. (2000) *Cities in a World Economy* (2nd edn). Thousand Oaks, CA: Pine Forge Press.

Savski, K. (2023) (Trans)languaging, power, and resistance: Bordering as discursive agency. *Language in Society* 1–23.

Sepulveda, L., Syrett, S. and Lyon, F. (2011) Population superdiversity and new migrant enterprise: The case of London. *Entrepreneurship & Regional Development* 23 (7-8), 469–497.

Schuerkens, U. (ed.) (2004) *Global Forces and Local Life-Worlds: Social Transformations*. Thousand Oaks, CA: Sage.

Smith, A. (1983) Nationalism and Social Theory. *British Journal of Sociology* 34, 19–38.

Smith, L. (2006) *Uses of Heritage*. London: Routledge.

Smith, M.P. (2017) Chapter 6: Transnationalism and the City. In M.P. Smith (ed.) *Explorations in Urban Theory* (pp. 157–174). New York: Routledge.

Soysal, L. (2001) Diversity of experience, experience of diversity: Turkish migrant youth culture in Berlin. *Cultural Dynamics* 13 (1), 5–28.

Stroud, C. (2015) Linguistic citizenship as utopia. *Multilingual Margins: A Journal of Multilingualism from the Periphery* 2 (2), 22–37.

Thrift, N.J. (1996) *Spatial Formations*. London: Sage.

Thrift, N.J. (1997) The still point: Resistance, expressive embodiment and dance. In S. Pile and M. Keith (eds) *Geographies of Resistance* (pp. 124–151). London: Routledge.

Thrift, N.J. (1999) Steps to an ecology of place. In D. Massey, J. Allen and P. Sarre (eds) *Human Geography Today* (pp. 295–322). Cambridge: Polity Press.

Tunbridge, J.E. and Ashworth, G.J. (1996) *Dissonant Heritage: The Management of the Past as a Resource in Conflict*. Chichester: Wiley.

Urry, J. (2000) *Sociology Beyond Societies: Mobilities for the Twenty-First Century*. London: Routledge.

Vertovec, S. (1996) Multiculturalism, culturalism and public incorporation. *Ethnic and Racial Studies* 19 (1), 49–69.

Vertovec, S. (2007) Super-diversity and its implications. *Ethnic and Racial Studies* 30 (6) 1024–1054.

Wang, C. (2012) Bridging borders in the global city: Negotiating sameness and difference in Hong Kong's skilled immigrants from mainland China. *Journal of International Migration and Integration* 13 (4), 565–581.

Wang, C. (2013) Place of desire: Skilled migration from mainland China to post-colonial Hong Kong. *Asia Pacific Viewpoint* 54 (3), 388–397.

Wessendorf, S. (2013) Commonplace diversity and the 'ethos of mixing': Perceptions of difference in a London neighbourhood. *Identities* 20 (4), 407–422.

White, E.J. (2002) Forging African diaspora places in Dublin's retro-global spaces: Minority making in a new global city. *City* 6 (2), 251–270.

Wilkins, A. (2019) *Migration, Work and Home-Making in the City: Dwelling and Belonging among Vietnamese Communities in London*. Abingdon: Routledge.

Wimmer, A. and Glick Schiller, N. (2002) Methodological nationalism and beyond: Nation-state building, migration and the social sciences. *Global Networks* 2 (4), 301–334.

Yalçin-Heckmann, L. (1997) The perils of ethnic associational life in Europe: Turkish migrants in Germany and France. In T. Modood and P. Werbner (eds) *The Politics of Multiculturalism in the New Europe: Racism, Identity, and Community* (p. 95–110). London: Zed Books.

Yeoh, B.S.A. (2015) Affective practices in the European city of encounter. *City* 19 (4), 545–551.

Yeoh, B.S.A. and Huang, S. (2000) 'Home' and 'Away': Foreign domestic workers and negotiations of diasporic identity in Singapore. *Women's Studies International Forum* 23 (4), 413–429.

Zhu, H. (2017) New orientation in identity in mobility. In S. Canagarajah (ed.) *The Routledge Handbook of Migration and Language* (pp. 117–132). Abingdon: Routledge.

Part 1

'Metrolingual Space': Cultural Translation, Language Ideologies and Diasporic Identities in a Global City

2 Negotiating New Migratory Identities through Multilingual Practices: The Case of Post-Crisis Italian Migrants in London

Giulia Pepe

Introduction

The 2008 economic crisis set in motion new migratory fluxes. Northern European countries, such as the UK, received significant migratory flows both from East Europe and from apparently economically stable southern countries, such as Portugal, Italy, Greece and Spain (King, 2017; Lafleur & Stanek, 2017). These movements have captured the attention of scholars and the media (King, 2017), but linguistic studies on these new migrants are still rare. In particular, the Italian case has so far not been properly addressed (Vedovelli, 2015). The main aim of this chapter is to present the key findings of a study on the linguistic repertoires and multilingual practices of a group of post-2008 crisis Italian migrants in London in relation to their negotiation and performance of new identities. It suggests that the migrants rely on the language resources acquired through migration to display new professional and social identities. Interestingly, we find not only differences – as theorised by recent studies on contemporary migration – but also similarities between old multilingual practices developed by post-war Italian migrants and post-2008 migrants' uses of their repertoires, despite the lack of contact between these two migration phases.

While empirically focusing on post-2008 Italian migration to London, the chapter also proposes an innovative consideration of Italian migration history. It starts with an overview of the history of Italian migration to

England and to London in particular. It then proceeds with a review of the relevant literature regarding the connection between identities negotiation and multilingual practices, and an introduction to the methodology applied to carry out the research. The main body of the chapter is devoted to the presentation of data and discussion of the research findings. The implications of this study for the research of transnational migration in global cities are discussed in the conclusion.

A New Flow, an Old Phenomenon: The History of Italian Emigration to England

Italy has a very long history of migration to England, which dates back to the end of the 18th century. In this period, Italian migrants were mostly living in poor conditions, being labourers and local artisans (Sponza, 1988, 2005). In 1863, the church of Saint Peter on Clerkenwell Road was founded and it became the centre of the community (Fortier, 1999, 2006). Already at the end of the 19th century, Italians in London were mostly employed in the hospitality sector (Sponza, 2005). However, the significant growth of Italian mass migration to England started immediately after WWII. Due to the agreements between the Italian and the British Labour ministers, Italians started to be recruited in bulk to be employed in brick factories (Barni, 2011). Therefore, they mainly moved to and settled in English industrial towns, such as Bedford and Peterborough (Barni, 2011), with most of them coming from the southern regions of Italy (Di Salvo, 2014, 2015, 2018; Guzzo, 2014). In those towns, Italians grouped in neighbourhoods, giving birth to the historical Italian communities, popularly called *Little Italies* (Gabaccia, 2006). Although most of the post-war migration was to those small industrial towns, a smaller number of post-WWII migrants settled in London as well, repopulating the area around the church of St. Peter and mainly opening food related businesses (Sponza, 2005). The post-WWII migration of Italians diminished within the span of two decades, but these migrants had already created strong communities, wherein cultural centres, Italian language schools, clubs and shops had developed.

Italian emigration has generated a vast production of popular images in the media, arts, films and literature (Gardaphé, 1996), resulting in a crystallisation of the image of the old migrants. The first image usually found in literature on the topic is connected to poverty and ignorance: poverty of the country of origin and poverty of the migrants who were generally employed in humble occupations. In the English context, Tosi (1991) highlights the extremely low number of middle-class migrants that arrived after WWII. The literature on this migration provides a standard sociolinguistic profile of Italian immigrants: mostly coming from the southern regions of Italy, illiterate, unemployed in Italy and employed in menial jobs in England, and speakers of their local dialects. Italy underwent a phase of Italianisation – understood as the spread of the Italian language in different contexts, from the most formal to the most personal ones – only at the beginning of the 1960s. Nevertheless, this process was relatively slow and most of the Italian population in the decades after WWII still preferred – and were more competent in – their local dialects than standard Italian. Italian dialects are Romance languages, each of them having their own phonetic, morphological and syntactical features which in many cases greatly differ from those of standard Italian.

The social and linguistic features which typically describe the post-WWII migration from Italy are emphasised by scholars (Conti, 2012; Gjergji, 2015; King *et al.*, 2014; McKay, 2015; Sacco, 2013; Scotto, 2015) when making sociocultural comparison between the post-WWII and post-2008 crisis Italian immigrants. The depiction of the new phase of immigrants has been dominated by the *brain drain* narrative (Tintori & Romei, 2017) that portrays them as highly educated (Sacco, 2013) young cosmopolitans (King *et al.*, 2014; Scotto, 2015) who suffered the stagnant sociocultural and economic situation of Italy (Conti, 2012), or highly educated professionals who moved more because they were tired of the Italian mindset rather than as economically driven migrants (Scotto, 2015). Compared to post-WWII migrants, post-crisis migrants are certainly more educated, as Italian levels of literacy and italianisation increased over the last 60 years. In 1950, when post-war migration reached its peak, 30% of the Southern Italian population was illiterate and this rate was even higher among low social class members, whereas in 2011, only 1% of the Italian population was completely illiterate (Istat, 2011).

The new flow of Italian migration worldwide, however, is far from being homogeneous (Ferrini, 2018), contrary to how Conti (2012), Sacco (2013) and Scotto (2015) describe it. This is especially the case for the Italian communities in London that have expanded greatly in the two-year period 2013–2015 (Tintori & Romei, 2017). In their 2017 report, *FondazioneMigrantes* claimed that migration had increased by 60.1% in the 2006–2016 decade (Licata, 2017), and the 2018 report (Licata, 2018) confirms this number. Moreover, the 2017 report confirmed the UK as the favourite destination for new Italian mobility (Licata, 2017). In March 2020, the EU Settlement Scheme released its quarterly statistics providing information on the number of EU citizens who had applied for Settlement and Pre-Settlement Status to remain in the UK after Brexit

(EU Settlement Scheme Statistics, March 2020). The document shows that about 350,000 Italians had applied for the Settlement Status Scheme. In terms of number of applicants, Italians are the third largest group after Poles and Romanians – although this does not include those who do not need the Status to remain in the UK permanently (i.e. those who have acquired British citizenship) and those who could not apply because they did not meet the criteria for the application. The Italian Consulate estimates that the real figure is much higher and suggests that more than 700,000 Italians are living in the UK (Degli Innocenti, 2018) and that most of them have settled in the capital. The Consulate also acknowledges that the majority of new Italian migrants do not register with AIRE (*Anagrafe Italiani Residenti all'Estero*), the official register of Italians living abroad.[1]

Observation of the Italian communities in London, as presented in this chapter, shows the existence of a whole range of Italians who left the country for diverse reasons and who come from extremely variable sociocultural, economic and educational backgrounds. Such a large expansion of the community in the last five years, and the lack of statistical data on the entire community, suggest the brain drain narrative in the mainstream media is untenable. There are indeed university graduates working in the financial and in other economically prestigious sectors, but also migrants who, despite their high level of education, are employed in menial jobs, owing to their lack of competence in English. The communities also include less-educated migrants, who mainly work in the hospitality sector and whose knowledge of English on arrival is usually very basic. In short, the post-crisis phase is characterised by a strong heterogeneity which prevents us from providing a simple antithetical image contrasting old and new migrants. The variety in education, social class, cultural background, regional origin, profession in the host country, and migratory sociocultural habits is then reflected in the diversity of linguistic competences and linguistic repertoires of post-crisis migrants.

Translanguaging: The Making of New Identities Through Multilingual Practices

Past theories believed individuals were 'characterised by coherence, rationality and continuity' (De Fina, 2016: 168–169) while post and late modern theories (Giddens, 1991, 1993) understand the self as 'fragmented, multivocal, discontinuous, and contradictory' (De Fina, 2016: 168–169). Individuals are now seen as entities who have access to 'inventories of identities' which they can display (2016: 169) and negotiate (De Fina, 2010). This interpretation led to an understanding of late modern migrants' lives as multifaceted and connected with multiple realities, with diverse contexts and with other speakers living in different countries and continents. Late modern migrants represent the possibility of living within multiple cultures and languages simultaneously. De Fina *et al.* maintain that social constructionism interprets identities as a process, happening in 'concrete and specific' interactions, which 'results from processes of negotiation' (2006: 2–3), and this offers an analytical model for new emerging identities.

Bucholtz and Hall (2005) theorised five principles which rule such processes: indexicality, emergence, relationality, partialness and positionality. Among these, the 'indexicality principle' is the most relevant for this study that focuses on sociolinguistic analysis. It is based on the notion of the *index*, which is a 'linguistic form that depends on the interactional context for its meaning' (Bucholtz & Hall, 2005: 594). The notion of indexicality implies the creation of connections between linguistic forms or multilingual practices – realised by the speakers in interactions – and sociocultural values and social meanings. The notion of indexicality recalls the theory of 'indexical order' (Silverstein, 2003) and 'orders of indexicality' (Blommaert, 2007). The scale of indexical orders explains how linguistic features go from being unnoticed and used only by a sociodemographically defined group of speakers (first-order of indexicality) to being understood – only by members of the group – as stereotypical identifiers of that group (second-order of indexicality) and becoming carriers of sociocultural meanings (third-order of indexicality), recognised by outsiders as well. The scale shows how, when features reach the 'third-order' (Johnstone *et al.*, 2006: 78) they then operate as typical elements in 'more reflexive identity work' (Johnstone *et al.*, 2006: 78). Thus, when the speakers are aware that the linguistic features or practices produced within the group have acquired meanings shared by non-members, they can experience appropriation of those features by strangers or promote meaning (or uses) shifts. This theoretical framework is centred on the idea that languages are sociocultural constructs of groups of speakers, and the process of language development is then interpreted as bidirectional, since the process of language construction 'also constructs the group itself' (Johnstone *et al.*, 2006: 79).

Indexical orders have been widely applied to the study of multilingual practices. For instance, Leimgruber (2012) suggests that, in Singaporeans' speech, the multilingual practice of language shifting has an indexical meaning. Therefore, multilingual practices convey metapragmatic and social meanings – understood by the group's members – in a second-order indexicality understanding, and conventionally recognised meanings on a third-order indexicality interpretation, as outsiders recognise the implications of such practice. The assumption behind this theorisation is that ideologies and everyday individuals' perceptions regarding sets of linguistic variants produce indexical associations, and, consequently, speakers can choose to adhere to a linguistic style in cases where they want to be associated with a sociocultural category, or they can choose to reject that style if they wish to disaffiliate. Bucholtz and Hall maintain that 'the use of linguistic structures and systems that are ideologically associated with specific personas and groups' (2005: 594) is an indexical process yielding identity relations that develop from interactions. Thus, identities are understood as the product of interactions between individuals and, hence, they are named *social identities* (Huot & Rudman, 2010). As Huot and Rudman explain, 'social identity reflects one's location within the social structure' (2010: 69). Some elements of social identity are naturally intrinsic and not modifiable (i.e. ethnicity and age), while other social identifications can be earned, constructed and acquired due to changes in individuals' statuses or conditions. This aspect gains relevance since one acquires a determined social identity, and this will affect individuals' personal identity, their views and how other people perceive them. Since individuals are builders and performers of identities (Goffman, 1959), their constructed identities are always being positioned in a social context and influenced by and related to sociocultural factors. The speakers, thus, become social actors performing roles, and these roles are built according to the social and cultural environment in which such performance happens, through the exploitation of indexes. As shown in the data analysis section, through the use of multilingual practices, with languages and translanguaging as indexes of sociocultural values and common migratory stories, speakers can negotiate and perform their new social identities.

In the last decade, the traditional structuralist approach, which focused on the grammatical mechanisms ruling the mixing of languages, was challenged by modern post-structuralist orientations that saw 'communication not in terms of separate languages, but rather in terms of heteroglossic and hybrid practice' (Fang & Shaobin, 2016: 21). 'Transnational' and 'glocal' are the key adjectives to describe late-modern migrants' lives (Duff, 2015; Roudometof, 2005; Schiller *et al.*, 1992). Transnationalism refuses essentialist ideas that see individuals as fixed units, carrying one essence that defines their entire being (Grillo,

1995). On the contrary, as in the case reported in this paper, identity is performed through the act of translanguaging that is interpreted as the mechanism leading the speakers to the construction of meaning and a 'sense of their social reality' (Mazzaferro, 2018: 6). García and Li define it as ways 'in which bilinguals use their complex semiotic repertoire to act, to know, and to be' (2014: 137). As transnationalism is living with one's 'feet in two societies' (Chaney, 1979: 209, in Schiller *et al.*, 1992), translanguaging is living with one's feet in two (or more) languages. Translanguaging stands as a possibility for migrants to start identity processes, by using all the linguistic resources at their disposal to share their stories, background and socio-cultural values with other migrants. The linguistic resources are indexes interpreted by multilingual speakers not only on the basis of their common culture, but also through the sense and meaning processes they themselves activate through their interactions (Li, 2011). Translanguaging is a continuous process the speakers rely on to perform different identities, to tell their story, and to share a common history with those involved in the interactions. The possibility of translanguaging is given by a shared linguistic repertoire, which, however, every speaker exploits in different ways (Paulsrud & Straszer, 2018).

Methods and Data

A combination of two methodological frameworks was adopted in the research presented in this chapter. I chose 'ethnography of speaking' (Bauman & Sherzer, 1974) to investigate the multilingual practices with which post-crisis migrants engage during in-group gatherings. Interpretative Phenomenological Analysis (IPA) (Smith & Osborn, 2003) was used to explore how these migrants perceive such practices and relate them to the processes of negotiation and performance of migration-related identities. The participants were selected from among my direct friends or acquaintances, using the snowball technique. The rationale behind this choice is that I required a friendly and relaxed environment to gather spontaneous data which would show natural everyday communications. To be selected, the participants needed to speak Italian as their mother tongue, to be aged between 18 and 35, and they needed to live in London. In total, 21 participants were recruited for the research. The aim of this study is not to provide generalisable findings on Italian migration, but to explore 'how participants are making sense of their personal and social world' (Smith & Osborn, 2003: 55). Therefore, even if such a sample selection method might have affected the generalisability of the findings, the frameworks adopted – and the post-positivist paradigm under which the research was carried out – prevented this from being a concern. Post-positivism derives from a shift from dualistic thinking, promoted by positivism, to the emphasis on multiplicity and complexity of humanity, and thus supports interpretive research which understands meaning, experience, and knowledge generated by humans as contradictory, multifaceted and fluid.

Participant observation of spontaneously organised events, such as home dinner parties, were undertaken for data collection. As member of the group investigated – I am a post-2008 Italian migrant who lives in London – it was fairly easy for me to recruit participants through a 'friend of friend' chain. In addition, some participants were my direct friends or acquaintances and, thus, it was possible to obtain a high level of intimacy and spontaneity during the recorded events. Dialogues were audio recorded, and then transcribed for analysis.[2] I highlighted the passages where participants engaged with translanguaging. Participants' spontaneous conversations led to the formulation of new hypotheses. Follow-up semi-structured interviews with 15 key participants were completed. Following IPA procedures, I analysed the transcript of each interview and grouped the key points in 'themes' (e.g. community feeling, negotiation of identities, attitudes towards translanguaging, etc.) These were then compared across interview transcripts to find common patterns. This chapter focuses on one of the themes: the negotiation and performance of identities and the relationship of these processes with participants' linguistic repertoires and the use of such repertoires.

The New *Lingua Della Giobba*: A New Linguistic Repertoire for Post-2008 Italian Migrants

In 1939, Prezzolini published a paper entitled *La lingua della giobba* that described the translingual style of Italian migrants in New York at the beginning of the 20th century. His empirical analysis provides a picture of the language mixing practices developed in New York's Little Italy, demonstrating the lexical outcomes of the contact between New York English and the dialects spoken in the Italian peninsula. The title itself is emblematic of this style: *lingua* means 'language', *della* 'of the', and *giobba* is an adapted and integrated loanword which means 'job' (Greavu, 2014; Haspelmath, 2009). It derives from the English word 'job' and it is orthographically adapted, since the voiced postalveolar affricate /ʤ/ is written according to the Italian grapheme system

(Bertinetto, 2010). Prezzolini (1939), through such graphemic adaptation, was loyal to the pronunciation of the migrants, who would utter these loanwords influenced by their (mainly southern) dialectal accents. Moreover, the Italian suffixal vowel /-a/ is added after the gemination of the plosive bilabial phoneme /b/. In his definition of *lingua della giobba*, Prezzolini highlights how this new translingual style was connected to poverty, lack of education and a mixture of dialectal varieties, which were the only languages spoken by Italian migrants at that time. He links this *lingua* to the fatigue of adapting to a new world. Prezzolini's reflection concerns the ontology of *giobba*, which diverges substantially from the notion of job. He writes that '*Giobba* well expresses the condition lived by many of our emigrants when they reached these harbours, and searched for any job, just to be able to eat. *Giobba* is the job one finds, without affection or spiritual interest' (Prezzolini, 1939: 122, author's translation). *Giobba* is thus an index of the experience of those migrants who escaped poverty and unemployment to find occupations in the USA, and who worked on their language, and their identity, to achieve mutual intelligibility with those coming from different regions of Italy, while struggling to integrate into the receiving society.

A remarkably similar repertoire was developed by post-war migrants in the UK (Guzzo, 2014; Panese, 1992; Rocchi, 2006). My study suggests that post-2008 migrants who arrive in London with low English competence, usually employed in the hospitality sector (restaurants, bars, hotels, catering companies), develop their own – new – *lingua della giobba*. They reproduce linguistic features, dynamics and mechanisms that indexically recall the style of post-war migrants, despite the lack of physical regular contact between these two phases of migrants. Such separation of the post-war and post-2008 phases emerged from my ethnography and was often mentioned by those who participated in the project. Not feeling confident speaking English, they seem keen to search for workplaces where other employees are Italian speakers who can help them with their work training or other job-related matters. These places are the perfect settings for the development of the new *lingua della giobba*. The segment below is an example, and, although the speaker was not recorded at work but during his interview, he reproduces an everyday typical conversation he has with an Italian colleague. Giulio[3] is a southern Italian migrant who arrived in London in 2016. He moved to London when he was offered a job as a baker for an Italian bakery. According to him, his knowledge of English is very low, although he has a secondary school diploma.

Segment 1. The English tools

01	Giulio	perchè mi risulterebbe abbastanza::	because it would be quite::: hard then
02		difficile poi comunque a lavoro per	anyway at work for instance all the
03		esempio tutti i nomi tutte le le le <.>	nouns all the the <.> tools everything
04		utensilerie tutto quello che ci serve	that we need we use everything
05		usiamo tutto tutto in inglese cioè io	everything in English I mean when I
06		quando vado da *nisbet* il fornitore io	go to *nisbet* the supplier I go to buy
07		vado a comprare *gloves* i *blue gloves*	*gloves* the *blue gloves* I go to buy the
08		vado a comprare il *blue roll* vado a	*blue roll* I go to buy the *soft brush* I
09		comprare il *soft brush* non vado a	don't go to buy the kitchen roll a:::nd
10		comprare la carta assorbente e:: il	the brush or the gloves I go to buy the
11		pennello o i guanti vado a comprare le	*soft sponges*
12		*soft sponge*	
13	Giulia	[giggling] le sai tutte benissimo	[giggling] you know them all very
14			well
15	Giulio	io per tagliare il pollo per tagliare le	to cut the chicken to cut the potatoes
16		patate chiedo a C** dov'è il *chopper*	I ask C** where is the *chopper* <...>
17		<...> cioè io sto sul *front* C** mi metto	I mean I'm on the *front* C** I put
18		sul *front* <.> o mi metto sul *back*?	myself on the *front* <.> or I go on the
19			*back*?

Giulio begins with justifying his translanguaging at work. He introduces the topic by saying that it would be difficult for him to shift from his *lingua della giobba* to a variety of monolingual Italian (lines 01–02). He then spontaneously provides examples suggesting the naturalness of such realisations. In lines 06–12, he relates his linguistic behaviour to a daily practice. The tools are 'bought' in English, and, therefore, the sense and the essence of those objects are provided by the English signifier, even in the conversations with his Italian colleagues. Giulio's language is practical and tangible. In this case, translanguaging becomes a way to abandon the time and place of the interview, to lead both the interviewee and the interviewer to a different space–time dimension. Through translanguaging, the participant concretely involves the listener into his migratory experience. Giulio continues reproducing an imaginary but plausible exchange with his colleague, C**, reporting examples of their daily exchanges. The conversation is rich in translanguaging elements, and it is a true expression of Giulio's *lingua della giobba* at his workplace. As we notice, contrary to post-war migrants' habit to adapt English nouns into Italian phonetic, he does not adapt the English words included in his translingual style. Later in his interview, Giulio claims that his style is completely different from the one of post-war migrants, asserting his right to challenge past associations – indexical meanings – translanguaging came to acquire within the Italian migration context.

Showing their newly acquired professionalism through multilingualism appears to be very important for some participants, even when they are not at work. In the following extract, Andrea, who works as a waiter for an Italian restaurant, demonstrates his new identity and his loyalty to his professional engagement to his brother, Stefano. As preliminary information, we need to know that Andrea moved due to scarce job possibilities in his own region. He chose London because he followed his brother's suggestion. His brother moved to London in 2010 to learn English and to study at post-graduate level. Translanguaging allows Andrea to play a character inspired by his professional self when he is at home and, most importantly, with this performance, Andrea shares his new self. The translanguaging lens allows us to enter Andrea's migration experience, showing his trajectory. Andrea is also representative of a considerable number of post-2008 migrants who migrated in search of fortune and professionalism, which they could not achieve in Italy, and who are generally excluded from the media and academic presentation of contemporary Italian migration.

Segment 2. Playing a character

01	Giulia	no tu sei pe:r <.> sei più subdolo	no you are fo::r <.> you are more sneaky
02		ma come tuo fratello	but you are like your brother
03	Stefano	più silenzioso	more silent
04	Giulia	Esatto	exactly
05	Andrea	io faccio i *side* di Nutella	I make some *sides* of Nutella
06	Giulia	io no grazie	not for me thanks
07	Andrea	te la metto *on the side*	I put it *on the side*
08	Giulia	[giggling] no no non la voglio	[giggling] no no I don't want it at all
09		proprio	

Andrea is here trying to persuade Giulia[4] to accept a topping for a dessert. Andrea's insistence consists of reproducing a very traditional Italian practice. Traditionally, in Italy, the guest is offered the biggest portion of food and this offer is repeated as a sign of kindness and politeness. In this case, Giulia plays the role of the guest. She is on the refusing side, and she is the one being served, along with Andrea's brother, Stefano. Therefore, due to his task, Andrea not only performs the host but also his waiter persona, by presenting his newly acquired professional identity. In line 05, he describes his action by engaging in translanguaging. This lexical insertion is common in his daily linguistic practice and, although he is now in a domestic environment, he resorts to his professional language, which serves a performative purpose. When Giulia declines his offer, he insists on it by returning to a classical translingual realisation (line 07). I would claim that, for this speaker, returning to English for this kind of realisation is a performative act. Andrea possibly uses this phrase in his everyday professional life, both with foreign customers and with the Italian staff he works with, and he sees these formulas as professional identity makers. By performing his professional persona, the speaker is including Giulia in his own world, sharing part of his daily routine and demonstrating his progress in the acquisition of the host country language and his ability to use it properly.

The relationship between translingual practices and professional identities is another theme picked up in the interviews. In Segment 3, Nicola discusses the value of English in relation to his professional world. Nicola is a southern Italian migrant who moved to London in 2013. He works as director of an Italian company that organises internships for Italian high-school students. Most of his co-workers are Italian.

Segment 3. Giving sense to who you are

01	Giulia	cioè secondo te l'inglese è una lingua	in your opinion does the English
02		che ha uno scopo lavorativo?	language have a professional
03			purpose?
04	Nicola	alcuni termini mi viene da usarli più	I find easier to use some terms in
05		semplicemente in inglese <.> cioè li	English <.> I mean I consider them
06		vedo più *effettivi* non so come dire	more *real* I don't know how to say
07	Giulia	efficaci?	effective?
08	Nicola	efficaci <.> [laughing] *effective*	effective <.> [laughing] *effective*
09	Giulia	[laughing]	[laughing]
10	Nicola	più efficaci in inglese	more effective in English
11	Giulia	ok	ok
12	Nicola	cioè ti ho detto *skills* prima	I mean I said *skills* before
13	Giulia	ha più senso dirlo in inglese?	does it make more sense to say it in
14			English?
15	Nicola	cioè l'altro giorno parlavo con un mio	I mean the other day I was talking
16		amico e gli dicevo *fatti quotare* invece	with a friend and I was saying *get a*
17		di fatti fare il preventivo dicevo *fatti*	*quote* instead of get a quote I was
18		*quotare* perchè alcuni termini un po'	saying *get a quote* because some
19		perchè mi piace ma alcuni termini	terms a little bit because I like it but
20		comunque mi danno veramente il	other terms really they give me the
21		senso:: *compagnia company* io dico	sense ::: *compagnia company* I
22		sempre la *compagnia* in Italia non si	always say *compagnia* in Italy you
23		dice *compagnia* si dice azienda io dico	don't say *compagnia* you say society
24		*direttore* in italiano è amministratore	I say *director* in Italian is
25		non sono direttore <.> quindi alcuni	administrator I'm not a director <.>
26		termini li sento veramente che in	so I feel that some terms in English
27		inglese sono più diretti danno più il	are more direct they give more the
28		senso di quello che fai	sense of what you do

The exploitation of English happens spontaneously in the first part of the segment. The formal register of the communicative situation (the interview) causes Nicola's doubt about the word chosen. In line 06, Nicola opts for a loanshift, recognising his translingual realisation only after my suggestion. By adapting the English word 'effective' into an existing Italian morphosyntactic lexical item, *effettivi*, he adds a new meaning to the Italian adjective. The consequent laugh suggests an agreement of the two speakers about what happened, and how important this episode is in an interview on the use of English in Italian migrants' speech. Without any solicitation, Nicola explains his point on the effectiveness of English since the transfer of English word meanings into Italian words helps him to create a fluid professional style. The concluding turn (lines 15–30) is extremely important to an understanding of the value attributed to translanguaging. For this speaker, English is more than a linguistic resource. It is a provider of sense, and by engaging with translanguaging, thus using their full linguistic repertoire, the speakers can explain their new world, and, in this case, their new professional world.

In line 12, Nicola mentions the word 'skills'. This item indexes a professional system which Italian migrants experience more in the host country than in the homeland. The assessment of workers' actual skills and the appreciation for them are elements that the participants believe are neglected in the Italian job market. It is important to specify that the reality of facts could differ, but the perception of the speakers is the only truth that matters for the present analysis. The deployment of the English language, then, is presented almost as a necessity for the description of a job market considered fairer and more skills-based than the Italian one. Resorting to translanguaging, for Nicola, is a way to obtain the real sense of his world (lines 20 and 21), and, hence, by accepting English influences on his linguistic behaviour, he can also deliver that sense. It shows here how translanguaging is an extremely important means to express speakers' interpretations of their world (Li, 2011), and an incredibly valuable tool for exploring speakers' diverse trajectories and evolution of their selves, and to understand speakers' processes of reflection on the indexical significance of such practice. Although Nicola works for an Italian company and speaks Italian with most of his co-workers, he still feels the urgency to rely on translanguaging to demonstrate his professionalism in more than one world, and in more than one language. Translanguaging is thus the clear expression of his transnationalism, his regular contact with two (and more) systems of professional values.

The following example demonstrates the important function translanguaging has in providing an adequate description of one's work. The inclusion of the English language seems crucial to better contextualising the job of these participants. In this segment, Ciro, a southern Italian migrant who moved to London in 2014 to find a job, had a conversation with Cristina, who went to London to improve her English for six months after she graduated from university and then stayed to find a job.

Segment 4. Accepting what you do (and what you are)

01	Giulia	e che fate a Londra? che lavoro fate?	and what do you do in London?
02			what's your job?
03	Ciro	attualmente?	at the moment?
04	Giulia	sì	Yes
05	Ciro	lavoro in uno *sho::p* <.> come te lo	I work in a *sho::p* <.> how I can
06		spiego non so come posso definirlo un	explain it I don't know how I can
07		bistrot?	define it a bistro?
08	Cristina	una catena?	a chain?
09	Ciro	lavoro in una catena che fa paste	I work for a chain that makes pasta
10	Cristina	*fast food* ma che fa *healthy food*	*fast food* but that makes *healthy food*
11			
12	Ciro	[sì fa solo	[yes
13		pasta ed è bar vende caffè e:: vende	we make only pastas and it's a bar it
14		insalate	sells coffees a::nd it sells salads
15	Giulia	ok e tu che fai?	ok and what do you do?
16	Cristina	io lavoro in un'agenzia che affitta	I work for an agency that rents rooms
17		camere però è molto diversa	but it's very different from the estate
18		dall'agente immobiliare in Italia <.> il	agent in Italy <.> my title is *letting*
19		mio titolo è *letting manager* anche se	*manager* even though I'm
20		mi vergogno di questo nome <..>	embarrassed about this name <..> the
21		l'altro giorno un ragazzo mi ha scritto	other day a guy wrote me M** is
22		M** è molto professionale e io ho	really professional and I thought
23		pensato a come faccio io le *viewing*	about how I do the *viewing* <.> that I
24		<.> che cioè proprio *professional* è	mean *professional* is something else
25		un'altra cosa	
26			

Ciro seems reluctant to engage with translanguaging. He pauses after using a translingual item (line 05) and then admits his incapability of describing the place he works for. While Ciro tries to avoid translanguaging, Cristina intervenes to help him (line 10), and she does it by engaging in translanguaging. Ciro, on the other hand, continues his explanation avoiding the practice. Interestingly, also, Cristina initially does not resort to translanguaging to describe her job (lines 16–18). She explains, though, that her profession does not coincide with the Italian way of understanding this job. This is relevant as she starts to show her acknowledgment of two professional dimensions, and this aspect is then translated into a linguistic issue. The reason for the lack of engagement with translanguaging is provided in lines 19–21. The speaker prefers not to use her English job title, as she does not adhere to the very particular brand of professionalism this job title seems to imply. She does not see a coherence between her daily professional duties and her English job title. According to Cristina, the set of values this title carries contrasts with her self-evaluation of her professionalism.

Becoming an Adult in a Migratory Context

For many Italians who left Italy after 2008, their migration coincided with their first step towards economic independence and implies a series of changes which determine a transformation of the individual at different levels (Bhugra & Becker, 2005). For most of the participants, finding an economically satisfactory job in Italy was difficult. Economic autonomy could only be gained in a foreign context. In addition, the Italian cultural system does not encourage independence even for those young people who do work. In many speakers' narratives, I found that the need for independence and the need to challenge Italian customs led to the decision to migrate. This migration was presented by the literature as a 'flight' of young people from a country subject to a gerontocracy (Montanari & Staniscia, 2017: 50), understood as a sociocultural situation in which much older people hold the decisional power. Scholars started to describe gerontocracy, and the more general cultural system that favours those who have already established their socioeconomic status, as an endemic issue of Italian society which only patently emerged in a moment of economic crisis and which forced thousands of young Italians to leave (Bartolini et al., 2017; King et al., 2016). If we accept that the true beginning of adulthood happens once children leave the parental home (Goldscheider & Torr, 2007), we can see a relation between migration and the passage from adolescence into adulthood.

Matteo moved to London in 2015 to find a job and now works as waiter for an Italian restaurant. He shares a flat with Andrea and Giulia, the researcher. In the house, he is usually considered the least mature since he moved two years after Andrea and Giulia. And in Italy, he was dependent on his mother. The dialogue presented in the segment below shows his willingness to be considered as a knowledgeable adult and his renegotiation of identity. Since the discussion is around a bottle of milk, Matteo's expertise on the quality of this product indexes his engagement with his migratory (and also professional) life. Understanding the differences between products and the new labels seems an obvious task, upon which, however, the process of adult independence is based. Demonstrating his expertise on the properties of the milk, Matteo tries to renegotiate not only his personal identity, but also his social identity as a migrant, as a person who left his parents' house to challenge himself with a new experience.

Segment 5. Proving to be an adult

01	Matteo	sì ma era *semi-skimmed*	yes but it was *semi-skimmed*
02	Andrea	e che cazzo c'entra?	what the hell does that have to do with it?
03	Giulia	beh meno animali che lo	well less animals that infect it
04		infettano	
05	Matteo	*semi-skimmed* è meglio	*semi-skimmed* is better
06	Giulia	e tra l'altro era tutto *skimmed*	and by the way it was whole *skimmed* I
07		penso	think
08	Matteo	*semi-skimmed*	*semi-skimmed*
09	Giulia	ma no era rosso	but no it was red
10	Matteo	eh *semi*	so *semi*
11	Giulia	no il rosso è *skimmed* <..>	no the red one is *skimmed* <..> wait I'll
12		aspetta che mi tolgo	move from the corner
13		dall'angolino	

In the previous turns of this conversation, Matteo told Giulia and Andrea, that he drank expired milk from a bottle in the fridge. This information had put him in a position of inferiority in front of migrants who appear to have more knowledge about everyday matters in the host country, and, thus, people who started the process of autonomy earlier than he did. His defence, hence, starts with a recourse to the English language (line 01). Translanguaging is here an index of Matteo's involvement in the real life of the host country. The centre of this discussion may appear trivial, but it is indeed indexically loaded. The recourse to translanguaging is effective to win his argument over Giulia, who supports Matteo (line 03–04), maintaining that, by being semi-skimmed, the milk could have hurt him less, owing to the lower levels of animal fats. However, the convergence and support does not last more than one turn. Giulia tries to reaffirm her role of the more competent and adult migrant, by pointing out that the bottle they are discussing contained skimmed milk (lines 06–07). Giulia's description of the colour of the bottle lid stops Matteo's attempt to reaffirm his expertise (line 09). Matteo, however, repositions himself as the knower of the labelling of the milk. Giulia's claim does not concern the type of bottle in the fridge, but it is a general statement on the colour-label system in the UK. Her turn, in line 11, represents the end of such an argument. Giulia reaffirms her social role of expert migrant, not allowing further discussions and changing the topic (lines 12–13); Matteo, hence, does not contribute with additional turns on this matter.

The relationship between adulthood, independence and English language is acknowledged by the informants in their interviews. In the following extract, I lead the participant towards a reflection on her recently acquired independence and maturity, and its link with her changed linguistic repertoire. Maria is a northern Italian migrant who arrived in

London in 2014, after she completed her post-graduate studies. She works for an American financial services company.

Segment 6. Becoming independent in another language

01	Giulia	è comunque stato un passaggio da:: una fase di infanzia a una vita da adulta?	it was anyway a passage fro::m a child stage to an adult life?
04	Maria	sì più o meno sì	yes more or less yes
05	Giulia	anche tante cose di responsabilità saranno cambiate no?	also many responsibilities must have changed, mustn't they?
07	Maria	ah sì quello sicuramente <.> sì dover avere a che fare o comunque amministrare cose anche in un contesto non italiano certe cose tipo la casa e va beh il *bank account* e boh tante cose	ah yes that surely <.> sure having to deal or anyway managing things in a non-Italian context also some things like the house and well the *bank account* I don't know many things

Maria agreed with me about the new responsibilities this life brings along with it. Maria stressed the context in which she had to take on obligations (line 08–10) and she used translanguaging (line 12) to exemplify the new tasks the adult life requires. She does not need to continue the list of burdens as, with the English item, she immediately identified the interesting (for my interview) semantic area, and, due to my belonging to the group, Maria relied on our shared knowledge and experience to establish an agreement on the extension and the indexicality of such an item. In the interview context, where one would not expect engagement with translanguaging due to the formality of the conversational situation, the use of a linguistic resource different from Italian, even if expressed with a lexical borrowing only, has a strong indexical meaning, as it reminds to the story of migration of such speaker, which she knows she shares with the interviewer. Indexicality here intervenes at two levels: English is the language that indexes adulthood for this speaker and all adult life related matters, while translanguaging indexes her passage to adulthood and her migratory experience at the same time. In the following segment, our discussion continues.

Segment 7. Becoming adults in another language

01	Giulia	però ad esempio se devi parlare della casa dell'affitto delle questioni di vita pratica	but for instance if you have to talk about the house the rent the matters of practical life
04	Maria	ah sì:: anche quelle <.> ah sì quello sicuramente se dovessi tornare in Italia e dovessi sbrigare delle faccende di tipo burocratico anche lì mi mancherebbe il vocabolario	ah yes also those <.> ah yes that for sure if I had to go back to Italy and I had to deal with bureaucratic matters also there I would not have the vocabulary

In asking this question, I was connecting my own experience with Maria's, following her suggestion reported in the previous segment. Maria explained here how having acquired independence in a foreign country has affected her linguistic repertoire. Therefore, she is justifying her translingual practices linked to the management of her new life by hypothesising a return to Italy and, thus, to monolingual Italian conversations (lines 05–06). This element is fundamental. In previous turns of the interview, not reported here due to space limitations, Maria presented herself as an independent woman, restless, free to behave as she wishes, and able to manage new aspects of her life. On the contrary, a return to Italy was imagined (at least linguistically) in negative terms. She focused on her linguistic disadvantage to implicitly express her ignorance of the Italian system in which she does not have experience of dealing with bureaucratic tasks. Later, Maria admitted that she had contradictory feelings towards the changes in her linguistic repertoire. In producing this last turn, Maria lowered her tone, communicating a certain sadness for her absence of vocabulary. On the one hand, she appreciated the power that learning English gave to her, but, on the other she regretted the loss of purism, of her perfect eloquence in her mother tongue. I have noted the same tendency in the participants with a very high level of education. In reality, though, all the migrants recorded engaged with translanguaging when discussing topics related to their adult life or everyday issues.

Conclusion

This chapter explored the sociocultural multilingual practices of a sample of post-2008 crisis Italian migrants in London, with the aim of exploring their identity construction processes and group dynamics. The data provided an insight into the mechanisms of identity negotiation and performance in discourse, within a migratory context. Through the sociolinguistic study of this new phase of migrants, it emerges that, in contrast to the media depiction of the post 2008 Italian immigrants as homogeneously highly educated and cosmopolitan professionals, in reality the increasingly enlarging Italian community in London is highly diverse. In addition, this study suggests that post-2008 Italian migrants distance themselves from their homeland's emigration past, rejecting to be associated with the previous generation of migrants. Nonetheless, they rely on linguistic practices which started their process of order of indexicality in the post-war years. The contemporary migrants involved in this research claim to develop new cultural habits and new forms of socialisation, distancing themselves from community-based forms of aggregation, promoted by post-war migrants, and preferring more individualised systems of connections with other migrants.

This study put forward two main arguments. First, the post-2008 migrants develop a new *lingua della giobba*. The old and new *lingua della giobba* differ in the realisation of multilingual practices. While post-war migrants tended to adapt loanwords into Italian morphology, post-2008 migrants prefer to create a translingual style that avoids morphological adaptation of nouns, although accepting adaptation of verbs. According to the participants, it is a language that can be used with other migrants, useful to display their new professionally acquired identities and to reflect on professionalism and job values. The engagement with this new *lingua della giobba* is a tool to perform a life in more than one world. Second, for post-2008 migrants, the new world, London, is not only the world of professionalism but also of adulthood. Translanguaging offers the possibility to show and negotiate your new adult self, but it almost becomes a necessity as well, since English is the language in which migrants acquired their independence. Translanguaging can be used with other migrants, who not only share a similar linguistic repertoire, meaning that comprehension can be achieved, but also share the same experiences. Engagement with translanguaging is an expression of such sharing.

Translanguaging is the element that links these migrants, and which represents and unifies the post-2008 crisis phase, despite its heterogeneity. This study provides an example for the exploration of contemporary migrant groups in London. In addition to post-2008 migration from Italy, several other European migrant communities in London were repopulated (as for instance the Greek-speaking or the Spanish-speaking community) after the financial crisis (King, 2017). A comparative study of different European migrants in the UK could show similarities and differences among these diverse cultural and linguistic groups. This would lead to a better understanding of the new London migratory scenario, extremely diversified and complex, and help scholars navigate new research perspectives. Recognising the potential of new European migrants' exploitation of their full linguistic and semiotic repertoire and exploring their real linguistic needs will help scholars and policy makers better comprehend these communities' dynamics. The translanguaging framework discussed in this chapter proves effective to investigate multilingualism from a different angle, with a focus on contemporary migrants' trajectories, as it acknowledges the complexity of late modern migrants' lives in more than one world.

Notes

(1)   These considerations were made by the former Italian General Consul, Massimiliano Mazzanti, in an interview held at the Italian Consulate in London on 30 June 2016.
(2)   The research was approved by the Research Ethics Committee of the University of Westminster. Participants were fully aware of being recorded as they had signed a Consent Form and a Participations Sheet before starting the ethnography. All the transcription conventions are listed in Appendix 2.1.
(3)   All the names of participants are pseudonyms. 'Giulia' is the name of the researcher and author of the chapter.
(4)   As insider researcher, I participate in the spontaneous conversations recorded and I analyse my linguistic behaviour along with that of my participants. In the following analyses, I address myself as 'Giulia' when I consider myself a participant.

Appendix 2.1

<.> one second pause
<..> two second pause
<…> longer pause
[overlapping
[contextualisation]
? questioning tone
! exclamation/raising of tone
italic non-standard Italian words (dialectal or mispronounced)
bold italic English insertions, loanwords and loanshifts
: elongation of sound
** omitted names of people involved and not involved in project or workplaces
+++ unintelligible recording

References

AAVV (2011) L'Italia in 150 Anni. *www.istat.it*. Available from: http://www3.istat.it/dati/catalogo/ 20120118_00/cap_7.pdf (accessed 24 July 2017).
Barni, M. (2011) Regno Unito. In M. Vedovelli (ed.) *Storia linguistica dell'emigrazione italiana nel mondo* (pp. 244–62). Rome: Carrocci.
Bartolini, L., Gropas, R. and Triandafyllidou, A. (2017) Drivers of highly skilled mobility from Southern Europe: Escaping the crisis and emancipating oneself. *Journal of Ethnic and Migration Studies* 43 (4), 652–673.
Bauman, R. and Sherzer, J. (1974) *Explorations in the Ethnography of Communication*. Cambridge: Cambridge University Press.
Bertinetto, P.M. (2010) Fonetica italiana. *Quaderni del laboratorio di linguistica* 9, 2–30.
Blommaert, J. (2007) Sociolinguistics and discourse analysis: Orders of indexicality and polycentricity. *Journal of Multicultural Discourses* 2 (2), 115–130.
Bhugra, D. and Becker, M.A. (2005) Migration, cultural bereavement and cultural identity. *World Psychiatry* 4 (1), 18–24.

Bucholtz, M. and Hall, K. (2005) Identity and interaction: A sociocultural linguistic approach. *Discourse Studies* 7 (4-5), 585–614.

Conti, F. (2012) The present significance of national identity issues: The case of Italian graduates in the UK. *Bulletin of Italian Politics* 4 (1), 5–22.

De Fina, A. (2010) The negotiation of identities. In M.A. Locher and S.L. Graham (eds) *Interpersonal Pragmatics* (pp. 205–224). Berlin: De Gruyter Mouton.

De Fina, A. (2016) Linguistic practices and transnational identities. In S. Preece (ed.) *The Routledge Handbook of Language and Identity* (pp. 163–178). London and New York: Routledge.

De Fina, A., Schiffrin, D. and Bamberg, M. (eds) (2006) *Discourse and Identity* (Vol. 23). Cambridge: Cambridge University Press.

Degli Innocenti, N. (2018) Brexit: 400mila italiani «sommersi» in corsa per diventare residenti. www.ilsole24ore.com. Available at https://www.ilsole24ore.com/art/mondo/2018-01-25/brexit-corsa-italiani-sommersi-diventare-residenti-161132.shtml?uuid=AErqqzoD (accessed 02 April 2019).

Di Salvo, M. (2014) Variazione linguistica e identita' regionale: I pugliesi di Cambrdige e Bedford. In R. Bombi and V. Orioles (eds) *Essere Italiani nel Mondo Globale Oggi: Riscoprire l'Appartenenza* (pp. 77–108). Udine: Forum.

Di Salvo, M. (2015) I pugliesi di Cambridge e i pugliesi di Bedford tra continuita' e variazione. *Italica* 92 (4), 919–936.

Di Salvo, M. (2018) Heritage language, identity, and education in Europe: Evidence from the UK. In P.P. Trifonas and T. Aravossitas (eds) *Handbook of Research and Practice in Heritage Language Education* (pp. 699–714). Toronto: Springer.

Duff, P.A. (2015) Transnationalism, multilingualism, and identity. *Annual Review of Applied Linguistics* 35, 57–80.

EU Settlement Scheme Statistics (April 2020) EU Settlement Scheme Statistics, April 2020, Experimental Statistics. https://assets.publishing.service.gov.uk/government/uploads/system/uploads/attachment_data/file/886174/eu-settlement-scheme-statistics-april-2020.pdf (accessed 5 June 2020).

Fang, Q. and Shaobin, M. (2016) Translingual creativities: A sociolinguistic case study of English lexical borrowings in Mandarin from perspectives of language contact. *Asian Englishes* 18 (1), 19–35.

Ferrini, C. (2018) Le lingue ei profili sociolinguistici dei neoemigrati italiani nel mondo: tra cervelli, braccia e ipotesi di 'innesti'. *Italian Canadiana* XXXII, 31–54.

Fortier, A.M. (1999) Re-membering places and the performance of belonging(s). *Theory, Culture and Society* 16 (2), 41–64.

Fortier, A.M. (2006) Community, belonging and intimate ethnicity. *Modern Italy* 11 (1), 63–77.

Gabaccia, D.R. (2006) Global geography of 'Little Italy': Italian neighbourhoods in comparative perspective. *Modern Italy* 11 (1), 9–24.

García, O. and Li, W. (2014) *Translanguaging. Language, Bilingualism and Education.* New York: Palgrave Macmillan.

Gardaphé, F.L. (1996) *Italian Signs, American Streets: The Evolution of Italian American Narrative.* Durham and London: Duke University Press.

Giddens, A. (1991) *Modernity and Self-identity: Self and Society in the Late Modern Age.* Standford: Standford University Press.

Giddens, A. (1993) Modernity, history, democracy. *Theory and Society* 22 (2), 289–292.

Gjergji, I. (2015) Cause, mete e figure sociali della nuova emigrazione italiana. In I. Gjergji (ed.) *La Nuova Emigrazione Italiana* (pp. 7–23). Venezia: Ca'Foscari.

Goffman, E. (1959) *The Presentation of Self in Everyday Life.* London: Penguin Books.

Goldscheider, F. and Torr, B. (2007) Leaving home in the transition to adulthood. In G. Ritzer (ed.) *The Blackwell Encyclopedia of Sociology* (pp. 2570–2574). Oxford: Blackwell Publishing.

Greavu, A. (2014) A classification of borrowings: Observations from Romanian/English contact. *Diversité et Identité Culturelle En Europe* 10 (2), 95–104

Grillo, T. (1995) Anti-essentialism and intersectionality: Tools to dismantle the master's house. *Berkeley Women's Law Journal* 10, 16–30.

Guzzo, S. (2014) *A Sociolinguistic Insight into the Italian Community in the UK: Workplace Language as an Identity Marker.* Newcastle: Cambridge Scholars Publishing.

Haspelmath, M. (2009) Lexical borrowing: Concepts and issues. In M. Haspelmath and U. Tadmor (eds) *Loanwords in the World's Languages: A Comparative Handbook* (pp. 35–54). Berlin: De Gruyter Mouton.

Huot, S. and Rudman D.L. (2010) The performances and places of identity: Conceptualizing intersections of occupation, identity and place in the process of migration. *Journal of Occupational Science* 17, 2, 68–77.

Istat (2011) L'Italia in 150 Anni. *www.istat.it*. Available from: http://www3.istat.it/dati/catalogo/ 20120118_00/cap_7.pdf

Johnstone, B., Andrus, J. and Danielson, A.E. (2006) Mobility, indexicality, and the enregisterment of 'Pittsburghese'. *Journal of English Linguistics* 34 (2), 77–104.

King, R. (2017) Theorising new European youth mobilities. *Population, Space and Place* 24 (1), 1–12.

King, R., Lulle, A., Conti, F. and Mueller, D. (2016) Eurocity London: A qualitative comparison of graduate migration from Germany, Italy and Latvia. *Comparative Migration Studies* 4 (1), 1–22.

King, R., Lulle, A., Conti, F., Mueller, D. and Scotto, G. (2014) The lure of London: A comparative study of recent graduate migration from Germany, Italy and Latvia. *Sussex Centre for Migration Research* Working Paper 75, 2–39.

Lafleur, J.M. and Stanek, M. (2017) EU migration and the economic crisis: Concepts and issues. In J.M. Lafleur and M. Stanek (eds) *South-north Migration of EU Citizens in Times of Crisis* (pp. 1–14). Switzerland: Springer.

Leimgruber, J. (2012) Singapore English: An indexical approach. *World Englishes* 31 (1), 1–14.

Li, W. (2011) Moment analysis and translanguaging space: Discursive construction of identities by multilingual Chinese youth in Britain. *Journal of Pragmatic* 43 (5), 1222–1235.

Licata, D. (ed.) (2017) *Rapporto Italiani nel mondo.* Rome: Tau editrice.

Licata, D. (ed.) (2018) *Rapporto Italiani nel mondo.* Rome: Tau editrice.

Livingston, A. (1919) La Merica Sanemagogna. *Romanic Review* 9, 206–226.

Mazzaferro, G. (2018) Translanguaging as everyday practice: An introduction. In G. Mazzaferro (ed.) *Translanguaging as Everyday Practice* (pp. 1–12). Springer.

McKay, S. (2015) Young Italians in London and in the UK. In I. Gjergji (ed.) *La Nuova Emigrazione Italiana. Cause, Mete e Figure Sociali* (pp. 71–81). Venice: Edizioni Ca'Foscari-Digital Publishing.

Montanari, A. and Staniscia, B. (2017) Young Italians on the move. European mobility in times of crisis. In B. Glorius and J. Domínguez-Mujica (eds) *European Mobility in Times of Crisis: The New Context of European South-North migration* (pp. 49–73). Bielefeld: Transcript-Verlag.

Nardo Cibele, A. (1900) Alcune parole usate dalla popolazione mista italiana e negra nelle 'fazende' di San Paolo nel Brasile. *Archivio per lo Studio delle Tradizioni Popolari* 19, 18–24.

Panese, M. (1992) Il code-switching come strategia comunicativa: Un'indagine della comunita' italiana a Londra. In A.A. Sobrero (ed.) *Il Dialetto nella Conversazione* (pp. 43–78). Galatina (LE): Congedo.

Paulsrud, B. and Straszer, B. (2018) 'We know the same languages and then we can mix them': A child's perspectives on everyday translanguaging in the family. In G. Mazzaferro (ed.) *Translanguaging as Everyday Practice* (pp. 49–68). Springer.

Prezzolini, G. (1939) La lingua della giobba. *Lingua Nostra* 1, 121–22.

Rocchi, L. (2006) La Lingua di chi è emigrato. Un'indagine tra la Sicilia e l'Inghilterra. *Altre Italie* 33, 129–158.

Roudometof, V. (2005) Transnationalism, cosmopolitanism and glocalization. *Current Sociology* 53 (1), 113–135.

Sacco, G. (2013) Italians in London. *European Scientific Journal* 9 (19), 582–593.

Schiller, N.G., Basch, L. and Blanc-Szanton, C. (1992) Transnationalism: A new analytic framework for understanding migration. *Annals of the New York Academy of Sciences* 645 (1), 1–24.

Scotto, G. (2015) From 'Emigrants' to 'Italians': What is new in Italian migration to London? *Modern Italy* 20 (2), 153–165.

Silverstein, M. (2003) Indexical order and the dialectics of sociolinguistic life. *Language & Communication* 23, 193–229.

Smith, J.A. and Osborn, M. (2003) Interpretative phenomenological analysis. In J.A. Smith (ed.) *Qualitative Psychology: A Practical Guide to Research Methods* (pp. 51–80). London: Sage Publications.

Sponza, L. (1988) *Italian Immigrants in Nineteenth-Century Britain: Realities and Images.* Leicester: Leicester University Press.

Sponza, L. (2005) Gli Italiani in Gran Bretagna. *Altreitalie* 30, 4–22.

Tintori, G. and Romei, V. (2017) Emigration from Italy after the crisis: The shortcomings of the brain drain narrative. In J.M. Lafleur and M. Stanek (eds) *South-North Migration of EU Citizens in Times of Crisis* (pp. 49–64). Switzerland: Springer International Publishing.

Tosi, A. (1991) *L'Italiano d'Oltremare. La lingua delle communita'italiane nei paesi anglofoni.* Florence: Giunti.

Vaughan, H.H. (1926) Italian and its dialects as spoken in the United States. *American Speech* 1, 431–435.

Vedovelli, M. (2015) La condizione linguistica dei neoemigrati Italiani nel mondo: problemi e prospettive. In D. Licata (ed.) *Rapporto Italiani nel Mondo* (pp. 204–210). Roma: Tau editrice.

3 'Sorry, I'm French': Frenchness as Uneasy Resource in the Construction of Home, Identity and Belonging among French Students in London

Saskia Huc-Hepher and Fabrice Lyczba

Introduction

This chapter interrogates how 'Frenchness' is performed and experienced among French undergraduates who have chosen to study in London, and how the notion of so-called 'national identity', which features so prominently in French political and media discourse, intersects with migratory processes of belonging and homemaking in ways that may further transform it. Focusing on students in the first year of their degrees,[1] it explores the complex role played by culture, language and the senses in this early stage of their mobility and diasporic identity construction.

But why French students? Anecdotally, prior to embarking on this project, the authors regularly noted transformations embodied by their own French students over the course of their undergraduate degrees (see Huc-Hepher, 2021b).[2] More objectively, when the field research for this study ended in 2019–20, France had the second-highest number of EU students enrolled at UK universities, with 13,675, compared to 13,965 for close first-place holders, Italy (Higher Education Statistics Agency, 2020). Among these French students, 2,655 were full-time undergraduates in London and over three-quarters of them were enrolled in just seven *central London* universities.[3] These figures confirm both the significance of the French student population in London and the premigration forces at play, whereby the perceived 'symbolic capital' (Bourdieu, 1994: 161) associated with prestigious(-sounding) central institutions appears to have guided the students' educational mobilities. Yet French students have largely eluded scholarly attention.[4]

Choosing to study at institutions based in London's 'superdiverse' heart (Vertovec, 2007), presents an opportunity for the French students to construct their own incarnation of a distinctive, symbolically charged, cosmopolitan identity (Conradson & Latham, 2007). For many, it is their first experience of living away from the family home, and doing so during their formative years encourages a form of 'vernacular cosmopolitanism' (Georgiou, 2013) through exposure to new cultural resources in the global city. However, it is a reinvented self which remains informed by the French primary habitus (as their choice of university, for instance, would suggest) and one whose capacity for transformation, irrespective of the London *situation* (Tsing, 2000), is hence restricted (Bourdieu, 2005; Duchêne-Lacroix & Koukoutsaki-Monnier, 2016; Oliver & O'Reilly, 2010). Ultimately, the emotionally 'shocking element of cultural interaction and encounter' (Walsh, 2012: 50) can give rise to a 'dislocation of habitus' (Hardy, 2012: 126), an unsettling sense of 'habitus hysteresis' (Bourdieu, 2000: 278), which in turn leads the students to embrace, exaggerate or contest their constructions of Frenchness. We therefore posit that Frenchness, as a self-reported marker of identity and difference, functions as a complex, ambiguous and dynamic resource in the students' belonging, which in fact coheres with the experience of older cross-Channel migrants (Benson, 2011; Huc-Hepher, 2021b) and warrants academic scrutiny. Despite the propensity for transformation among this young cohort, Frenchness is seen to shape the space where belonging is constructed both through cracks and crevasses in their originary understanding of 'national identity' *and* through the *reification* of key elements of this identity. In a continuous, glacier-like process of fracturing and solidifying, a salient feature of their belonging and homemaking project emerges: its fundamental *unease*.

So, as the London experience provokes fissures in hegemonic understandings of Frenchness, leading some to dispute essentialist notions of 'being French', the students' fluid and often paradoxical embodiment of cultural identity is a catalyst for their unease. At times, veritable fractures develop, such as a fundamental unease with discordant articulations of regional, national, ethnic and/or racialised inflections of Frenchness. But unease also manifests when navigating the adopted London field, where a 'French identity' per se is re-solidified discursively in ways that challenge the cosmopolitan quest for 'being different together' (De Backer, 2019). In casting doubt over traditional, monochrome definitions of identity through their belonging project, the students *simultaneously* undermine, reconfigure and perform Frenchness.

A Contextual Backdrop: Hegemonic Frenchness and Translocality

In 21st-century France, so-called 'national identity' has been the object of 'a public reckoning that borders on a full-scale moral panic' (Silverstein, 2018: 7). Beyond the Sarkozy-government-led *Grand débat sur l'identité nationale* (2009–10), an endeavour which ultimately proved oxymoronic (Ratinaud & Marchand, 2012), efforts to establish a state-sponsored '[n]eorepublican discourse' (Leruth, 1998) on 'French identity' continue to fuel debate. This narrative has resulted in 'the hegemonic rise of an exclusivist understanding of the concepts of the Republic' (Mondon, 2015: 407), which foregrounds '*laïcité*' (secularism *à la française*) and an assimilationist form of integration that negates multicultural 'communitarianism' ('*le communautarisme*'). In the name of egalitarian universalism, therefore, attempts to erase ethnic, gender, regional, language and class differences are legitimated (Bauberot, 2008; Chabal, 2010, 2015, 2017; Hajjat, 2012; Lapeyronnie, 2010; Leruth, 1998; Noiriel, 2007).

This hegemonic conception of 'Republicanism' as a unified and unifying national fabrication of 'Frenchness', and as France's clearest articulation of 'banal nationalism' (Billig, 1995), is nevertheless challenged by numerous studies. Following what postcolonial historians have dubbed a 'paroxysmal crisis in France in terms of the redefinition of the nation's rapport with respect to its own identity' (Bancel, 2013: 208), Silverstein (2018) argues that the legacy of colonialism in contemporary France, particularly resistance to decolonising national identity, is key to understanding how this discourse of Republicanism is complicit in the rise of 'Republic racism' (Dubois, 2000), 'virtuous racism' (Guénif-Souilamas, 2006) or 'respectable racism' (Wolfreys, 2018). In other words, the discourse of universal Frenchness serves to fuel contemporary forms of social exclusion and discrimination (Simon, 2006). Sociological studies consequently reveal French national identity as fractured, with 'visible minorities' (Montague, 2013) marginalised by colour-blind Republicanism and demanding greater recognition of diversity. They show whiteness to play a concealed, yet potent, role in restricting access to multiple aspects of French national identity: to citizenship rights (Beaman, 2015, 2018), cultural life (Escafré-Dublet, 2019) and even French Republican values themselves (Murphy, 2011). Frenchness thus emerges as a site of unreconciled postcolonial tensions, where dynamic trajectories of belonging cohabit unharmoniously and where minorities seek to reclaim it as an identity *inclusive* of diversity (La Documentation française, 2009; Maalouf, 2001; Mballo & Bourget, 2018).

Problematising the question further, a major survey on heritage and diversity in France (INED/INSEE, 2016) showed that beyond postcolonial debates, French 'national identity' is constantly revisited, questioned and re-imagined by diverse mobility experiences and territorial ties that accommodate 'plural allegiances' within Frenchness (see Simon, 2012).[5] Importantly, belonging and French national identity were found to be (re) defined in contemporary France by multiple regional, national and/or international mobility trajectories, potentially simultaneously. When 'to be here' is different from 'to be from here' (Sencébé, 2004), mobility, territory and origins engage in dialogue and delineate multiple identity possibilities (Guérin-Pace, 2009) in a nimble dance between 'territories to which we belong' and 'territories that belong to us' (Filippova & Guérin-Pace, 2008). The façade of 'a' French national identity – referred to here as 'hegemonic Frenchness' – therefore appears increasingly flimsy and disconnected from lived experience, with a range of dynamic territorial, socioeconomic, ethnic and linguistic (Filhon, 2011) processes eroding and reshaping it. In this context, the mobility of French people *outside* France, estimated at some 200,000 per year (Temporal & Brutel, 2016), though largely ignored in French national-identity and migration discourse (Gonzalez, 2014), further threatens the façade of hegemonic Frenchness as it fundamentally 'interrogates [French people's] relationship to the nation' (Gonzalez, 2014: 15) and opens the door to Frenchness – as a symbolic 'territory that belong[s]' to French migrants – being redefined by their encounter with 'territories to which they belong'.

Within this tortuous landscape of belonging, and building on the homemaking turn in migration studies, we hypothesise that France's physical closeness to the UK, combined with the nations' historical connection and disjuncture, only reinforces the sense of London as a 'translocality' (Giclis, 2009: 275, citing Appadurai, 1995). We argue that the postmigration field constitutes a localised in-between space where relations encompass both new London sociabilities and profound affective and sensorial links to precise premigration filial, linguistic, gustatory and olfactory 'placehoods'. Gielis's description of the diasporic field as a 'continuum of place' (Gielis, 2009: 282), corresponding to a 'state of "inbetweenness"' spanning 'here' and 'there', in which migrants construct home and belonging (Gielis, 2009: 282), is particularly apt for a population whose link with the originary 'home' is not just maintained through media or everyday practices and rituals, but also by a material presence and frequent visits – a population suggestively named 'Eurostars' and 'super-movers' in Adrian Favell's analysis of EU migrants in Europe (2006, 2008). For French student migrants in London, the construction of a 'cosmopolitan continuum' (Ong, 2009) is a quotidian experience rendered both banal and peculiarly dynamic by geographic proximity, complicating 'the messy reality of their lived experience' (Huc-Hepher, 2021b: 5) in 21st-century global London.

Dis-located from their family home and driven by desires for new horizons, our French undergraduates in London formulate, and then experience, migration imaginings in which 'home' is the unspoken beating heart. But their mobility is complicated by a context where homesickness is curable, budget permitting, by a hop on the Eurostar. Consequently, 'homecoming' (Dürrschmidt, 2016) often takes place alongside home-*making*, and the students must navigate a 'transnational habitus' (Nedelcu, 2012), spanning both geographical and psychological divides. Their transition from being supported children-at-home to autonomous adults-away-from-home makes their London belonging particularly fraught and uneasy. At this formative period in their lives, we therefore ask how much the students are at home in their (diasporic) French identity; how Frenchness helps or hinders belonging; and how/where they are at home – or not – as they embark on their three-year degrees in London.

Methodological Minutiae

The findings we present correspond to stage one of our longitudinal, mixed-methods study, designed to monitor French students' identity transformation over the three-year duration of their degree programmes, commencing September 2017. The data collection process began with a targeted online survey, circulated in the students' first term. It comprised a combination of quantitative-style yes/no, Moreno-scale and multiple-choice questions, together with open questions for qualitative responses. The questionnaire was designed to allow findings of scale to triangulate our interview data and provide a structured written framework redistributable at strategic points over students' degrees, hence constituting a reliable mechanism for recording response patterns vertically, over time, and horizontally, across students.

One of the first hurdles encountered when designing the methodology was how to conceptualise and apply 'Frenchness'. For ease and practicability, we targeted students based on their university-registered country of domicile. This had the advantage of objectivity, removing researcher bias regarding the definition of Frenchness, while broadening recruitment to non-French nationals with recent lived histories in France, regardless of family background. Yet, it excluded students who might self-identify as French but who, whatever their prior mobility trajectory, were living in London prior to enrolling on their university course. Both the call for participation and questionnaire were written in French, which added an element of self-selection, as the French language served as an imperfect, but experientially sound, proxy for self-identification with Frenchness.[6] It was anticipated that use of the French language would also prompt more spontaneous, hence potentially more candid responses. Adding narrative richness to the survey data, we conducted one-to-one semi-structured interviews with students who, in the questionnaire, had volunteered to take part in follow-up discussions. These conversations lasted around 40 minutes each and were also chiefly conducted in French, on university premises, in the second semester of the students' first year.[7]

The biggest challenge was low response rates. Despite the targeted approach and involvement of three London universities, only 24 students responded to the initial survey, 14 in 2017–18 and 10 in 2018–19 when we repeated the call.[8] The questionnaire sample was skewed towards women, and most respondents self-identified as 'white' (17), with four stating 'mixed' heritage and one 'black'. There was an almost even split between Catholics and respondents with 'no religion'. Among this cohort, only a third (8) were interviewed, of whom five were women.[9] This thwarted any aspirations for quantitative breadth and potency, but given the ethnographic grounding of the study, the data collected was deemed worthy of analysis and dissemination.

At Home in Their French Identity? A Tale of Uneasy Ambiguity

In this section, we concentrate primarily on the results of our initial questionnaire and subsequently on interview data, arguing that at this early migration stage, respondents' French identity is firm in some respects, more oscillatory in others, and above all replete with ambiguity. In the survey, stability was repeatedly combined with fluidity; cultural and ethnic identity with civic and linguistic identity; collective 'national identity' with individuated iterations; and rhetoric with practice.

Most students self-identified as 'French', with answers ranging from 'very French' to 'somewhat French', though two selected 'not very French'.[10] The French–British Moreno scale produced both 'French, not British' responses and 'as much French as British', despite all respondents living in France pre-migration and only one having a British parent. 'EU' and

'London' epithets generated even greater ambivalence. Most respondents felt 'as much French as European', or 'as much French as London', with both ends of the scale also represented. Overall, self-identification with Frenchness remained strong and was thus testament to a persistent 'primary identity' (Valdez & Golash-Boza, 2018: 1) or primary habitus, which contributed to postmigration 'boundary-making' (Leurs & Ponzanesi, 2018: 11), especially in relation to the 'British' alternative. Crucially, Frenchness emerged as fluid and dynamically related to the London field. Such malleability suggested a selfhood in flux, interpretable either as migration trigger or early outcome of immersion in London, and thus indicative of a destabilising hysteresis effect (Bourdieu, 2000; Hardy, 2012).

When probing the civic, cultural and ethnic dimensions of Frenchness, further ambiguities arose. None of the respondents agreed that 'to be French one should be born in France', and many rejected this 'very strongly', with similar unanimity expressed against the statement that 'to be French it is important to have French ancestors'. But when asked whether France was defined by 'its people, not its values', a question often used to measure identification with 'ethnic' articulations of national identity, responses were split. These mixed findings confirmed the anticipated individuated understandings of Frenchness among the undergraduates and their resistance to categorisation into a single profile. Family mobility trajectories and personal lived experience were seen to affect identity more than abstract allegiances to inherited or civic nationhood. Melanie,[11] for instance, indicated that she felt 'somewhat French' (but also 'as much French as Londoner') and *completely* disagreed with the ancestry premise, doubtless linked to her parents' migration to France (from Poland and Algeria). Yet, she also *somewhat agreed* that 'France is defined by its people, not its values' – potentially self-excluding herself from Frenchness. Melanie's self-declared 'Jewish' faith, family heritage and self-identified 'white' ethnicity were thus interweaving into a complex tapestry of Frenchness.

Kerian, whose heritage is also mixed ('Moroccan, Algerian, Breton and Scottish'), was one of very few to report feeling 'more British than French' – despite having never lived in Britain – and 'not very French' – after a lifetime, so far, in France. This agentive rejection of Frenchness, possibly a reaction to premigration prejudice, as discussed in the interview, chimes with recent statistics on young French people's changing views on such core French values as *laïcité* and its potentially discriminatory function (Ifop, 2021). Indeed, our data revealed widespread uneasiness regarding the outdated *Français de souche*[12] concept and uncertainty regarding the role of 'values', such as *laïcité*, in identity construction. For, confirming our expectations, the universalist discourse of 'hegemonic Frenchness' (defined above and experienced by respondents in France within the framework of 'Republican values') fails to recognise the fluidities and complex trajectories of our respondents.[13] As Kerian elaborated, 'What I've been through, whether in my family or personally, has made me the person I am today... It happened in France...but it could've happened anywhere'.

Notwithstanding respondents' ambivalence towards 'French values' and openness to multiculturalism (evidenced by strong agreement that 'immigration is good for society' and strong disagreement that 'French culture is endangered by immigration'), premigration universalist ideologies *were* paradoxically operationalised in response to statements about different integration models. Students favoured cultural 'assimilation' over other models, and the French language was considered a key marker of national identity, with no-one disagreeing that 'to be French it is important to speak French'. Shedding light on the students' underlying motivations for studying in London, most respondents perceived France as a globalised country, but where difference is problematic. In a similar vein, and countering French public opinion, all bar one opposed France's burqa ban and there was wide endorsement of 'foreign-sounding' accents. Overall, the majority of our survey respondents expressed a strong sense of civic French identity (French-speaking, assimilationist, globally open), but this was generally at odds with their disidentification from France's blanket *laïcité* and 'colorblind racial ideology' (Beaman, 2018: 12).

These findings therefore disrupt what has emerged as the central bedrock principle of current French hegemonic conceptions of French identity: *laïcité*, and its concomitant erasure of difference. Indeed, opposition to *laïcité* transpired to be a factor of distinction legitimating the students' London project. Whereas France's Republican egalitarian ideals were seen to whitewash racial, ethnic and/or faith-based differences, the postmigration field was perceived as a space that embraced difference and multiculturalism. This proved to be fundamental to the London experience and created an ideological rift between our respondents and their loved ones left behind. In our survey and interview data, London was defined as 'tolerant', open-minded, welcoming of change and difference, especially religious. Conversely, France tended to be described as intolerant, incomprehensible, inward-looking and retrograde, with no discernible difference whether respondents were from small towns or large cities. Kerian (from Paris), for instance, was clear about this:

> In France I had problems because I've got a beard, I've got tattoos, I'm homosexual... so because of all this it was hard in France. And I knew it was more open-minded here, more tolerant of homosexuality; people love tattoos here, everyone's got tattoos in England...[14]

Respondents often associated 'tolerance' with modernity and internationalism, both of which were deemed to be materialised in London. Contrastingly, France was considered 'intolerant' due to associations with tradition and resistance to change. This subjective reframing of the pre-migration space points towards nascent ideological transformation and critique, both fundamental to the new home-making project on which the students were embarking. Importantly, these attitudes were often linked to an expressed need for social and personal distinction, London mobility being driven by a desire to follow one's own path, to mature and reinvent oneself. Adding another strand of ambiguity to the self-identification process, therefore, a tension between collective, inherited nationalism and individualised, agentive cosmopolitanism was conveyed (Alemán & Woods, 2018). Not only – in a typically *Bildungsroman* manner (Cicchelli, 2008) – did participants perceive their migratory trajectory as an *original* and *highly personal* (ad)venture which distinguished them from non-movers in France, but it sometimes also led to further distinction from other London-French migrants.

In our interviews, Benjamin, for example, explained how he decided to migrate to London 'from the countryside' to study business management as a last-minute solution, after an administrative grade-calculation error thwarted his plans to study music in France. His London imaginings were articulated as an intimate voyage of re-discovery for a 'truer' self, connected with his father's business career: 'I found myself with nothing... But it wasn't necessarily a bad thing... it made me realise what I was passionate about, that I was attached to business, because my whole childhood was spent in my father's shop'. Although his mobility meant abandoning plans 'two years in the making', Benjamin presented it as 'an opportunity': to learn English, to 'open up to the international dimension', to experience 'difference'. But in his self-portrayal, English-language proficiency was foregrounded as key in the quest for *cosmopolitan distinction*. Significantly, Benjamin, who played rugby for his university team, initially considered other French speakers to be a threat to this quest, as demonstrated by his denouncing of 'Parisian' players to his (non-French) captain for 'speaking in French behind everyone's back'. Their in-group linguistic practices were perceived both as a transgression of the sporting *esprit de corps* and his personal objective to give London – and the English language – a chance, being integral to his search for a reinvented self.

For others, 'Frenchness' functioned as a symbolic site of twofold distinction: it was rejected in pursuit of 'cosmopolitanism' and praxially embraced as a reaction to the London/English field. Pierre, for instance, after feeling alienated in his first year at a provincial business school in

France, had sought the comfort of like-mindedness in London. His pre-existing cosmopolitan outlook, cultivated through a migratory background and attendance at an international bilingual school in Paris, meant he was ill at ease studying 'with French people, who were not very open-minded'. Curiously categorical that French migrants are indifferent about French culture and their French identity, claiming they 'forget it', he juxtaposed this assertion with a description of the regular, deliberately *French*-themed wine-and-cheese parties he held with his group of clearly demarcated French friends in London (Figure 3.1): 'French red wine, French cheese. I mean, we're not going to eat cheddar'. There was consequently a contradiction between Pierre's (cosmopolitan) discourse and (clichéd, purportedly nationality-defining) practices that eluded him, suggestive of a Frenchness performed rather than perceived, and so deeply engrained as to become invisible (Bourdieu, 1994; Bourdieu, [1972]2000). This dichotomy evidenced Frenchness being used as a resource in response to a need for cultural distinction, despite the normative interpretation of 'Frenchness' displayed, which in fact belied participants' rejection of 'French values' and self-professed search for an open, multicultural society epitomised by London.

The data presented in this section have revealed the complexities, ambiguities and paradoxes affecting French identity construction in the still comparatively unfamiliar diasporic context. While there was

Figure 3.1 French wine and cheese, north London, June 2022 (photo by Fabrice Lyczba)

negation of France's stagnant and insular outlook, a strong identification with Frenchness was demonstrated through socialising praxis and reported conceptions of self. As a result, the students found themselves in an uneasy position of agentive distancing – physical and conceptual – from their French identity and pre-reflexive, almost stereotypical, embodiment thereof. This left them in a fundamentally ambiguous state, what Bourdieu would term an unsettling cleft habitus (Bourdieu, 2004; Thatcher & Halvorsrud, 2016): both alienated from their Frenchness and relying on it for their (re)construction of home, belonging and self.

French(ness) and *Terroir* in Student Cosmopolitan Belonging

In spite of participants' criticisms of national belonging, profound attachment to Frenchness was expressed through gestures of 'banal nationalism' (Billig, 1995), some overt, like Pierre's monthly wine-and-cheese parties, others subtler. Hélène, who lamented not hearing a 'typically English accent' enough in London because her circle of friends was predominantly international, reported regularly visiting the library to read the French newspaper, *Le Monde*, declaring 'it would be good to have another one like *Le Figaro* or *Les Echos*'. Yasmine claimed feeling 'closer to British culture than French culture', while lauding France's literary tradition: 'the only thing I'm really proud of is French literature and the French language'. Likewise, Benjamin was unapologetic regarding his 'attachment to the [French] language... there's a wealth, whether in theatre, literature, music... it's a cultural attachment really. Yes, I'm nationalistic about my homeland; I'm proud to say I'm French'. Echoing this, Pierre undermined his original contention that French migrants are indifferent about their Frenchness, by envisaging a UK-based future in which he would transmit French history and values to his imagined children: 'so mummy's English, sure, but daddy's French, and daddy's country is the land of the Rights of Man, it's one of the oldest countries in the world and one of the founding countries of the EU'. Even Kerian, whose experience of discrimination in France made him reluctant to embrace a French identity, admitted being 'proud [... and] happy to be French'.

However, the ambiguity at the core of respondents' French identity was complicated by a tension between belonging to the nation state and a more personally meaningful regional space. Although the notion of Frenchness is validated institutionally – through passports, UK university records, local voting rights, etc. – and self-assigned by participants through their allusions to the French language as a key constituent of Frenchness, *regional* belonging was equally strong. Constructed primarily around sensoriality, for example in the form of sounds – including local dialects – and smells, a deep connection to a localised space imparted a regional 'placehood', arguably at odds with national allegiances.

In particular, students from non-Parisian backgrounds testified to profound regional and familial belongings.[15] Yasmine expressed 'a closer tie with [her southeast] hometown than with France in general, because … I associate it with my family, my friends, my childhood and teenage years… So it's linked to memories'. Like Yasmine, Rose, who grew up between Lille, Calais and London, has migrant heritage: Pakistani on her father's side, Spanish-French on her mother's. She self-identified as French 'without hesitation' and allegedly did 'not feel at all Calaisian', since Calais is for her the archetypal closed-minded, economically depressed small town that London's dynamic diversity had relegated to the background of her diasporic identity. And yet, regardless of the upward social mobility facilitated through her geographic mobility, Calais remained an affective and linguistic anchor. Rose described how 'we used to spend every holiday in Calais. So, Calais is, after all, where my grandparents were, and where my grandfather lives. It's my home. Calais, it's a dialect; it's difficult for me to speak French even today'.

Thus, in the performativity of Frenchness through family and language, *terroir* was deployed by our respondents in ways that are close to the roles 'terroir' plays in Demossier's study of French wine culture (2011, 685) as both a 'tool leading to homogeneity and rootedness, while supplying a means … to respond to globalization'.[16] Benjamin was indeed keen to share how his entire family, over several generations, were born within a 25-mile radius in southwest France and were 'really *from* that area, like, hardcore' – a distinction rooting his London belonging project *contra* French-speaking 'Parisians' in his London rugby team. Recalling the London–Paris 'moral geographies' described by Mulholland and Ryan (2017: 143), the non-Parisian students used *terroir* as a means of distinction from the French capital and of diasporic selfhood and 'placehood' in superdiverse London. Theirs was again a paradoxical paradigm where intuitive local pride competed with rationalised cosmopolitan desire in the search for postmigration belonging. Beyond 'bidimensional' (Ryder *et al.*, 2000) and 'translocal' (Gielis, 2009) emplacement, therefore, 'multilocal' (Duchêne-Lacroix & Koukoutsaki-Monnier, 2016) or 'polytopical' (Huc-Hepher, 2021b: 85) forms of belonging were observed, giving rise to an uneasy sense of self across the in-between space.

At times, however, primal connections to the 'mother-tongue' and the motherland could compromise students' embedding in London in the same way that the intrinsically physical and sensory functions of the

Figure 3.2 View towards the Lauragais, Tarn-et-Garonne (France), August 2022 (photo by Saskia Huc-Hepher)

tongue, nose and ear eased Pierre's belonging in the early phase of his migration. Benjamin's longing to belong in London remained haunted by sensory longing for the comforting sounds and smells of the localised pre-migration habitat (Figure 3.2). He evoked the 'Autan wind ... that comes from the Mediterranean ... and blows between the Massif Central and the Pyrenees', and the 'smell of the Lauragais, of the region ... which intersects with the Tarn, the Lot and the Haute-Garonne ... it's my home scent, when I go out, it's like when you go to the seaside and you smell the scent of the sea'. But this peculiarly powerful olfactory incarnation of home was irretrievable in London and constituted an absence that fundamentally compromised his diasporic belonging.[17]

Whether through the ritual cheese-and-wine parties, the familiar smells and sounds of the Lauragais, the inflections of Calaisian words or the initial embracing of English among all our participants, it is the phenomenological and the local, rather than an abstract national construct, that creates a *sense* of (un)belonging in the diasporic field/space and habitus/self. We explore below how these sensory factors also function as powerful mechanisms for displacement upon *arrival* in the capital.

An Uneasy Sense of Home in London

In the emotionally unsatiated postmigration space, the symbolic power of national and/or regional tastes, sounds and smells serves as affective nourishment (Waskul & Vannini, 2008) and contributes to the construction of 'convivialism' (Gilroy, 2004). Through cheese-and-wine parties, a shared 'sensory order' (Waskul & Vannini, 2008) is created, whereby an emotional attachment is formed, both across the transnational time-space – creating a diasporic sense of home – and between the students. However, this same sensory order can also give rise to an uneasy sensation of alienation and dislocation on initial confrontation with the postmigration field, that is, 'habitus hysteresis'.

As seen with all our respondents, language is critical in the construction of diasporic belonging. English proficiency featured prominently in all respondents' narratives, either as premigration trigger or postmigration goal. Early contact with English often paved the way for migration and English fluency constituted a major element of the students' sought-after 'mobility capital' (Murphy-Lejeune, 2002: 51). Kerian, like others, explicitly connected the English language with nascent mobility imaginings:

> I've had this dream of living in England since I was six ... I think I was watching a cartoon [in English] ... I told my mother: 'Mum, I want to go to England' ... When I started having English lessons with my mum's friend and realised I really liked it, I told her: 'I don't think there's a place for me here', meaning France, '...I don't think I belong here'.

For Kerian, it was contact with English through premigration media that planted the mobility seed, having awoken his sense of dis-placement in the 'homeland'. His growing linguistic capital also represented a resource in achieving distinction socially and in relation to his family (whom he described as too 'poor' to afford a private English tutor and too 'lazy' to watch films with French subtitles). For others, such as Benjamin, English was associated with deficiency, both personally, as described above, and institutionally, the French education system being deemed ineffective in language teaching. This was made apparent upon Benjamin's arrival in London, when his sensory disorientation was profound, despite years of learning English in France:

> the underground map ... is super complicated with its 15 lines; I thought: 'OK, where do I go now?'... I was quite lost at first ... on public transport, but mainly because of the language ... I'm very attached to the French language and speaking French ... So arriving in England and not being able to express myself was very frustrating. At first, I almost never talked.

Benjamin's juxtaposition of the bewildering effects of navigating the physical cityscape alongside the frustrations of negotiating the London soundscape is telling. It reveals the alienating potency of both, and the inextricable link between language, identity and belonging. French allowed Benjamin to feel at home in his selfhood, whereas English rendered him a perpetual outsider. Indeed, most students oscillated between longing for an elusive English soundscape and finding comfort in their French mother-tongue.

Julie, for example, expressed a desire to access English through friendships: 'I would love to have English friends, I would, but frankly I've no idea how'. Meanwhile, she recognised an inexplicable pull towards other French people: 'it feels like there's [always] a French person following me around'. Except at university, the London linguistic soundscape remained predominantly French, forcing an unexpected and uneasy reckoning that served as a barrier to emplacement. For Yasmine, the home comforts of speaking French also proved irresistible, 'immediately switch[ing] to French' with her 'only French friend here'. And this was the case 'even if there are people speaking English around' them, 'because there are things you simply can't express in English and language does create a connection'. Although immersion in the English soundscape was a key premigration driver, speaking *French* was central to the lived experience of London, and to diasporic kinship and homemaking. From this embodied linguistic paradox, a sense of unease in the surrogate 'home' ensued.

The senses also prompted an uneasy embodied paradox in Hélène. Despite lauding the 'open-minded', 'tolerant' and 'more international' characteristics of London, and acknowledging its transformative force, purportedly rendering her 'more tolerant and patient', Hélène's account exposed odour as a powerful othering tool which undermined her multiculturalist rhetoric. As her anecdote demonstrates, the olfactory served as much to inhibit feeling at home in the postmigration space as it did to cement it in the premigration space for Benjamin (Classen, 1992):[18]

> I arrived to the building of my accommodation and it was awful because it was in the basement – because a lot of people live in the basement in London – I don't know if you do, but I don't know how people do because I can't, really, it's not possible for me... I had a mini flat, so it was like a flat with a common bathroom and common kitchen, and we were six, three bedrooms, and I had a bedroom with two other people. And it was... Indian people, so it was smelling very hard... the food I mean, because the kitchen was next to the room... and I wanted to open the window and the girl told me 'Yeah, but be careful because when it's raining in London we have bugs in the room, and it's raining a lot in London so we can have a lot of bugs'. And I was like 'What...? Are you kidding me? I'm not going to live in the basement with bugs'. So, I went to see the reception, and I told them I was claustrophobic, and it's true that in the room I wasn't feeling great, and they found me another room; now I am in another building, with only the bathroom and the room, and with only one girl and she's Spanish so we have the same way of thinking...

Of initial relevance here is the repulsiveness dominating Hélène's testimony, and understanding how such revulsion was constructed culturally.

From the claustrophobia caused by the lower-ground-floor dwelling (such as Figure 3.3, prohibited by law in France),[19] via the 'unfamiliar' smells considered 'unpleasant', to the invasive threat of insects from outside: they all paint a picture of what is 'alien' and hence disturbing.

Apparently unaware that the estrangement she felt, enclosed in the basement at the mercy of the bugs and other residents, was comparable to the othering she projected onto the space and its inhabitants, Hélène's language is simultaneously banal (the hygiene risk of infestation) and opprobrious (for others, living with bugs is acceptable, but not for me). This distinctive form of repulsion and othering is heightened when coupled with the conclusion of the anecdote: the new roommate was 'Spanish so we have the same way of thinking'.[20] For Hélène, then, although London represents a long and enviable history of (multi)cultural encounter, it is only a first step on her journey to openness.

It is the 'politics of smell', however, that constitutes the main hurdle. Hélène's identification of a causal relationship between Indian heritage and unpleasant odours corroborates her continued prejudice: 'it was… Indian people, so it was smelling very hard'. Despite claiming to be more

Figure 3.3 Basement accommodation, central London, June 2022 (photo by Fabrice Lyczba)

open-minded and 'tolerant' than her non-moving French friends, her words belie the sentiment. She is quick to correct herself: 'the food I mean, because the kitchen was next to the room', but the slight has been uttered and the latent xenophobia brought to bear. This spontaneous coupling of malodour and national identity is – somewhat ironically – a xenophobic trope used commonly by the British press in relation to the French (Huc-Hepher, 2019) and deployed regularly in French political discourse regarding France's migrant communities, as demonstrated explicitly by former Presidents Jacques Chirac and Nicolas Sarkozy who, respectively, notoriously referred to 'the noise and smell' of 'foreigners' (Chirac's, 1991 Orléans speech) and a resolve 'to clean the housing estates with a jet washer' (Sarkozy, 2005). Odour, 'foreignness' and dirtiness associations thus have precedent and frame the repulsion nexus to which Hélène attests. Significantly, also intrinsic to the definition of dirtiness – the corollary of unpleasant smells – is darkness, which renders Hélène's comment an evocation of discrimination beyond the xenophobic – into the realm of racism. This is illustrated by Hélène's comfortableness sharing her home with a 'like-minded' Spanish student, but uneasiness living with 'Indian' peers – who were potentially British with South Asian heritage. The superseding of the room-mates' potential *Britishness* by their embodied '*Indianness*' raises the suspicion that what drives the feeling of being more *at home* with the *Spanish*, Western European student could actually be, in this toxic mix of cleanliness, odours, and the sense of the foreign, a pre-migration 'structuring structure' (Bourdieu, [1972]2000: 256) of *whiteness* (White Western European-ness) – regardless of Hélène's conviction that her London project is evidence of a performance of cosmopolitanism *that distinguishes her* from her French background. Hélène thus seems to articulate an unsettled, possibly evolving notion of cosmopolitanism, still structured by racial, colonialising, and sensory essentialism carried over from the French primary habitus that the London field has not yet had time to reframe and potentially reform.

This anecdote consequently bears witness to a complex and conflicted sense of home on arrival in London. Inner and outer, self and other, confinement and openness, repugnance and allegiance collide on a triadic backdrop of sensorially triggered fear: claustrophobia, entomophobia and xenophobia, identifiable as a hysteresis effect. At this arrival stage of her migration, Hélène's deep-seated anxieties, doubtless reinforced by being far away from the support networks *of home*, disclosed an unease which was fundamentally incompatible with being *at home* in London. Other respondents' negotiations with their sensory definition of 'Frenchness', from the tastes of French cheese and wine to the sounds of the language, were arguably less contentious, but just as powerfully fraught with the contradictions and ambiguities that render the construction of belonging singularly uneasy.

Conclusion

The empirical evidence explored in this chapter has confirmed that the London location is not immaterial to French undergraduate mobility. The students' migration was as much a place-bound project as an educational one, with the appeal of London portrayed, in survey and interview data, through its perceived multiculturalism, openness and modernity. The students' desire to enact this cosmopolitan ideal through their degree mobility and quest for a reinvention of self, facilitated by the global city, emerged as a means to escape the constraints of the premigration nation state and its purportedly outdated, divisive values. Yet, at the same time, the students were seen to put French national and/or regional identity and inherited ideologies to use in the pursuit of distinction and belonging. As Benjamin expressed regarding his hesitancy in contributing to class discussions: 'sorry, I'm French' – both a plea for recognition of linguistic incompleteness and vulnerability and a form of sociocultural distinction in relation to his peers. Frenchness repeatedly served as a marker of difference, pride and frailty in the London milieu.

Immersion in the postmigration space gave rise to the discovery that, notwithstanding efforts to belong and to embrace the local language and culture, there was a profound longing for, and attachment to, the premigration habitat. Yet, this longing was not for a France left behind, nor an abstract notion of civic belonging and nationhood, but rather for a regionally localised and personal space, replete with the comforting sounds and smells of childhood. The pre-reflexive potency of the senses also unearthed deep-seated anxieties which shed light on unconscious prejudice – racism even – lurking in the shadows of habitus. The fissuring and redefinition of Frenchness that arises in and through mobility was hence brought to bear in different, yet related, ways.

While the transnational space epitomised the migrations and cultural flows of superdiverse global cities, it was simultaneously conducive to dislocation and porous to discrimination. The students' premigration imaginings transpired to be at odds with their lived experience of studying and living in London, prompting a hysteresis effect which resulted in complex reworkings of what being French meant. In short, the students' first-year London sojourns were characterised by unease as their constructions of self, of belonging and of home were defined by patterns of ambiguity and embodied paradox that left them with a cleft habitus. They found themselves both alienated from and irrevocably at home in their French cultural identity – actively engaged in re-imagining the contours of Frenchness to fit their deeply personal, developing, and as yet uncertain London belonging projects.

Notes

(1) This chapter presents the initial results of a multi-strand, longitudinal study conducted in 2017–19: 'The London Transformation Project', which investigates shifts in cultural and national identity among French undergraduate students in London universities. Our ultimate aim is to understand how identity and belonging are performed, experienced and constructed in the superdiverse context of London over time, with a focus on how French national identity (often essentialised) is actually constructed as a *malleable* resource and deployed in critical, creative ways through the students' cosmopolitan distinction and uneasy search for belonging. Although beyond the remit of this chapter, in their second year, the same students were invited to attend a focus group and bring a material object to represent 'home', as well as a photograph of 'their London'. Repeated circulation of the questionnaire and follow-up interviews were projected for their final year, but the global pandemic ultimately impacted take-up.

(2) The authors are both based in London. One is a French male (now with British citizenship) and the other a British female (now with French citizenship). They have been observers of French undergraduate mobility for a number of years, given their role in higher education and the constant influx of French students.

(3) The number of French students enrolled at London universities in 2019–20 represented an increase of 12.5% from 2014–15 and the fifth fastest growth. Students were dispersed across central London institutions as follows: King's College London (610), UCL (570), University of the Arts London (275), Imperial (230), the London School of Economics (145), Queen Mary (140) and the University of Westminster (110). By comparison, the population of Italian students was less concentrated, with 12 London HEIs drawing 80% of them, including Goldsmiths, the University of Greenwich and London Metropolitan University (Higher Education Statistics Agency, 2020).

(4) Research to date on French students has investigated how short-term Erasmus mobilities of French (and other) students across Europe influence academic results and professional trajectories, with some, albeit limited, consideration of identity (Ballatore, 2010; Cardwell, 2019; Erlich, Agulhon, and Office national de la vie étudiante (OVE) 2012; Papatsiba, 2003). Elizabeth Murphy-Lejeune's ethnographic work on Erasmus students (2007), rich as it is, does not focus on constructions of Frenchness. Overall, there is an absence of research on French students enrolled in programmes abroad for over a year – corresponding to the UN-approved statistical definition of 'migrant' – despite the growth in this population in London and despite valuable contributions from International Student Migration/Mobility (ISM) research (see, for example, Suzanne Beech's work on social networks (2015), Russell King and Parjati Raghuram's (2013) useful mapping of the ISM field and its research agenda and Bilecen and Mol's collection of articles on inequalities in international academic mobility (2017)).

(5) The survey, entitled *Trajectories and Origins: The Diversity of Populations in France*, was conducted by Ined (the French Institute for Demographic Studies) and Insee (the French National Institute of Statistics and Economics Studies) in 2008–09 among 22,000 members of the French population and built on previous enquiries into the impact of place and territory on definitions of Frenchness (Ville & Guérin-Pace, 2005).

(6) All survey questions and responses cited in this chapter have been translated into English by the authors.

(7) Choice of interview language was left to the participants. All but one chose French.

(8) All London universities were approached for help in disseminating the call to participation, but only two responded positively: University of Westminster and University of Roehampton. One student from the London campus of the French university Dauphine-Paris participated through contact via the International Students House.

(9) We concentrate on data collected from two cohorts of respondents during year one of their undergraduate studies, in October–November 2017 and October–November 2018, with interview data (audio-recorded, transcribed and translated) in March 2018 and March 2019. As such, the analysis presented here does not seek to monitor the process of transformation, but instead interrogates the students' uneasy negotiations of their national and cultural identity, belonging and homemaking at the outset of their migratory experience.

(10) It is important to note that the two respondents who identified least with Frenchness *also* self-identified as 'visible minorities', i.e. as 'mixed' in their ethnic origins and with at least partly North-African families (the postcolonial implications of which are not to be underestimated). As indicated above, multiple studies have shown how disidentification from Frenchness is linked to experiences of racialised marginalisation in France, leading to more conflicted forms of belonging.

(11) All interviewees have been given pseudonyms to protect their anonymity.

(12) The French word 'souche' literally means (tree) 'stump', functioning as a metaphor for 'French' heritage or origins in a similar way that 'roots' are used to suggest ancestral belonging, or 'branches' are used in family 'trees'. However, it is important to note that use of the term 'Français de souche' has been the subject of fierce public debate in France, having been adopted by Marine Le Pen's far right party and often serving as a proxy for whiteness, rather than citizenship.

(13) As the work of McCrone and Bechhofer (2010: 924) has shown, albeit in the context of Scottish national identity formations, 'the distinction between ethnic and civic has more to do with opposing styles of arguments than with measurable concepts' and, in practice, researchers are often confronted with 'a subtler combination of the two'.

(14) The idea of London as a social space where homosexuality and tattoos are positively normalised was reported by Huc-Hepher's respondents almost a decade earlier (2021b), which substantiates the continued resistance to change perceived in France and the commonality of the sentiment among the French diaspora more broadly.

(15) None of our respondents from Paris expressed similar attachment to a regional sense of identity. Premigration belonging was for them uniformly presented as 'French' (rather than 'Parisian').

(16) The term *terroir* is difficult to translate owing to its semantic scope and inherent malleability in French. Priscilla Parkhurst Ferguson legitimately defines *terroir* as 'this fidelity to the land, this rootedness', associating it with (regional/local) authenticity (2004: 23). However, chiming with Marion Demossier (2011) above, John P. Murphy (2018: 146) disputes the authenticity claim, drawing attention to its strategic use for

'the branding of French cultural identity'. Given this pliability, we have chosen to retain the term in French.

(17) Indeed, Benjamin abandoned his London studies after his second year and returned to his hometown. In later data collection not included in this chapter, Benjamin went on to identify language as the chief obstacle to belonging in London, confiding that over time he was speaking 'French more', seeing 'more French friends' and visiting family in France every two weeks. Rather than struggling to watch TV in English, he 'preferred not to get stressed out and to just watch it in French'. Like other French migrants in London (Huc-Hepher, 2021a), it was his self-reported inability to articulate his thoughts in a manner commensurate with his intellect, and the anxiety involved in English decoding/encoding processes, that caused Benjamin's unease: 'I always have this frustration of not being able to express myself fully, or say exactly what I want in English, even if I've acquired a good level of English now ... it'll never be at the same level as my mother-tongue'. Ultimately, it was his lack of linguistic ease that was the catalyst for Benjamin's degree abandonment and return migration.

(18) This interview was conducted in English, at the request of the student, keen to practise her English.

(19) Whether the respondent's categorical rejection of basement accommodation is rooted in the national or the regional spatiality of her primary habitus/habitat is unclear. However, the 'Carrez Law' stating that basements are, by definition, unfit for human habitation (Sénat, 2013), together with statistics indicating that 66% of people occupy detached houses in France (Statista, 2020a), compared to only 24% in the UK (Statista, 2020b), suggest that inhabiting the subterranean areas of properties might be relatively alien to the French mindset. Article L. 1331-22 of the French Public Health Act (Code de la Santé Publique, CSP) states that 'cellars, basements, attics ... and other premises are by definition unfit for human habitation and cannot be used for the purpose of accommodation'. A 2013 official addendum by the Health Ministry further clarifies it, while attics may be transformed into habitable spaces, 'for basements, as these are defined by being underground, they are by nature unfit for human habitation and no transformation may change their nature' (Sénat, 2013).

(20) It is relevant that the words 'who is Spanish' are added by Hélène throughout the interview every time she speaks about 'my roommate', as if that national difference was *the* key identifier and somehow worthy of being repeatedly foregrounded.

References

Alemán, J. and Woods, D. (2018) Inductive constructivism and national identities: Letting the data speak. *Nations and Nationalism* 24 (4), 1023–1045. https://doi.org/10.1111/nana.12320.

Appadurai, A. (1995) The production of locality. In R. Fardon (ed.) *Counterworks: Managing the Diversity of Knowledge* (pp. 204–225). London: Routledge.

Backer (de), M. (2019) 'Being different together' in public space: Young people, everyday cosmopolitanism and parochial atmospheres. *Social & Cultural Geography.* https://doi.org/10.1080/14649365.2019.1594352.

Ballatore, M. (2010) Etudiants sans Frontières? Pratiques Étudiantes Dans Un Contexte 'Étranger'. Une Comparaison Angleterre/France/Italie. In Y. Neyrat (ed.) *Les Cultures Étudiantes: Socio-Anthropologie de l'univers Étudiant* (pp. 247–268). Paris: L'Harmattan.

Bancel, N. (2013) France, 2005: A postcolonial turning point. *French Cultural Studies* 24 (2), 208–218. https://doi.org/10.1177/0957155813477794.

Bauberot, J. (2008) Cultural transfer and national identity in French laicity. *Diogenes* 218, 17–26.

Beaman, J. (2015) Boundaries of Frenchness: Cultural citizenship and France's middle-class North African second-generation. *Identities* 22 (1), 36–52. https://doi.org/10.1080/1070289X.2014.931235.

Beaman, J. (2018) Are French people white?: Towards an understanding of whiteness in Republican France. *Identities* 26 (5), 1–17. https://doi.org/10.1080/1070289X.2018.1543831.

Beech, S.E (2015) International student mobility: The role of social networks. *Social & Cultural Geography* 16 (3), 332–350. https://doi.org/10.1080/14649365.2014.983961

Benson, M. (2011) *The British in Rural France*. Manchester: Manchester University Press.

Bilecen, B. and Mol, C.V.M. (2017) Introduction: International academic mobility and inequalities. *Journal of Ethnic and Migration Studies* 43 (8), 1241–1255. https://doi.org/10.1080/1369183X.2017.1300225.

Billig, M. (1995) *Banal Nationalism*. London: Sage.

Bourdieu, P. ([1972]2000) *Esquisse d'une théorie de la pratique*. Paris: Le Seuil.

Bourdieu, P. (1994) *Raisons Pratiques: Sur La Théorie de l'action*. Paris: Le Seuil.

Bourdieu, P. (2000) *Esquisse d'une Théorie de La Pratique* (1st edn. 1972). Paris: Le Seuil.

Bourdieu, P. (2004) *Esquisse pour une auto-analyse*. Paris: Raisons d'agir.

Bourdieu, P. (2005) Habitus. In J. Hillier and E. Rooksby (eds) *Habitus: A Sense of Place* (2nd edn). Aldershot: Ashgate.

Cardwell, P.J. (2019) Does studying abroad help academic achievement? *European Journal of Higher Education* 1–17. https://doi.org/10.1080/21568235.2019.1573695.

Chabal, E. (2010) Writing the French national narrative in the twenty-first century. *The Historical Journal* 53 (2), 495–516.

Chabal, E. (2015) *A Divided Republic: Nation, State and Citizenship in Contemporary France*. Cambridge: Cambridge University Press.

Chabal, E. (2017) From the Banlieue to the Burkini: The many lives of French Republicanism. *Modern & Contemporary France* 25 (1), 68–74. https://doi.org/10.1080/09639489.2016.1246164.

Chirac J. (1991) Discours d'Orléans, in Guyotat Regis, 'Le débat sur l'immigration Le maire de Paris: "Il y a overdose"', *Le Monde*, 21 June 1991.

Cicchelli, V. (2008) Connaître Les Autres Pour Mieux Se Connaître: Les Séjours Erasmus, Une Bildung Contemporaine. In F. Dervin and M. Byram (eds) *Échanges et Mobilités Académiques: Quel Bilan?* (pp. 139–163). Paris: L'Harmattan.

Classen C. (1992) The odor of the Other: Olfactory symbolism and cultural categories. *Ethos: Journal of the Society for Psychological Anthropology* 20 (2), 133–166. https://doi.org/10.1525/eth.1992.20.2.02a00010

Conradson, D. and Latham, A. (2007) The affective possibilities of London: Antipodean transnationals and the overseas experience. *Mobilities* 2 (2), 231–254.

Demossier, M. (2011) Beyond Terroir: Territorial construction, hegemonic discourses, and French wine culture. *Journal of the Royal Anthropological Institute* 17 (4), 685–705.

Duchêne Lacroix, C. and Koukoutsaki-Monnier, A. (2016) Mapping the social space of transnational migrants on the basis of their (supra)national belongings: The case of French citizens in Berlin. *Identities* 23 (2), 136–154. https://doi.org/10.1080/1070289X.2015.1008000.

Dubois, L. (2000) La République Métissée: Citizenship, colonialism, and the borders of French history. *Cultural Studies* 14 (January), 15–34. https://doi.org/10.1080/095023800334968.

Dürrschmidt, J. (2016) The irresolvable unease about be-longing: Exploring globalized dynamics of homecoming. *European Journal of Cultural Studies* 19 (5), 495–510. https://doi.org/10.1177/1367549416631553.

Erlich, Valérie, Catherine Agulhon, and Office national de la vie étudiante (OVE) (*2012) *Les Mobilités Étudiantes*. Paris: La documentation française.

Escafré-Dublet, A. (2019) The whiteness of cultural boundaries in France. *Identities Journal Blog* (blog). 25 September 2019. http://www.identitiesjournal.com/1/post/2019/09/the-whiteness-of-cultural-boundaries-in-france.html.

Favell, A. (2006) London as Eurocity: French free movers in the economic capital of Europe. In M.P. Smith and A. Favell (eds) *The Human Face of Global Mobility: International Highly Skilled Migration in Europe, North America and the Asia-Pacific* (pp. 247–274). New Brunswick: Transaction Publishers.

Favell, A. (2008) *Eurostars and Eurocities*. Oxford: Blackwell.

Filhon, A. (2011) Appartenances Régionales et Sentiments Nationaux: Le Rôle de La Langue. *Ethnologie Française* 41 (1), 141–49.

Filippova, E. and Guérin-Pace, F. (2008) Les territoires qui nous appartiennent, les territoires auxquels nous appartenons. In F. Guérin-Pace and Flipppova *Ces lieux qui nous habitent: Identité des territoires, territoires des identités* (pp. 13–36). Ined-Editions de l'Aube.

Georgiou, M. (2013) *Media and the City: Cosmopolitanism and Difference*. Cambridge: Polity Press.

Gielis, R. (2009) A global sense of migrant places: Towards a place perspective in the study of migrant transnationalism. *Global Networks* 9 (2), 271–287.

Gilroy, P. (2004) *After Empire: Melancholia or Convivial Culture?* London: Routledge.

Gonzalez, J. (2014) 'Trop d'émigrés? Regards Sur Ceux Qui Partent de France'. Fondapol. http://www.fondapol.org/etude/julien-gonzalez-trop-emigres-regards-sur-ceux-qui-partent-de-france/.

Guénif-Souilamas, N. (2006) The other French exception: virtuous racism and the war of the sexes in postcolonial France. *French Politics, Culture & Society* 24 (3), 23–41.

Guérin-Pace, F. (2009) La Diversité Des Ancrages Territoriaux Au Regard Des Parcours Migratoires. In F. Guérin-Pace, O. Samuel and I. Ville (eds) *En Quête d'appartenances: L'enquête Histoire de Vie Sur La Construction Des Identités* (pp. 145–164). Paris: Ined. https://www.ined.fr/fr/publications/grandes-enquetes/en-quete-d-appartenances/#tabs-2.

Hajjat, A. (2012) *Les frontières de 'l'identité nationale': l'injonction à l'assimilation en France métropolitaine et coloniale*. Paris: Découverte.

Hardy, C. (2012) 'Hysteresis'. In M. Grenfell (ed.) *Pierre Bourdieu – Key Concepts* (pp. 126–149). Durham: Acumen.

Higher Education Statistics Agency (2020) Where Do HE Students Come from? | HESA. 2020. https://www.hesa.ac.uk/data-and-analysis/students/where-from.

Huc-Hepher, S. (2019) Sometimes there's racism towards the French here: Xenophobic microaggressions in pre-2016 London as articulations of symbolic violence. *National Identities*: 1–25. https://doi.org/10.1080/14608944.2019.1649250.

Huc-Hepher, S. (2021a) Navigating the London-French transnational space: The losses and gains of language as embodied and embedded symbolic capital. *Languages* 6 (1), 57. https://doi.org/10.3390/languages6010057

Huc-Hepher, S. (2021b) *French London: A Blended Ethnography of A Migrant City.* *Manchester.* Manchester University Press.

Ifop (2021) Étude Ifop pour Lycra et le Droit de Vivre réalisée par questionnaire auto-administré en ligne 15 au 20 janvier 2021 auprès d'un échantillon de 1 006 personnes, représentatif de la population lycéenne âgée de 15 ans et plus. Available from https://www.leddv.fr/wp-content/uploads/1_PPT_IFOP_LICRA_2021.03.02.pdf (accessed 17/04/2021).

INED/INSEE (2016) Trajectoires et origines: enquête sur la diversité des populations en France. Paris: Ined. https://www.ined.fr/fr/publications/grandes-enquetes/trajectoires-et-origines/.

King, R. and Raghuram, R. (2013) International Student migration: mapping the field and new research agendas. *Population, Space and Place* 19 (2), 127–137. https://doi.org/10.1002/psp.1746.

La Documentation française (2009) *La France au pluriel.* Cahiers français 352. La documentation française. http://www.ladocumentationfrancaise.fr/catalogue/3303330403525/.

Lapeyronnie, D. (2010) Le débat sur l'identité nationale: vers un renouvellement de notre modèle d'intégration? *Regards sur l'actualité* 358: 39–51.

Leruth, M.F. (1998) The neorepublican discourse on French national identity. *French Politics and Society* 16 (4), 46–61.

Leurs, K. and Ponzanesi, S. (2018) Connected migrants: Encapsulation and cosmopolitanization. *Popular Communication* 16 (1), 4–20.

Maalouf, A. (2001) *Les Identités Meurtrières.* Grasset. Paris.

Mballo, R. and Bourget, C. (2018) Comment Peut-on Être Française et Musulmane? Lallab Face à l'identité Nationale. *French Cultural Studies* 29 (3), 254–264. https://doi.org/10.1177/0957155818774482.

McCrone, D. and Bechhofer, F. (2010) Claiming national identity. *Ethnic and Racial Studies* 33 (6), 921–948. https://doi.org/10.1080/01419870903457199.

Mondon, A. (2015) The French Secular hypocrisy: The extreme right, the republic and the battle for hegemony. *Patterns of Prejudice* 49 (4), 392–413. https://doi.org/10.1080/0031322X.2015.1069063.

Montague, D. (2013) Communitarianism, discourse and political opportunity in Republican France. *French Cultural Studies* 24 (2), 219–230. https://doi.org/10.1177/0957155813477806.

Mulholland, J. and Ryan, L. (2017) London is a much more interesting place than Paris: place comparison and moral geographies of highly skilled migrants. In M. Van Riemsdijk and Q. Wang (eds) *Rethinking International Skilled Migration* (pp. 135–153). Abingdon: Routledge.

Murphy, J.P. (2011) Baguettes, berets and burning cars: The 2005 riots and the question of race in contemporary France. *French Cultural Studies* 22 (1), 33–49. https://doi.org/10.1177/0957155810386678.

Murphy, J.P. (2018) Foie gras in the freezer: Picard Surgelés and the branding of French culinary identity. *Food and Foodways* 26 (2), 146–169. https://doi.org/10.1080/07409710.2018.1454774.

Murphy-Lejeune, E. (2002) *Student Mobility and Narrative in Europe: The New Strangers.* New York: Routledge

Nedelcu, M. (2012) Migrants' new transnational habitus: Rethinking migration through a cosmopolitan lens in the digital age. *Journal of Ethnic and Migration Studies* 38 (9), 1339–1356.

Noiriel, G. (2007) À quoi sert 'l'identité nationale'. Passé & présent. Marseille: Agone.

Oliver, C. and O'Reilly, K. (2010) A Bourdieusian analysis of class and migration: Habitus and the individualizing process. *Sociology* 44 (1), 49–66. https://doi.org/10.1177/0038038 509351627.

Ong, J. (2009) The cosmopolitan continuum: Locating cosmopolitanism in media and cultural studies. *Media, Culture & Society* 31 (3), 449–466.

Papatsiba, V. (2003) *Des étudiants européens. «Erasmus» et l'aventure de l'altérité.* Berne: Peter Lang. http://www.persee.fr/doc/rfp_0556-7807_2004_num_149_1_3186.

Parkhurst F.P. (2004) *Accounting for Taste.* Chicago: University of Chicago Press.

Ratinaud, P. and Marchand, P. (2012) Recherche improbable d'une homogène diversité: le débat sur l'identité nationale. *Langages* 187, 93–108.

Ryder A.G., Alden L.E. and Paulhus D.L. (2000) Is acculturation unidimensional or bidimensional? A head-to-head comparison in the prediction of personality, self-identity, and adjustement. *Journal of Personality and Social Psychology* 79 (1), 49–65. https://doi.org/10.1037/0022-3514.79.1.49.

Sarkozy N. (2005) in Cosnay F. (2010) 'On va nettoyer au Karcher la cité' *Europe 1* (21 Sept. 2010). https://www.europe1.fr/politique/On-va-nettoyer-au-Karcher-la-cite-287906

Sénat (2013) https://www.senat.fr/questions/base/2013/qSEQ130606772.html (accessed 17 June 2021).

Sencébé, Y. (2004) Être Ici, Être d'ici: Formes d'appartenance Dans Le Diois (Drôme). *Ethnologie Française* 34 (1), 23–29.

Silverstein, P.A. (2018) *Postcolonial France: Race, Islam, and the Future of the Republic.* London: Pluto Press.

Simon, D. (2006) Separated by common ground? Bringing (post)development and (post) colonialism together. *The Geographical Journal* 172 (1), 10–21.

Simon, P. (2012) *French National Identity and Integration: Who Belongs to the National Community?'* Washington DC: Migration Policy Institute.

Statista (2020a) *Share of French people living in a detached house 2009–2018.* Statista Research Department. Available from https://www.statista.com/statistics/950081/share-population-living-houses-france/ (accessed 14/04/2021)

Statista (2020b) *United Kingdom: Housing Conditions by Dwelling Type 2018.* Statista Research Department. Available from https://www.statista.com/statistics/503705/distribution-of-the-population-in-the-uk-by-dwelling-type/#:~:text=In%20given %20year%2C%2060.8%20percent,with%2024%20percent%20occupancy%20rate (accessed 14/04/2021).

Temporal, F. and Brutel, C. (2016) La mesure des flux migratoires entre la France et l'étranger: et si on parlait (aussi) d'émigration? *Revue européenne des migrations internationales* 32 (3 & 4), 215–229. https://doi.org/10.4000/remi.8270.

Thatcher, J. and Halvorsrud, K. (2016) Migrating habitus: a comparative case study of Polish and South African migrants in the UK. In J. Thatcher, N. Ingram, C. Burke and J. Arahams (eds) *Bourdieu: The Next Generation. The Development of Bourdieu's Intellectual Heritage in Contemporary UK Sociology.* New York: Routledge.

Tsing, A. (2000) The global situation. *Cultural Anthropology* 15 (3), 327–360.

Valdez, Z. and Golash-Boza, T. (2018) Master status or intersectional identity? Undocumented students' sense of belonging on a college campus. *Identities:* 1–19. https://doi.org/10.1080/1070289X.2018.1534452.

Vertovec, S.(2007) Super-diversity and its implications. *Ethnic and Racial Studies* 30 (6) (1 November 2007), 1024–54. https://doi.org/10.1080/01419870701599465.

Ville, I. and Guérin-Pace, F. (2005) Interroger les identités: l'élaboration d'une enquête en France' *Population* 60 (3), 277–305.

Walsh, K. (2012) Emotion and migration: British transnationals in Dubai. *Environment and Planning D: Society and Space* 30, 43–59. https://doi.org/10.1068/d12409.

Waskul D.D. and Vannini P. (2008) Smell, odor, and somatic work: Sense-making and sensory management. *Social Psychology Quarterly* 71 (1), 53–71. https://doi.org/10.1177/019027250807100107

Wolfreys, J. (2018) *Republic of Islamophobia: The Rise of Respectable Racism in France.* New York: Oxford University Press.

4 Alevi Kurds in the UK: Paving the Way Towards Recognition of a New Ethno-Religious Identity

Umit Cetin and Celia Jenkins

Introduction

The aim of this chapter is to develop a profile of the London Alevi Kurds,[1] tracing the context of their departure from Turkey and their transition in the UK from a marginalised, hidden community to one gaining official recognition, something that has yet to be achieved in Turkey. We argue that the boundaries of Alevi identity are fluid and contested depending on the context, politics and power of those who are defining it. This is the case emically and etically in both Turkey and the UK in terms of whether Alevism is seen as a culture or a religion and whether it is part of Islam or distinct from it. Following recent debates on Alevi identity, we share the preference to capture its complexity through describing Kurdish Alevism as an ethno-religious identity (Aydın, 2020; Gezik & Gultekin, 2019; Jenkins *et al.*, 2018). To see the emergence, and recognition, of the ethno-religious identity of Alevi Kurds in London, the chapter locates that community in a transnational context (Cosan-Eke, 2014; Emre-Cetin, 2018; Ozkul, 2019), briefly outlining the pre-migration history and experiences of Alevis in Turkey and their context of departure. This is necessary in understanding their conditions and experiences of settlement in the UK. Following a history of persecuted exclusion in Turkey (Cetin, 2014), Alevis migrated in large numbers first to Germany and then other mainland European countries and more recently since the late 1980s to the UK where, like their continental counterparts, they became a hidden and marginalised community, a position that has substantially changed more recently.

In this chapter, we explore the social consequences of both the experience of marginalisation and subsequent process of attaining recognition for the first and second generations. In particular, we examine the crucial agentic role of the İngiltere Alevi Kültür Merkezi-Cemevi (İAKM-C henceforward, and translated as the London Alevi Cultural Centre and Cemevi) and the national Britanya Alevi Federasyonu (BAF henceforward, and translated as the British Alevi Federation) in the past decade or so in establishing Alevis as a distinct community in London and the UK, seeking official recognition in a way that has yet to be achieved in Turkey. It is important here to briefly outline the establishment of the İAKM-C and BAF as without them it is doubtful that the Alevi community could have achieved so much. The main hub of Alevi activity from the early 1990s was the İAKM-C which was based in Hackney in a former textile factory and very much focused on the religious role of the cemevi (which means place of worship for Alevis) and was important as a place to hold Alevi funerals and religious and cultural events as well as courses in Turkish, saz and semah (Geaves, 2003). In the early 2000s, there was a change of leadership and the Chair of the İAKM-C was very proactive in expanding the membership and the scope of the Centre's activities. The İAKM-C was the original power base and hub but once the organisation expanded and Alevis began to settle outside London, new associations were set up across the country. The İAKM-C leadership went on to establish the BAF in 2013 to provide an umbrella organisation for the 17 national associations across London and nationwide in places such as Leicester, Doncaster, Edinburgh and Bournemouth (AleviNet). The Chair of the İAKM-C went on to be the Chair of BAF and was instrumental in mobilising Alevis in the UK and forging connections with Alevi organisations transnationally.

In working closely with the community over many years, we have conceptualised London Alevi Kurds as an ethno-religious community. They offer a unique case of how contextual and especially agentic factors work together to produce new forms of identity, which, in the case of the Alevi Kurds, is best described as an ethno-religious one due to its distinct ethnic and religious characteristics. We have noted that describing Alevism depends very much on whose perspective is taken, as Alevism's origins and its religious character have always been a subject of intense contestation (Cetin & Jenkins, 2023; Sokefeld, 2008). For example, a Kurdish nationalist perspective would place Alevism's roots in the ancient religion of Kurds, namely Zoroastrianism, whereas nationalist Turks will see Alevism as stemming from ancient Turkish roots in Shamanism (Van Bruinessen, 2017) while others, both inside (a minority) and outside of

Alevism, argue it was, or still is, a heterodox form of Islam. Moreover, these definitions are constantly changing depending on what course Kurdish and Turkish identity politics follows.[2] However, as a working definition we define 'Alevi' as an umbrella term used to refer to various ethno-religious groups who describe themselves as Alevi and who come from central Turkey (Jenkins *et al.*, 2018: 1).[3]

The Construction of Ethno-Religious Identities

Fenton (2010) argues that a theory of ethnicity is a theory of contexts that provide conditions for situationally relevant ethnic identities to come into being. This allows members of the ethnic group to give specific meanings, relevance and functions to what they view as the primordial elements of their ethnicity. Similarly, Morawska (2011) argues for a flexible and syncretic notion of ethnicity that can be a primordial, situational and a socially constructed experience dependent each and together upon their interaction with the host environment. This approach to ethnicity that sees it as an interplay between internal and external processes is adopted here as we trace how an Alevi Kurd identity emerged in the political and historical context of the Alevi experience in Turkey and evolved within the context of migration and the Alevi Kurd diaspora in London.

However, our other contention is that Alevi identity with its interplay between ethnicity and religion cannot be grasped simply by using the concepts of religion or ethnicity alone; rather it is a complex interplay between ethnic and religious identity. This conception is shared by other researchers on Alevism (Arakelova, 2010; Aydın, 2018; Gezik & Gultekin, 2019) although not always expressed as such (e.g. Karaosmanoglu, 2013). Most of the existing references to an ethno-religious identity relate to Alevis and Alevism in Turkey, whereas our research explores the ethno-religious identity in the diaspora context of London and the UK (Cetin, 2014; Cetin *et al.*, 2020; Jenkins *et al.*, 2018; Cetin & Jenkins, 2023). In that sense, we argue that transnational links and diasporic contexts add a different layer to the complexity of ethno-religious identity. In the case of the Alevi diaspora in London, we contend that the ethnic identity of Alevi Kurds has facilitated a deeper association with a religious identity which has provided an opportunity for Kurdish and Turkish Alevis to unite.

The difficulties in defining Alevism purely in ethnic terms can be seen with language. Language is one of the most visible features by which ethnic boundaries are maintained as it links 'past and present generations in a peculiarly sensitive web of intimacy and mutuality' and thus ethnic identity is comprised of cultural acts which can only be fully understood through the 'linguistic system to which they are naturally related' (Fishman, 1997: 65). For the members of an ethnic group, language is a medium that links them to the collectivity and through which assimilation into the dominant group can be enforced or resisted. For example, in Turkey the state has banned the Kurdish language with the aim of assimilating Kurds into Turkishness but Kurds resist by continuing to speak their own language (Yeğen, 2007). However, as Enloe (1996) contends, language cannot be the only marker to distinguish one ethnic group from another as can be seen in the case of Alevis who speak different languages (Kurdish and Turkish) but still see themselves as Alevi.

There are also problems in defining Alevis purely in terms of religion. Religion is an important marker of the boundaries of an ethnic group because it is a visible characteristic by which not only the internal/emic ethnic identity is maintained and reproduced by the members but also assimilation into other groups is resisted (Andrews, 1989; Enloe, 1996; Fenton, 2010; Knott, 1992; Smith, 1998). Thus, the religious beliefs of groups within a national border can have a major influence on inter-ethnic relationships, both constructively and harmfully, the latter particularly when the dominant religious group uses violence to enforce assimilation (Enloe, 1996). However, religion cannot be the sole determinant of ethnicity as one religion is shared by more than one ethnic group. For example, Islam is shared by both Turkish and Kurdish ethnic groups in Turkey but the latter have experienced discrimination and exclusion in spite of their shared beliefs (Turkmen, 2019). Furthermore, one ethnic group can adopt two different religions or follow different sects within a religion that can at times intensify the conflict between, and within, ethnic groups such as the tensions between Alevi Turks and Sunni-Turks where the ethnic marker of religion cuts across the ethnicity of national identity.

For these reasons, our analysis of Alevi Kurd identity, or more accurately set of identities within Alevism, has shifted towards the 'ethnoreligious' as the preferred conceptual framework because it is impossible to capture the essential aspects of the community without it (Aydın, 2018; Cetin, 2014). Arakelova (2010) describes ethno-religious identity as a shift from a purely religious identity, which can cut across ethnic groups, to a new identity that is dependent on a range of characteristics including religion, culture, language and so on, but most importantly depends on members of the community choosing to belong to this new ethno-religious group. According to Arakelova, the process of new ethno-religious formation has three stages: firstly, dissociation from the existing religious group; secondly, members forming a closed community of believers with a new syncretic system of beliefs reinforced by the practice of endogamy; and thirdly, this new religious identity becoming transformed into a new ethnic group differentiated by its religious markers of identity. As an example, Arakelova suggests that Alevi Kurds may feel closer to Alevi Turks than they do to Sunni-Turks or Kurds (Geaves, 2003). In Turkey, Alevi may be a 'preferred identity' for both Turks and Kurds although this can change depending upon national and political events and a group's attitude to them (Cetin, 2014). Here there is a complex interplay between different affiliations and identities (for example, left-wing, secular, Turkish nationalist, Kurdish nationalist), the emphasis on which can change in different circumstances.

The idea of ethno-religious identity is adopted by Gultekin (2019) in his analysis of the struggles of Alevi Kurds from Dersim[4] to gain state recognition of their religious and national identity in Turkey. He suggests that Alevi Kurd identity:

> involves intersected cultural boundaries between Alevism and Kurdishness [...] in that both identities gain new socio-political and ethno-religious aspects. Kurdish Alevis share many similarities with other Alevi communities. However, they have their own socio-religious organisations, sacred place practices, mythological discourses and rituals. Although Kurdish Alevis now tend to define themselves as Kurds, their cultural heritage gives rise to many differences compared with other Kurdish communities and Kurdish nationalist politics. (Gultekin, 2019: 5)

Alevi Kurdishness here implies both a religious and ethnic identity with the appreciation of a common cultural identity and, as will become clear, also often a political one. Gultekin, like Arakelova, is describing the process of religion-building to forge a distinctive new ethno-religious identity (Kurd but equally Alevi), and relevant for our discussion is his suggestion that they have continued building their ethno-religious identity to gain recognition in their countries of settlement too. We shall use the case of the London Alevi Kurd community organisations to demonstrate their leadership role in the formation of ethno-religious identities and how ethnicity and religion become entwined within a transnational context.

The analysis in this chapter is based on extensive ethnographic and participatory action research by the authors conducted over the last 12 years with and for the İAKM-C and since 2013 with the BAF, and our research testifies to the importance of their agentic role in effecting change. Cetin (2014) conducted an ethnographic study starting in 2009 on the high incidence of suicide among Alevi Kurdish second-generation young men, something which was unusual in the transnational Alevi community. As a member of the Alevi community himself, he was witnessing the changes in the community associations first-hand. He had unique access to and support from the community to conduct ethnographic field-work to try and understand the underlying causation of the deaths by suicide. Over an extended period of time, he interviewed community leaders, religious leaders, parents and friends of those who had died by suicide, observed at funerals and community events and benefitted from informal conversations with members of the community. Much of his research informs this analysis of the development of the London Alevi Kurds as a unique community (Cetin, 2014, 2015). As a result of the continued concerns about Alevi youth, the then Chair of İAKM-C asked the University of Westminster for help to address the perceived negative identity of the second generation. This was in 2010 and Jenkins joined Cetin to undertake participatory action research (Truman, 2004) with the İAKM-C to find, develop and monitor solutions to this problem.

The participatory action research involved three main stages: identifying the problem, identifying and implementing solutions, and monitoring outcomes (Truman, 2004). The first stage entailed preliminary meetings with the İAKM-C committee and focus group discussions with Alevi youth to understand their perspectives and discuss potential solutions. Alevi young people suggested that Alevism lessons in religious education (RE) classes at school might help themselves and their peers to clarify their religious identity as Alevis and understand more about Alevism. This then became an agreed strategy. The second phase required extensive meetings with local schools and authorities for permission to include Alevism lessons in the RE curriculum and then planning, designing and teaching the lessons. The third phase has involved talking to teachers, parents, leaders and members of the community and, where available, official responses to the Alevism lessons to monitor their impact and to assess their usefulness to schools and the transnational Alevi community. Currently the research is evaluating the changes occurring within the London Alevi community to redefine Alevism and how it is practised in the UK to make it more relevant to second and future generations. Overall, extensive interviews and conversations have been conducted with the London Alevi community and religious leaders, members, parents and schools. These were supplemented by observations, working party planning meetings, observing lessons and attending school and community events, staff development sessions and meetings with European Alevis and academics working in the field. Additionally, we drew on local Turkish newspapers reporting on events. It is not always possible to be precise about the source of the data that has informed the analysis in this chapter but wherever possible we have tried to validate our impressions and understanding through cross-checking findings with key informants.

The Emergence of an Ethno-Religious Identity and New Religious Freedom among the First-Generation Alevis in London

In order to situate the settlement of the London Alevi Kurds, it is important to briefly explain their context of departure from Turkey, their country of origin. There are approximately 15–20 million Alevis in Turkey, about 5 million of whom are Alevi Kurds who speak the Kurdish and Zaza languages and are also known for historical reasons as Kızılbaş[5] (van Bruinessen, 1997; Yilmaz, 2020). These Alevi Kurds who settled in London originate mainly from the central and south-eastern regions of Turkey. The scope of the present research is limited to Alevis who speak (or have traditionally spoken) Kurmanji (a dialect of Kurdish also known as Northern Kurdish) and Zaza, both Indo-European languages and part of the Iranian language group (Koçan & Öncü, 2004; Yilmaz, 2020). We refer to both of these groups as Alevi Kurds because most of the people we met in our research defined themselves this way. Turkish official ideology defines citizenship on the basis of religion and ethnicity: Sunni Islam and ethnically Turkish are together the dominant form of identity and this excludes all other ethno-religious groups such as Alevis (Koçan & Öncü, 2004), leaving them without any official status and invisible in government statistics (Erman & Göker, 2000). There is no doubt that Alevi identity in general, and Alevi Kurdish identity in particular, has been forged in the dynamic between external political and cultural events (a history of persecution and massacres, the attempted assimilation by the Turkish state, and the conflictual relations between Kurds and the Turkish state) and internal attempts to maintain and define an Alevi identity, and even to deny it or at least subscribe to a secularised version of it. This broader context of persecution explains the migration of Kurdish Alevis in larger numbers to the UK in the late 1980s and why they mostly chose to hide their religious identity in their countries of settlement (Sokefeld, 2008.)

Historically, the UK was not a popular choice for settlement migration to Europe, unlike Germany and France, which have more established Alevi communities. The earliest migration of the Alevis to the UK can be traced back to the 1960s which corresponds to the migration patterns of other groups such as Turks who migrated to Western developed countries to meet the demands for cheap labour (Atay, 2010; Issa & Atbas, 2016). Although a small community was formed in London, nevertheless the UK is a relatively new destination of settlement for Alevis and Kurds who started migrating in meaningful numbers in the late 1980s as asylum-seekers due to the military coup in Turkey and state pressure on Alevi Kurds to fight against the Partiya Karkeren Kurdistan (translated as

Kurdistan Workers' Party, PKK), which meant they needed to find a safe country (Demir, 2012; Enneli *et al.*, 2005). The largest wave of migration to the UK occurred briefly in 1989 as refugees left the Malatya, Maraş, Sivas and Kayseri provinces.[6] They chose the UK in large numbers because there were no visa requirements (Wahlbeck, 1999). However, on 23 June 1989 the British government introduced a visa requirement which effectively curtailed the number of migrants arriving from Turkey. Subsequently, migration continued for those who could bring their families through chain migration as a result of the Family Reunification Law but for those without family already here, they were reliant on either the Ankara Treaty,[7] if they met its stringent terms, or people-smuggling (Cetin, 2014).

The Alevi Kurds who arrived in Britain in the late 1980s were mainly married men and, while some were economic migrants (Demir, 2012), the majority arrived as refugees to escape persecution. Whereas their primordial identity as Alevi had been viewed negatively by the Turkish state and the majority Sunni population, for those who claimed asylum on the grounds of religious persecution, Alevi became a positive situational identity in gaining refugee status in Britain. Since the British asylum policy was organised around 'communitarianism', it enabled the ethnic and religious groups to organise themselves as communities within a multi-cultural context (Whalbeck, 1989).[8] However, that some Alevi Kurds emphasised their ethnic Kurdish identity, some their political identity as engaging in left-wing parties, and others their religious identity in applying for asylum, suggests the articulation of multi-layered identities (Cetin, 2014; Fenton, 2010). At the same time, selective acculturation into British society occurred because they maintained strong transnational attachments to their own communities of origin in Turkey as well as to their ethnic cultural norms, values and resources (Morawska, 2009; Ozkul, 2019).

According to Cetin (2014, 2016), this was evident from their settlement patterns in London which mirrored their city/village of origin, and their process of adaptation tended towards assimilation into their own ethnic community rather than into mainstream (British) society: a process that Morawska (2009: 18) describes as 'ethnic-path adaptation within their own communities'. Many worked at the textile factories that were local to them which offered low-paid, low-skilled and labour-intensive jobs. Once they were granted refugee status they were able to bring their families over from Turkey due to family reunification rights and their wives also worked in the textile factories or did piece-work at home. They lived on council estates mainly in the London Boroughs of Enfield, Islington, Hackney and Haringey. Despite their working and living conditions, the first-generation Alevi Kurds considered themselves to be successful in many ways. For example, they sent remittances home to the family in Turkey and used any capital they had saved to start their own businesses when the textile industry started to decline. The majority of them eventually bought their own homes in better areas of London, moving out of social housing. Moreover, they felt successful because they could exercise cultural and political agency in support of transnational Alevi and Kurdish politics.[9] However, they remained a largely hidden community in London and had no presence in UK official statistics where they were grouped as Turkish (Cetin, 2014).

The Role of the İAKM-C and BAF in the Construction of a New Alevi[10] Ethno-Religious Identity

Based on our collaborative research findings over the past 12 years, we are now in a position to present the development of the politics of recognition and construction of a new Alevi ethno-religious identity in London and the UK through the efforts of the İAKM-C and later the BAF. Since the late 1990s, the İAKM-C has become increasingly important in serving religious needs as its primary function and, in the process, in defining Alevism in this new context. In an interview in July 2018, the first Chair of BAF (who was also the Chair of İAKM-C previously) explained how the central role of the İAKM-C was to hold religious ceremonies, especially funerals because Alevis did not want to hold their funerals in mosques (Zirh, 2012). Given the occasional ethnic tensions between Turkish and Kurdish Alevis, as well as the different national and political allegiances within the community, the leadership had hoped to unite all Alevis by prioritising its religious functions as a key element in the establishment of the İAKM-C. However, a religious identity that might typically be associated with a sense of belonging within a community did not fully succeed in creating or reflecting a cohesive sense of that belonging; rather it was also gradually establishing a difference between Turkish Alevis and the Kurdish and leftist communities. Interestingly, Cetin's interviews with the first-generation Alevis confirmed that the original İAKM-C management[11] tended to attract those who defined themselves as Turkish and Alevi, distinguishing themselves from the Kurds and 'politicised' (that is, leftist) Alevi Turks.

There is a general view among the Alevi community that the İAKM-C was initially established with the encouragement of the Turkish state with an aim to divide and weaken the social formation that largely supported Kurdish political movements. In addition, many Alevi Kurds have traditionally been secular, strongly opposed to religion and much more inclined to engage with left-wing politics and embrace equality issues. They saw Alevism as a cultural tradition and defended secularism in all spheres of life. For these reasons the management did not want Alevi Kurds as members of the İAKM-C. This process of marginalisation of Alevi Kurds within the İAKM-C was described as follows by one of Cetin's (2014) participants:

Of course Alevi is our religion and culture and I wanted to be a member [of the centre]. But I did not feel like going there. It does not appeal to me politically and ethnically. For example they were promoting Turkish nationalism up until recently, so they did not want the Kurds to go there. (Zafer)[12]

Another participant also reflected these sentiments in his experience of the İAKM-C:

When the community centre was first opened I went there to be a member. I filled in a form but two months later I was told that my application was declined. I said why? The management of that time told me that I was too political and dangerous for them. They told me that this was just a cultural centre. (Remzi)[13]

These participants represented the general feeling of both the Alevi Kurds and Alevi leftists whose main reason for fleeing the country was the conflict with the Turkish state and vigilante groups that oppressed the Kurds, Alevis and leftists. We argue that this represents a turning point where this constituency of Alevis expressed their desire to forge their own ethno-religious community.

As the number of Alevi Kurd migrants in the UK increased, so did their status within the London Kurdish community. Having been a 'twice minority' religiously and ethnically in Turkey, they became the majority in the London Kurdish community (Demir, 2012), representing an important reversal of their marginalised status in Turkey. Most of them knew very little about Alevism as a religion because it had been forbidden in Turkey but now in London they could enjoy the fact that they were no longer under pressure to conceal their Alevism. They could begin to explore, develop and express their faith freely thus re-imagining it in religious as well as cultural and political terms. However, with the perceived Turkish state-friendly original management of the İAKM-C in the 1990s, it was not surprising that the Alevi Kurds mostly attended Kurdish community centres instead. Once the leadership at the İAKM-C had shifted to accommodate the Kurdish majority towards the end of the 1990s, Demir (2017) notes that in a range of responses to its de-Turkification there came what she describes as a 'repositioning of religion' within the

London Alevi community. As part of their strategy of dissociation from the influence of the Turkish state associated with Sunni Islam, Alevi Kurds increasingly emphasised the importance of their religion. Demir reports, however, that her participants, who were mostly leaders in the London Kurdish community, expressed some ambivalence as to whether this repositioning in favour of a religious identity entailed Alevi Kurds dissociating themselves from their Kurdish identity too. This is reflected in the fragmentation of the Alevi Kurdish community with some associating exclusively with the Kurdish community centres, some with the Alevi centres only and yet others attending both or neither.

It is interesting to compare this with Arakelova's (2010) process of transformation from a religious to an ethno-religious formation. In the case of the İAKM-C's 'repositioning of religion' we can see some evidence of travel in the opposite direction. Here an ethno-political Kurdish identity became superseded by an ethno-religious one more centred on identification as Alevi, although this included Kurdish ethnic and cultural aspects. However, the fragmentation in the community also suggests the possibility of different directions of travel. This was reflected in how individual members associated themselves with the respective organisations and community centres which influenced how they defined their identity. For example, some Alevis are moving towards an exclusively ethnic identity because they prefer to maintain a secular 'rational' orientation and see the religious turn as a backward step. These people are more likely to attend Kurdish community centres. Conversely, some Alevis are welcoming the chance to redefine their religious identity and therefore associate more with the İAKM-C.

Alevi Practices of Religious Expression in the UK

What characterised the first-generation's experience of settling in London in the 1990s was the process of starting a new life with opportunities for themselves and their children which were previously unimaginable in Turkey. The first Chair of BAF reflected that: 'The first generation knew where they were coming to, they knew where they were from and their roots' (Interview with the Chair of the Alevi Federation, July 2018). In this respect, they fitted the pattern of 'segregated integration' first described by Cetin (2014). While the first generation mostly associated within the community, memories of being treated as a 'twice minority' in Turkey made them circumspect about revealing their Alevi identity to outsiders (Jenkins, 2020). It was also, as we have seen, an identity that was in many senses being rediscovered, re-imagined and evolving as an ethno-religious one. As in Turkey, there were no official statistics to describe Alevis in the UK and, consequently, most Alevis were still defined etically by others, which meant that they were assumed to be religiously Muslim and ethnically Turkish or Kurdish, hence rendering them invisible as Alevi in the receiving country (Jenkins & Cetin, 2018; Massicard, 2009). Nevertheless, the first generation were positively disposed towards the state and education in particular as providing security and future prospects for their children. One father of seven children expressed these aspirations when he said:

> We had a dream, I mean we thought we are now in Europe and our children can now have a good education, at least get a degree. [...] I always reminded my children that we did not have the opportunity to go to school in Turkey. (Hasan in Cetin, 2014)

Parents did not anticipate the real difficulties and challenges the second generation might face when they started school and crossed ethnic and religious boundaries. They had great confidence that schools would help their children to succeed without requiring any parental intervention, other than to provide for them materially. Some parents could speak English and did support their children to do well at school and their children have gone on to enter professions or establish their own businesses (Cetin, 2017). However, many Alevi Kurd children struggled academically, especially when they reached secondary level, and many attended economically deprived neighbourhood schools which lacked the resources to provide much support. The boys in particular were more likely to underachieve, truant and get mixed up in gangs and inter-ethnic conflicts (Cetin, 2020). Eventually, a minority ended up being excluded from school, engaging in gangs, drugs and petty crime and, once their lives had spiralled downwards and they could see no future, a few would die by suicide (Cetin, 2014, 2020).

Alevi Kurd pupils were invisible in schools where most teachers and peers did not know they were Alevi. Moreover, most Alevi children did not know enough about their religion to be able to explain their identity to others (Cetin, 2014; Jenkins, 2020; Jenkins & Cetin, 2018). This identity confusion was compounded by parents registering their children for school as 'Turkish' and 'Muslim' because that was written on their national identity cards and also because they did not want their children to face possible discrimination from teachers and peers. Teachers and other pupils would therefore treat them as Turkish and Muslim and they would struggle to explain the difference, often resorting to describing themselves as 'sort of Muslim' (Jenkins & Cetin, 2018). Alevi Kurd pupils felt marginalised and excluded from their school community and this adversely affected their achievement, behaviour and sense of belonging. The İAKM-C became increasingly concerned about the second generation, especially the boys, but more generally they were anxious about what they perceived as the 'negative identity' of the second generation and what could be done about it. By the early Noughties, the İAKM-C approached local councils, schools, health providers, social services and other faith communities in an effort to find solutions. This engagement with local agencies represented a key driver on the part of the İAKM-C towards integration, recognition and acceptance in British society (Jenkins, 2020; Jenkins & Cetin, 2018).

In post 1980s Turkey, the introduction of compulsory RE classes teaching exclusively Sunni Islam and the event of the Sivas massacre of Alevis, coupled with the refusal to recognise Alevism, prompted a strong reaction by Alevis worldwide. Whereas they had previously been hidden communities in their countries of settlement, they now became visible through protests, identity politics and establishing local, national and European Alevi associations (Sökefeld, 2008). The Alevi revival provided the impetus for Alevis to assert their identity and rights for recognition as a religion also in their countries of settlement (Cosan-Eke, 2014; Massicard, 2009). A key driver for institutional recognition across Europe was their campaign for Alevism lessons in state schools in the receiving countries (Karakaya-Stump, 2018). Germany was the first to provide Alevism lessons in some federal states in 2002, thereby officially endorsing Alevism as a religion and as distinct from Islam through what Sökefeld (2008) describes as a new politics of recognition.

With the collaboration of local schools and the University of Westminster, the İAKM-C began a successful campaign to design and introduce Alevism lessons in RE classes in schools so that their own and other children would learn about Alevism (see Figure 4.1). This represents a key example of the İAKM-C's strategy of religion-building and framing the content of Alevism to reflect their own interpretation (Arakalova, 2010; Gultekin, 2019). In 2011, the first primary school launched the lessons and in 2013, the first secondary school began the lessons and this success sparked considerable interest not only in the local community but also in the wider Alevi community transnationally. Parents wanted other schools where their children were registered to also introduce the lessons and it generated interest and conversations in families and with community centres about Alevism (Jenkins & Cetin, 2018). The lessons gave the pupils a greater sense of belonging and a way of explaining their identity and the schools teaching Alevism lessons conferred legitimacy on it as a

Figure 4.1 An Alevism lesson with year 9 at Highbury Grove School in Islington, March 2014 (photo by the BAF with permission from the school)

religion, raising their profile in local communities. The Chair of BAF described the position of the second generation like this:

> They couldn't explain who they were. This is where RE lessons came in, our children couldn't explain their background, religion and heritage[…] Since the community started talking about Alevism lessons at schools, even if they didn't have any at their own school, it made a huge unbelievable impact, in a positive manner. For example, parents and children now easily say they are Alevi. They got rid of that lack of identity. If people say what is Alevi? These children can say I am Alevi. (Chair BAF, July 2018)

The increased visibility and understanding of Alevism as a religion made a real difference to Alevi pupils. One of the secondary school pupils who was part of the first cohort to have Alevism lessons expressed the difference this made to his experience in school:

> Everywhere we Alevis are a minority, people don't know about us but when they learn about Alevism, they accept it and you get a lot more respect. (Cem, Focus group, Highbury Grove[14] pupils, April, 2017)

Parents too felt more engaged in their children's education through the schools' recognition of their religion. In interviews with parents, they explained how they felt better understood now:

> the schools used to ask us if we were Muslim and I used to hesitate to respond as we are Kurdish Alevi. At this new school, the school reassured me that they knew what Alevism was. (Fatma, July, 2018 in Jenkins, 2020)

Importantly, the İAKM-C (and subsequently the BAF), in claiming separate Alevism lessons in RE classes, had achieved both a dissociation from

Islam, which ran counter to the official ideology of Alevism in Turkey, and a distinctive religious identity for the UK community to be counted as Alevi. As such, the RE lessons played a critical role in redefining how Alevism as a religion is constructed in the UK.

The Britanya Alevi Federasyonu, established in 2013, grew out of the İAKM-C and was set up as an umbrella organisation to liaise between the national network of community centres and to direct their campaigns.[15] Following the success of the Alevism lessons in British schools, the BAF took their success to the next level through gaining official recognition as a religion by the Charity Commission in 2015.[16] There is a thriving Alevi Youth Federation and new Alevi associations in some London universities as young people feel more confident and secure in their identity. The BAF have achieved official recognition and increased visibility through a three-pronged strategy consisting of Alevism lessons in schools, representation at local and national government levels and separation of Alevism from Islam that has forged a modern brand of Alevism (Sökefeld, 2008). Integration into political life in London included canvassing for Alevi councillors, Mayors and MPs in areas with a significant Alevi population and cooperating with local organisations to resolve local issues.[17] Moreover, they instigated an All-Party Parliamentary Group which first met at the House of Commons in 2013 to lobby for recognition of Alevis' human and religious rights. A further successful campaign was launched around the same time to include Alevism as a religion in the 2021 National Census classification to enable them to be counted and described in the UK (see Figure 4.2).[18]

In summary, the Alevi community centres in London and the UK have played a pivotal role in successfully dissociating Alevism from Sunni Islam and establishing a new modernised ethno-religious Alevi identity which aspires to be supra-ethnic and able to fit in with the norms of the country of settlement. The role of the Alevi associations, the İAKM-C and BAF in particular, has been crucial in this transformation although Sökefeld notes in relation to the German context that the institutionalised separation of Alevism from Islam is more an achievement of the associations than necessarily believed by their members. While identity continues to depend heavily on asserting a difference from and intersection with other identities, and upon the local and transnational sociopolitical and cultural context (Sökefeld, 2008), Alevi identity is captured in the intersection of fluid ethno-religious boundaries and ultimately its status is reflected in how individuals choose to express it meaningfully in their lives.

Figure 4.2 The Alevi campaign for inclusion as a religion in the national census (photo taken by the BAF, February 2021)

Concluding Remarks

The syncretic perspective on ethnic formation which stresses the interplay of primordial, circumstantial and constructed components (Fenton, 2010; Morawksa, 2011) has been usefully employed to understand the ethnic identity and practices of the London-based Alevi community in its transition from the margins of British society to an officially recognised religious group. This chapter addresses three main arguments. Firstly, it describes the crucial role of the London İAKM-C and BAF in forging a new ethno-religious identity, albeit with some fluidity of boundaries (the different emphasis on Alevi and Kurd), thereby confirming other researchers' evidence of this trend (Aydın, 2020; Demir, 2017; Gultekin, 2019). It describes the shift towards dissociation from Sunni Islam and so the formation of a new ethno-religious group with its own defined Alevi identity, thereby confirming aspects of Arakelova's (2010) thesis. In the case of the UK Alevi Kurds, there has been a shift for many in favour of emphasising an Alevi identity which incorporates a Kurdish identity in reframing Alevism as a distinct religion but without losing sight of their Kurdishness.

Secondly, it demonstrates the importance of the transnational context in understanding the experience of Alevis in London and the UK. The first-generation Alevi migrants in the 1990s mostly emphasised their Kurdish or leftist identity, belonged to Kurdish community centres and engaged in leftist politics with their Alevi identity as of secondary or of only cultural significance. It is with the influence of the İAKM and later the BAF that the first generation began to develop a clearer Alevi ethno-religious identity which incorporated Kurdishness. The second generation also suffered the consequences of marginalisation at school because nobody knew about their religion assuming them to be Turkish or Kurdish Muslims and they experienced problems with underachievement and dis-affection. For them Alevism constituted an absent identity. The struggle for recognition of Alevis across Europe was spurred on by events in Turkey in reaction to the introduction of compulsory RE lessons based exclusively on Sunni Islam, massacres and the discrimination of Alevis, and the refusal to recognise Alevism as a distinct identity. It is also the case that the more established Alevi communities in Germany and other countries of settlement were a key influence on how British Alevis developed their strategies for recognition in the UK. For example, the politics of recogni-tion in the UK follows a similar pattern to Germany (Sökefeld, 2008) and was mostly achieved as a result of the work of the İAKM-C and subse-quently the BAF. According to Sökefeld, this strategy had three prongs which we have illustrated through the London Alevis. These consisted of getting involved and cooperating with local organisations and agencies; gaining representation in local authorities and electing MPs; and, most importantly, in introducing Alevism lessons into the RE curriculum in schools. This has enabled them to gain recognition at national level and to be counted in the national census as a distinct religion from 2021 onwards.[19]

Thirdly, in the process of making advances in terms of the official recognition and integration of Alevis in the UK, it is also clear that London Alevis feel a real sense of belonging in their local communities. For exam-ple, in relation to the Covid-19 pandemic, the BAF took responsibility for providing a food bank, meal delivery services and other resources for the local communities and service providers in the area, rather than just exclu-sively for their own members. Further, their acceptance as part of British society as a distinct faith group is illustrated by the fact that they were invited to a commemoration for the late Queen attended by religious lead-ers the day before her funeral. Like other migrant communities, Alevis in London and the UK continue to work out their sense of place and belong-ing in a context which broadly facilitates diversity and inclusion, enabling them to forge their ethno-religious identities and feel a sense of belonging in a way that is not possible in Turkey.

Notes

(1) While Alevis can be both Turkish or Kurdish ethnically, the majority of the UK Alevi community is in fact Kurdish and the term 'Alevi' is how the Britanya Alevi Federasyonu (British Alevi Federation) defines itself although it caters for Turkish and Kurdish as well as other ethnic background Alevis. In this paper we shall make a distinction between Alevi Turks and Alevi Kurds only when it is necessary to distinguish between them.

(2) This view is one that is largely rejected by the Alevi associations in the UK. In Turkey it has been favoured by the Turkish authorities as a justification for denying Alevism as a distinct religion and the recognition of Alevi places of worship. Other writers, for example, Karakaya-Stump (2019) and Aydın (2018) argue against attributing any primordial identity to Alevism.

(3) We do not intend to enter into a discussion of the origins of Alevism as a religion so here we offer an emic explanation of what is Alevism provided in a leaflet written by the BAF.

(4) Dersim, or Tunceli as it has been renamed by the Turkish state is the only province where Alevis are in the majority.

(5) The term was originally used by the Sunni Muslims as a pejorative term but later came to be reclaimed by Alevis as a badge of pride

(6) Several factors were involved but the most important was the fear generated by the memory of the 1978 Maraş massacre of Alevi Kurds by the ultra-nationalist fascist group, the Grey Wolves. When right-wing nationalist Islamists gained significant power in the local elections of 1989, Alevi Kurds feared that what had happened in 1978 could happen again.

(7) Since the early 2000s, migration has been through the terms of the Ankara Treaty which was set up in 1963 between the European Union and Turkey to allow migrants from Turkey to work in these countries and formed the main channel of transnational migration (Bilecen, 2022).

(8) For a detailed examination of the British asylum policies of that era, see Whalbeck (1989)

(9) From 2014–17, Jenkins et al. conducted a funded census-like survey of the Alevi Federation Membership to collect information about their lives and experience in the UK in order to support their inclusion in the National Census in 2021. See the Report to the British Academy https://www.thebritishacademy.ac.uk/funding/ba-lever-hulme-small-research-grants/past-awards/2013-14/

(10) To reiterate our point here, the London Alevi community was ethnically mixed but overwhelmingly comprised Alevi Kurds, as one of the largest Alevi communities outside of Turkey. Hence Alevi refers predominantly to Alevi Kurds in this section too.

(11) We suggest that the early management committee tended to be seen as state-friendly but they were not exclusively Turkish. This reflected their desire to keep Alevis away from the Kurdish and leftist organisations.

(12) First-generation Alevi Kurd male who is now in his 70s. All the names of interviewees have been changed unless permission has been explicitly given to use their real names.

(13) A first-generation Alevi Kurd male now in his 60s.

(14) This is the real name of the school, included here with permission of the school.

(15) There are 17 Alevi Cultural Centres and cemevis serving people in the UK. These centres are based in Wood Green (London), Glasgow, Leicester, Croydon, Harrow, Northamptonshire, York, Newcastle, Liverpool, Bournemouth, Nottingham,

Doncaster, Hull, Sheffield, Edinburgh, Manchester, Newport and Enfield (London). (BAF)

(16) See http://www.alevinet.org/MAP.aspx?pid=AleviNewsEventsArticles_en-GB&aid=nn_150209782_92832609

(17) Currently there is an Alevi Kurdish MP in the UK Parliament. The current Mayor of Enfield and previous Mayors of Haringey and Enfield were also Alevi. There are three councillors in Haringey, two in Hackney and twelve in Enfield.

(18) Following a meeting with the Office of National Statistics, it was confirmed that Alevism would appear in the dropdown menu for 'Other religions'. https://londragazete.com/english/197324/baf-launched-a-campaign-to-be-included-in-the-2021-census/

(19) See this link http://alevinet.org/MAP.aspx?pid=Haberler_en-GB&aid=nn_301060676_109173189

References

Andrews, P.A. (ed.) (1989) *Ethnic Groups in the Republic of Turkey*. Wiesbaden: Reichert.

Arakelova, V. (2010) Ethno-religious communities: To the problem of identity markers. *Iran & the Caucasus* 14 (1), 1–17

Atay, T. (2010) 'Ethnicity within ethnicity' among the Turkish-Speaking immigrants in London. *Insight Turkey* 12 (1), 123–138.

Aydın, S. (2018) The emergence of Alevism as an ethno-religious identity. *National Identities* 20 (1), 9–29.*

Aydın, S. (2020) A survey of the roots and history of Kurdish Alevism: What are the divergences and convergences between Kurdish Alevi groups in Turkey? *Kurdish Studies* 8 (1), 17–42. https://doi.org/10.33182/ks.v8i1.551

Bilecen, T. (2022) Ankara Anlaşması: Türkiye'den Birleşik Krallık'a Yeni Bir Politik Göç Akını mı? *Çalışma ve Toplum* 2 (73), 887–904.

Cetin, U. (2014) Anomic disaffection: A sociological study of youth suicide within the Alevi-Kurdish community in London. PhD thesis, University of Essex, UK.

Cetin, U. (2016) Durkheim, ethnography and transnational communities: Researching young male suicide in the London Alevi-Kurdish community. *Ethnography* 17 (2), 250–277. https://doi.org/10.1177/1466138115586583.

Cetin, U. (2017) Cosmopolitanism and the relevance of 'zombie concepts': The case of anomic suicide amongst Alevi Kurd youth. *The British Journal of Sociology* 68 (2), 145–166. https://doi.org/10.1111/1468-4446.12234

Cetin, U. (2020) Unregulated Desires: Anomie, the 'Rainbow Underclass' and Second-generation Alevi Kurdish Gangs in London. *Kurdish Studies* 8 (1), 185–208. https://doi.org/10.33182/ks.v8i1.541

Cetin, U. and Jenkins, C. (2023) Alevi Kurds in the UK: Community formation and integration. In A. Arkilic and B. Senay (eds) *Routledge Handbook of Turkey's Diasporas*. Abingdon: Routledge.

Cetin, U., Jenkins, C. and Aydın, S. (2020) Editorial: Alevi Kurds: History, politics and identity. *Kurdish Studies* 8 (1), 1–6. https://doi.org/10.33182/ks.v8i1.558

Cosan-Eke, D. (2014) Transnational communities: Alevi immigrants in Europe. *Alevilik-Bektaşilik Araştırmaları Dergisi [The Journal of Alevi Bektasi Research]* 10, 167–194.

Demir, I. (2012) Battling with Memleket in London: The Kurdish diaspora's engagement with Turkey. *Journal of Ethnic and Migration Studies* 38 (5). https://doi.org/10.1080/1369183X.2012.667996

Demir, I. (2017) Shedding an ethnic identity in diaspora: de-Turkification and the transnational discursive struggles of the Kurdish diaspora. *Critical Discourse Studies* 14 (3), 276–291. https://doi.org/10.1080/17405904.2017.1284686.

Emre-Cetin, K.B. (2018) Communicative ethnocide and Alevi television in the Turkish context. *Media, Culture & Society* 40 (7), 1008–1023

Enneli, P., Modood, T. and Bradley, H.K. (2005) *Young Turks and Kurds: A Set of Invisible Disadvantaged Groups.* York: Joseph Rowntree Foundation.

Enloe, C. (1996) Ethnic soldiers. In J. Hutchinson and D.A. Smith (eds) *Ethnicity* (pp. 282–285). Oxford: Oxford University Press.

Erman, T. and Göker, E. (2000) Alevi politics in contemporary Turkey. *Middle Eastern Studies* 36 (4), 99–118.

Fenton, S. (2010) *Ethnicity* (2nd edn). Cambridge: Polity Press.

Fishman (1977) Language and ethnicity. In H. Giles (ed.) *Language, Ethnicity and Intergroup Relations* (pp. 15–52). London: Academic Press.

Geaves, R. (2003) Religion and ethnicity: Community formation in the British Alevi Community. *Numen* 50 (1), 52–70.

Gezik, E. (2012) *Alevi Kürtler* [Alevi Kurds] (3rd edn). Istanbul: İletişim Yayınları.

Gezik, E. and Gultekin, A.K. (2019) (eds) *Kurdish Alevis and the Case of Dersim: Historical and Contemporary Insights.* Lanham, MD: Lexington Books.

Göner, Ö. (2005) The transformation of the Alevi collective identity. *Cultural Dynamics* 17 (2), 107–134.

Gültekin, A.K. (2019) Kurdish Alevism: Creating new ways of practicing the religion. Working Paper Series of the HCAS 'Multiple Secularities – Beyond the West, Beyond Modernities' 18. Leipzig University.

Issa, T. and Atbaş, E. (2016) Alevi communities in Europe: Construction of identity and integration. In T. Issa (ed.) *Alevis in Europe: Voices of Migration, Culture and Identity* (pp. 189–203). Abingdon: Routledge.

Jenkins, C. (2020) 'Aspirational Capital' and transformations in first-generation Alevi-Kurdish parents' involvement with their children's education in the UK. *Kurdish Studies* 8 (1), 163–184. https://doi.org/10.33182/ks.v8i1.545

Jenkins, C. and Cetin, U. (2018) From a 'sort of Muslim' to 'proud to be Alevi': The Alevi religion and identity project combating the negative identity among second-generation Alevis in the UK. *National Identities* 20 (1), 105–123.*

Jenkins, C., Aydın, S. and Cetin, U. (2018) Editorial. *National Identities* 20 (1), 1–7. https://doi.org/10.1080/14608944.2016.1244934.*

Karakaya-Stump, A. (2018) The AKP, sectarianism, and the Alevis' struggle for equal rights in Turkey. *National Identities* 20 (1), 53–67.*

Karakaya-Stump, A. (2019) *The Kizilbash-Alevis in Ottoman Anatolia. Sufism, Politics and Community.* Edinburgh: University of Edinburgh Press.

Karaosmanoglu, K. (2013) Beyond essentialism: Negotiating Alevi identity in urban Turkey. *Identities* 20 (5), 580–597.

Knott, K. (1992) The role of religious studies in understanding the ethnic experience. *Community Religions Project Research Paper.* Leeds: University of Leeds.

Koçan, G. and Öncü, A. (2004) Citizen Alevi in Turkey: Beyond confirmation and denial. *Journal of Historical Sociology* 17 (4), 464–489.

Massicard, E. (2009) The repression of the Koçgiri rebellion, 1920–1921. *Online Encyclopaedia of Mass Violence* [online]. Available at: http://www.massviolence. org.

McDowall, D. (2002) Asylum seekers from Turkey II. *Report written for Asylum Aid.*

Morawska, E. (2011) Ethnicity as a primordial-situational-constructed experience: Different times, different places, different constellations. *Studies in Contemporary Jewry* XXV, 3–25.

Morawska, E. (2009) *A Sociology of Immigration: (Re)making Multifaceted America.* Basingstoke: Palgrave Macmillan.

Özkul, D. (2019) The making of a transnational religion: Alevi movement in Germany and the World Alevi union. *British Journal of Middle Eastern Studies* 46 (2), 259–273. https://doi.org/10.1080/13530194.2019.1569304.

Shankland, D. (2003) *The Alevis in Turkey: The Emergence of A Secular Islamic Tradition.* London: Routledge.

Smith, R.C. (1998) Transnational localities: Community, technology and the politics of membership within the context of Mexico and US migration. Transnationalism from below. *Comparative Urban and Community Research* 6, 196–238.

Sökefeld, M. (2008) *Struggling for Recognition: The Alevi Movement in Germany and in Transnational Space.* New York: Berghahn Books Publication.

Truman, C. (ed.) (2004) *Social Research and Social Justice.* London: Palgrave.

Turkmen, G. (2019) Civil war and religion: Turkey. *Oxford Research Encyclopaedia of Politics.* Online Publication.

van Bruinessen, M. (1997) 'Aslını inkâr eden haramzādedir': The debate on the ethnic identity of the Kurdish Alevis. In K. Kehl-Bodrogi, B. Kellner-Heinkele and A. Otter-Beaujean (eds) *Syncretistic Religious Communities in the Near East* (pp. 1–23). Leiden: Brill.

Wahlbeck, O. (1999) *Kurdish Diasporas.* Basingstoke: Macmillan Press Ltd.

Whalbeck (1989) Community work and exile politics: Kurdish Refugee associations in London, *Journal of Refugee Studies* II (3).

Yeğen, M. (2007) Turkish nationalism and the Kurdish question. *Ethnic and Racial Studies* 30 (1), 119–151.

Yilmaz, B. (2020) Language attitudes and religion: Alevi Kurds in the UK. *Kurdish Studies* 8 (1), 163–184. https://doi.org/10.33182/ks.v8i1.545

Zirh, B. (2012) Following the dead beyond the 'nation': A map for transnational Alevi funerary routes from Europe to Turkey. *Ethnic and Racial Studies* 35 (10), 1758–1774. https://doi.org/10.1080/01419870.2012.659274.

*All the articles cited from this special issue of the journal *National Identities* are also available as a book. Jenkins, C., Aydin, S. and Cetin, U. (eds) (2018) *Contested Boundaries: Alevism as an Ethno-religious Identity.* Abingdon: Routledge.

Part 2

'Performative Space': Visualising, Sounding and Acting Identities in a Transnational Field

5 Performing Black Beauty: The Congolese Community in London

Benedetta Morsiani

Introduction

The chapter examines the cultural practice of the *Miss Congo Beauty Pageant UK*, aiming to reveal the dynamic sociocultural and political meanings embedded within it. The case study highlights two major issues of investigation. Firstly, it demonstrates how the young London Congolese produce a contemporary form of cultural representation of 'traditional' Congolese customs and values and display a transnational and 'imaginary' sense of belonging to the Democratic Republic of Congo (DRC). Secondly, it illustrates how the cultural practice is transformed into an arena where everyday concerns affecting the young London Congolese and other Black African diasporas are expressed. The pageant arena serves to contest conservative beliefs perpetuated by elders, tackling and advancing controversial disputes regarding Black African women's rights, gender equality and sociocultural stigmas. Additionally, notions of Black beauty and the 'natural' body are embraced as alternatives to conventional Western beauty ideals. Therefore, the meaningful and contradictory site of *Miss Congo UK* enables the public performance of 'new' racial, ethnic and gender identities and the configuration of a progressive mentality among young London Congolese.

The chapter is divided into three main sections. The first main section discusses the transformation of beauty competitions into sites of identity production and cultural agency, especially among minority groups. Next, it introduces the Congolese migration to the UK and settlement in London, and the *Miss Congo Beauty Pageant UK* as a major activity of the communities. The methodology used is also introduced. The main part of the chapter is devoted to a fine-grained ethnography and in-depth analysis of the *Miss Congo Beauty Pageant UK* final gala night of the 2017 competition. It pays particular attention to some of the rituals incorporated in the show's seg-ments and performed on stage by young contestants and other performers.

Performing Beauty as a Process of Cultural Production

Beauty pageants represent an extremely popular phenomenon that span many different countries at a local, national and international level, and acquire standard characteristics within the most diverse societies and cultures (Cohen *et al.*, 1996). A similar format is followed, usually once a year. It begins with a process of selection of the participants, who then embark upon a period of rehearsal until the final public event where each contestant performs and is judged in front of an audience. The winner is finally selected to serve as a symbolic representation of the community's or nation's collective identity during the following year.

The rich and interdisciplinary literature on beauty pageants points out how these competitions should be considered not merely as forms of enter-tainment, but as dynamic places where specific sociocultural groups define, modify and represent their cultural meanings (King O'Riain, 2008). Drawing on 13 beauty pageant case studies from very different cultural contexts worldwide, Cohen *et al.* (1996) argue that pageants have a con-troversial nature, evoking passionate interest and engagement with politi-cal issues: 'struggles over beauty contests are also struggles over the power to control and contain meanings mapped onto the bodies of competitors' (Cohen *et al.*, 1996: 9). Similarly, Banet-Weiser's work on pageants in the USA highlights how these are 'profoundly political arena[s], in the sense that the presentation and reinvention of femininity that takes place on the beauty pageant stage produces political subjects' (Banet-Weiser, 1999: 3).

Beauty pageants are thus very interesting cultural sites where local iden-tity and culture are publicly performed and made visible (Cohen *et al.*, 1996), where meanings of race, ethnicity (Craig, 2002), class, gender and nationalism are rearticulated, and where conceptions of conventional, nationalised 'femininity' and idealised 'beautiful' bodies are reflected (Balogun, 2012). Pageants also provide a discursive space to produce moral, religious (Faria, 2010) and global dynamics (Crawford *et al.*, 2008). It is not surprising that national and international beauty contests have frequently represented sites of controversy, often being interpreted as cultural forms of oppression both in Western and non-Western countries (King O'Riain, 2008). Some studies emphasise the objectification and commodification of women's bodies. These see pageants as exploitative spaces of profit-making that perpetuate patriarchal images of unrealistic beauty and bodily appear-ances and that indicate a loss of women's purity and modesty (Faludi, 1992).

While the potentially damaging consequences and well-argued critiques embedded within the beauty pageant spectacle should be taken seriously, the culture, time and context in which these competitions take place must also be considered. Pageants can be received in conflicting ways among diverse societies within different individual and collective circumstances (Crawford *et al.*, 2008). Beauty contests featuring numerous racial, ethnic and diasporic communities, organised by and for individuals who belong to those specific minority groups, can become valuable vehicles in rearticulating cultural authenticity and difference (McAllister, 1996).

Maxine Leeds Craig, in *Ain't I a Beauty Queen?: Black Women, Beauty, and the Politics of Race* (Craig, 2002), highlights that African American beauty pageants in the 1960s represented fundamental sites of cultural agency, where notions of Black beauty were directly used as a counter-response to dominant representations of Western beauty. Pageants served as arenas for Black African women to contest centuries of stereotypically racist depictions of them as ugly, vulgar and sexually available (Craig, 2002). The display of their natural beauty, that put Blackness and African 'authenticity' at its centre, developed as part of the symbolic repertoire against racial exclusion and the assertion of racial difference (Faria, 2010).

The mushrooming of beauty competitions among diasporic minority groups similarly resulted from an active reaction against the exclusion experienced in host societies. These competitions stood as a validation that ethnic women and their cultures should be considered equally beautiful to women belonging to dominant cultures. Pageants were produced for symbolic resistance and to claim greater acceptance (Faria, 2010). Organisers, participants and audiences belonging to the same racial, ethnic or national group have frequently experienced beauty competitions as cultural forms which imaginatively express a connection to their distant, original homelands, and display 'authenticity' (Mani, 2006). The pageant can be defined as 'a local adaptation, a refashioning of a dominant cultural form to the particular needs for representation within the community' (Borland, 1996: 75). Diasporic transnational beauty competitions particularly operate to reproduce sociocultural norms involving gendered, racial and ethnic ideals and to raise awareness around cultural identity stories while revealing internal conflicts and differences between diasporas (Faria, 2010). The performance of beauty contests deserves, therefore, to be analysed at the local level and in connection with those specificities that characterise each social group (Crawford *et al.*, 2008).

It is within this background that Miss Congo Beauty Pageant UK is analysed. The Congolese pageant represents not a mere runway performance where young Congolese women are judged on their beauty, but rather a safe public sphere where young participants are able to voice their individual everyday experiences, interests and ambitions, and where the audience can reflect on ordinary social life issues affecting their own communities. It involves a participant selection process, an intense training period and a final public event ending with the queen's coronation. During the castings, participants are interviewed both in groups and individually and selected only if they can show genuine interest in wanting to know more about their cultural heritage and getting involved with community work. The training process, usually spanning a period of three months preceding the final event, involves a series of workshops to prepare the contestants for the final show, mainly aiming at motivating the personal development of the young participants. These activities include dance classes, life and self-confidence coaching sessions as well as educational lectures on the history, culture and politics of the DRC.

Congolese Migration to the UK and Settlement in London

Compared to Anglophone Black African diasporas, the history of Congolese migration to the UK for political reasons is a more recent phenomenon: it began in the late 1980s and reached its highest level in the 1990s and 2000s. The collapse of the state followed by the overthrow of Mobutu's regime by L.D. Kabila's armed rebellion in 1997, the Second Congo War (1998–2003), and the implementation of very restricted immigration policies in Belgium, France and Switzerland brought many Congolese to seek asylum in the UK. Furthermore, the UK became the major destination for other Congolese groups. These 'Euro–Congolese', mostly from France, Belgium, The Netherlands and Spain, saw the UK as a less discriminatory environment and with a better labour market (Garbin & Pampu, 2009).

Although remaining a 'minority within a minority' compared to Anglophone Black African groups linked to British colonial history, the Congolese community[1] represent the biggest Francophone African group among the Central and Western Francophone African groups, settled in the country (Garbin, 2014). The two oldest districts to have hosted the highest number of Congolese are Tottenham in north London and Newham in east London (Styan, 2003). However, the community has progressively expanded in many other neighbourhoods of north, east and south London (Pachi et al., 2010).

Miss Congo Beauty Pageant UK

To analyse the Congolese, London-based, annual beauty competition *Miss Congo Beauty Pageant UK,* the chapter[2] applies a multi-sited ethnographic approach, advocated by George Marcus, which traces 'a cultural formation across and within multiple sites of activity' (Marcus, 1995). In so doing, it follows *people* (young migrants); *things* (fashion garments), *metaphors* (signs, symbols and images), *stories* (memories and everyday life narratives), *lives* and *biographies* and *conflicts* related to the beauty pageant. Observational written field notes, mainly taken during other community events and gatherings, and face-to-face, in-depth, semi-structured interviews[3] were combined with virtual fieldwork, involving the analysis of data collected from a variety of media sources, such as social networking spaces, web channels and weblogs. The multi-sited approach suits well the investigation of young diasporic individuals' everyday lives in London since they are increasingly mobile, live in many places without having specific areas of gathering and their cultural events are often temporary, short-lived phenomena, spanning across the metropolis.

The community event, which takes place every year, is today organised and promoted by its main founder Luke, owner of *Disk and Jockey Entertainment*, a Congolese events management company. Luke is a 33-year-old Congolese who describes himself as 'an entrepreneur, a businessman, an event organiser', who is also the founder of the *Voice of Congo*, a Congolese diaspora-based web news platform. The beauty competition was initially held in conjunction with the Congo annual independence celebration on the evening of 30 June. It was only from 2013 that the *Miss Congo Beauty Pageant UK* became a community event per se. Up to the present day, the organisational team is composed by a small group of young London Congolese men and women. These are considered to be intellectual experts in their fields and successful professional figures within the young community. Along with Luke, they lead the casting and training process of the pageant as well as participating in the final event either as performers, hosts or judges.

The event has significantly been cast by research informants as a 'cultural pageant', insisting mainly on the intellectual dimension of the contest, in order to portray a well-educated, middle-class and open-minded trajectory of the communities. Such interpretation was made very clear to the contestants from the casting process documented in the *Official Miss Congo UK* YouTube channel. As expressed by one of the organisers, Vava Tampa, a community political activist founder of the charity *Save the Congo*:

> *Miss Congo* is definitely not just about you being pretty, believe me we had so many pretty girls applying. We want more than prettiness, we want substance! So here are a couple of hints: you need to be informed and aware of what is going on across the world, you should mention

watching the news and read papers, learn about new Congolese stuff! This is gonna be beyond being gorgeous and 'having the body' or being 'pretty', is gonna be beyond all of that! You need to have what people say in French – and forgive me because I am gonna sound very colonial – the *bagage intellectuel* (intellectual baggage, knowledge). This is gonna be about bringing that *bagage intellectuel* which can also simply mean 'having something in your mind'. So just go home and look around and be sure to come back and bring that here! (Official Miss Congo, 2017)

In accordance with this, during the training process, organisers were mostly oriented to stimulate candidates' intellectual abilities and to assess young women's determination to become active agents of improvement both in the London diaspora and back home. Contestants were offered educational lectures on the history, culture and politics of the DRC, with the aim of expanding young women's knowledge and passion about their Congolese heritage. In Luke's words in interview: 'we want to teach them everything they need to know on the Congo' (Interview: 21 April 2017). This was also evidenced by Vava on the *Official Miss Congo UK* YouTube channel: 'only when you understand your story, your history, where you come from, where you were before, only when you enter that image it becomes much easier to kind of dream large and big and to sort of being "confident"' (Official Miss Congo, 2017).

Miss Congo Beauty Pageant UK 2017 Final Gala Night

The *Miss Congo Beauty Pageant UK 2017* final gala night was held in the 'prestigious' Stratford Town Hall venue, in Newham, on the evening of 1 April, from 7pm to 12am. It was promoted on the official pageant online booklet as: 'A gala night to celebrate Congolese beauty and empower Congolese women. One of the most prestigious African beauty pageants in Europe', involving 'beauty, knowledge, power, talent and culture'.

It featured nine young Congolese women between 18 and 25 years of age, who were mainly university students settled in London. Very few of them were born in the DRC and only one was born in London. The majority were born and grew up in other European countries such as France, Belgium, The Netherlands and Germany before moving to London, and had never visited the DRC.

The event was sold out and attended by both generations of London Congolese. These were mainly family members and friends as well as community leaders and businesspeople who had come to support contestants for the title. Members of the audience also included individuals from other Black/African diasporas such as Nigerians, Ghanaians, African–Caribbean, Ugandans and Sierra Leoneans.

The final gala night followed a standard format of segments similar to other beauty pageants: traditional dress catwalks, a talent show, questions and answers, and an evening gown catwalk ending with the winner's coronation. In addition to the young contestants' appearances, performances and speeches, music concerts and a poetry recital also took place, together with short speeches by the former *Miss Congo UK*, other African beauty queens, members of the audience and those promoting upcoming Congolese events.

Embodying racial and ethnic 'authenticity'

The pageant talent show segment was opened by 31-year-old British Congolese man JJ Bola. He is a well-established poet, writer, educator and political activist of the young community and that evening he performed one of his spoken word pieces, *Something Beautiful*:

Something beautiful is happening.

Right here, right now, in this room.

Lifting the gloom from our consciousness,

(...)

Something beautiful is happening.

(...)

I dreamed, when I was two, my grandmother sat me

on her knee and said *mokili oyo ezali ya yo*

na maloba na yo oko komisa yango kitoko.[4]

And just like you, I didn't understand what was

she said, but the feeling stayed with me

and when I got older, I asked my father and he

replied your grandmother talked because she

didn't have much time left.

I haven't seen her since,

but wherever she is, she stays with me.

A woman that I never knew.

On that day,

something beautiful happened.

When I first wrote poetry,

(…)

I knew both where I was going

and where I had come from.

Where I belong,

(…)

Because like the universe, I am mostly darkness,

and darkness dwells alone,

in the corners of dimly lit rooms

or the backs of your mind.

Darkness is unknown, undiscovered,

Unrelenting (Bola, 2015)

The piece is taken from JJ Bola's poetry collection entitled WORD. It reflects a story of self-discovery: from the dreamed attachment to the homeland where he encounters his Congolese grandmother in his imagination, to his perpetual search for identity in conversation with his Congolese father in London. He is aware of having partially lost his Congolese, Black African roots, highlighting his inability to understand the native language, Lingala, expressing the problem to many other young Congolese in the audience who probably share similar feelings. The figure of his grandmother could also be interpreted as a metaphorical reference to the 'myth of Mama Africa', the collective idea that the ancestral African continent exists as a nurturing spirit inside every Black individual (de Santana Pinho, 2010). The poem plays a symbolic connecting role with African cultural memories while also echoing a conflicting 'double consciousness' (Du Bois, 1903), of being both Black African and British in one body. JJ Bola's performance during the pageant could be described as a multi-sensory experience, emphasised by his tall and strong bodily presence, the escalation and sudden drop of the tone of his voice, the very fast or very concise pace of his reading and the gesture of his right hand often close to the chest. In so doing, JJ Bola probably aimed to resonate a collective transnational narrative, performing for the Black African communities, defining his own racial and ethnic identities (Craig, 2002).

Once JJ Bola left the stage, the nine contestants were then individually reintroduced by the hosts for the talent show segment. Each young woman was allotted 15–25 minutes to perform their acts, elaborated and rehearsed during the training. These ranged from singing to spoken word poetry, and stand-up comedy to dramatic monologue.[5] During the question-and-answer segment (Figure 5.1), judges addressed questions to each contestant mostly concerning the homeland, such as history, geography, politics, religion, gender empowerment, cultural production, charitable work and future plans. Some contenders were asked, for instance, to give the number and the names of all the neighbouring states bordering with the DRC, to explain the reasons for the geographical proximity of the capital of the DRC (Kinshasa) and the capital of the Republic of Congo (Brazzaville),[6] while others were asked to give personal opinions on why the DRC has not yet had a woman as President or describe who was the religious leader, Kimpa Vita.[7] The last common question addressed to all was to explain individual action plans if they were crowned as winners.

The pageant segments described above clearly attempted to present a night of cultural 'authenticity' (McAllister, 1996), with the 'authentic' notion relating to how cultural identities are constructed in the present (Schackt, 2005). Sets of traditional Congolese cultural practices and knowledge, such as the display of folk fashion clothes, dance movements, poetry enacted and discussions of key information regarding the homeland, were 'preserved' and 'reinvigorated' (Schackt, 2005) by the contestants and other performers, and exercised within a communal gaze (King O'Riain, 2008).

Figurer 5.1 Contestants on stage during the question-and-answer segment (photo credit Letitia Kamayi)

In displaying a spectacle that had many 'authentic' elements of the Congolese heritage, organisers and performers satisfied audience expectations that they were taking part in an 'originary' story. The staged performance of racialised and ethnicised bodies became allegorical signifiers of a Congolese cultural identity as well as of a communal Black African selfhood. The finals were designed to represent and celebrate the very essence of what it means to be Congolese, African and Black in the diaspora, and therefore produced as a vehicle to reclaim a transnational narrative of everyday experiences.

Crowning a Queen with 'A Cause to Fight For': A Symbolic Statement

Towards a cultural change

With a throne in the middle of the stage, the contest concluded as all pageant organisers, judges, former *Miss Congo UK* winners, other beauty queens and hosts clambered on stage to announce the final results. Twenty-two-year-old student Horcelie Sinda Wa Mbongo was proclaimed as the new queen, becoming the new 'ambassador' of the young Congolese community. Significantly, the final public crowning of *Miss Congo UK 2017* symbolised a strong socio–cultural and political gesture. Being affected by the HIV virus and well-focused on her 'cause to fight for', the winner embodied a quite controversial mentality and cultural shift among young London Congolese. The queen was chosen not only as a symbol of 'authentic' culture but also as a symbol of cultural progress.

During the talent show segment of the finals, Horcelie had performed a semi-autobiographical play, written by herself (Figure 5.2). The play was set in a secondary school in Kinshasa and was acted out in collaboration with two other 17-year-old Black African girls, affiliated to Horcelie's church. The first scene included the appearance into the ballroom of the Townhall and on stage of the three young women interpreting 15-year-old classmates during an ordinary day at school. They were all dressed in female school uniforms composed of white shirts and knee length dark blue skirts. The play's dialogue revealed that the young girl played by Horcelie was experiencing verbal abuse and discrimination for her health condition by the two schoolmates.

The second scene of the play portrayed Horcelie reciting a monologue, *The gift of time as suffering*:

> The daytime stood still was the day I knew myself well. It was then I saw everything I missed (...) Time treats us all differently. For some kindly and others harshly (...) And forgiveness (...) When time is asking you and

Figure 5.2 Horcelie's performance of a semi-autobiographical play written by herself (photo credit Letitia Kamayi)

I to forgive it is difficult to surrender to it freely. But even if it means crying, I must cry. Even if it means dying, I must die (…) Time whispered in my ears, though they've done you wrong you must forgive (…) *Kombo na nga Horcelie. Ba boti na nga ba kolisa nga na maloba oyo; kozongisa mabe na mabe te. Libisa ba oyo ba sala yo mabe. Mwana tango abotamaka na pasi ayebaka pasi te.*[8] (…) In this human life pain is inevitable but a gift to the human soul. A gift to the wise, a gift to the poor, a gift of mine. This innocent cry of a new-born child is my new beginning, the definition of my name.

Hi, my name is Horcelie Sinda Wa Mbongo and I am one among other 2.5 million children in Africa that were born HIV positive. My bravery is not telling you that I am positive, but my bravery is that I chose to live as HIV positive woman (…).

Horcelie's performance aimed to describe the everyday experiences, characterised by many difficulties, of living with HIV in Africa and among its diasporas. It emphasised how HIV positive Congolese and Black African individuals are still victims of a deep social stigma which results in bullying and discriminatory behaviour, bringing suffering and isolation from a young age. Horcelie's final poem also embodied a spiritual message, referring to the role played by Christian beliefs in her life and the significance of learning how to truly forgive. Performing on stage, in her own narrative, became a form of prayer.

In the play, Horcelie alluded more precisely to her own childhood experience of social discrimination in the DRC. She remembered what school peers have said or done to her during childhood when she was not aware of her condition.

> We had no idea I was positive, but some spots started to appear on my skin (…) I went to school, and (…) when you are early for school in the Congo you have to (…) stand beside one girl or one boy and wait to get in (…) Nobody wanted to stand next to me and they were saying stuff about my spots and they thought they would catch the same and they did not want any contact with me (…) I had to stay at home (…) until all the spots kind of disappeared. I did no blood test in the Congo; I don't know if it was because my mum couldn't afford it or because everyone kept telling me that it was nothing (…). So, traditionally they would take a (…) yellow rock and they would crash it down to make a sort of yellow liquid and they would add water and other herbal stuff. (…) they put this cream onto my skin and the spots surprisingly disappeared (…). Only when I grew up, I realised the reason why I had those spots on my skin. (Interview: 19 June 2017)

Similar memories of verbal and physical segregation experienced in the Congo were evoked in the first scene of the play, when the two classmates derogatively described Horcelie's character as 'the girl with AIDS', mentioning that they had to wash their hands after touching her or to avoid touching or speaking to her for fear of catching the disease. Significantly, the spectacle of the pageant represented a platform to finally disclose her disease to friends and relatives who were not aware of it. Some discovered Horcelie's story at the finals and others after hearing her interviews with Africa BBC and BBC Afrique. These online reports were discussed internationally, not only in the UK but also in Denmark, Michigan (US), Makurdi (Nigeria), Sierra Leone, Abu Dhabi (United Arab Emirates) and Doha (Qatar).

Horcelie is today a health and HIV and AIDS campaigner within the Black African diaspora in London. The beauty pageant represented a battlefield for Horcelie to articulate cultural and political agency. Winning it and being in the 'spotlight' for some time acted as a reinforced springboard for her campaign on raising local and global awareness of AIDS and HIV and speaking about her story. She is now actively participating in talk shows, volunteering activities and church cultural events organised by and outside the community in London, Manchester, Birmingham, etc. Her story and activism were featured in Black African and other magazines, for example *Mambo* (Figure 5.3), as part of HIV Prevention campaigns in England.

The healthier lifestyle magazine for Africans   Issue 19 - Winter 2017

mambo

MISS
CONGO
UK
Horcelie inspiring
her community.

THE CHANCE
TO BEAT
HIV IS IN
SIGHT
Rates are
falling +
new ways
to stop
HIV

ZOE'S
GHANA
KITCHEN
Pop-up
success
for the
queen
of cuisine

MAMBO
CULTURE
New music,
theatre
and books

PLUS
CHRISTMAS
HEALTH SUPPORT

Figure 5.3 Horcelie featured on magazines as a health and HIV and AIDS campaigner (image credit *Mambo* Magazine)

Furthermore, in 2018, Horcelie founded a Congolese health and well-being community organisation, *Lobiko ya Congo*,[9] based on educational lectures to open the discussion not only on HIV/AIDS but also on mental health, sickle cell disease, diabetes, disabilities, etc, which affect the Black African diaspora. Horcelie's symbolic coronation at the pageant as a leading 'ambassador' of the young London Congolese community signified a willingness from the organisers and judges to trace a counter-story on how to deal with HIV/AIDS and other health issues, therefore portraying a forward-thinking narrative of the young London Congolese community.

Questioning the Community's Ideologies and Trying to Subvert Global Standards of Beauty

In opposition to many national and international pageants which request participants to meet quantifiable bodily measurements, such as specific heights, weights and sizes, bodily specifications were one of the least important aspects required to participate in *Miss Congo UK* and to be selected as queen of the year. The Congolese competition thereby criticised the strict boundaries placed on women's bodies in standard pageants (Oberhauser *et al.*, 2017), indicating that international beauty concepts should include a broader variety of appearance ideals (Balogun, 2012). As testified by the experience of Anna, one of the pageant participants I interviewed: 'I am 5'10 and quite curvy and I am not typically model or pageant material' (Interview: 15 April 2017).

Although Anna was the only young Congolese woman with a curvaceous body, while all the other contestants were relatively slim, tall and sporty, her presence, and the claimed openness towards other women with similar shaped bodies, demonstrated the willingness of the organisers to promote diversity and naturalness. Because cultural aspects were central to the pageant, young women were not excluded based on their looks, nor selected for their 'thinness and tallness', but rather for their interest in appreciating their Congolese background and actively influencing a progressive mentality within the community. As testified by Horcelie in her interview: 'we were all different body sizes and that's what Miss Congo is trying to show (...) We had curvy girls, we had some short girls, and I am also not tall enough to be a model. [The pageant] mostly [focuses] on how much you want to know about your own community' (Interview: 19 June 2017).

Importantly, *Miss Congo UK*'s inclusivity sought to push forward the community's ideologies on beauty expectations. In conversation with other contestants, it emerged that, until recently, the Congolese diaspora's preferences with regard to women's appearances have been deeply influenced by Western criteria of beauty, not only concerning body measurements, but also regarding other physical attributes such as skin tonality and hair texture and colour. According to Lucrèce, the winner of the 2016 competition, women with 'fair skin and straight hair' have always been considered 'more beautiful and attractive' in the DRC and the Congolese European diasporas: 'mixed race girls, especially mixed with Whites, have usually been favourite!' (Interview: 25 May 2017). For this reason, older generations of Congolese women and men would commonly bleach their skin using very popular cream products.

In this regard, during the talent segment, young Congolese contestant Victoria Bangu, performed a poem entitled *You are pretty, but...*, which targeted the skin lightening issue. Its symbolic sociocultural and political message was to openly persuade the Black African members of the audience to be proud of the beauty of their skin and of their 'Blackness' as a whole. Victoria opened her talent act by highlighting to everyone that 'no matter what shade you are, you should always know that you are beautiful!' and she continued to recite:

'You are pretty, but... you'd be prettier if you was lighter!' he said to me. – I was sixteen then, I am now twenty-four, but those very words are haunting me for the longest of time. – Why is everyone in the Congolese community trying to be yellow? (...) For you see, no matter how light you become and (...) what your tone is, your kids when you birth them *bako funda yo!*[10] – How are we to raise our daughters and our sons to appreciate their melanin, (...) the skin they are in, if we're yet to understand that beauty is not defined solely by the shade your skin is in (...) 'cause you're Black, Black is beautiful to a shade that is unrecognisable. For we are coming newer shades, let's embrace it, proclaim it!'. (Miss Congo Beauty Pageant UK, 2017)

In accordance with Victoria's performance, several studies demonstrate that skin whitening is a widespread habit which extends across races, ethnicities, gender and age. The use of bleaching cosmetics aims to reduce or interrupt the physiological production of the melanic pigmentation of the natural skin (Abraham, 2017). Despite the severe side effects resulting from the use of skin lightening products, the practice is extensively used in numerous African countries, especially among the dark-skinned sub-Saharan African population and Black African diasporas in the West (Petit *et al.*, 2006).

This very complex habit results from the collective cultural assumption that, as expressed by Lucrèce, 'lighter skin is better than darker skin' (Interview: 25 May 2017). Giovanni Vassallo underlines that the mass consumption of expensive bleaching cosmetics in the DRC indicates that a big section of the population seems to believe that 'whiter' is 'more beautiful and healthier', with light-skinned pop stars such as Beyoncé often taken as a reference point (Vassallo, 2011). These cultural beliefs are deeply reinforced by billboard advertising, print and electronic media messages in Africa which still often portray White-skinned individuals as 'icons' of beauty (de Souza, 2008). Thus, the percentage of Congolese people who have experienced collateral effects from voluntary de-pigmentation is very high (Vassallo, 2011).

Contributing factors to the spread of the concept of skin bleaching throughout the African continent and its diasporas can be found in history and, consequently, in individuals' cultural memories. During the slave trade and colonisation, White supremacist and hegemonic ideologies, based on the assumption that Western cultures were 'racially superior' to other cultures and dark skin had an 'inferior' social meaning, strongly shaped a 'colour caste system' (White, 2005: 295) which divided social groups, where an order 'from high to low parallels the skin colour from light to dark' (Westerhof, 1997: 574). Next to Whites in the social structure, were (and still are) mixed-race individuals, estimated to be of a superior class to the full-blooded Africans (Cooper, 2016). These ideas persist among the Congolese and endorse 'a hierarchy that suggests the more European one's features – the lighter one's skin, the less ethnic one's facial features and the straighter and longer one's hair – the greater one's social value' (White, 2005: 295). The system has, consequently, institutionalised racist dynamics and incentivised the internalisation of self-hatred and low-esteem behaviour within Black African communities and their diasporas (White, 2005).

Drawing on Frantz Fanon's seminal work (1952), the skin bleaching phenomenon developed in Africa and its diaspora can be related to the inferiority complex of Blacks in relation to Whites perpetuated during colonialism (Begedou, 2014). Fanon examines how the complex of inferiority was indoctrinated by colonists into the minds of the colonised through psychological mechanisms of racism. 'Whiteness' was a symbol of purity, justice, truth, virginity, defining what it meant to be civilised, modern and human, while 'Blackness' represented the exact contrary, a symbol of ugliness, sin, darkness, immorality, ignorance and inferiority. Colonised subjects inevitably began (or were forced) to identify themselves through the eyes of colonisers. They experienced a dynamic of internalisation of this inferiority, which Fanon calls 'epidermalization', where their self-esteem and self-motivation evaporated. Black men started to emulate their oppressors, to wear 'White masks' in an attempt to 'turn White': pushing away the negative connotation of Blackness to gain recognition and be accepted as men by the colonisers (Fanon, 1952; Sardar, 2008).

The legacy of slavery and colonialism has profoundly shaped the ways in which many Black Africans have come to see themselves and experience their everyday lives. Many have maintained this 'distorted view' believing in their 'ugliness' and in the possibility of being 'beautiful' and less discriminated against only through a lighter skin colour (Begedou, 2014). Explanations behind skin bleaching, therefore, include an assumed direct connection between light skin and beauty, health, and advanced social status (Kamagaju *et al.*, 2016). The practice has for a long time been experienced as a means of becoming more attractive, accepted, and economically strengthened, with Africans in Europe not only continuing the practice but also spreading it among individuals who never performed it in their native countries (Petit *et al.*, 2006).

Similar to skin bleaching, Black Africans also modify their natural hair towards Eurocentric standards. Within the aforementioned coloured caste system, natural hair, together with skin colour and facial features, carries deep historical and social baggage (White, 2005). As expressed by Lucrèce in her interview, Congolese often use unhealthy and expensive chemical products to relax the hair texture and obtain a straightened hairstyle and/or to dye the natural colour and switch it to a lighter one. Adding hair extensions or wearing full scalp wigs is also a common habit. Regarding her mother's generation of Congolese women, Lucrèce noted: 'first thing is the hair, they usually have very eye-catching and bold hairstyles (...) they would do a very bright blond sort of thing but also sometimes red, sometimes they would dye their hair using the colours of the DRC flag' (Interview: 25 May 2017). However, a difference between generations was also pointed out: 'this is not everyone because now actually, so many young people are ditching those trends and just go for who they are!' (Interview: 25 May 2017).

Accordingly, the *Miss Congo UK* pageant aimed to highlight a generational distinction within the communities regarding how a stereotypically beautiful Congolese woman should look, thereby embracing a counter-story on beauty standards. It sought to symbolically support younger generations to eliminate the negative bleaching and straightening cultural habits. Self-representation of the body, involving how a woman wears her hair, dresses and uses cosmetics, whether she decides to use skin-lightening creams or not and whether to straighten her hair or not, is strictly connected to the cultural values of her community (Faria, 2010). Although some contestants still straightened their hair, the winners of both the 2016 and 2017 competitions had very dark skin and natural curly hair, embodying a naturalness, appreciation and symbolic pride in their origins and aesthetics. In discussing natural beauty with Lucrèce, she stated: 'I did not see myself winning so when I won, I thought "Wow so that actually means that I am beautiful!"' (Interview: 25 May 2017).

The forward-looking story of younger London Congolese was manifested during the community event, and its metaphorical meanings have probably been shaped by the current social debate on beauty standards. Western criteria in relation to bodily appearances are slowly shifting towards a wider global diversity and inclusivity, as reported daily in the media. The relative exposure to more diverse beauty images, especially in cyberspace, seems to inspire young Black Congolese women to recognise, appreciate and embrace their physical and cultural features. In Lucrèce's experience:

> On the internet you see a lot of documentaries about people who tell how they used to bleach their skin and relax their hair but now they've stopped and maybe part of it is because we can actually see darker skinned models or actresses with natural hair in magazines (...) this is helping us to see the beauty of our colour, of who we are and how we were born (...) because how can you appreciate yourself if you don't see yourself in magazines that are considered beauty magazines? (Interview: 25 May 2017).

Occasionally, *Miss Congo UK* contestants themselves became promoters of 'new' standards of natural beauty images, displaying their dark skin and curly hair. For example, Lucrèce got involved with the promotion of *Knatural*, a Caribbean London-based hair brand which specialises in the production of human hair extensions for Black women. The brand aims to encourage Black women to enhance and embrace their natural hair textures and Lucrèce featured as one of the models on the company catalogue. She posed on the front page with a product called 'Afro-kinky', referring to the type of Afro hair textures which most Black women naturally have.

As Lucrèce's personal experience in London testifies, Black women can, therefore, assume an important role in the daily proliferation of cultural meanings. In positioning themselves as active agents in the production of Black natural beauty images, they acknowledge their racial and ethnic identities and reshape notions of Black 'womanhood' and 'femininity'. Lucrèce's contribution, in particular, has confirmed the idea that race and ethnicity are socially rearticulated during day-to-day cultural life, and are co-constructed with gender rather than being the products of nature, entirely constituted biologically in the body. More generally, European and American beauty standards reified in Miss Universe and Miss World competitions were subverted by the story embedded in *Miss Congo UK*. The pageant has attempted to symbolically challenge Western conceptions of bodily appearances, showing how the performance of racial, ethnic and gender identities is always demarcated through a fluid interaction between individual practices and collective actions (Craig, 2002).

Conclusion

A major cultural practice, *Miss Congo Beauty Pageant UK*, organised every year by the London Congolese diaspora, was investigated in this chapter. Special focus was given to the illustration of the 2017 final gala night, with three foremost poetry and theatrical performances analysed in detail.

Miss Congo Beauty Pageant UK resulted in a fascinating cultural site where local identities were publicly transformed and made visible not only to the eyes of Congolese but also to many other Black African London diasporas. On the one hand, through the performative act of their spoken words and bodily gestures, young London Congolese showcased a pride in racial and ethnic 'authenticity' and transnational attachment to the homeland. On the other hand, however, they simultaneously openly challenged Black African older generations' core values and habits towards fundamental sociocultural and political issues such as gender inequality, health misconceptions and stigmas and Westernised beauty standards. The analysis of this case study, therefore, demonstrated how a cultural practice organised by a specific diasporic group bears larger implications for the understanding of life histories and everyday experiences of other ethnic minorities in London.

Notes

(1) According to the latest Census of the Office for National Statistics of 2011, the DRC Congolese in London numbered 10,388. However, a 2006 report by the International Organization for Migration (IOM) estimated between 20,000 to 40,000 Congolese officially settled in the UK, with 13,000 to 17,000 Congolese estimated to be living in the Greater London area. Therefore, it remains very difficult to estimate the precise number of the Congolese population currently living in the UK and London, as it is likely to be higher than what official statistics convey.

(2) The data based on which this chapter is written come from a more in-depth case study analysis of the *Miss Congo Beauty Pageant UK 2017,* as part of my PhD thesis 'Performing cultural identities and transnational 'imaginaries': fashion and beauty practices as diasporic spaces among young London Congolese' (Morsiani, 2019).

(3) The interviewees for this case study were 14 young Congolese women and men, between 20–30 years of age, who were mainly university students, political activists and entrepreneurs and acted as contest's organisers, contestants, and attendees.

(4) English translation: 'The world is yours, in your words you can make it beautiful'.

(5) A spoken word poetry and a monologue performed by two of the contestants are analysed later in this chapter.

(6) The proximity and rivalry between the two African capitals lies in colonial roots, when the capitals were established in the 19th century. The French and the Belgian colonial empires were competing for the conquest of the strategical geographical area, the last possible point where ivory, rubber and other goods could be carried by ships on the Congo River and the best spot to build railways to the Atlantic Ocean. When France founded the capital city of Brazzaville on the northern bank of the Congo River, in 1880, King Leopold II ordered his own explorer Henry Morton Stanley to establish Léopoldville on the southern Congo riverbank, in 1881 (Pakenham, 2015). The legacy of European imperialism has brought these twin capitals to be the symbol of the current strong competition between the two Congos (Burke, 2017).

(7) Kimpa Vita was a Congolese woman who lived between the 17th and 18th centuries. She founded and led the Antonian Movement, a mass Christian and political movement with thousands of followers, which aimed to end a long-lasting civil war and

restore the broken monarchy of the Kingdom of Kongo. It also represented a popular movement which fought against the slave trade. The Antonian movement was violently suppressed and Kimpa Vita was burned as heretic in 1706 (Thornton, 1998).

(8) English translation: 'My name is Horcelie. My parents taught me this lesson; not to seek revenge. But there is so much pain. Through pain a child is conceived but pain is not known to their child'.

(9) English translation: *Aid for Congo*.

(10) English translation: 'They will tell on you!' or 'they will accuse you!'.

References

Abraham, M.R. (2017) Dark is Beautiful: The battle to end the world's obsession with lighter skin. The Guardian. Access and quality see: https://www.theguardian.com/inequality/2017/sep/04/dark-is-beautiful-battle-to-end-worlds-obsession-with-lighter-skin (accessed November 2017).

Balogun, O.M. (2012) Cultural and cosmopolitan: Idealized femininity and embodied nationalism in Nigerian beauty pageants. *Gender and Society* 26 (3), 357–381.

Banet-Weiser, S. (1999) *The Most Beautiful Girl in the World: Beauty Pageants and National Identity*. Berkeley, CA: University of California Press.

Begedou, K. (2014) Decolonizing the mind and fostering self-esteem: Fanon and Morrison on skin lightening practices in the African diaspora. In *NAAAS & Affiliates Conference Monographs* (pp. 1–18). Virginia, USA: National Association of African American Studies.

Bola, J.J. (2015) *Word*. London: African Renaissance.

Borland, K. (1996) The India bonita of Monimbo: The politics of ethnic identity in the new Nicaragua. In C.B. Cohen, R. Wilk and B. Stoeltje (eds) *Beauty Queens on the Global Stage: Gender, Contests, and Power* (pp. 75–88). New York: Routledge.

Burke, J. (2017) Face-off over the Congo: The long rivalry between Kinshasa and Brazzaville, The Guardian. Access and quality see: https://www.theguardian.com/cities/2017/jan/17/congo-rivalry-kinshasa-brazzaville-river-drc (accessed December 2017).

Cohen, B.C., Wilk, R. and Stoeltje, B. (1996) *Beauty Queens on the Global Stage: Gender, Contests, and Power*. New York: Routledge.

Cooper, H. (2016) Where beauty means bleached skin. *The New York Times*. Access and quality see: https://www.nytimes.com/2016/11/26/fashion/skin-bleaching-south-africa-women.html (accessed November 2017).

Craig, M.L. (2002) *Ain't I a Beauty Queen?: Black Women, Beauty, and the Politics of Race*. Oxford: Oxford University Press.

Crawford, M., Kerwin, G., Gurung, A., Khati, D., Jha, P. and Regmi, A.C. (2008) Globalizing beauty: Attitudes toward beauty pageants among Nepali women. *Feminism and Psychology* 18 (1), 61–86.

de Santana Pinho, P. (2010) *Mama Africa: Reinventing blackness in Bahia*. Durham, Durham, NC: Duke University Press.

de Souza, M.M. (2008) The concept of skin bleaching in Africa and its devastating health implications. *Clinics in Dermatology* 26 (1), 27–29.

Du Bois, W.E.B. (1903) *The Souls of Black Folk*. New York: Fawcett Publications.

Faludi, S. (1992) *Backlash: The Undeclared War Against American Women*. New York: Anchor Books.

Fanon, F. (1952) *Peau Noire, Masques Blancs*. Paris: Éditions du Seuil.

Faria, C. (2010) Contesting Miss South Sudan: Gender and nation-building in diasporic discourse. *International Feminist Journal of Politics* 12 (2), 222–243.

Garbin, D. (2014) Regrounding the sacred: Transnational religion, place making and the politics of diaspora among the Congolese in London and Atlanta. *Global Networks* 14 (3), 363–382.

Garbin, D. and Pampu, W. (2009) *Roots and Routes. Congolese Diaspora in Multicultural Britain*. London: Cronem/Corego.

Godin, M. and Doná, G. (2016) 'Refugee Voices', New Social Media and Politics of Representation: Young Congolese in the Diaspora and Beyond'. *Refuge: Canada's Journal on Refugees* 32 (1), 60–71.

International Organization For Migration (2006) *D.R. Congo. Mapping Exercise*, London: International Organization for Migration.

Kamagaju, L. *et al.* (2016) Survey on skin-lightening practices and cosmetics in Kigali, Rwanda. *International Journal of Dermatology* 55 (1), 45–51.

King O'Riain, R.C. (2008) Making the perfect queen: The cultural production of identities in beauty pageants. *Sociology Compass* 2 (1), 74–83.

Mani, B. (2006) Beauty queens: Gender, ethnicity, and transnational modernities at the Miss India USA pageant. *Positions: East Asia Cultures Critique* 14 (3), 717–747.

Marcus, G.E. (1995) Ethnography in/of the World System: The Emergence of Multi-Sited Ethnography. *Annual Review of Anthropology* 24 (1995), 95–117.

McAllister, C. (1996) Authenticity and Guatemala's Maya Queen. In B.C. Cohen, R. Wilk and B. Stoeltje (eds) *Beauty Queens on the Global Stage: Gender, Contests, and Power* (pp. 105–124). New York: Routledge.

Miss Congo Beauty Pageant UK (2017) Talent Segment Part 1. Facebook. Access and quality see: https://www.facebook.com/Misscongouk/videos/1452896661439028/ (accessed 15 December 2017).

Morsiani, B. (2019) Performing cultural identities and transnational 'imaginaries': Fashion and beauty practices as diasporic spaces among young London Congolese. Published PhD, University of Westminster.

Oberhauser, A.M., Fluri, J.L., Whitson, R. and Mollett, S. (2017) *Feminist Spaces: Gender and Geography in a Global Context*. Abingdon: Routledge.

Office For National Statistics (2011) *'QS213EW – Country of birth'*. Available from: https://www.nomisweb.co.uk/census/2011/QS213EW/view/2013265927?cols=measures (accessed 10 February 2016).

Official Miss Congo (2017) ROAD To #MissCongoUK2017. Youtube. Access and quality see: https://www.youtube.com/watch?v=jaXz0UtBt9U (accessed 16 November 2017).

Pakenham, T. (2015) *The Scramble For Africa*. London: Abacus.

Pachi, D., Garbin, D. and Barrett, M. (2010) Processes of political (and civic) engagement and participation in the London area: Views from British Bangladeshi and Congolese youth. Paper presented at the 6th CRONEM Conference on Living Together – Civic, Political and Cultural Engagement Among Migrants, Minorities and National Populations: Multidisciplinary Perspectives. (Guildford, 29–30 June).

Petit, A., Cohen-Ludmann, C., Clevenbergh, P., Bergmann, J.F. and Dubertret, L. (2006) Skin lightening and its complications among African people living in Paris. *Journal of the American Academy of Dermatology* 55 (5), 873–878.

Sardar, Z. (2008) Foreword to Black Skin, White Masks. Ziauddin Sardar website. Access and quality see: https://ziauddinsardar.com/articles/forward-black-skin-white-masks (accessed July 2018).

Schackt, J. (2005) Mayahood through beauty: Indian beauty pageants in Guatemala. *Bulletin of Latin American Research* 24 (3), 269–287.

Styan, D. (2003) La Nouvelle Vague? Recent Francophone African Settlement in London. In K. Koser (ed.) *New African Diasporas* (pp. 1–16). Abingdon: Routledge.

Thornton, J. (1998) *The Kongolese Saint Anthony: Dona Beatriz Kimpa Vita and the Antonian Movement, 1684–1706.* Cambridge: Cambridge University Press.

Vassallo, G. (2011) The use of skin whitening products among African people: Research in Italy and the Congo. In A. de Witt-Paul and M. Crouch (eds) *Fashion Forward* (pp. 279–286). Oxford: Inter–Disciplinary Press.

Westerhof, W. (1997) A few more grains of melanin. *International Journal of Dermatology* 36 (1997), 573–574.

White, S.B. (2005) Releasing the pursuit of bouncin' and behavin' hair: Natural hair as an Afrocentric feminist aesthetic for beauty. *International Journal of Media and Cultural Politics* 1 (3), 295–308.

6 Articulating the Subjectivities of British Chinese Women through Art and Material Objects

Denise Kwan

Introduction

The subjectivities of British Chinese women have been overlooked in public life and academic research in the UK, despite their tenacious agency and invaluable contribution to the British Chinese as a cohort. Mainstream theories found within migration studies have tended to portray Chinese migration from an economic perspective and, as a discipline, it has traditionally assumed a gender-neutral perspective (Benton & Gomez, 2008; Christiansen, 2003; Wang, 2000). This 'neutrality' limits the notion of the migrant who is imagined as an individual male unburdened by domestic work. This view of migration marginalises female migratory narratives and has meant that the experiences of British Chinese women have historically been the 'minority of the minority' (Hsiao, 2014). The lack of a gendered consideration ignores how ethnic identifications are entangled among gendered dynamics as 'gendered identities can take on racialized elements' (Parker, 1995: 136). A solely socioeconomic vantage of the British Chinese makes it difficult to view the lived experience; rather the individuals are reduced to identity categories pertaining to 'race', 'gender', 'age', 'language', which risks a reductive perspective on the lived experiences.

To heighten the visibility of migrant Chinese women and nurture a view of their lived subjectivities, this chapter makes a necessary case for the use of participatory art methods with first-generation British Chinese women. In this study, the women use Cantonese as a common language to converse; however, many of the women possess abilities in wider languages such as Vietnamese, Mandarin and Hakka, thus highlighting the multiplicity of migratory routes for these women. The research reported in this chapter is part of a wider project with British Chinese women across two generations (Kwan, 2019); however, for the context of this chapter, I will specifically focus on the creative insights from the first generation, referring to those who migrated from and via Hong Kong during the post-war period in Britain. The insights in this chapter are informed and shaped by a participatory art collaboration with the Chinese Women's Group at Haringey Chinese Community Centre, London. As an artist and researcher working with an ethnographic sensibility, I facilitated art workshops for eight months and, in this time, the workshops evolved into an informal bilingual Cantonese-English art school where the women explored collage and printmaking to articulate their journeys and selfhood.

Historically, the visual discourse of Chineseness in Britain has been dominated by representations that epitomise the racial fetishistic Western gaze of the museum (Clunas, 1998). This fetishistic gaze reveals itself through the framing of 'Chinese' material objects in British museums that highlight an imperialistic taste for an 'exotic' material aesthetic without acknowledgement of its migratory journey and origin. This hyper visibility and mythically constructed 'China' in Britain sits in contrast to the invisibility of everyday Chinese diasporic experiences, specifically those of women. The creative methodology adopted in this project can be viewed as a strategy to counter the homogenising and racial fetishistic gaze of 'China' seen in British museums. The use of participatory art methods highlights the enriched possibilities of experiential research methods that amplify lesser heard migrant voices. It highlights the limits of purely linguistic modes of expression and traditional interview contexts as methods of understanding our social world. Such a materially embodied position articulated through art making and objects acts as a creative and subversive strategy to disrupt and revise relations of power and representation. It offers a counter narrative to nation-state discourses of Chinese identity to present a diasporic account of the lives of Chinese women in Britain in order to imaginatively create and articulate the parameters of their agency and desires on their terms.

Materially Embodied Visions of British Chinese Women

The creative insights produced by the British Chinese women in this research are viewed through a theoretical concept, Materially Embodied Visions, which has been specifically devised for this study. Materially Embodied Visions acts as a concept to give visibility to the actions of women and to situate their bodily experiences and thus transform the cultural parameters of their representation. Informed by the emerging literature that draws people's attention to the nexus between migration and material culture (Basu & Coleman, 2008; Wang, 2016), Materially Embodied Visions combines concepts borrowed from material culture and visual culture to orientate a view of British Chinese women through their material worlds and art making. To foreground a feminist embodiment perspective and capture these relations of power through visual making, I employ 'situated knowledges' (Haraway, 1991) as an integral idea that conceptualises the dynamics between vision, power and positionality. While a material culture theory of objectification acknowledges an inherent people–object entanglement, it is not an abstracted notion of 'culture' that creates material expressions, but rather culture is created through materiality (Miller, 1987; Tilley, 2006). Using a material culture focus to understand the everyday subjectivities of British Chinese women offers a critical contrast to the collection and fetishisation of Chinese material objects as represented in many public museums of Britain.

As a concept, Materially Embodied Visions epitomises a feminist 'view from below' as a strategy to disrupt the bodies of knowledge that have been constructed about British Chinese identities through museum and material culture. The conceptual term attempts to illuminate the insights between the subjectivities of British Chinese women and the emerging articulation of themselves through their material worlds and art making. A perspective of material culture presents an opportunity for women to reverse the relations of power and, through objects and storytelling, women are afforded a context to speak about their journeys, desires and aspirations.

In this chapter, the voices of the women will be structured under the following thematic sections: (1) 'Discarding Dissonance' which explores the way in which specific personal objects are actively forgotten; in contrast (2) 'Embracing Recall' traces the significance of material objects in taking ownership of the past to empower oneself; (3) 'My stones will become diamonds' offers an in-depth analysis of a personal account of one of the women; while (4) 'A Floating Sisterhood' emphasises the fluid yet robust structure of support that the women operate with and for each other. Together, they illustrate strongly how British Chinese women articulate their subjectivities through the vehicle of art and material objects.

In total, 10–15 first-generation women from Haringey Chinese Centre participated in this project. Established in 1987, the Haringey Chinese Centre[1] has played an important role in the local Chinese community.[2] They self-described as a group of 'overseas brides' and, broadly, they shared similar backgrounds; all the women were married with adult children. Many of the women shared similar employment experiences and few had completed a full formal education. On arriving in the UK, they recalled working in the catering profession or taking on sewing work as flexible employment to juggle alongside early motherhood. All the women were fluent in Cantonese and had varying abilities in English, Mandarin and Vietnamese.

As an artist of British Chinese heritage, the participatory art methods adopted in this project were inspired by my own mother's pyjamas that she brought to Britain as part of her migratory wardrobe during the 1980s. To better understand her migratory story, I began to ask my mother about the story of her pyjamas. Drawing on this intergenerational process as inspiration, I adopted collage and experimental art writing as strategies to give visibility to her migratory story and material world. Subsequently, this personal process of collaging formed the wider methodology I used with first generation women to form the bilingual art school.[3]

The use of visual methodologies is informed by the overlapping relationship between anthropology and art. Examining the crossover between art and anthropology, Roger Sasni (2015) explains that ethnography can offer artists the theoretical and practical tools to facilitate and assist creative participation which informs the methodological term visual ethnography. Ethnographic principles of participant-observation and a 'thick description' of social interactions are hallmarks of the methodology. For the artist, an ethnographic sensibility can support and establish relations of participation. As these socially engaged art projects evolve, they can initiate change in the social world as they can create 'unprecedented relations between different actors, generating new alliances and communities – in other words, help re-imagine and rebuild the social at a local level' (Sasni, 2015: 13). Visual ethnography becomes a way to view people as active participants in producing knowledge about their own experiences. In this project, the use of creative methods challenges the way the Chinese in Britain have been framed by occupational and economic terms, rather than through cultural or creative pursuits. By assigning to particular bodies a machine-like capacity for work but an inherent lack of creativity constructs them [the Chinese] as essentially 'Other', denies their status as fully human and questions their very ability to participate in the social and cultural realm (Yeh, 2014: 1207).

The use of visual methodologies provides a platform to articulate overlooked experiences on a broader level and to dismantle power structures. A creative methodology can 'build coalition across groups and challenge dominant ideologies' (Leavy, 2009: 13). The representation of British Chinese women has consequences for the perception of the British Chinese and the Chinese diaspora at large. The racialising imagery of Fu Manchu (Clegg, 1994) and the fetishistic gaze represented by 'Chinese' objects in British museums projects nation–state notions of identity; it constructs a Chinese identity as orientating from a geographically bound 'China' and overlooks the nuanced experiences of diasporic Chinese in Britain.

British Chinese Women: A Context

The British Chinese comprise Chinese ethnicities from Hong Kong, Malaysia, Singapore, Vietnam, Taiwan and China. Due to the colonial status of Hong Kong, the predominant group of Chinese in Britain are from Hong Kong and hence they are a substantial and long-standing sub-group of the Chinese in Britain among all the ethnic groups.[4] The policies of the post-war era, namely the 1948 British Nationality Act and 1962 Commonwealth Immigrants Act, were two pieces of legislation that shaped the character of the Chinese in Britain. Through these policies, individuals were able to apply for their kin to join them and the presence of women transformed a previous bachelor society into a settled society and gave rise to the second generation of the British born Chinese.[5] Many of the first generation arrived during the post-war boom of immigration and through kin-based chain migration. While the first-generation Cantonese speaking women form a substantial portion of the British Chinese population, research on their gendered experiences has been scant.

Published 20 years after the initial Chinese post-war boom, the Home Affairs Report of 1986 was the first formal attempt to identify the social challenges of the Chinese in Britain. This report has been influential in shaping perceptions of the Chinese (Christiansen, 2003; Song, 1995). It adopted a strong assimilatory tone without thorough recognition of the structural barriers that framed British Chinese experiences. Throughout the report, there was little recognition of how the socioeconomic challenges of migrant men and women are gendered in experience. Specifically, the findings emphasised the difficulty faced by women; in turn this presented a de-humanising image of the migrant Chinese woman as 'helpless' and 'victim'. Several aspects of Chinese life in Britain render many Chinese women extremely isolated as described by Dummet and Lo (1984).

> Lacking command of English, they cannot play any part in or understand their children's education [...] they are likely to have little time with their husbands [...] they are dependent on their husbands for finances, which can often lead to squabbles or even more serious martial breaches [...] in the worst cases the consequences can include mental breakdown and child battering. (1984: 16)

Since the Home Affairs Report of 1986, there have been a few instances of research solely focused on the experiences of British Chinese women. These accounts have explored the experiences of British Chinese women through the context of self-employment and labour (Song, 1995) and adjustment needs of mothers in the process of settlement (Yuen, 2008), while Lee *et al.* (2002) called for a greater recognition of the multiple migratory routes and various class statuses within the Chinese women immigrants.[6] In among the scant amount of material relating to British Chinese women, these accounts are certainly invaluable starting points.

The majority of British Chinese women from the post-war cohort have experienced few employment opportunities outside catering and in turn this has impacted their collective sense of political and social assertion. The private nature of family-owned business in Britain is less conducive to inciting collective political action and therefore the lack of an overt political identity could be attributed to the socioeconomic parameters experienced by the British Chinese. Despite this, British Chinese women have achieved settlement in the face of challenges from a British government that has not fully recognised their social needs and structural inequalities. Their settlement is a testimony to their own personal determination against the odds. This exposes the institutional racial prejudice that underscores the lives of British Chinese women where the 'problem' cannot be viewed as 'cultural' but rather as related to policies and structural forces, which play an intrinsic role in the engineering of challenges encountered by British Chinese women.

Certainly, the sites of employment and the domestic are influential in shaping a migrant woman's subjectivity; however, to solely focus on these parameters would be to restrict our understanding of their agency in society. Furthermore, traditional social science methods of using life-history interviews (Lee *et al.*, 2002; Song, 1995) and narrative inquiry (Yuen, 2008) have a propensity to only produce insights that focus on the socioeconomic parameters of the women's lives, which to some extent, can confine and reproduce the parameters of the women through their social circumstance and role as 'worker' or 'mother'.

To build upon the existing research into British Chinese women and to further capture their untold agency, it is crucial to consider how British Chinese women can be understood in and outside of the family and employment. From a methodological stance, this chapter advocates the use of participatory art methods as a meaningful strategy to challenge stereotypes that surround the academic and public understanding of women from a Chinese heritage. Through the context of art methods, the women are presented with wider and experimental parameters to express their tenacity, humour and desires and therefore the prospect of art enables the women to re-imagine and articulate their agency from their personal and embodied vantage point.

Discarding Dissonance

Drawing on the concept of Materially Embodied Visions, while objects and art making offer a way to articulate 'a view from below', the women participants expressed a greater affinity to situate their subjectivities through art making than through personal material objects. Only a few women wanted to publicly recount the challenge of migration through past objects and interviews. Many of the women remarked that they had not kept the initial possessions that had travelled with them; these items had been lost, worn out, pawned or replaced and overall, it appeared that the women did not publicly express much sentimental attachment to these initial objects.[7]

In contrast, the process of art making was a significant method of self-articulation, rather than talking about oneself through past migratory objects. The absence of migratory objects from the women can be interpreted as exercising a level of 'active forgetting' (Carsten, 1995) and 'selective remembering' (Connerton, 2008). The lack of migratory past objects expressed a desire to disengage from the past and instead project their hopes into the future as a place of betterment and contentment. This lack of attachment to past objects also highlighted that perhaps for this group of women, the process of recounting their lives through old objects was a restrictive process that would only frame their identity within the terms of the past and migratory hardship.

For one woman participant, the project functioned as an opportunity to donate her personal possessions. Collected from her home, one of the participants Jenny (aged 63 at the time of the interview) arrived with an armful of objects.[8] All the objects inhabited a similar persona; a kitsch-like aesthetic with mass-produced items portraying a decorative and colourful Asian appearance. Among the paraphernalia, a figurine stood out, it was a bulbous plastic cartoon figurine of a girl and boy dressed in traditional Chinese clothing beaming with large smiles. Connected at the hip, they appeared to be a newly married couple soaring in unison towards a bright and hopeful future. Curious as to the story of this object, I inquired about the origin of the object, to which Jenny remarked, 'I don't want it, you have it for the study. If you don't want it, then put it into the bin. It reminds me of my marriage and it wasn't very happy so I don't want it'. Jenny's insistence to give away her object suggested a desire to discard the item and productively manage the memory. During a workshop session, the nature of her marriage emerged as her experience as a young overseas bride became more vivid, which was crucially always inflected with humour.

Encouraged by her family to marry and create a better life abroad, Jenny's arrival in Britain was the first time she had met her husband. On arriving in Britain, she realised her husband had embellished his achievements, but as a woman with little education and no financial means to leave her husband and return to Hong Kong, she was left with no option but to remain in her unhappy marriage. Jenny had been given gold jewellery as a wedding dowry in case of emergencies, but she explained that it had been sold to aid everyday living as she recalled her initial arrival,

> My mother at the time said, 'You can choose from millions and thousands of men, you better not choose a broken light bulb!' But then I got here, he had nothing. I went through the wrong door, I gambled and lost. My mum wouldn't allow me to go back, she said I was a married girl, I couldn't go back. You go through your in-laws' door and the pressure starts. My parents had lots of daughters, why did they need me as well?

Margery Wolf (1972) describes the status of daughters in Chinese society as akin to 'spilt water and like water, she may never return' (1972: 34). For Jenny and other young overseas brides in similar situations, this pressure intensified. Unable to visit her natal family, she stressed the difficulty of fulfilling the expectations of her husband's family while also acclimatising to a new culture and language. The learning curve was steep, 'I had to learn everything. Had to learn the money, roads, cook dinner, look after kids, washing clothes, it sent me into a tailspin'. Jenny's list of domestic work signalled a new phase of womanhood and her new identity as a mother. Like many of the women in the group, Jenny juggled the responsibilities of raising the family and lowly paid work such as ad-hoc sewing work, which required little language ability.

The expectation on the migrant bride was not only to marry but more importantly to reproduce the next generation of her husband's family. Marriage is ladened with reproductive expectations; as Wolf reminds us, one of the most fundamental roles expected of a daughter-in-law is to reproduce the paternal family line, ideally through the conception of a son. Only when she begins her own 'uterine family' (Wolf, 1972) can she establish her belonging in her husband's family which highlights the daughter-in-law's ambivalent position in the patriarchal family structure.

The figurine, though cheerful and child-like, harboured another reality. The object was a witness of the past and the figurine presented her past in a light that was too frank and resisted a light-hearted account of her history. As a memento from the past, it spoke too directly to stories of past struggles. For Jenny, the practice of active forgetting manifested itself in the desire to discard specific objects to control the dissonance of her life. Jenny's strategy echoes Carsten's notion of active forgetting and in doing so, forgetting becomes productive as it enabled her to reinvent herself and this afforded her a renewed freedom in her retirement years.

Embracing Recall

In contrast to the majority of the Women's Group, the English teacher of the Women's Group, Lanan (aged 78), was one of the few people to publicly share their migratory experience through material objects. As a Chinese Vietnamese woman, her migratory journey marked her as distinctive to the rest of the women in the group who predominately arrived in the UK via Hong Kong and the Southern regions of China. Lanan's demotion from a middle-class citizen to a refugee was narrated through her possessions. To recount her story as a mother of three children fleeing Vietnam, Lanan recalled the various things that accompanied the month-long boat trip from Vietnam to Hong Kong, and eventually to Britain.

To board the ship, Lanan was only allowed to take one bag and inside it contained a host of items that affirmed the family's sense of selfhood. These objects included a Vietnamese household register (should the family be refused entry to Hong Kong and need to return to Vietnam), birth certificates, and permission letters, but the most precious was a series of family photographs (Figure 6.1). Wrapped in several layers of plastic, they had been gifted by her mother who said, 'If you survive the journey, wherever you go, look at the photos and you can see us'. Lanan's family photographs depicted another world. Aged brown photographs show the family relaxing in their large garden or dressed in their best clothes for a proud studio portrait. Lanan emphasised that her family presented themselves as a modern Asian family, her father in a modern Western suit, her mother dressed in a traditional Chinese two-piece. Photographed in a studio, this world depicted through the photographs was one of relative ease and dignity in contrast to their status as refugees.

The most contested possession was a series of black and white photographs taken of the family on arriving in Hong Kong after a month on board the boat. Taken for the practical purpose of cataloguing the arrival of refugees, the photograph reduces people to an administrative number. Unlike the previous studio portrait, Lanan stood in front of a blank wall. Like a specimen for analysis, her eyes are fixed and stoic as she stares

Figure 6.1 'Family and refugee photographs', 2019 (photo credit Denise Kwan)

straight ahead. Given the nature of the photograph, Lanan and her refugee counterparts dubbed these as their 'prisoner's photographs'. This sense of dehumanisation was captured as the photograph led Lanan to reflect on the loss of her former identity.

> In my whole life, I was born to a wealthy family and had a good education until the age of twenty-one and then straight to work and had a good job. I've never been treated poorly. At that time, I think wow, they treat me like a prisoner...Really sad (laughs).

> I can guarantee you, if you ask one hundred Vietnamese families, I suppose one hundred per cent would say, 'No sorry we didn't keep those pictures' (…) Some even say, 'Why keep this, that's a very bloody memory, we don't want to keep it!' I say, 'That's history, that's world wide history!' Some say they don't want to remember those years because it was a very sad memory.

The photograph captured the powerlessness of her situation at its most pronounced. Unlike the family studio portraits, Lanan's identity was hidden through the mechanical gaze as her portrait underlined the dehumanisation of her situation and status. Lanan recognised that the keeping of these photographs and their difficult memories was unusual among her Vietnamese counterparts; instead, many would choose not to hold on to these objects as a method of internal preservation.

However, as she settled into life in the UK, these photographs enabled Lanan to reclaim and reconstruct a difficult part of her personal history. Without these photographs, that transition would remain vacant and hollow. Objects become material anchors to make sense of the displacement she experienced as a mother of three children. While these photographs are viewed as fraught mementoes by her counterparts, these objects carefully preserved among paper and plastic sheets have enabled Lanan to claim her place in history. In retelling her story through these photographs, she reconstructed her selfhood not as a victim, but as a survivor.

'My Stones Will Become Diamonds'

Unlike the significance that Lanan gave her refugee photographs, the other participants in the Women's Group publicly expressed less sentimental value in relation to their migratory possessions. This difference was especially heightened during an art workshop themed on visualising their feelings and life prior to migration. Unsure how to proceed with the task, one of the participants asked Anna, aged 65, as the president of the group, how best to illustrate her gruelling village life.

Raised in rural Hong Kong, Anna was the first-born female of her family which presented her with a double disadvantage. She recalled a challenging upbringing where she took on much of the housework and recalled having to raise herself and her siblings, describing herself as, 'I am born of the sky and raised by the sky'. Overburdened with caring for her siblings from a young age, she gave up her education at the age of 13 to enable the continuation of her siblings' education. As she was unable to complete her studies, her mother was keen to find her a suitor. Anna refused marriage and planned to join her father in Britain to work alongside him in catering; however, her father remained highly sceptical: 'You are a girl and if you are married when you arrive in Britain then you will be likewise useless'. Despite her father's doubts, Anna was determined to support her family financially and she arrived in the UK as a teenage girl to work alongside her father in catering.

The scepticism of her father highlighted a gendered preconception that it is men who travel to foreign lands while women remain in the domestic space. To interfere with this gendered conception of space brings attention to a woman's body. Moving the female body into the male space of travel and trade highlights a woman's sexuality, specifically in this case it raised the concern that Anna would be married into another family and unable to financially assist her natal family. Her determination to join her father as an economic migrant challenged the gendered binary of male/

female, public/domestic and work/family. In this scenario, it was the daughter who assumed the traditional role of a son and the expectation to support the family through economic migration.

Confident in her pragmatism, Anna strongly asserted that, as women, they need not concern themselves with past hardships because the past should reside in the past. Anna launched into a mini manifesto. She rose out of her chair to tell the group of the way she overcame her own trials by remaining focused on the future. The message was: one need not revisit old memories of difficulty and negativity; it is more productive to focus on creating a positive future.

On hearing this, Lanan joined in the conversation and suggested that old hardships and trials have a place in our lives and, therefore, they should be included in the art collages. Therefore, two positions emerged: the past has a valuable place in our lives; or one only needs to focus on the future. This ideological stance was reflected through Anna as her collage (Figure 6.2) captured this sense of positive future dynamism.

In presenting her collage, Anna announced to the group that her life motto was to 'turn stones into diamonds' and through the collage she brought this manifesto into life. Selecting the textures from mono-printing and magazine imagery, Anna's collage grew tall into the sky as her ambition gathers strength and voracity. Dark and scratchy forms inhabit the ground representing the rocks, stones and pebbles and, as the collage grows, the colours become brighter and more vivid in their conviction. The textures and surfaces are more dazzling and more spectacular as shards of light splinter off the dulled hues. Gathering energy, they appear as particles generating momentum as they cascade upwards, resembling the dazzle of fireworks. They eventually explode and transform into multicoloured jewels in shades of jade and crimson among the glitter of diamonds. They cascade and swirl with a hypnotic focus as these diamonds find themselves poised on an elegant hand, a comfortable cradle, the resting place of hard toil. Rising up to speak about her collage, Anna articulates her sense of agency through her work with the wider group.

> Anna: This is the point of my story and the conclusion is here. My conclusion is, this is rock, my life before was like a stone, sturdy and barren. My hope is...I've struggled so much...I hope in the future that I can turn a rock into diamonds! From the inside the rock is an explosion and from the explosion, there are bright diamonds! The light is beaming out. I can go around the world on this light. That is my manifesto, tomorrow will be better, my stones will become diamonds!

> Members of the group: Your dreams have come true!

Figure 6.2 'Tomorrow will be better', 2019 (photo credit Denise Kwan).

Anna: Not everything has come true but good things have come to me. I thank the gods. I have a roof over my head, so I am sheltered from the rain. My rice bucket has rice so I can cook dinner. My purse has 20 pounds so I can buy plenty of groceries. So I am very content. Thank you god.

Members of the group: So now you have lots of diamonds?!

Anna: I have some, it's just not a lot! (laughs) But there are lots of diamonds in rocks and in my garden there is a lot of rock!

The material of stone was a metaphor of her previous life, restrained by gendered expectations to marry and abide by patriarchal conventions; however the destruction of this stone brought forth a new existence, a transformed self, forged through migration. Her determination to succeed transforms the unforgiving stone into a glittering spectacle. Through art making, she fully captured her personal agency as she narrated her self-hood with a fantastical tenacity. Just as she had created a new life in Britain, the collage functioned in a similar fashion, because in both scenarios, Anna was starting from a blank page onto which she inscribed her ambitions.

Like Anna's collage, many of the collages of the Women's Group resembled an account of their migratory aspirations as fantastical visual narratives and this became a collective aesthetic of the collages. Leafing through newspapers and magazines, the women projected their desires and selected imagery that fitted their aspirations; often imagery of new material goods were present such as stately homes and new cars. Clearly, the pursuit of a new future was entangled with material goods and stability.

For this group of women, the process of collage making revealed a palpable tendency to project an optimistic future. This outlook would be difficult to articulate through old migratory possessions, which would only recount the past. As embodied by their collages, their intention was to look towards the future and strive towards a material stability that is focused on acquiring the new, rather than maintaining the old. To continue their settlement, it appeared it was more important to lessen their attachment to their own initial migratory hardships. Instead, art making enabled the women to articulate and visualise their ambition and desire unencumbered by social circumstance.

Though Jenny had a difficult marriage, this was not the story that she visualised in her a group collage (Figure 6.3). Her collage imagined a glamorous wedding for all the women; at the centre of the page are rows of women dressed in white bridal wear while the men are dressed in red tailcoats. Food and drink are plentiful and abundant as they show a vast selection of Western and Eastern cuisine. Images of new cars and beauty creams dart around the collage while a mother with a child smiles out from the corner of the page. An overall air of dynamism and anticipation is accumulated in the collection of images.

Two of the group members, Jenny and Ying (aged 67) describe their visual collage:

> Ying: We are getting married, after the marriage we have a huge party and we've invited so many sisters. Even Jenny brought along her new boy-friend! (laughs). These women are all us and we are all sisters, and these

Figure 6.3 'Group Collage 1', 2019 (photo credit Denise Kwan)

all the brothers and they are driving the car. This is a Rolls Royce! But they drove the wrong car and ended up driving a broken-down car! (laughs) We wanted to go in the Rolls Royce but ended up in the broken-down car!

Members of the group: You better not get in! The bride better not get in if the car's like that!

Ying: And there is food, there's everything to eat. There's champagne and wine and after food, we start the music. Sister Jenny comes out and performs for us and performs ballet.

Jenny: Who are these two? [Pointing to two figures].

Members of the group: They are the audience!

Jenny: Maybe they are watching me perform?

Members of the group: They are thinking sister Jenny is so beautiful!

The art workshops became live sites of meaning making where the women instinctually formed groups; each person would be responsible for specific tasks related to the physical making of the collage, whether that was selecting, cutting or attaching images. Through the visual and the symbolic, their stories were released from the mundanity of common-sense reality. Instead through their collective visual making and feedback, they weaved together a narrative of spontaneity which was responsive to change and adaptation; the threads were loose and pliable.

In this alternative realm illustrated by the collage, Jenny did not tolerate her unhappy marital fate. Instead, she was single and embarked on a new courtship while she pursued her passion for dancing. However, this idealisation was never far from reality's reach, as the pot of Olay cream was a light-hearted reminder of her age. While the women set their sights on a Rolls Royce, it was the 'broken-down car' which they settled for instead. In these ways, these short and humorous anecdotes encapsulated their migratory aspirations and their attempt to strive for the best while having to make do with a lot less.

Their collective visual narratives diverged from the personal stories which they shared through the interview process. Their interviews often referred to periods of self-sacrifice, long hours of toil and gendered challenges which were exacerbated by the loneliness and challenges of migration. The need to adhere to speaking logically about oneself can subdue stories and restrain the ability to speak in metaphorical and fantastical ways. Outside of the usual time-space and social constraints, their desires were unencumbered; within their imagination resided an account of their desire and humour more vivid than the socioeconomics that framed their lived experiences.

A Floating Sisterhood

At the top of the collage in Figure 6.4 are dark shadowy figures wandering aimlessly in a barren landscape. Facing away from us, we only see their backs as they walk away from us towards a destination that is not in view; where have they come from and where are they going? In contrast, the images below depict a more hopeful scene; the sun dawns on a lonely canoe with two people in it and again they face away, as though searching and looking for a destination far away in the distance. We turn a page and on the other side shows a distinct contrast as glamour and people populate the collage. In relation to her group collage, Jenny explained the narrative:

> This is about the future and not knowing what to do, we are floating and don't know where the destination is, we are looking forward and then eventually, thankfully, we saw some houses but, thankfully, besides us there are some friends helping us along. Look, there are friendships everywhere! Look, we've arrived now and see how happy we are in every step. We even have face powder on, look! (...) We are learning to grow vegetables and we even have fans! Our friendship networks are becoming stronger and bigger!

Their sense of sisterhood created a point of knowledge sharing and this was reflected in their collective art making. Voluntarily, they formed

Figure 6.4 'Group Collage 2', 2019 (photo credit Denise Kwan)

smaller groups to complete the artwork and through the process of col-
lecting images, the collage narrative grew from the image selection. The
women's desire to make together underlined their sense of shared culture.
Anna says, 'We share secrets…we come here to talk and we talk about our
husbands, isn't that a secret?! We talk about our daughters'. Their informal social time with each other cannot be labelled as trivial 'gossip'; rather
the sharing of information was essential in creating a supportive network.
From this position, they inhabited and shared a flexible structure of power
as Yuet Lan (aged 68) puts it:

> Everyone knows different things and have different skills, and so our
> friendship is good, it makes us more powerful. We create more power
> because when we are together, we are more powerful. More skills and
> more ideas and because I might know something that maybe she doesn't
> know. More power. By coming together, it builds the strength of the
> group and makes the group more powerful and stronger.

In this way, power was not a vertical notion assigned from above and received by those who were powerless; instead, her articulation of power resembled a horizontal form of skill sharing. This sharing referred to everyday matters such as navigating transport, the health system or simply a space to share domestic frustration. As a group of women that felt socially encumbered by their English language, the group functioned as an opportunity where the women could share information to overcome such barriers. A network of support and sharing was formed by the women to create an infrastructure of power in the continual settlement of their lives.

The Women's Group resembled Wolf's (1972) concept of the uterine family. Wolf describes the uterine family as a female response to the lack of women-centred spaces in traditional Chinese patriarchal society, 'The uterine family has no ideology, no formal structure, and no public existence. It is built out of sentiment and loyalties that die with its members, but it is no less real for all that' (1972: 37). Among informal conversations with other women, they could retrieve advice and temporarily inhabit a roving female space, as Wolf puts it.

Like Wolf's uterine family, there was little public knowledge about the Women's Group. the women may have mentioned the activities of the Women's Group to their families but often only informally, in passing. The existence of the group relied on recommendations from the women; an interesting dance activity, a cookery class, or a weekend trip out of London. The English lessons certainly gave a focus to the group, but the broader more essential function of the group was the bringing together of women and, in this way, they offered support and power to each other.

Conclusion

A gendered understanding of the British Chinese illustrated the challenges faced by migrant first-generation Chinese women. Contrary to the restricted findings of the Home Affairs Report of 1986 and its depiction of British Chinese women as passive and dependent, this chapter reinforced the tenacity they exerted in the face of obstacles and the vital role of women in familial and economic settlement. To speak about the British Chinese and any migrant community, it is vital to consider the invaluable role of women and the multiple roles and agency they enact within the family and society in pursuit of settlement and stability.

Many of the women valued creative expression over a verbal articulation of themselves through past objects; they did not publicly want to talk about themselves in the past tense through old things. Rather their sense of agency as migrant women was better facilitated through art making where they could visualise ambitious futures for themselves.

In this study, the concept of Materially Embodied Visions disrupted the constructed knowledge of British Chinese women and challenged the one-dimensional view of British Chinese women as 'subordinate' or 'victims'. This conceptual term brings forward a deeper perspective into the ways that the women articulate their agency, journeys and ambitions through art making and on their own terms. During interviews and conversations, the women often expressed their struggles as mothers and workers; however, in the process of art making the women often represented their identities with humour and exuberance, a far cry from their verbal articulations. Art making provided the women with a greater spectrum to assert a positive reaffirmation and fantastical re-imaginations of their identities and desires.

The process of making enabled the women to assert their imaginations and visualise their agency without constraint. The popularity of creative expression cannot, however, be viewed as wholly unproblematic as their preference for art making could also be read as a strategy to 'keep face', as the women were given an opportunity to sidestep recounting the challenging phase of settlement. Nonetheless, art making afforded the women an expansive space to inscribe their desire and agency as women with a wider scope. The women's artwork carved out a symbolic space and, through the act of making, they spoke to each other about their lives as lived and imagined.

Through art making the women constructed another version of their stories; one that was agile to their desires, a version which would otherwise remain buried under the pressure of articulating oneself in a formalised interview setting. Through the visual and the symbolic, the women's stories were released from the mundanity of commonsense reality. From this vantage point, the artworks captured their aspirations outside the confines of socio-economic and time-space constraints. The visual narratives were not simply individual accounts, but they are a record of a cohort of British Chinese women as a female community where they marked their points of symmetry and angles of divergence to each other. The process of art making mirrored the migratory journey because in both scenarios, the women construct with a blank page. Though the sisterhood is an ephemeral structure, we capture a glimpse of their form and vibrancy through the artwork of these British Chinese women.

Notes

(1) As a centre, it caters to a range of generational needs as it provides a range of activities including Chinese Language School, luncheon club, housing support and advice service, computing training, leisure outings, and health classes.

(2) Located in North London, it is a well-respected centre among families and individuals in the area. This centre was one of the few in London that ran a women-centred space. The Women's Group has run for nearly ten years and as a group, they were predominantly Cantonese speaking and their ages ranged between 60–82 years old (at the time that the research was conducted).

(3) To build a skill-based reciprocal relationship, I attended their group and volunteered as an English co-teacher and, gradually over time, I began to run fortnightly art workshops which resembled the format of an art school. Being a second generation British-born Chinese, I had a reasonable command of Cantonese, though I encountered difficulty in expressing more nuanced ideas. The president of the Women's Group identified my difficulty with Cantonese and suggested that the art workshops be delivered bi-lingually in English and Cantonese.

(4) Highlighted in the 1986 Runnymede Home Affairs Report, most first-generation Chinese derived from Cantonese speaking regions of Hong Kong and Southern China; as well there was a substantial Hakka-speaking minority among others with diverse dialects who are second time migrants from Southeast Asia, including Malaysia, Vietnam and Singapore.

(5) The narrative of the Chinese in Britain started as exclusively male-centric as Chinese migration began in 1851 when Chinese male seafarers working onboard the East India Company were beginning to arrive at the docklands of London Limehouse, Liverpool, Cardiff (Benton & Gomez, 2008). These seafarers mostly understood themselves as sojourners who would make their living abroad and send family remittances with the view to eventually return to their country.

(6) Lee *et al.* (2002) identified three groups of Chinese women: (1) overseas brides; (2) women who migrated with their families or 'college wives'; and (3) independent migrants. Those with the appropriate resources were able to negotiate familial and employment structures to their advantage and viewed migration as a liberating adventure, while those who possessed fewer resources carried the burden of labour inside and outside of the home.

(7) Some participants were baffled about the invitation to discuss their experiences through personal possessions. One woman remarked, 'It's really weird that someone wants to interview random Chinese women about their belongings'. As a second-generation woman, this highlighted the bias of my initial assumption of the sentimental value attached to these initial objects.

(8) All participants in the study have been given pseudonyms.

References

Basu, P. and Coleman S. (2008) Introduction: Migrant worlds, material cultures. *Mobilities* 3 (3), 313–330.

Benton, G. and Gomez, E. (2008) *The Chinese in Britain, 1800-Present, Economy, Transnationalism, Identity*. London: Palgrave Macmillan.

Carsten, J. (1995) The politics of forgetting: Migration, kinship and memory on the periphery of the southeast Asian state. *The Journal of the Royal Anthropological Institute* 1 (2), 317–335.

Christiansen, F. (2003) *Chinatown, Europe: An Exploration of Overseas Chinese Identity in the 1990s*. London: Routledge.

Clegg, J. (1994) *Fu Manchu and the 'Yellow Peril': The Making of a Racist Myth*. Stoke-on-Trent: Trentham Books.

Clunas, C. (1998) China in Britain, the Imperial collections. In T. Barringer and T. Flynn (eds) *Colonialism and the Object: Empire, Material Culture, and the Museum* (pp. 41–51). London: Routledge.

Connerton, P. (2008) Seven types of forgetting. *Memory Studies* 1 (1), 59–71.

Dummett, A. and Lo, J. (eds) (1986) *The Chinese Community in Britain: The Home Affairs Committee Report in Context*. London: The Runnymede Trust.

Haraway, D. (1991) *Simians, Cyborgs and Women, The Reinvention of Nature*. Great Britain: Free Association Books.

Hsiao, Y. (2014) *Women in British Chinese Writings: Subjectivity, Identity and Hybridity*. Oxford: Chartridge Books.

Leavy, P. (2009) *Method Meets Art, Arts-Based Research Practice*. New York: The Guildford Press.

Lee, M., Chan, A., Bradby, H. and Green, G. (2002) Chinese migrant women and families in Britain. *Women's Studies International Forum* 25 (6), 607–618.

Miller, D. (1987) *Material Culture and Mass Consumption*. Oxford: Blackwell Publishers.

Parker, D. (1995) *Through Different Eyes: The Cultural Identities of Young Chinese People in Britain*. Aldershot: Avebury.

Parker, D. (1998) Emerging British Chinese identities. In E. Sinn (ed.) *The Last Half Century of Chinese Overseas* (pp. 91–114). Hong Kong: Hong Kong University Press.

Tilley, C., Keane, W., Kuchler, S., Rowlands, M. and Spyer, P. (2006) *Handbook of Material Culture*. London: SAGE Publications.

Sasni, R. (2015) *Art, Anthropology and the Gift*. London: Bloomsbury Academic.

Song, M. (1995) Between 'The Front' and 'The Back' Chinese women's work in family business. *Women's Studies International Forum* 18 (3), 285–298.

Wang, Gungwu. (2000) *The Chinese Overseas, From Earthbound China to the Quest for Autonomy*. Cambridge, MA: Harvard University Press.

Wang, C. (2016) Introduction: The 'material turn' in migration studies. *Modern Languages Open* 0 (0). https://doi.org/10.3828/mlo.v0i0.88.

Wolf, M. (1972) *Women and the Family in Rural Taiwan*. Stanford, CA: Stanford University Press.

Kwan, D. (2019) Dressing Up, dressing down! situating identities and negotiating otherness through the bodies of British Chinese women. *British Journal of Chinese Studies*, 9 (1), 117–159. https://doi.org/10.51661/bjocs.v9i1.28

Yeh, D. (2014) Contesting the 'model minority': Racialization, youth culture and 'British Chinese'/ 'Oriental' night. *Ethnic and Racial Studies* 37 (7), 1197–1210.

Yuen, J.K.S. (2008) The moon in foreign countries is particularly round and bright, narratives of Chinese immigrant women in the UK. *Compare, A Journal of Comparative and International Education* 38 (3), 295–306.

7 Negotiating Diasporic Identities in Glocal Heritage Discourses: The Case of the Chinese New Year Celebration in London

Cangbai Wang

Introduction

When discussing cultural diversity and living heritage in Britain, Stuart Hall (1999) raised the important question of 'whose heritage' in relation to the interpretation and ownership of heritage in British society. He called for a critical examination of the 'whole concept of "British Heritage" from the perspective of multicultural Britain, which has been emerging since the end of World War II' (Hall, 1999: 3), and a redefinition of the nation and re-imagination of 'Britishness' in a more profoundly inclusive manner. More specifically, he criticised what he called the 'retrospective, nationalised and traditionalised conception of culture' (Hall, 1999: 4), which gives undue emphasis to the preservation of artefacts authorised as valuable in relation to the national past and the representation of the British version of tradition. To change the mainstream heritage discourse that has ignored the cultural tradition of ethnic minorities, Hall called for a new agenda that represents the cultural complexity of Britain, the basic building block of which is 'the demand that the majority, mainstream versions of the Heritage should revise their own self-conceptions and rewrite the margins into the centre, the outside into the inside' (Hall, 1999: 10).

Hall's thesis on multicultural heritage is ground-breaking for research into race, ethnicity and culture in Britain and other Western countries. However, there is a tendency in his argument to emphasise 'the political implications of the container notion of society ... [in which] the social fabric and the integrity of social institutions and the cultural norms that support them are seen as contained within state borders' (Glick Schiller & Çağlar, 2011: 64). The world we live in today has become much more globalised than it was 20 years ago, displaying what Blommaert (2005: 126) has called 'layered simultaneity' in time and space. International migration is therefore no longer a linear process of movement from home country to host country,[1] and from emigration to settlement. Instead, migrants are increasingly mobile and transnational subjects who tend to maintain social and cultural connections with more than one place (Appadurai, 1996; Basch et al., 1994; Hannerz, 1996; Ong & Nonini, 1997; Urry, 2007). In addition, the technologies of international travel and long-distance communication have become cheaper (if still unequal) and more easily accessible, allowing migrants to develop and maintain multiple ties and transnational social networks (Vertovec, 2004; Wilding, 2006). For instance, the wide use of Facebook, Twitter, YouTube and other digital platforms enables migrants to maintain connections with their families back home even, as described in this chapter, when physical travel was restricted or suspended during the Covid-19 pandemic. It is therefore necessary to go beyond 'methodological nationalism' in academic inquiries (Beck, 2007; Smith, 1983; Wimmer & Glick Schiller, 2002) to explore the complex ways in which migrants negotiate heritage discourses in the home and host countries in a transnational social field characterised by spatial and temporal 'simultaneity' (Levitt & Glick Schiller, 2004: 1003).

When it comes to the study of diasporic heritage, I would argue that it is more meaningful to see transnational migrants as 'double marginal subjects' who constantly engage with the heritage discourse of both the host and the home countries from the diasporic periphery. In contrast to earlier literature that sees marginality as something negative associated with alienation, frustration and loss, recent research in cultural studies has realised the potential power of marginality as a resource of creativity and a site for representing ethnic, racial and cultural differences and contesting hegemonies (Osumare, 2001). For this research that focuses on migration and heritage, the differentiation made by Bennett (1993) between 'encapsulated marginals' and 'constructive marginals' is particularly useful. The former refers to victims of marginality, feeling detached and frustrated with being unable to meet the (sometimes conflicting) requirement of both home and host cultures; the latter benefits from the position of in-betweenness which grants migrants the freedom and flexibility to negotiate social connections and cultural practices from both the home and the host countries. Being 'part of social networks both here (in the

new country of residence) and there (in the former country of residence)'
(Gielis, 2009: 271), migrants are empowered by a sense of agency to construct new identities and achieve 'social anchoring' (Grzymala-Kazlowska,
2017) through the positioning of 'constructive marginality'. In the field of
cultural heritage, there is a growing body of literature that focuses on
heritage-making associated with transnational migration and diaspora
(Ang, 2011; Basu & Coleman, 2008; Byrne, 2016, 2022; Wang, 2016,
2021). These works have problematised, rather than stabilised, the nationalised and territorialised understanding of cultural heritage and identities.
In the context of Britain, it has come to the realisation of scholars that
'British heritage is the heritage of a nation of nations, shaped through
waves of migration and diaspora, wide-ranging imperial histories and
contemporary flows of globalisation' (Littler & Naidoo, 2005: 2). A transnational perspective to cultural heritage 'opens up a range of tensions
which trouble the intimate interrelationship that presumably exists among
(national) identity, memory and heritage' (Ang, 2011: 82). Indeed, only by
going beyond the binary dichotomies of 'national and transnational',
'minority and majority', 'immigrant and local' and 'outsider and insider'
in conceptualising heritage-making (Huc-Hepher, 2021; Wang, 2016)
could we fully understand the new dynamic and complex ownership of
cultural heritage in the 'super-diverse' (Vertovec, 2007) sociocultural condition of 21st-century Britain.

Informed by the most recent debate in relation to migration and heritage discussed above and through a case study of the annual Chinese New
Year Celebration (CNYC) in London, this chapter proposes 'glocal heritage discourses' as a new analytical framework for investigating the living
heritage of migrants in Britain. In his pioneering research of the global–
local problematic, Robertson (1995) put forward the notion of 'glocalisation' to transcend the tendency to cast the idea of localisation as a form of
opposition to the hegemonically global. As he put it:

> The global is not in and of itself counterposed to the local. Rather, what
> is often referred to as the local is essentially included within the global ...
> In this respect globalization, defined in its most general sense as the com-
> pression of the world as whole, involves the linking of localities. But it
> also involves the 'invention' of locality, in the same general sense as the
> idea of the invention of tradition (Hobsbawn & Ranger, 1983), as well as
> its 'imagination' (cf. Anderson, 1983). ... On top of that, the very ability
> to identify 'home', directly or indirectly, is contingent upon the (con-
> tested) construction and organization of interlaced categories of space
> and time 'by making what were once distant cultures visible and present
> through spectacular shows'. (Robertson, 1995: 35)

'Glocalisation' offers a useful concept for the analysis of links between global forces and 'local life-worlds' (Schuerkens, 2004). It is particularly relevant to research into heritage-making and identity construction of transnational migrants in urban space. As geographer Doreen Massey (1994: 169) has put it, '[t]he identity of a place does not derive from some internalised history. It derives, in large part, precisely from the specificity of its interactions with the "outside"'. Similarly, Ayşe Çağlar and Nina Glick Schiller (2011: 5) argued, 'to some degree all cities have been restructured and rescaled by processes in which the global and local are more than intertwined; they are part and parcel of the same ongoing processes of reconstructing and reimagining place'. A glocal perspective enables us to pay attention to the grounded subjectivity of migrants without losing sight of the ways in which place identity and the place of heritage-making are connected to a broader network of social, cultural and financial linkages that is forged by mobility. By examining the heritage-making of migrants in a glocal context, it 'reveals some of the internal tensions and contradictions in the very idea of diaspora, which exemplify the multifaceted complexities of identity formation in the contemporary globalised world, which cannot be contained within the cultural and geographical confines of the nation-state' (Ang, 2011: 82).

This chapter investigates how diasporic heritage-making becomes a glocal exercise imbricated in connections with multiple spaces, times and scales. It contributes to research into migration and heritage in three specific ways. First, it illustrates how migrants painstakingly deal with the 'authorised heritage discourse' (Smith, 2006) of both the host and home countries in the process of innovative diasporic heritage-making in urban spaces. Second, it unveils a 'double heritagisation' process that underprops and characterises the heritage activities of migrants in global cities. As shown in this case study, through simultaneous use of the strategy of 'blending' and 'authenticating', the organisers of the CNYC have invented a new cultural tradition (Hobsbawn & Ranger, 1983) built on the localisation of a diasporic heritage and the globalisation of a local tradition. By doing so, they not only reclaim power and cultural ownership but also make a 'contribution to the contemporary reinvention of urban life' (Çağlar & Glick Schiller, 2011: 81). Third, it shows that migrants are not marginalised subjects shaped by the positioning of a specific locality. Instead, by reassembling economic, cultural and political capital in a transnational space, migrants, at least members of the business elites, become transnational agents in urban politics. It must be said that it is not my intention here to argue for the representativeness of the finding of this chapter for conceptualising heritage practices of the entire British Chinese community in all its diversity. The Chinese in Britain are highly fluid and fragmented in terms of migration trajectory, linguistic affiliation, occupation and class status as well as political identities (Benton & Gomez, 2008). The ways in which people perceive and deal with heritage also vary greatly (see Chapter 11 for a study of everyday food heritage experienced differently by different groups of users from the British Chinese communities). However, a case study of the CNYC, initiated by a group of business leaders based in London's Chinatown and actively participated in by people from across ethnic communities in London and beyond, sheds new light on the complex process of how migrants engage with identity negotiation and articulation in urban space. This chapter provides compelling evidence that the annual CNYC in London is more than a show for the entertainment of local and international audiences. It is a highly empowering cultural exercise that produces a 'glocal imagination' of roots, places and belongings and expresses a 'flexible citizenship' (Ong, 1999) of the British Chinese, and by extension, many other ethnic minorities in the UK.

The Chinese New Year Celebration in London

Although Chinese settlement in the UK emerged as early as the late 19th century, large-scale Chinese migration to the UK took place only after World War II. The 1948 British Nationality Act gave commonwealth citizens the automatic right to work and settle in the UK. In the next two decades, a large number of agricultural workers from the New Territories of Hong Kong arrived in the UK seeking opportunities for a better life (Parker, 1998). The 1970s and 1980s saw a significant rise in the number of Chinese migrating from Southeast Asia, which is the biggest source of post-war Chinese migration to the UK from outside Mainland China, Hong Kong and Taiwan (Benton & Gomez, 2008). Between the late 1970s and 1990s, 22,000 Vietnamese refugees were admitted to the UK, among whom at least 70–85% were ethnic Chinese (Benton & Gomez, 2008; Pieke, 1998). Later, according to the 2022 Census of England and Wales, the number of Chinese in England and Wales increased from 393,141 in 2011 to 445,619 in 2021, making up about 0.7% of the UK population.[2] The actual size of the Chinese population in the UK is even larger if Chinese tourists and business visitors, as well as undocumented migrants, are counted. Approximately two-thirds of Chinese in Britain were born outside the UK, with the majority coming from Hong Kong, mainland China and Southeast Asia. It is estimated that the total number of Chinese in Britain reached 700,000 as of 2020, with the Greater London area being home to the largest Chinese population in the UK.[3]

The Chinese New Year, also called the 'Spring Festival',[4] is the most important annual festive event widely celebrated in China and among Chinese communities overseas, including the Chinese in Britain. The Chinese New Year, which is not an official public holiday in the UK, had at first been celebrated in the domestic space of British Chinese families. It was not until 1985 that the first public celebration of the Chinese New Year emerged in London. The celebration was organised by the London Chinatown Chinese Association (LCCA 伦敦华埠商会), a voluntary body founded in 1978 by a group of Chinese business leaders for the purpose of 'developing and expanding businesses in Chinatown and representing British Chinese to engage effectively with the British government' (The Official website of LCCA, no date).[5] In the first years after it was launched, the CNYC was held in Gerrard Street and the neighbouring streets, the heart of Chinatown,[6] and celebrated mainly by ethnic Chinese working in Chinese shops, restaurants and other businesses in Chinatown (Newell, 1989). Local amateur Chinese artists and school children were invited each year to perform traditional Chinese singing and dancing to a small Chinese audience on a platform set up in Gerrard Street.[7] In 2000, Chu-Ting Tang, the then newly elected chair of the LCCA, proposed moving the site of the CNYC from Chinatown to Trafalgar Square, one of London's most iconic public spaces. With the support of the London Mayor, Ken Livingstone, Trafalgar Square hosted its first CNYC in 2002, and it has become the central stage of this annual event ever since. During the Chinese New Year in 2017, a spectacular light show was for the first time held at the London Eye, one of London's most famous landmarks, marking the expansion of the celebration to the South Bank.[8] The CNYC in London has been widely covered by the media and is regarded by some as 'the largest Chinese New Year celebration outside Asia',[9] with the reported number of visitors reaching more than 700,000 per day.[10]

The one-day celebration usually takes place over the first weekend of the Chinese New Year. A routine schedule is followed each year. It kicks off at 10am with a costume parade that starts in Charing Cross Road and Shaftesbury Avenue and proceeds through the streets to Trafalgar Square. Featuring a dragon dance and a lion dance, performers from diverse cultural and ethnic backgrounds participate in the parade, dressed up in colourful Chinese festival costumes. Following this spectacular parade, live performances of traditional Chinese song and dance, opera, martial arts, acrobatics and so on are staged on purpose-built stages in Leicester Square, Shaftesbury Avenue and Charing Cross Road. Shops and restaurants in Chinatown are decorated with red lanterns, and an open-air market is set up around the Chinatown area to sell Chinese snacks, handicrafts, traditional souvenirs and festival decorations to visitors. The highlight of the celebration is the New Year gala which takes place on a big stage in Trafalgar Square. The performance usually begins at around 12 noon, after firecrackers and an eye-dotting new lion ceremony, and it continues for more than six hours. The one-day celebration ends with a fireworks display in Leicester Square.

In 2021, to follow local lockdown rules prompted by the Covid-19 pandemic, the LCCA cancelled the CNYC.[11] Instead, it put on a 90-minute virtual celebration of the New Year of the Golden Ox, aired via its YouTube channel, London Live and Youku (the equivalent to YouTube in China). The in-person celebration was cancelled again in 2022 for the same reason. The LCCA however managed to put on a lion dance and a night market at Newport Place in Chinatown on New Year's Eve, with a video screen set up at the side of the square to show pre-recorded performances.[12] The 2021 online Chinese New Year Celebration serves as the analytical focus of this chapter. It is supplemented by the Commemorative Issue of the 2021 Chinese New Year Celebration published by LCCA, interviews with senior members of LCCA,[13] informal participant observation at on-site Chinese New Year celebrations held before the pandemic, as well as media reports of the event by both Chinese and English language newspapers published in the past five years.

Negotiating Glocal Cultural Heritage Discourses

The 1985 launch of the CNYC in London coincided with the Soho area being officially named 'Chinatown' by Westminster City Council. Since the 1950s, the Soho area in central London had attracted an increasing number of Chinese immigrants to set up Chinese catering businesses and these thrived in post-war London. This was followed by the rapid growth of Chinese shops and businesses including Chinese bookshops, barbershops, accounting services, travel agencies, legal centres, Chinese medicine shops, gambling clubs and so on (Benton & Gomez, 2008). The 1970s witnessed a rise in the adoption of multiculturalism by many Western countries, including Britain, as a new policy for increased recognition and accommodation of non-white immigrant cultures and identities (Bissoondath, 1994; Kymlicka, 2012). Multiculturalism also entered cultural discourse and directly impacted on the ways in which urban space was perceived and organised. While Chinatowns continued to be seen by many as ghettos of the Oriental 'other', they have also increasingly become resource for urban regeneration and multicultural asset for tourist development in the eyes of both city authorities and Chinatowns' Chinese business elites. North American Chinatowns, notably those established in major metropolis such as New York, San Francisco, Los Angeles and Vancouver, underwent major makeovers in the 1970s and the 1980s. Exaggerated Chinese architecture such as Chinese-style gates and signs and banners in Chinese and English with 'oriental' fonts were introduced to create ethnicised urban space as the object of consumption by the white middle-class tourists (Anderson, 1995; Light & Wong, 1975; Umbach & Wishnoff, 2008). Given this context, in 1985, Westminster City Council, which had taken charge of the development of the Soho area, invested £235,000 in the Chinatown transformation project, including setting up three Chinese gates (two on Gerrard Street and one on Macclesfield Street), a pavilion at Newport Place and a pair of stone lions in the centre of Gerrard Street, as well as putting up bilingual (Chinese and English) street signs and pedestrianising the main streets. Following the makeover project, the local council formally named the area 'Chinatown' and had its official boundaries inscribed into the tourist map of central London (Christiansen, 2003: 179).

As shown above, the launch of the CNYC in London was not an isolated incident. Instead, it was part and parcel of a re-branding project led by the local council and Chinese business leaders who intended to strategically promote London's multicultural identity and economic development. Furthermore, it became a unique form of 'cultural capital' (Bourdieu, 1986) used by the London Mayor, Ken Livingstone, to formulate and project 'an appropriate metropolitan "brand image" – a brand image which trades heavily upon both the city's dynamic multiculturalism and its economic and infrastructural commitment to global capitalism' (Livingstone, 2000, cited in Dowdall, 2003: 328) that was considered essential for re-establishing London as a key node in the global economy at the beginning of the 21st century. Together with other festivals and carnivals organised by ethnic minorities in London (Bell, 2007), the CNYC held in London's Chinatown 'has become an integral part of what makes it a world class city' (City of Westminster, 2003: 1-3). In his congratulatory letter to the organisers of the 2018 Chinese New Year celebration, Sadiq Khan, the current Mayor of London, said:

> Chinese New Year is always a joyous time in the city's cultural calendar … Over the past year, I have enjoyed meeting with members of London's Chinese community as well as the many Chinese businesses around the capital and hope to visit China during my Mayoralty to strengthen economic and cultural ties with this great nation. London is open to all people and all communities. That's why I'm so proud of the Chinese New Year festivities here in the capital, which are the largest of their kind

outside of China and entertain hundreds of thousands of Londoners from all communities, as well as visitors to our city.[14]

Since 2002, the mayor's office has contributed to the event budget every year, including paying for the police fees, the hiring fees for the venue, road traffic management and so on, and the rest of the funding is raised by the LCCA from commercial sponsors.[15] The Chinatown transformation project and the CNYC have also received endorsements from the British government and the British Royal Family. Since 1985, members of the British Royal Family have paid several official visits to Chinatown. The most recent one was made by the royal couple, the then Prince of Wales and Duchess of Cornwall, now the King and Queen Consort, who visited Chinatown during the 2022 Chinese New Year (Figure 7.1), a visit that was 'designed as a boost to the community, whose businesses have suffered in Covid lockdown and whose members have endured rising racist abuse as a result of the pandemic'.[16]

While the CNYC has been endorsed by the UK authorities, it has also received strong support from the central government of the People's Republic of China (PRC), which plays an instrumental role in supporting LCCA to put on the New Year gala at Trafalgar Square. Since 2009, the Chinese government has dispatched, via the Office of Overseas Chinese Affairs of the State Council, singing and dancing troupes made up of top Chinese artists to come to London to perform to the public during the

Figure 7.1 Prince Charles eye-dotted a new lion when he visited London's Chinatown during Chinese New Year, 1 February 2022 (photo courtesy of Xiao Ma)

festival.[17] The gala has become the signature programme of this annual event. Dispatching Chinese artists to perform in London was part of a state-led global cultural project of China under the name of 'Cultures of China-Festivals of Spring' (文化中国-四海同春). Since 2009, the Chinese state has dispatched 81 troupes to conduct 176 visits worldwide (including to Hong Kong and Macao), and the number of performances had reached 483 by 2021.[18] The purposes of this cultural project are best explained in the address given by Tan Tianxing, deputy director of the Office of Overseas Chinese Affairs of the PRC, at the 2018 opening ceremony of the London Chinese New Year Celebration at Trafalgar Square[19]:

> The Chinese New Year is the most important traditional festival of the Chinese people. The annual celebration of Chinese New Year carries the deeply cherished national emotion and crystallises enduring love and attachment to the family and to the nation. To celebrate the Chinese New Year together with overseas Chinese around the world and with the public of the host countries who love Chinese culture, we dispatched six art troupes to 29 cities in 14 different countries as well as Hong Kong and Macao.[20]

'Cultures of China-Festivals of Spring' was developed hand in hand with another high-profile cultural project called 'Happy Chinese New Year' (欢乐春节) led by the Ministry of Culture and Tourism of the PRC.[21] While the former was aimed at 'serving the diasporic Chinese' by supporting the celebration of Chinese New Year in diasporic Chinese communities around the world, with the intention of enhancing connections between the Chinese overseas and the homeland,[22] the latter targets international audiences more broadly with the purpose of spreading China's cultural influences and promoting the global image of China through the media of cultural performance. These activities contribute to what Lee (2017) called an emerging 'global China':

> Global China is taking myriad forms, ranging from foreign direct investment, labor export, and multilateral financial institutions for building cross-regional infrastructure to the globalisation of Chinese civil society organisations, creation of global media networks, and global joint ventures in higher education, to name just a few examples. (Lee, 2017: xiv)

Since the beginning of the new millennium, the Chinese state has increasingly resorted to cultural heritage as a new vehicle to expand Chinese influence and to strengthen the attachment of Chinese diaspora to the homeland. Ien Ang (2011) discussed how, by emphasising the shared, real or imagined, ethnic and linguistic connections between China and the Chinese overseas, the Chinese government has given rise to 'transnational nationalism', or more precisely, 'national transnationalism', among the Chinese overseas. This 'heritage turn' is perhaps best exemplified by the boom in state-led building of 'Overseas Chinese Museums' in the PRC (Wang, 2021). Since the late 1990s, more than 20 museums specialising in the history of Chinese Overseas have been set up across China. By including the objects and cultural practices of diasporic Chinese in the official definition of 'Chinese culture heritage' and staging the previously marginalised diasporic Chinese in China's museum space, it has not only reshaped people's knowledge about global Chinese migration but also stimulated a cultural reimagination of China through the prism of cultural heritage.

As discussed above, the birth and success of the CNYC in London needs to be understood in glocal discourses characterised by the intersection of the rise of multiculturalism in Britain and the cultural expansion of China on the global stage. It is perhaps best illustrated by the new Chinese gate established on Wardour Street in Chinatown in January 2016, just before the annual celebration of the Chinese New Year. In contrast to the three 1986 gates, which were designed by a British architect, the new gate was designed and assembled by China's top craftsmen in Beijing and sponsored by several Chinese companies in the UK. Leaders of LCCA hosted the opening ceremony alongside HRH The Duke of York, the Chinese Ambassador to the UK and other distinguished guests. The new gate, applauded as 'the largest of its kind in the UK',[23] can be interpreted as a new landmark that signifies the unalleviated significance of 'glocal heritage discourses' to China and Britain in the new millennium. Consideration of the dual discourses brings to light the complexity and dynamics in the heritage-making of Chinese diaspora in a transnational space, offering a useful opportunity to examine the ways in which migrants engage with identity construction and place-making through heritage in a global city.

London's Chinese New Year Celebration as a 'Double Heritagisation' Process

The celebration of Chinese New Year in London is a two-fold operation involving Chinese migrants reinforcing their roots in the host society and re-connecting with the Chinese homeland. The complex negotiation with different categories of time and space inherent in this practice reminds us of McFarlane's notion of 'translocal assemblages' (2009: 566). It refers to the processes of disassemblage and reassemblage of 'history, labour, materiality and performance' in the interaction between the local and the global, accompanied by the formation of a double form of identity which helps 'link our interest in subjectivity with broader socio-political issues' (Oakes & Schein, 2006: xiii). Researching the CNYC in London unveils a 'double heritagisation' process involving simultaneous use of two distinctive yet mutually complementing strategies by the Chinese business leaders associated with LCCA in their glocal heritage-making practice.

The strategy of 'blending'

One strategy is what I call 'blending', referring to the ways in which migrants perform the process of 'fitting-in' of their diasporic cultural practices into the mainstream cultural traditions of the host society, without losing ethnic and cultural differences. It corresponds to the process of making the global local in the sense of demonstrating the 'mainstreaming' of migrants to the host society, either by demonstrating how the cultural tradition of migrants has been accepted as part of British tradition or telling the successful story of how migrant communities are recognised and honoured by the authorities for their social and economic contribution to British society.

The exercise of 'blending' starts with relocating the central stage of the CNYC from Chinatown to Trafalgar Square. When Mr Tang first proposed the idea, it was opposed by many members of LCCA who worried that the move would not only add financial strain to the association but also take away visitors and business from Chinatown.[24] To convince people that this was the right decision, Tang argued that 'it will be forever an event for the Chinese immigrants alone if we celebrate the Chinese New Year within Chinatown. Only after we do the festival in the iconic place of Trafalgar Square could it be accepted by the mainstream society and become a global event'.[25] When asked what it meant to her to move the central stage of the celebrations from Chinatown to Trafalgar Square, Christine Yau, the vice-chairman of the LCCA, said:

> We want to share it with [the] wider community. Because Chinatown, you know, is quite small, they say it's a Chinatown event, but this is different. ... I think we were very lucky to be able to use the Square to engage people from all over the country. And we also have people from different counties to join us, not only the Londoners. So, it was very important. It enabled us to share our culture.[26]

Hosting CNYC in Trafalgar Square symbolises the emerging 'mainstreaming' of one migration group into global London and to multicultural Britain. Indeed, over the years, the CNYC has become not only a major festival for the British Chinese, but also 'an integral part of the London event calendar and is the biggest outdoor event in London' (Official website of LCCA, no date), attended by hundreds of thousands of people from diverse ethnic and cultural backgrounds. Among the participants each year, only 10% or so have been ethnic Chinese, while the rest have been local British and visitors from Europe and beyond.[27] Every year, the Mayor of London, the Lord Mayor of Westminster, the Member of Parliament for the Cities of London and Westminster, the Chinese ambassador to the UK and other VIP guests have attended the gala staged at Trafalgar Square and made opening speeches. The event has also received congratulatory letters from the Queen and the Prime Minister. In his greeting message to LCCA prior to the 2021 celebration, then Prime Minister Boris Johnson said:

> I am aware it has not been an easy decision to suspend preparation for a public celebration this year, which has become an integral part of the London event calendar ... I appreciate all the Association does to strengthen and serve the British Chinese community and beyond, promoting Chinese culture in the UK and deepening exchanges and friendships between people of all races and backgrounds.[28]

An analysis of the 2021 virtual celebration of the Chinese New Year of the Golden Ox reveals further how the strategy of 'blending' was used. Transnational migrants often reach out to virtual places, either representations of familiar physical places in the virtual world or new virtual realities as communities of imagination and interest, to form a global sense of place (Gielis, 2009: 282). The 2021 online celebration of the CNYC belongs to the second type of 'virtual reality' created by migrants. First, the logo of the event, appearing on the first page of the online programme (Figure 7.2), featured the image of an Ox on the right and Nelson's Column on the left, both surrounded by 'auspicious clouds'. In the middle of the page the English words 'Chinese New Year 2021' are printed against a red background. Both the pattern of the clouds and the red colour symbolise 'happiness' and 'luck' in Chinese culture. In addition, the way in which Nelson's Column – arguably an architectural icon of British military prowess and sovereignty – is depicted within a Chinese lantern conveys the intermingling of the cultures and the transnational cooperation within the single element of the semiotic orchestration. The virtual celebration started with a 5-minute videorecording of a lion dance. Interestingly, it featured one 'Chinese lion' dressed in red and yellow, the colours of the national flag of the PRC, and a 'British lion' in a dress of red, white, and blue, the colours of the Union Flag (Figure 7.3). Together,

Figure 7.2 The logo of the 2021 Chinese New Year online celebration. A screenshot from https://www.youtube.com/watch?v=h1VGkHotwAY&t=39s, taken by the author

Figure 7.3 Lion dance performed at Trafalgar Square (photo courtesy of Eric Lee/ LCCA)

the lion dance duet signifies the friendship and collaboration between China and Britain that are at two ends of the transnational journey of the Chinese in Britain.

In addition to the use of visual metaphors such as the iconic image of the Ox, the Nelson's Column and the pattern of auspicious clouds, the strategy of 'blending' was also employed in the selection of local artists who have featured in the New Year gala each year. For example, Emmy the Great, the Hong Kong-born mixed UK-Chinese heritage singer, was invited to sing several songs with her band at Trafalgar Square in 2013.[29] In 2018, the festival featured UK-born mixed UK–Chinese heritage TV personality and fashion stylist Gok Wan. While no explanation for the selection of artists was given publicly by the LCCA, their presence could be said to embody and celebrate the fusion of two cultures. This was also the case for the 2021 virtual celebration of the CNYC. The show was hosted by two bilingual presenters: Mr Bo Wang, an internationally renowned tenor, born in China and educated in China and the UK, and Ms Phoebe Haines, an award-winning British Mezzo Soprano who speaks fluent Mandarin and has performed widely in China and worked together with British Chinese musicians. While Wang wore a western suit, Haines wore a Qipao (a traditional Chinese dress). Throughout the programme, they acted as hosts and introduced acts in both Chinese and English. The show also featured a song performance by Allan Chan who rose to fame in the Voice UK 2020. He was also the first Chinese artist to perform for the Prime Minister and other MPs and guests at No. 10 Downing Street as an Ambassador for LCCA in 2019.[30]

The 'blending effect' is perhaps best symbolised by the successful story of Chu-Ting Tang. Born in the New Territory of Hong Kong, Tang moved to the UK in 1975 at the age of 22. After working in the catering industry for decades, he now owns several high-end Chinese restaurants in London and has expanded his business to real estate and tourism. As chair of the LCCA, he has played a leading role in communicating with the local authorities, promoting Chinatown and safeguarding the reputation and interests of Chinese businesses in difficult times, such as during the 2001 foot and mouth disease crisis[31] and the most recent Covid-19 pandemic.[32] His most notable achievement is certainly initiating and organising the CNYC in Trafalgar Square which, in the words of Tang, 'enhances the status of the Chinese communities'.[33] In 2011, Tang was awarded an OBE (Officer of the Order of the British Empire) for his 'services to Chinese people in Chinatown'.[34] In 2016, LCCA was also honoured by the Office of Overseas Chinese Affairs of the PRC for its contribution to the wellbeing of the Chinese overseas in the UK. In his speech at the award ceremony in Beijing, Tang said: 'We are very pleased to be recognised by both the mainstream British society and the motherland'.[35]

The strategy of 'authenticating'

The other strategy is what I call 'authenticating', referring to the ways in which migrants proclaim and perform 'lingering on' in their own cultural heritage through re-enacting, in reality or metaphorically, distinctive cultural practices from the home country. It is aimed at making the local global in the sense of telling the story of how the place-making of migrants has been shaped by not only the sociocultural context where they are located but also their connections with the home country despite the diasporic nature of their existence. While the concept of 'authenticity' emphasises the state of being true, 'authenticating' focuses on the negotiated process of becoming authentic via embodied activities such as staged performances in public spaces (Ateljevic & Doorne, 2005; Xie, 2011; Zhu, 2015). Here, 'authenticating' is not only a technique that is used by the event organisers to attract and impress the local audiences by making what were once distant cultures visible and present through spectacular shows. It is also, and perhaps more importantly, a way to construct a sense of 'constructive marginality' by proactively enacting their connections with the home country. When China is becoming a significant power with increasing influences globally, how to navigate relations with the 'homeland' for their own interests has become an important part of identification and place-making for Chinese diasporas.

Indeed, although the red lanterns that filled the space of Chinatown and Trafalgar Square during the festival may have helped create an authentic atmosphere of Chinese culture, it was the staged performances put on by Chinese artists in Trafalgar Square that effectively created a sense of 'experiential authenticity' (Wang, 1999) among the Chinese diaspora and the London audiences. According to Ms Yau, vice-chairperson of the LCCA, this is one of the key factors for the success of the CNYC. It is through the bodily engagement with the sensorial experience of watching the acts in the square, purchasing Chinese artefacts, and smelling and tasting Chinese food in the market, that the audiences established a sense of 'real' in relation to what this particular cultural tradition of China is about and how much it means to the Chinese communities. As Ms Yau put it:

> Not a lot of people understand our culture; well, some people do, you know, they read enough. But to see it actually in front of your eyes, the sort of colour and to actually see people from China performing and to meet the Chinese here face to face, and have the chance to interact, is important.

We also have families with young children who are half-Chinese. Quite a lot I've spoken to, they were quite surprised that, Chinese New Year is like this, celebrated this way. They have no idea.[36]

When on-site celebration in physical urban spaces became impossible due to Covid-19 restrictions, the performance staged online became the most important tool used by the event organisers to produce a powerful, albeit ephemeral, sensation that authenticates China. The 2021 online programme was made up of video recordings of selected acts put on by the 'Cultures of China-Festivals of Spring' performing troupe in their visits to London before the pandemic and supplemented by a small number of pre-recorded performances by local artists. Space does not allow for a detailed analysis of the performance of each act. However, a brief glance at their titles reveals key features of the performances and ideas behind the show. Out of the 13 acts aired online, nine were performed by Chinese artists, whose performance portrayed and celebrated the cultural and ethnic diversity of China. The main acts included, for instance: 'Yi Wind and Fire', a dance about the love stories of young men and women of the *Yi* ethnic group performed by Guizhou Song and Dance Theatre; 'The Song of Spring', a song performed by a band from Inner Mongolia called *Jixiangsanbao*; 'Long Tassels Drum', a dance celebrating harvest in a *Han* Chinese village, performed by Beijing-based China Oriental Performing Arts Group; 'Why are Flowers so Red', a Uyghur dance performed by Shanghai Theatre Academy; 'I come from Baesha', a dance representing the life of Baesha *Miao* ethnic group performed by Guizhou Song and Dance Theatre (Figure 7.4); 'Animal-Style Boxing', a martial arts act performed by Henan Shaolin Temple Monks. The finale was a song called 'Ode to the Motherland', a well-known patriotic song in China, performed by a choir with Bo Wang as the lead singer.

The acts put on by the Chinese artists inevitably represented an official view of Chinese culture and Chinese society. By eulogising ethnic harmony and glorifying people's happiness, the acts are intended to project a positive image of China to international audiences. However, this study does not seek to interrogate the extent to which the image of China communicated by these acts is generously 'authentic' or how it is interpreted by the audiences, as answering these questions goes beyond its scope. Rather, it asks the question of how the event organisers have made use of staged performance as a vehicle to engage with the authorised heritage discourse of the home country, and how, by doing this, they enhance their own social and economic status, give visibility to the Chinese in Britain, and construct a desirable identity as 'constructive marginals' (Bennett, 1993). In other

Figure 7.4 Stage performance of *Miao* ethnic minority dance 'I come from Baesha' (photo courtesy of Jon Mo/LCCA)

words, what really matters here is the action of performance itself rather than what is performed. It is through the performance that the dual process of 'blending in authenticating' and 'authenticating in blending' is activated and sustained. By looking into the 'double heritagisation' process undertaken by migrants, this study makes explicit the fluid and multifaceted complexities of identity formation among the Chinese business leaders and wider British Chinese communities in a transnational context.

Conclusion

Stuart Hall (1999) raised the important question of 'whose heritage' when discussing cultural traditions in Britain. To what extent has the landscape of British cultural heritage changed since his article was first published? Is Hall's thesis still valid today? And can we develop new perspectives that could capture new issues on migration and heritage in 21st-century Britain? It is not the aim of this chapter to answer all these questions, but they require further and fuller investigation. However, revisiting Hall's thesis offers a useful starting point for the research presented in this chapter.

Firstly, building upon Hall's argument on migration and heritage, and through a case study of the CNYC in London, this study proposed the notion of 'glocal heritage discourses' as a new framework to re-conceptualise heritage-making and identity construction among migrants in Britain. As geographer Doreen Massey (1994: 156) put it, '[w]hat we need, it seems to me, is a global sense of the local, a global sense of place'. A glocal perspective shifted the focus of analysis away from how migrants interact with the heritage discourse of the host country alone to the process in which they engage with the heritage discourse of both the host and the home countries simultaneously, enabling us 'to think beyond dichotomies and mutually exclusive notions of local and transnational ties, and to recognise immigrants as agents who are able to forge their belonging and multiple attachments' (Ehrkamp, 2005: 348). As shown in this case study, the Chinese in Britain have navigated agilely between the discourse of multiculturalism that has been on the rise since the 1970s in Britain, and the discourse of 'global China' promoted by the Chinese state as an emerging world power. The findings have demonstrated what Michael Peter Smith (2005: 235) called 'Transnationalism "from in-between"' in the sense of how migrants as 'translocal subjects' mediate between transnational forces 'from the global' and 'from the local'. It is at the intersection of local and global that transnational migrants, as in the case of the Chinese in Britain, found the very inspiration for innovative heritage-making and the seed of success in anchoring themselves as diasporic subjects.

Secondly, this research has demonstrated that the heritage-making of transnational migrants is a 'double heritagisation' process, a highly dynamic and complex process involving negotiation with multiple centres and interactions between here and there. It has shown that 'instead of operating with local/global dichotomies, it may be more useful to think of subjects in terms of "relatively mobile and fixed transnationals"' (Yeoh, 2005: 410). Through simultaneous use of the strategy of 'blending' and 'authenticating', the organisers of the CNYC have invented a new tradition and a new locality in global London. The annual CNYC, produced by and producing crisscrossing sociocultural as well as political-economic relations, operating both outside and within the borders of nation-states, has unsettled traditional understandings of heritage and values seen from the framework of a single nation-state, be it Britain or China. By doing this, the CNYC has contributed to the reinvention of London's urban life that has been underpinned by 'multidimensional, encompassing social, economic and political relations as well as cultural and interpersonal networks and technological linkages' (Smith, 2005: 235).

Thirdly, this study has brought to light the agency of migrants who are conscious of 'the opportunity structures that the diasporic condition entails, which must include both the restrictive consequences of deterritorialization and reterritorialization and the creative potential of the multiplicity of connectivity … in both local and transnational contexts' (Li & Zhu, 2013: 44). Migrants are not merely marginalised subjects whose culture is either denied or undervalued by the mainstream society. Rather, as shown by this case study, migrants are able to carve out new space for constructing desirable identities through innovative heritage practices. However, the agency of migrants is far from being autonomous. It is imbricated in global-local dynamics shaped by shifting political and economic relations within and between nation-states. At a time when Britain and China are entering a new stage of development of their mutual relations,[37] the ways in which Chinese migrants, and Chinese business leaders in particular, engage with 'double heritagisation' may change considerably in the post-pandemic and post-Brexit era. Despite these changes, however, migrants will continue to make painstaking efforts to engage with 'glocal heritage discourses' to create a more inclusive and open understanding and practice of cultural heritage and identities in global cities.

Notes

(1)   The term 'home country' and 'host country' are used here as descriptive terms rather than analytical ones. 'Home country' refers to either the country where migrants were born or the ancestorial homeland of the descendants of early migrants. The term 'host country' refers to the country where migrants have physically settled or naturalised.

(2)   Office for National Statistics (ONS) https://www.ons.gov.uk/peoplepopulationand community/culturalidentity/ethnicity/bulletins/ethnicgroupenglandandwales/census2021 (accessed 19 December 2022).

(3)   Embassy of the People's Republic of China in the UK, 'the Basic Information on Population Distribution of Chinese Students, Employees of Chinese enterprises and the Ethnic Chinese in Britain' (中国驻英国大使馆:《在英留学生、中资企业、华侨华人等群体基本分布情况), 20 May 2021. https://www.fmprc.gov.cn/ce/ceuk/chn/lsfwxx/ t1877042.htm (accessed 16 July 2022).

(4)   The festival starts on the first day of the Chinese lunar calendar each year and lasts for two weeks. It is the biggest national holiday in China when people spend time together with their families. As it is based on the Chinese lunar calendar, the Chinese New Year dates vary slightly between years, but it usually comes during the period from 21 January to 20 February in the Gregorian calendar.

(5)   Originally called 'London Chinatown Neighbourhood Association', LCCA took charge of services such as government liaison and building good relations with Westminster City Council and Metropolitan Police to improve the street scenes and security for local Chinese businesses and safeguard the rights of Chinese business and Chinese people.

(6) The first 'Chinatown' in the UK was formed in the late 19th century in Limehouse, hosting transient sailors employed by British shipping companies to work in the Britain-Far East trade. By the 1880s, the Limehouse district had become the centre of the small Chinese population with mixed Chinese households and businesses concentrated mainly on two streets: Limehouse Causeway and Pennyfields (Benton & Gomez, 2008).

(7) Mong Mai, interviewed by Saskia Bünte, 3025: China Exchange, The Making of Chinatown Oral History Project, 2019, City of Westminster Archives.

(8) 'London Eye Decorated with Lanterns and Coloured Streamers, Celebrating Chinese New Year with the Whole World' (伦敦眼张灯结彩　普天同庆春节), Nee Hao Magazine: British Chinese & East Asian culture, 10 January 2017, https://www.neehao.co.uk/chinese-new-year-celebrations-and-london-eye-switch-on-chinatown-london (accessed 20 August 2022).

(9) Visit London: Official Visitor Guide, https://www.visitlondon.com/things-to-do/event/4733685-chinese-new-year-in-london (accessed 21 August 2022).

(10) Christine Yau, interviewed by Freya Aitken-Turff, 3025: China Exchange, The Making of Chinatown Oral History Project, 2019, City of Westminster Archives; Zhai Lu (翟璐) 'London Hosted Grand Chinese New Year Celebration, Happily Welcome the Year of Dog' (伦敦举行盛大春节庆典　喜迎狗年"旺"声一片), 19 February 2018, https://www.chinanews.com.cn/gj/2018/02-19/8450635.shtml (accessed 16 August 2022).

(11) LCCA managed to put on the CNYC in Trafalgar Square in January 2020, with the support of a group of Chinese singers and dancers from Guizhou province as well as local artists. Although coronavirus had started to spread inside China, it was not considered a threat to public activities in the UK at that time.

(12) Jack Saddler, London's Chinese New Year Celebrations Have Been Scaled Back Due to Covid, 13 January 2022, https://secretldn.com/london-chinese-new-year-parade (accessed 21 August 2022).

(13) The interviews were conducted by China Exchange, a charity based in London's Chinatown, for its 'Made in Chinatown' project. The oral recordings were subsequently stored in Westminster City Archive for the use of the public.

(14) 'London to Welcome Chinese Yew Year of the Dog on Sunday', London and Partners, Friday 16 February 2018, https://media.londonandpartners.com/news/london-to-welcome-in-chinese-new-year-of-the-dog-on-sunday (accessed 10 July 2022).

(15) 'The largest celebration outside of Asia', BBC, 2014.11.13 https://www.bbc.co.uk/london/content/articles/2009/01/22/cny_planning_feature.shtml (accessed 15 July 2022).

(16) Robert Jobson, 'Charles and Camilla celebrate Lunar New Year In London's Chinatown', 2 February 2022, Evening Standard, https://www.standard.co.uk/news/uk/prince-charles-camilla-chinatown-visit-london-chinese-lunar-new-year-b980102.html (accessed 18 July 2022).

(17) Since 2019, the delegation of Chinese performance troupes has been led by the All-China Federation of Returned Overseas Chinese of the PRC.

(18) LCCA, Highlights of Cultural China-Festivals of Spring (文化中国.四海同春 文化艺术精品), 2021, p. 82.

(19) Zhai Lu (翟璐), 'London Hosted Grand Chinese New Year Celebration, Happily Welcome the Year of Dog' (伦敦举行盛大春节庆典　喜迎狗年"旺"声一片), 19 February 2018, https://www.chinanews.com.cn/gj/2018/02-19/8450635.shtml (accessed 16 August 2022).

(20) All Chinese-language newspapers and other forms of publications cited in this chapter have been translated into English by the author.

(21) International Communication and Collaboration Bureau, Ministry of Culture and Tourism of the PRC (文化和旅游部国际交流合作局), 'Retrospective Exhibition on the Fifth Anniversary of Happy Chinese New Year' ('欢乐春节' 五周年回顾展举办), 3 March 2014, Official website of the Ministry of Culture and Tourism of the PRC, https://www.mct.gov.cn/whzx/tpxw/201403/t20140303_829537.htm (accessed 23 August 2022). Ma Siwei (马思伟), '2022 Happy Chinese New Year Global Programme Launched' (2022年 '欢乐春节' 全球活动启动), 27 January 2022, Official website of the Ministry of Culture and Tourism of the PRC, https://www.mct.gov.cn/whzx/whyw/202201/t20220127_930764.htm (accessed 23 August 2022).

(22) LCCA (伦敦华埠商会), *Highlights of Cultural China-Festivals of Spring* (文化中国.四海同春 文化艺术精品), 2021, p. 82.

(23) 'Chinatown Welcomes Iconic New Gate on Wardour Street', 5 January 2016, https://www.shaftesbury.co.uk/en/media/press-releases/2016/Chinese-Gate-Release.html (accessed 29 August 2022).

(24) Christine Yau, interviewed by Freya Aitken-Turff, 3025: China Exchange, The Making of Chinatown Oral History Project, 2019, City of Westminster Archives.

(25) Yan Zhengyu (严振羽), 'Chu-Ting Tang OBE: Obsessed with Chinese Culture, Attachment to the Motherland' (大英帝国官佐勋章获得者邓柱廷: 心系中华文化 胸怀桑梓真情), Nouvelles d'Europe (UK Edition) 欧洲时报 (英国版), 18 March 2016 http://www.oushinet.com/static/content/qj/qjnews/2016-03-18/795973898645536768.html (accessed 25 August 2022).

(26) Christine Yau, interviewed by Freya Aitken-Turff, 3025: China Exchange, The Making of Chinatown Oral History Project, 2019, City of Westminster Archives.

(27) 'LCCA: Let the Chinese New Year becomes one of UK's Festivals' (伦敦华埠商会: 让中国春节成为英国人的节日), 12 June 2016, http://www.gqb.gov.cn/news/2016/0612/39463.shtml, accessed 5 September 2022.

(28) LCCA, *Commemorative Issue on 2021 Chinese New Year*, 2021, p. 5.

(29) 'London Hosted Grand Events to Celebrate the Year of Snake' (伦敦举办盛大庆典欢迎蛇年春节), BBC, 10 February 2013, https://www.bbc.com/ukchina/simp/uk_life/2013/02/130210_cny_celebration (accessed 27 August 2022).

(30) Artist Spotlight: One interview with Alan Chan, 14 March 2018, https://www.acm.ac.uk/artist-spotlight-interview-with-alan-chan (accessed 27 August 2022).

(31) When the UK government accused China of illegally exporting beef meat, under the leadership of Tang, LCCA rallied a few thousand people to protest in front of the Ministry of Agriculture. In the end, the Ministry of Agriculture gave a statement saying that there was no evidence in the accusation and publicly apologised to the Chinese community. Chu-Ting Tang, interviewed by Shuang Wu, 3025: China Exchange, The Making of Chinatown Oral History Project, 2019, City of Westminster Archives. Yan Zhengyu (严振羽), 'Chu-Ting Tang OBE: Obsessed with Chinese Culture, Attachment to the Motherland' (大英帝国官佐勋章获得者邓柱廷: 心系中华文化 胸怀桑梓真情), Nouvelles d'Europe (UK edition) 欧洲时报 (英国版), 18 March 2016, http://www.oushinet.com/static/content/qj/qjnews/2016-03-18/795973898645536768.html (accessed 25 August 2022).

(32) Ye Zhuang (叶庄), 'In the Time of Pandemic, There is No "Half-time Break" for the Leader of Overseas Chinese Communities' (疫情之下, 这位侨领没有 '中场休息.'), *Xinmin Evening News* (新民晚报), 6 July 2020, https://paper.xinmin.cn/html/xmwb/2020-07-06/19/74105.html

(33) Chu-Ting Tang, interviewed by Shuang Wu, 3025: China Exchange, The Making of Chinatown Oral History Project, 2019, City of Westminster Archives.

(34) Yan Zhengyu (严振羽), 'Chu-Ting Tang OBE: Obsessed with Chinese Culture, Attachment to the Motherland' (大英帝国官佐勋章获得者邓柱廷：心系中华文化　胸怀桑梓真情), Nouvelles d'Europe (UK edition) 欧洲时报 (英国版), 18 March 2016, http://www.oushinet.com/static/content/qj/qjnews/2016-03-18/795973898645536768.html (accessed 25 August 2022).

(35) 'LCCA: Let the Chinese New Year becomes one of UK's Festivals' (伦敦华埠商会：让中国春节成为英国人的节日), 12 June 2016, http://www.gqb.gov.cn/news/2016/0612/39463.shtml (accessed 5 September 2022).

(36) Christine Yau, interviewed by Freya Aitken-Turff, 3025: China Exchange, The Making of Chinatown Oral History Project, 2019, City of Westminster Archives.

(37) In his first foreign policy speech on 29 November 2022, the UK Prime Minister Rishi Sunak said the so-called 'golden era' of relations with China, referring to closer economic ties under former Prime Minister David Cameron, was over. China was seen by the new administration as a systemic challenge to Britain's values and interests. See https://www.bbc.co.uk/news/uk-politics-63787877 (accessed 21 December 2022).

References

Anderson, B. (1983) *Imagined Communities: Reflections on The Origin and Spread of Nationalism*. New York: Verso.

Anderson, K.J. (1995) *Vancouver's Chinatown: Racial Discourse in Canada, 1875–1980.* Montreal: McGill-Queen's University Press.

Ang, I. (2011) Unsettling the national: Heritage and diaspora. In H. Anheier and Y.R. Isar (eds) *Heritage, Memory and Identity* (pp. 82–94). London: Sage.

Appadurai, A. (1996) *Modernity at Large: Cultural Dimensions of Globalization.* Minneapolis, MN: University of Minnesota Press.

Ateljevic, I. and Doorne, S. (2005) Dialectics of authentication: Performing 'exotic otherness' in a backpacker enclave of Dali, China. *Journal of Tourism and Cultural Change* 3 (1), 1–17.

Basu, P. and Coleman, S. (2008) Migrant worlds, material cultures. *Mobilities* 3 (3), 313–330.

Basch, L., Glick Schiller, N. and Szanton, B.C. (1994) *Nations Unbound. Transnational Projects, Postcolonial Predicaments, and Deterritorialized Nation-States.* Basel: Gordon and Breach Publishers.

Beck, U. (2007) Beyond class and nation: Reframing social inequalities in a globalizing world. *British Journal of Sociology* 58 (4), 679–705.

Bell, D. (2007) The hospitable city: Social relations in commercial spaces. *Progress in Human Geography* 31 (7), 7–22.

Benton, G. and Gomez, E.T. (2008) *The Chinese in Britain, 1800-present: Economy, Transnationalism, Identity.* Basingstoke: Palgrave Macmillan.

Bennett, J.M. (1993) Cultural marginality: Identity issues in intercultural training. In R.M. Paige (ed.) *Education for the Intercultural Experience* (pp. 109–135). Yarmouth, ME: Intercultural Press.

Bissoondath, N. (1994) *Selling Illusions: The Cult of Multiculturalism in Canada* (p. 17). Toronto: Penguin.

Blommaert, J. (2005) *Discourse: A Critical Introduction*. Cambridge: Cambridge University Press.

Bourdieu, P. (1986). The forms of capital. In J.G. Richardson (ed.) *Handbook for Theory and Research for the Sociology of Education*. Westport, CT: Greenwood: pp. 241–258.

Brickell, K. and Datta, A. (2011a). Introduction: translocal geographies. In K. Brickell and A. Datta (eds) *Translocal Geographies: Spaces, Places, Connections* (pp. 3–20). Farnham: Ashgate.

Byrne, D. (2016) Heritage corridors: Transnational flows and the built environment of migration. *Journal of Ethnic and Migration Studies* 42 (14), 2360–2378.

Byrne, D. (2022) *The Heritage Corridor: A Transnational Approach to the Heritage of Chinese Migration*. Abingdon: Routledge.

Çağlar, A. and Glick Schiller, N. (2011) Introduction. In N. Glick Schiller and A. Çağlar (eds) *Locating Migration: Rescaling Cities and Migrants*. Ithaca: Cornell University Press.

Christiansen, F. (2003) *Chinatown, Europe: An Exploration of Overseas Chinese Identity in the 1990s*. New York: RoutledgeCurzon.

City of Westminster (2003) *Chinatown Action Plan: Consulting on the Future of Chinatown*. London, United Kingdom.

Dowdall, P. (2003) Writing the 'architecture' of the global city Globalization and the birth of modern London. *City* 7 (3), 327–348.

Ehrkamp, P. (2005) Placing identities: Transnational practices and local attachments of Turkish immigrants in Germany. *Journal of Ethnic and Migration Studies* 31 (2), 345–364.

Gielis, R. (2009) A global sense of migrant places: Towards a place perspective in the study of migrant transnationalism. *Global Networks* 9 (2), 271–287.

Glick Schiller, N. and Çağlar, A. (2011) Chapter 4: Locality and Globality Building a Comparative Analytical Framework in Migration and Urban Studies. In N. Glick and A. Çağla (eds) *Locating Migration: Rescaling Cities and Migrants*. Ithaca: Cornell University Press.

Grzymala-Kazlowska, A. (2017) From connecting to social anchoring: Adaptation and 'settlement' of Polish migrants in the UK. *Journal of Ethnic and Migration Studies* 44 (2), 252–269.

Guarnizo, L.E. and Smith, M.P. (1998) The locations of transnationalism. In M.P. Smith and L.E. Guarnizo (eds) *Transnationalism from Below* (p. 3–34). New Brunswick, London: Transaction Publishers.

Hall, S. (1999) Whose heritage?: Un-settling 'the heritage', re-imagining the post-nation. *Third Text* 13 (49), 3–13.

Hannerz, U. (1996) *Transnational Connections*. London: Routledge.

Hobsbawm, E. and Ranger, T. (eds) (1983) *The Invention of Tradition*. Cambridge: Cambridge University Press.

Huc-Hepher, S. (2021) Queering the web archive: A xenofeminist approach to gender, function, language and culture in the London French Special Collection. *Humanities and Social Science Communications* 8, 298. https://doi.org/10.1057/s41599-021-00967-8

Kymlicka, W. (2012) *Multiculturalism: Success, Failure, and the Future*. Washington, DC: Migration Policy Institute.

Lee, C.K. (2017) *The Specter of Global China: Politics, Labor, and Foreign Investment in Africa*. Chicago, IL: The University of Chicago Press.

Levitt, P. and Glick Schiller, N. (2004) Conceptualizing simultaneity: A transnational social field perspective on society. *Annual Review of Sociology* 33, 129–156.

Light, I. and Wong, C. (1975) Protest or work: Dilemmas of the tourist industry in American Chinatowns. *The American Journal of Sociology* 6, 1360–1361.

Littler, J. and Naidoo, R. (eds) (2005) *The Politics of Heritage: The Legacies of Race.* London: Routledge.

Li, Wei and Zhu, Hua (2013) Diaspora: Multilingual and intercultural communication across time and space. *AILA Review* 26, 42–56.

Livingstone, K. (2000) London's a great international brand that has to be managed carefully. *The Independent*, 15 August.

LCCA (no date) Who is the London Chinatown Chinese Association? *London Chinatown Chinese Association.* Available from http://www.lccauk.com/ [accessed 21 April 2021].

Massey, D. (1994) *Space, Place and Gender.* Oxford: Polity Press.

McFarlane, C. (2009) Translocal assemblages: space, power and social movements. *Geoforum* 40 (4), 561–567.

Newell, V. (1989) A note on the Chinese New Year Celebration in London and its socio-economic background. *Western Folklore* 48 (1), 61–66.

Oakes, T. and Schein, L. (eds) (2006) *Translocal China. Linkages, Identities, and the Reimaging of Space.* London: Routledge.

Ong, A. (1999) *Flexible Citizenship: The Cultural Logics of Transnationality.* Durham, NC: Duke University Press.

Ong, A. and Nonini, D. (eds) (1997) *Ungrounded Empires: The Cultural Politics of Modern Chinese Transnationalism.* New York: Routledge.

Osumare, H. (2001) Beat streets in the global hood: Connective marginalities of the hip hop globe. *The Journal of American Culture* 24 (1-2), 71–181.

Parker, D. (1998) Chinese people in Britain: Histories, futures and identities. In G. Benton and F. Pieke (eds) *The Chinese in Europe* (pp. 67–95). London: Palgrave Macmillan.

Pieke, F.N. (1998) Introduction. In G. Benton and F. Pieke (eds) *The Chinese in Europe.* London: Palgrave Macmillan.

Robertson, R. (1995) Glocalization: Time-space and homogeneity-heterogeneity. In M. Featherstone, S. Lash and R. Robertson (eds) *Global Modernities.* London: Sage.

Schuerkens, U. (ed.) (2004) *Global Forces and Local Life-Worlds: Social Transformations.* Thousand Oaks, CA: Sage.

Smith, A. (1983) Nationalism and social theory. *British Journal of Sociology* 34, 19–38.

Smith, L. (2006) *Uses of Heritage.* New York: Routledge.

Smith, M.P. (2005) Transnational urbanism revisited. *Journal of Ethnic and Migration Studies* 31 (2), 235–244.

Umbach, G. ('Fritz') and Wishnoff, D. (2008) Strategic self-orientalism: Urban planning policies and the shaping of New York City's Chinatown, 1950–2005. *Journal of Planning History* 7 (3), 214–238.

Urry, J. (2007) *Mobilities.* Cambridge: Polity.

Vertovec, S. (2004) Migration and other modes of transnationalism: Towards conceptual cross-fertilization. *International Migration Review* 38, 970–001.

Vertovec, S. (2007) Super-diversity and its implications. *Ethnic and Racial Studies* 30 (6), 1024–1054.

Visit London (2021) Chinese New Year 2022 in London – Special Event – visitlondon.com. *visitlondon.com.* Available from https://www.visitlondon.com/things-to-do/event/4733685-chinese-new-year-in-london [accessed 21 April 2021].

Wang, C. (2016) Introduction: The material turn in migration studies. *Modern Languages Open.* http://doi.org/10.3828/mlo.v0i0.88

Wang, C. (2021) *Museum Representations of Chinese Diasporas: Migration Histories and the Cultural Heritage of the Homeland.* Abingdon: Routledge.

Wang, N. (1999) Rethinking authenticity in tourism experience. *Annals of Tourism Research* 26 (2), 349–370.

Wilding, R. (2006) 'Virtual' intimacies? Families communicating across transnational contexts. *Global Networks: A Journal of Transnational Affairs* 6 (2), 125–142.

Wimmer, A. and Glick Schiller, N. (2002) Methodological nationalism and beyond: Nation-state building, migration and the social sciences. *Global Networks* 2 (4), 301–334.

Xie, P.F. (2011) *Authenticating Ethnic Tourism.* Bristol: Channel View Publications.

Yeoh, B.S.A. (2005) Observations on transnational urbanism: Possibilities, politics and costs of simultaneity. *Journal of Ethnic and Migration Studies* 31 (2), 409–413.

Zhu, Y. (2015) Cultural effects of authenticity: Contested heritage practices in China. *International Journal of Heritage Studies* 21 (6), 594–608.

8 Performing the Symbiotic Relationship Between the Adapted Mosque and its Congregation

Julie Marsh

Introduction

The portrayal of mosques in the United Kingdom by mainstream media often involves presenting a single mosque as a representative of the entire Muslim community. When Islamic sites of worship are reduced to representation, a wider unhelpful discourse can develop that likens them all to each other and does not take into account the diversity of the Muslim diaspora in Britain. In addition, previous academic studies on Muslim sites of worship have mostly been theological and sociological and fail to examine the lived experience of the mosque. This chapter argues that a mosque cannot be represented because the acts of worship within it are fundamental to its existence. For this reason, the research conducted as part of this study should not be regarded as a representation of a space, and still less of individual worshippers, but rather as an attempt to 'perform' the mosque as it actually exists. This argument can be found in the findings from *Assembly*, a research project made and performed in three adapted mosques in London: Brick Lane Mosque, originally a Huguenot church, then a synagogue before becoming a mosque for the Bangladeshi diaspora; Old Kent Road Mosque, a conversion of a former pub to serve a predominantly Nigerian community; and Harrow Central Mosque, which used to occupy a pair of semi-detached houses acquired by a group of Pakistani immigrants. These chosen case studies reflect the architectural multiplicity, social diversity, and performativity of the adapted British Mosque.

Grass-rooted, designed and in many cases built by its users, the adapted mosque reflects the symbiotic relationship between buildings and diaspora communities. According to Historic England's website, there are estimated to be around 1500 mosques in Britain – the majority are formed from houses or other converted buildings, with fewer than 20% purpose-built. Any group can start a mosque by establishing congregational worship in any space they designate as being for prayer. Consequently, worship spaces serve as meeting places for these religious communities, fostering social cohesion and a sense of identity in the diaspora. These places of worship are considered cultural heritage because they provide essential activities for these minority groups, but not necessarily because they are architecturally or historically significant. The buildings range from adapted houses, shops, cinemas, pubs and other former places of worship. It is an organic process of architectural development, highly responsive to the immediate circumstances of the migrant communities. These mosques are in a continuous state of flux; as the community grows and their needs change, the buildings are continuously adapted to meet these changes. The process of mosque-making extends beyond simply importing Muslim culture; 'it is a vehicle through which their collective religious and cultural identity can be established a new' (Saleem *et al.*, 2021: 56). The decades after the independence and partition of India in 1947 saw large-scale Muslim migration from India, Pakistan and Bangladesh into Britain's industrial towns and cities of the Midlands, northern England and London. From the 1970s onwards, these early migrants were joined by further Muslim migration from Africa, the Middle East and Southeast Asia. As a result of leaving behind their cultural and social roots, these Muslim communities had to reconstruct the social and religious culture they had been dislocated from. This 'placemaking' was accomplished through the mosque, serving as a conduit for community coalescence and a vehicle for establishing a new religious and cultural identity.

A number of theoretical strands have arisen out of this research that centre on questions of space and its representation, including Doreen Massey's *For Space* (2005). In rejecting attempts to collapse space into representation, Massey raises pressing questions about how representational foundations of visual arts practice work. Artist and art theorist Barbara Bolt, who has a similar non-representational position in *Art Beyond Representation* (2004), asks, 'is it possible, for example, to think of our productions outside the paradigm of representation?' (Bolt, 2004: 12). Questions such as these prompted this research to take account of increasingly non-, or perhaps *more-than-*, representational understandings of place. Doreen Massey argues that place is not a quality of space, nor is space a surface across which we travel, nor is it representable as a fixed and discrete entity. Massey conceptualises place/space as a meeting point of inter-relations that do not necessarily exist within the same physical site. She provides a perspective on place as an ongoing and perpetually incomplete process, encouraging us to approach it outward-looking rather than inward-looking. Massey's key point is that space is unrepresentable since, to fix a representation of space, one needs to extricate it from the temporal to analyse it.

This understanding supports the broader philosophical shift towards understanding the mosque as emergent, relational, unfixed and beyond representational regimes. The *Assembly* project attempts to achieve this using the methodology 'site-integrity', a particular but original mode of site-specific practice that potentiates 'a dynamic exchange between site, artist, device, and community' (Marsh, 2019). Made with and for each faith community, this methodology enables an ethical and sensitive exploration of the dynamics of users in a site-specific context. This artistic fieldwork enacts a performance of place 'using ingeniously constructed camera motorised rigs to first film the space and then to play back those same images in a captivating encounter with the one-to-oneness of time and space' (Raban, 2018: 11). Miwon Kwon's *In One Place after Another: Site-Specific Art and Locational Identity* (2004) describes three forms of site-specificity, each encompassing different modes of inhabiting and interacting with place: phenomenological, institutional and discursive. Each of these paradigms can be applied to an analysis of *Assembly* as the phenomenological (physical location), institutional (religious/social structures) and discursive (theological and social within a ritual space). This research expands Kwon's three paradigms by proposing a fourth: 'the performative'. This fourth paradigm differentiates from other modes of site-specific practice through a dynamic material exchange between the site, artist, device and congregation. This exchange is based on relations; as relations change, space and place are also in constant flux.

Practical Methodology

Technically, the context of this research lies in the origins of early cinema, with reference to the Lumière Brothers' Cinématographe (a three-in-one device that could record, develop and project). *Assembly* builds upon this technique via the development of a recording/display device that is mobile. This new approach enacts a performance of space that cannot be separated from the temporal. Site-integrity performs place using motorised recording/display devices in situ, enabling an exact transfer of scale and time as the image maps the architectural site. As the title of this research suggests, site-integral artworks are informed, shaped and determined by the religious, social, political, architectural and institutional discourses present in the mosque.

Focusing on Jumu'ah (congregational) prayers, a film made one week was typically played back for the congregation after prayers the following Friday. As in camera mode, the device moves back and forth between the entrance and the Mihrab – but this time projecting footage of the congregation down into the hall. This filmic representation of the religious practice can then be experienced in the architectural site as 'a kind of matching of the world with its representations or, rather, a bringing of the two into critical conjunction' (Hamlyn, 2003: 53). The automated rig is designed to obtain a 1:1 ratio between image and site. The result is uncanny: mapped precisely to the mosque floor, the projected image of the carpet disappears into the actual carpet. The congregation, returning as observers, watch ghostly illusions of themselves at prayer, moving slowly across the hall (Figure 8.1). As the image moves through the physical space, the controlled motorisation creates an effect of only the frame moving, revealing, and concealing the architectural site below. With *Assembly*, rather than simply representing Muslim prayer, the aim was a series of artworks

Figure 8.1 Congregation members observe the moving projection in the main prayer hall at Brick Lane Mosque, 2018 (photo courtesy of Fuller-Rowell, J.)

centred on the congregation that convey a deeper, more multifaceted sense of the 'experience'.

Performing Religious Identities in Three London Mosques

Assembly was born out of a study of congregational prayer Jamaat (meaning *Assembly*), initially through a residency at Brick Lane Mosque, East London, in 2018–19. Brick Lane Mosque was chosen as a case study as it symbolises the overlapping migration histories of the East End. Initially built in 1743 as the Neuve Eglise, a Protestant chapel for Huguenot refugees, it became Spitalfields Great Synagogue in 1898 and, as local communities changed, was sold in 1976 to the Bangladeshi Muslim community and became Brick Lane Mosque. Brick Lane is at the heart of London's Bangladeshi-Sylheti community, and the mosque is embedded in the city's neighbourhoods and social fabric. The area has been vital in shaping a unique British-Bangladeshi identity, with Bengali migration stretching as far back as the 17th century. At the start of the project at Brick Lane Mosque, a consultation period with the religious scholars lasted several months. I also developed links with Everyday Muslims and the Inclusive Mosque Initiative, who served as ethical consultants on best working practices within this traditional mosque. This resulted in a clear framework: the filming process needed to be non-intrusive; therefore, the worshippers were filmed discreetly from above using a silent, automated device (Figure 8.2). The work also presented a significant technical challenge in terms of programming the rig to handle the scale and time of the projection within the physical site. I worked with a technical engineer and coders to develop a recording/display device that not only reproduced the image but also physically moved through the space in synchronised time. Due to the heritage status of the building, the rig could not be permanently fixed into the room and therefore had to be designed to be freestanding and automated. The filming process reflected the architectural modifications made to the gallery over the main prayer hall, which was adapted into a second floor of additional prayer space. An eight-sided lightwell was created by repositioning the original Georgian panelling, allowing worshippers to see the mihrab below. The filming rig was designed to span the width of this light well and was lowered into place before prayer and removed directly after by congregation members.

With the technology tested and a method of operation established, a second residency took place at Old Kent Road Mosque in 2019–21. In the early 1960s, a transient community of Nigerians came to London to study. Initially staying only for short periods, it wasn't until the 1980s that a

Figure 8.2 Documentation of rig filming in the main prayer hall at Brick Lane Mosque, 2018 (photo courtesy of Fuller-Rowell, J.)

more permanent community began to form, giving rise to the Muslim Association of Nigeria UK (MAN UK). A further 10 years passed before MAN UK acquired their first place of worship, the Old Kent Road Mosque. This building had previously been a Victorian public house, and the bar and function room quickly transformed into two identically sized prayer spaces for both men and women. The building's layout provides a provision of equality for both the male and female congregation, with the front entrance giving access to the women's section.

At the start of the project, the mosque committee nominated a steering group with representatives from the women, men, youth, elders and madrasah to work directly with congregation members to maintain focus and momentum throughout the project. Due to the mosque's non-heritage status, the filming rig was attached directly to the ceiling in both the primary and female prayer rooms spanning the entire width of both spaces. This also meant that both rigs in the main and female prayer space could be installed directly above and below each other, effectively mirroring the area. Therefore, the finished films were identical in duration and, if viewed side by side, ran for the same length of time. Covid-19 severely impacted the residency and culminated with a socially distanced site performance and *virtual screening* as part of Visit My Mosque 2020 in collaboration with the Muslim Council of Britain.

The third residency took place at Harrow Central Mosque in 2020–21. Originally adapted from a pair of semi-detached 1930s houses, the community was founded in the 1980s. After many modifications and enlargements, however, the house mosque could no longer accommodate the local Muslim community. In 1999, the congregation purchased an adjacent piece of land, and the project culminated in a substantial, purpose-built mosque after 12 years of fundraising and community-led construction. Harrow Central Mosque is now one of the largest purpose-built mosques in the UK. It marks an evolutionary step in mosque-making, with improvised structures replaced by purpose-built mosques. The prayer space in most British mosques is divided between men and women, despite no religious requirement for this. Whenever the women's prayer room is separate, a video link is used to follow the prayer in the men's prayer hall. In Harrow Mosque, the women's prayer space is located on a gallery level overlooking the men's prayer hall. Unfortunately, I could not access this space throughout the project due to the worsening pandemic and tighter restrictions on congregational prayer. The female congregation members were not allowed in the mosque during this time, therefore, a site performance was held for a minimal portion of the congregation under strict observance of social distancing rules. The following observations of the work were made during this time. They communicated a deep connection with the work as the pandemic challenged their sense of community and unity. A socially distanced performance in the main prayer hall finally took place in December 2020 for a limited number of the congregation.

Insights and Challenges of Making Art in Islamic Sites of Worship

Among the most challenging aspects of the research was finding the right balance between what was and wasn't appropriate to do in a mosque. For example, while it was necessary to turn off all the lights to see the projected image during testing (outside prayer times), some worshippers ignored the film and turned the lights on. This gentle reminder highlighted that a mosque is a place of prayer, not an art gallery. Many congregation members were curious about the artwork's intention at the beginning of the project. They discussed whether the artwork portrayed Islam positively or negatively and raised their concerns over the art's impact on their religious practices. In time, the congregation grew less anxious and became more involved in the development of the artwork.

The Friday congregational prayer was chosen to film in all three residencies because that is when people who might attend different mosques during the week go to the mosque they call their own– usually standing in the same position, more out of habit than for any religious reason. After filming, members of the congregation, therefore, knew where to look for images of themselves as the projections moved slowly across the hall during playback. The ability to see themselves objectively, as it were, prompted many to reflect on the practice of prayer, their movements, and so on. In each mosque, I was allowed to make the work as an artist, but as a woman, I was denied access to the main prayer hall during these prayer times. Therefore, male members of the congregation became more involved with the filming process by lowering the rig into place and turning on the sound recording equipment. Their involvement built trust and connection within the community, and they began to refer to the artwork as 'our' film.

At Brick Lane Mosque, opening the mosque for the congregation to see the work meant that women could enter the main prayer hall. It was outside of prayer time, but it was a part of the mosque they had never seen before. The men were also permitted to enter the female prayer space, but they declined. It was not the initial intention of the work, but it raised questions about the separation of worshippers by temporarily dissolving the religious/social boundaries. At the end of each residency, *Assembly* allowed the mosques to fulfil their mission to work closely with the wider community, members of different faith and non-faith by opening the artwork and site to a public audience. The moving floor projection – a record and a trace of worship – allowed others to experience prayer in situ via the artwork.

Unity, Ownership and Empowerment Within the Congregations

The most striking result of the project was that it gave the congregation a new view of themselves at prayer. Within Islam, moments of self-reflection are seen as essential to spiritual growth because: 'Reflection is the lamp of the heart. If it departs, the heart will have no light'. (Abd Allah ibn Alawi Attas). Some scholars have noted that the repetition of prayers in Islam gives them power and, far from rendering them meaningless, repetition makes them more powerful (Haeri, 2013). The patterns of repetition mediate between individuals and their deity, between individuals themselves, and ultimately reproduce the community they form. *Assembly* investigates the relationships between people and place and argues for the importance of belonging and locality to how people define themselves through place and unity. As one congregation member observes:

> you get an impression of everyone in the congregation doing it together, in unison, like everyone in the whole world at this time is praying towards one direction, which is a Muslim, and you get that sense of brotherhood and highlights a point, you know everyone is trying to work together, for a good thing. (Congregation feedback)

Responses ranged from deep philosophical inquiry to a more observational mode of 'living everyday life' and religious observance as an extension of it. Watching the ghostly images of themselves shot from above, many were suddenly aware of actions that had been unconscious or routine and found in them an unexpected interest and beauty. 'Usually, you're a part of it, so you don't get to watch yourself, prayer is very normal for us, second hand, but seeing it, watching it, it's a different kind of feeling'. People generally had an alternative sense of themselves and their relationship to the imam and the space. As one congregation member explained: 'The projection opened my eyes to the physical act of prayer. Of movement and repetition. Because my view or senses are often fixed on a focal point (the imam), I didn't really consider my own movements until seeing the image of myself in prayer'. Due to the exact transfer of time and scale, the film captures a precise relationship between body and space, helped by the fact that the people it addresses are part of the film.

The temporal dimension of each site performance is a vital component of the experience, as it is a re-projection of the same architectural space in synchronised time. This has a considerable effect on the mosque community as the artwork deconstructs the familiar frame of reference, subsequently affecting the congregations' material relationship with the physical site of the mosque prayer rooms. The 'conflict between representation as "illusion" and the "real" object could now be seen as one strategy for initiating a philosophical/aesthetic discourse in the experience of the work' (Le Grice, 1977). Ontologically, there can be no split between representation and the real; however, we experience the 'realness of the real' and the 'image-ness of the image', and *Assembly* pays attention to this. Worshippers experienced 'themselves' in the active sense, interacting directly with their image as they performed ritual prayer, movement and repetition. Congregation members questioned how their projected image of themselves corresponded to the physical space and how the image mediated their perception of the actual space. Worshippers could orient themselves to their image, watching their 'projected image of self' move over

Figure 8.3 Congregation member interacts with the projection in the female prayer space at Brick Lane Mosque, 2018 (photo courtesy of Fuller-Rowell, J.)

their physical body (Figure 8.3). One worshipper described their bodily expectation as they 'felt' the projected image pass over them,

> Experiencing the image of my own body and feeling it physically move over me was a strange feeling; I felt removed from the experience yet at the same time I was made more aware of the space around me and the movements of my body in prayer. (Congregation feedback)

This reflexivity allows the congregation to examine their performative practice and reflect on their religion philosophically. The Mosque community is not a fixed entity but is continually being made and re-produced by ritual. This same insight is extended through *Assembly* to the building where these prayers are held. Rather than placing the viewer in a fixed position, they are placed in the middle of a dynamic, changing environment. The idea of space being a fluid, continual and open-ended experiencing of an environment forces this artwork to reconsider itself as a spatial practice, 'if art is also an event in continual resistance to closure: art then is the name of the object of an encounter itself, and indeed of that which is produced by the encounter' (O'Sullivan, 2006: 2). Therefore, thinking about practice in terms of an event is not simply the unfolding of a sequence of activities within a 'privileged' and territorialised space of the gallery; the art experience needs to be rethought or re-experienced in terms of a changing live space. Site-integrity shifts from 'site as subject' to 'site-specific performance' by using dual-motorised rigs to record and 're-present' moving images in the very site of their making. *Assembly* also challenges ideas about what should take place in a sacred space. Performing *Assembly* in the mosque (rather than in a gallery) enabled the congregation to take ownership of the project and prevented the artwork from being experienced out of context. 'If *Assembly* were to be shown in a gallery, it would take on an entirely different meaning, one we wouldn't be comfortable with' said Naima Khan of the Inclusive Mosque Initiative. 'However, the bird's-eye view used to create the footage – fittingly called the "god shot" in the film industry – shows us ourselves in a unique and unfamiliar way that's worth experiencing' (Kahn, 2018: 12).

The project unexpectedly expanded at Old Kent Road and Harrow Mosque after being interrupted by Covid-19. Although the planned public site performances were cancelled, a series of socially distanced events took place after restrictions were relaxed. This was a profound moment for the congregation at Old Kent Road Mosque, who hadn't been able to join in congregational prayer for over three months. 'I know you didn't intend it, but the time that we are in makes it more impactful; I am taken back to a time when we could be together in unison'. This response from a congregation member demonstrates the importance of the physical act of Muslim prayer and its power to induce a haptic memory of embodied unison. Another worshipper at Harrow Mosque was particularly moved by 'the community doing the same thing at the same time, all together in the same space; it's something we haven't had for a while'. The site performance at Old Kent Road was given further poignancy due to its imminent demolition. The pre-recorded film made for this research was the last performance of congregational prayer to take place in the building. This recording now serves as an archive of this community's evolutionary journey.

Assembly found a way to connect and engage both prayer spaces, highlighting the differences in size, atmosphere and location (particularly in the case of Brick Lane Mosque, where the female congregation worshipped in what was previously the wine cellar), simultaneously uniting them in the act of prayer. The site-integral artworks stand passive in what they are but incredibly alive in what they narrate – the machine becomes the mediator. Both installations functioned as a self-making apparatus, arguing more about the triumph of lived space over representational space. The process of making *Assembly* went beyond my original project vision, reflecting each mosque's social and cultural structures. It impacted custom and practice within the community, enabling men and women to see part of their mosque they had never seen before. In most cases, this was the first-time female congregation members had stood in the main prayer hall, so comparisons between the two prayer spaces became a topic of conversation,

> The artwork reflects the contrast between prayer sites by mirror imaging the difference; the area for men upstairs, which is such a wonderfully open physical space, is full in the film, whereas the more confined space for us is all but empty in the film. (Congregation feedback)

Some female congregation members voiced concerns about equality of provision, with many wanting future access to the main prayer hall. In contrast, others explained why they prefer to pray in a separate space.

Dialogue, Respect and Tolerance within the Wider Communities

The *Assembly* project was made with and for the mosque congregations. Being fully embedded in the creative process resulted in greater agency and a desire to share the work with external audiences through a series of public site-performances, as Imam Kamal Hussain from Brick Lane Mosque discusses:

> It's a new way for non-Muslims to come and see how we Muslims pray and congregate together. It is a visual and audio experience and an opportunity to learn and understand Islam through dialogue, discussion, and social interaction. I'm sure people will get a moving experience out of it. (Imam Kamal Hussain, Brick Lane Mosque)

Rather than presenting an idea or image of what a mosque is or can be, the installation created an opportunity for new audiences to experience the mosque first-hand. Places generate their own fields of meaning as soon as we pay attention to them. According to Keith Basso in *'Wisdom Sits in Places: Notes on a Western Apache Landscape'* (1996), individuals and places interact through a process he calls 'interanimation'. A place is brought to life, 'animated by the thoughts and feelings of persons who attend to them' (Basso, 1996: 56). He states that relationships with places are 'most richly lived and surely felt' when people step back from their everyday experiences and attend self-consciously to them (Basso, 1996).

Due to the enthusiasm and confidence of the mosque community, the site performance allowed the public to engage in meaningful dialogue with the congregation (Figure 8.4). A YouGov Poll commissioned by the Muslim Council of Britain (MCB) reported that almost 90% of Britons hadn't been inside a mosque in recent years. By hosting *Assembly*, the

Figure 8.4 Public audience viewing the moving floor projection from the gallery at Brick Lane Mosque, 2018 (photo courtesy of Clifford, J)

mosque is no longer seen as a 'strict no-go area' outside of the Muslim community, so attendees can understand the religious practices without feeling like voyeuristic observers. As a member of the public describes, 'I was always curious to see and know what was taking place, but it was a strict no-go area. Having the opportunity to witness prayer through *Assembly* and not feel as though I was intruding was incredible. I found it a rare, meditative, and moving experience'.

The congregation's openness to discuss and debate their religion helped expand their awareness of their religious/cultural practices and the public perception of persons outside their faith. *Assembly*, therefore, could be seen as an instrument for community cohesion and understanding; a congregation member observed, 'With this kind of project, it is a way to bring people in and let them see we are like normal people practising faith'. *Assembly* reflects the diversity of the Muslim diaspora through sharing their private acts of combined worship in good faith. This site-specific, collaborative practice offers dialogue and scholarly exchange between multiple parties and perspectives, most notably providing Muslim communities with a voice to share their wisdom and valuable insights. The event also provided a platform for associated parties, such as Interfaith UK, the Muslim Council of Britain, and the Inclusive Mosque Initiative, to build relationships and create a sense of solidarity with each mosque.

Assembly provided an opportunity to share cultures and establish deeper relationships with the younger generation via site performances for local school visits. These events provide an opportunity for local school children to learn about the Islamic faith and culture while at the same time instilling a sense of belonging and pride in the madrasah pupils as they show the visiting children 'their mosque'. One mother reflects on how important art is for children to share their identities, especially when they have different cultural backgrounds, 'I loved seeing the children playing in and around the films, and I loved Stella's friends clearly being both proud to show her round the mosque and also simply enjoying being together'. Allowing children to share in a confident exchange with their friends is incredibly valuable, as Julian Morant, the headmaster of Christ Church C of E Primary School, comments:

> We had over 40 children, staff, and parents attend the film installation; they were all positive about the experience and engaged with it really well. They have come back to school and talked so positively about it; it certainly worked in the context of being made and displayed in the mosque, which was special. (Julian Morant, Christ Church CoE)

In another external development, the Muslim Council of Britain, as part of Visit My Mosque 2020, invited the public 'virtually' into Old Kent Road Mosque during the pandemic. I worked closely with the Old Kent Road community to create an online tour as part of this event, with a performance of *Assembly* presented via a live stream. This allowed the mosque community to virtually experience congregational prayer after two months without access to the mosque. After the film was streamed, I joined a Q&A with Muslim Council of Britain members, scholars and wider communities to discuss the nature and role of the virtual in Islamic religious practice. In the age of globalisation, where people have become 'disembedded' from concrete space and time, localities can be imagined as articulated movements in networks of social relations and understandings (Massey, 1991). The locality is not static, and the virtual manifestation of *Assembly* uses technology to mobilise and reconfigure time, space and place.

Preserving the History and Heritage of Adapted Mosques

Beyond its social resonance, *Assembly* has architectural significance, as evidenced by the V&A's decision to embrace this research in *Three British Mosques*, an exhibition curated by Shahed Saleem and the Victoria & Albert Museum for the Venice Architecture Biennale 2021. Responding to the theme 'How will we live together?' set by Lebanese architect Hashim Sarkis the V&A pavilion explored three case studies that illuminate stories of immigration, identity and community aspiration. The pavilion looks at the self-built and often undocumented world of adapted mosques, offering an attempt to record and celebrate mosque-making through three British mosques. The exhibition presented a 1:1 reconstruction of their highly decorative mihrabs, minbars and other architectural elements. These 3D replicas illustrated how material culture facilitates worship and reinforces cultural and religious identities.

The research findings from the *Assembly* project were shown as part of the exhibition, representing the intangible religious and cultural practices specific to each mosque. I was also commissioned to interview congregation members, allowing individual worshippers to tell personal stories. The *Three British Mosques* exhibition balanced the architectural vernacular of the self-built mosque with the community's lived representation and practices. The exhibition highlights how the building, the people, and their culture are interwoven and interlinked so that neither can be extracted without acknowledging the presence of the other. 'Migrant communities, their histories, their artefacts, the buildings they make, their aesthetics are usually unrecorded and unrepresented by the institutions that traditionally act as the gatekeepers to cultural value and historical significance' (Saleem, 2020: 47). The V&A through the Venice Biennale recognises and celebrates Britain's adapted mosque and diasporic and migrant history. Performing the 'live worlds' in which they are situated and the narratives of daily life they articulate, revealing architecture that this lived experience and embodied knowledge produces. The digital artefacts from this exhibition have now entered the V&A's permanent collection, providing an opportunity to preserve the history and heritage of each congregation and its place of prayer. Without this research, a significant period of informal religious architecture would have been lost.

Conclusion

This chapter began by describing the limitations of the representation of Islamic prayer sites within the mainstream media and academic research. *Assembly* opposes fixed representation and advocates the importance of artistic fieldwork to 'perform' mosques' religious and cultural identities. Through the 'site-integrity' methodology, this research makes a broader argument about the triumph of lived space over representational space. Drawing on space, place and identity theories, this research examines and feeds into the context of site-specific art and proposes a new paradigm, 'the performative', which artists could use to actively engage the site, community and audience within the creation and reception of artworks.

This research has found a way to 'perform' space and situate the congregation in the meaning-making of the place – all three site-specific artworks function as a place/self-making apparatus. The encounter of art in a Muslim prayer space brings a self-reflexive aesthetic experience activated by ritual. By uncovering the role of communities in shaping and negotiating their faith spaces, the research demonstrates that the adaptive reuse of buildings by diaspora communities fosters social cohesion and a sense of identity. The impact of the *Assembly* project is not limited to the mosque communities thanks to their willingness to engage with others outside their faith. The site-specific artworks were open to the local community, school groups and other parties. The congregation welcomed the wider communities in a confident exchange of culture; as one public member commented, 'it was an exceptional and moving experience, especially the way the congregation interacted with us; it was wonderful how they welcomed us into their space'. This shows how art can challenge social perceptions that might have existed unconsciously, providing a platform for discussion, respect and understanding.

References

Bolt, B. (2004) *Art Beyond Representation: The Performative Power of the Image.* London: Bloomsbury.

Basso, K. (1996) Wisdom sits in places: Notes on a western Apache landscape. In Basso and S. Feld (eds) *Senses of Place.* Santa Fe, NM: School of American Research Press.

Connolly, M. (2009) *The Place of Artists' Cinema: Space, Site and Screen.* Bristol: Intellect.

Haeri, N. (2013) *The Private Performance of 'Salat' Prayers: Repetition, Time, and Meaning.* Anthropological Quarterly, Vol. 86, No.1, pp. 5–34 the George Washington University Institute for Ethnographic Research.

Hamlyn, N. (2003) Film Art Phenomena British Film Institute.

Historic England (2018) British Islamic heritage celebrated by Historic England. Available at: https://historicengland.org.uk/whats-new/news/mosques-listed/ (accessed 8 January 2023).

Kwon, M. (2004) *One Place after Another: Site-Specific Art and Locational Identity.* Cambridge, MA: MIT Press.

Le Grice, M (1977) *Abstract Film and Beyond.* Cambridge, MA: MIT Press.

Marsh, J (2019) Site-integrity a dynamic exchange between site, artist, device and audience. *Journal for Artistic Research* 19.

Kahn, N. (2018) *The Most Vigilant Witness* – essay exhibition catalogue.

Massey, D. (1991) A global sense of place. *Marxism Today* (June 1991).

Massey, D. (2005) *For Space.* London: Sage.

Morris, R. ([1978] 1993) *The Present Tense of Space in Robert Morris Continuous Project Altered Daily: The Writings of Robert Morris*. Cambridge, MA: MIT Press.

O'Sullivan, S. (2006) *Art Encounters Deleuze and Guattari – Thought Beyond Representation*. New York: Palgrave Macmillan.

Raban, W. (2018) Introduction: Site-integrity catalogue.

Saleem, S. (2018) *The British Mosque: An Architectural and Social History*. Swindon: Historic England.

Saleem, S. (2020) Exhibiting self-built British mosques: Between the digital and the physical. *Journal of Civic Architecture* 6.

Saleem, S., Turner, C. and Kilgallon, E. (2021) *British Mosques*. London: Foolscap Editions.

Part 3

'Heritagisation Space': Collecting, Remembering and Transmitting the Past for a Shared Future

9 Spaces of Heritagisation: The UK Indian Communities and Memorials of War

Susan L.T. Ashley

This chapter inspects the ways that 'heritage' is mobilised through spaces and language of memorialisation. It focuses on war memorials in London and Brighton as sites of official and unofficial meaning-making activities by the Indian communities in the UK. Heritage is examined here not just as buildings or preserved landscapes, but as expressions, identities and cultural practices linked to the past. The chapter explores how memorial-ising discourses have asserted different forms of belonging and citizenship through these 'heritagisation spaces'. The two case studies used are the Memorial Gates near Hyde Park Corner in London, commemorating the armed forces of the British Empire in the World Wars, and the Chattri Memorial, Brighton, which honours those Indians who fought in the First World War. Employing historical, visual and ethnographic methods, the tangible monuments and the changing nature of the memorialising perfor-mances carried out around the monuments were studied. The research was part of a sequence of AHRC-supported qualitative projects from 2014 to 2019 '(Multi)Cultural Heritage' that inspected how non-dominant immigrant groups engage with and build a sense of 'heritage' in their adopted homes in the UK. The chapter documents the particular heritage-making at work within public memorialisation, addressing how meaning was conveyed both through the physicality of the sites and memorials as objects, and through the embodied activities within the spaces by the Indian communities. It analyses how differing valuations of heritage are voiced and enacted within these material forms and immaterial practices. It argues that differing representations and performances of postcolonial citizenship emerge within the publicness and visibility that shape 'heri-tagised' spaces of memorial.

Monument-building, aimed to render ideas about events and people as significant, can be situated within the broader literature on space and place making, and heritage. Numerous studies explore how the construction of meaning-full places (landscapes, monuments and sites) and the performance of commemorative activities in those locations, reinforces collective forms of memory and identity. Through meaning-making such spaces are transformed into places. From the foundational work on *landmarks* by Halbwachs (1992) and *lieux de mémoire* by Nora (1989), such places have been clearly demonstrated as mnemonic devices for expressing shared values, collective narratives and colonising the future with things we value today as our 'heritage' (Drozdzewski *et al.*, 2016; Osborne, 2001; Waterton, 2005).

Key to this analysis of how belonging and citizenship perform through memorialising is an engagement with the conceptualising of 'spaces' both as Arendtian 'spaces of appearance', and as a more Foucauldian 'space of surveillance' (Marquez, 2012). The first deals with locations that potentially generate a sense of collective action and resistance through shared visibility, and the second connotes sites which impose control and normalisation through their visibility. In both cases the 'publicness' of being in space, under observation of others, compels people to act in particular ways, and in this case perform heritage in different ways through memorialisation.

But in addition, these cases also allow us to use a postcolonial analysis of monuments as spaces of heritage, taking into consideration how power acts differently within such sites when minoritised bodies are involved – something neither Arendt nor Foucault properly accounted for. The added lens examines the dynamics of citizenship and belonging within a postcolonial framing, both an orientalist perspective and asymmetric binary distinctions between UK Indian practices as coloniser and colonised as per Said (1978), and hybrid relations as per Bhabha (1994), which implies the creation of a 'Third Space' of difference involving ambivalence, hybridity and/or mimicry, partly adaptive and partly disruptive.

Such sites of memorialising clearly act as 'heritagisation' spaces where the past is 'remembered, treasured and transmitted to the public and to the next generation, not only through the media of words but also the silent "talking" of objects' (as discussed by Wang and Lamb's introduction in Chapter 1). But argued below is that heritagisation is not that simple, and does not only involve representation and transmission, which implies the unencumbered passing on of knowledge about the past. Instead, 'heritagisation spaces' also entail performances and translanguaging that might endorse or challenge, adapt or transmute, those embedded and dominant narratives. Such spaces, hosting material and immaterial 'in-public' positioning, serve as both Foucauldian sites of surveillance and control, *and* as Arendtian sites of appearance and contestation, within an ambivalent colonising frame. The ritual enactment of stories, identities and values within spaces of heritage can validate new shapes and ideas through public performances in relation to the fixed older formation. Thus memorials, as heritage spaces and objects, become the platform for multiple interpretations of the past, as well as plural identities and values and, through heritagisation processes, can endorse different modes of belonging and citizen status.

War Monuments in the UK

War memorials are a noticeable part of public space in the UK, commemorating the past with monumental presence in towns and villages across the country, and acting as sites for remembrance activities. They are an inherent part of the 'affective infrastructure' that shapes national memory and national heritage (Crang & Tolia-Kelly, 2010). Most memorials in the UK were erected by local initiatives that decided what, where and who would be commemorated, and their desired remembrance tended to be the loss of young local men. These symbolic objects and practices structured what was considered 'normal' ways of commemoration and remembrance.

Such monuments made, and still make, a public claim to knowledge and status, generally representing the views of the dominant elites of the time. They typically commemorate a white and Eurocentric history of war (Wilson, 2013). They are solid structures that are rarely removed, thus the views of the time are projected into the future – which was the original aim of their erection, for 'time immemorial'. Their meanings arise from the structures' design, their place in the wider landscape and through the official public activities that take place around them (Smyth, 2019). Drozdzewski *et al.* argue that the spatiality of memory, or its solid 'a-where-ness', is of prime importance to the way such memorialisation functions. They note:

> The place of memory, its physical locale linking memory to territory, and the metaphoric and atmospheric places of memory created through the performance and practice of commemorative events rely on the bounding of memory to specific geographic places....[O]fficial designation imbues these places with significance to the nation through things like monuments, memorials and historical plaques. (Drozdzewski *et al.*, 2019: 266)

Such spaces – of memorial – rely on official designation and coordination of ritual events to continue to mark such locations as important to the local or national memory. In the United Kingdom, the shape of Great War monuments, and the actions and values conveyed in Remembrance Day ceremonies, remain the same today, and are jealously protected from change, 'lest we forget'. Drozdzewski *et al.* (2019) point out that material memorials 'need' to be visited and actively remembered to maintain their original meanings and impact, otherwise they are merely stones in the landscape. By reappearing each year as given and normal, the ritual events of memorialising activities continue to be 'protected from social criticism, and thus are able to demarcate behaviours and mould identities' (Ibarra-Colado, 2006: 473). Such monuments and ritual activities not only make material statements about collective historical events, but importantly they reinforce the characteristics and behaviours of those who 'belong' to the nation (Drozdzewski *et al.*, 2019).

While a multitude of First and Second World War monuments remember the war dead in small centres across the country, nationalist monuments to war were assembled in London. National war monuments, erected with strategic motivations, tend to be a particular focus of nation-building narratives. As Quentin Stevens notes:

> The physical commemorative landscape of a capital city is a matter of great national significance. A constellation of memorials provides a strong, visible, legible representation of national identity and values, lending a nation both historical and conceptual grounding, and also creates a stage for rituals that reinforce and extend national meanings. (2015: 39)

War monuments hold prestigious locations at the centre of Empire in central London, near Buckingham Palace. There they represent celebratory narratives of sacrifice and valour as part of British collective memory. Such national war memorials, erected with strategic, nation-building motivations, are the focus in most capitals of Western and Commonwealth countries (Ndletyana & Webb, 2017). Most emphasise and justify how the state treats the importance of peace and war (Stevens, 2015).

The idea that nations and people of the British Empire, now Commonwealth, contributed significantly to the war effort has been historically under-acknowledged and rarely represented. The greater recognition of non-white, non-European soldiers did not truly emerge in the broader public sphere until the four years of the UK First World War centenary (2014–2018) when a more global and nuanced understanding of the history of those wars was acknowledged. Recent research has inspected the significance of this from historical, social, cultural, architectural and political perspectives (e.g. Hallam & Hockey, 2020; Harvey, 2017; King, 2014). However, while recent commemorations of women and minorities has broadened the audiences for this subject, most rituals of memorialisation ignore internal struggles by minoritised groups and still tend to keep hidden the violence of the nation-state itself (Stevens, 2015: 60).

Indian Communities in the UK

Within this broader context of the war monument landscape, this chapter seeks to understand the memorialising spaces and actions of Indian[1] communities in the UK. The Indian presence in the UK has a long history that coincides with the British push into the Indian subcontinent via the East India Company in the 17th century (see Lawson, 2014). Subsequent trade and military interventions in India, including direct British rule over the region from 1858 to 1947, resulted in Indians of multiple ethnicities and religions working for, with and under the authority of the British Empire. From that period emigrants such as seamen and domestics, as well as elites, emigrated to the UK. Deployment by the British of almost 1 million Indian soldiers in Europe and the Middle East to bolster efforts during the First World War also brought Indian servicemen onto English shores (Omissi, 1994).

Mass immigration to the UK from India began after the Second World War, along with many other inhabitants of the British Empire, with government policies to attract migrants into industries and public services such as nursing (Visram, 1986). The 1948 British Nationality Act extended citizenship and immigration privileges to the 'new' Commonwealth countries of India, Pakistan and Ceylon, although subsequent regulations attempted to put controls on immigrant numbers (Uche, 2017). This growing population was bolstered by events such as the expulsion of South Asians from Uganda in 1972, where almost 60,000 Ugandan Indians were forced to leave, about half migrating to Britain (Uche, 2017). They had historically formed a merchant class, shaped by colonial tripartite policies, and brought what has tended to be described as both a conservatism and a Britishness that helped them flourish economically and socially in the UK (Herbert, 2012). From the 2000s ethnic Indian immigrants tended to be well educated and professional classes (Somerville & Dhudwar, 2010), with the 2011 census reporting 1.4 million people identifying with the Indian ethnic group or 2.5% of the population, and 1.1 million with the Pakistani ethnic group or 2.0% of the national population (Institute of Race Relations, 2020).

By introducing the subjectivities and activities of these large communities of the UK into our ideas of what can constitute 'heritage' in the UK, then, what might be considered 'normal' sites and practices of remembrance can be challenged. The idea of war monuments in the UK built specifically for soldiers of Empire was itself a rare situation – the two case studies, the Memorial Gates in London and the Chattri Indian Memorial near Brighton, are the primary examples in relation to soldiers of Indian origin. Their dissimilar symbolic, material and imaginary codes contest what is accepted and valued as British heritage and draw attention to the long history of Indian presence as citizens in the UK.

Spaces of Indian Memorialising

To explore these ideas, the chapter next draws on research into heritagisation processes at these two unique but similar spaces in the UK, describing the fixed monuments, their environ, the formalised rituals and the informal activities at each. A final section analyses and compares the effects of the two cases in relation to differing conceptualisations of 'space', and how this enacts divergent forms of citizenship by the Indian communities.

Memorialising at both locations was understood as both the formal material monument and the ritualised practices there, as well as the informal space-creating practices of people at the sites: both structural and subjective aspects of social action that express a signification of place (Bourdieu & Wacquant, 1992). Inspected in each case was its emplacement in space (the monument), and ethnographic scrutiny of discourses and experiential encounters at the site (practices). The goal of the research was to assemble multiple cognitive and experiential types of knowledge (McIlvenny & Noy, 2011). Bringing both objective and subjective elements together enabled the analysis of how memorial objects and practices constituted and validated what was considered heritage in its changing dimensions.

Lefebvre (1991) reflects this interest in the differences between structured systems and emergent or 'lived' systems in his theorising about the social production of space. Within the formalised space of remembrance certain practices are reiterated while other activities adopt 'habits of the body' that unconsciously employ tacit ways of behaving. In the case studies described below, while constrained within the 'conceived' space of monumental structures, the memorialising rituals embedded both routines and habits of the body within a 'perceived' space, with tacit ways of doing, but as well, incorporate imaginings of doing or 'lived' spaces (Dale, 2005: 657).

Both spheres were examined in the case studies, the Memorial Gates in London and the Chattri Memorial in Brighton, both important sites of heritage for Indian communities in the UK. Described next are the locations, features and remembrance activities at each. In both cases an ethnographic approach was taken in the research, which involved invited attendance at both ceremonies and added interviews with organisers. Observations of the memorial structures, procedures and participants were augmented by on-the-spot and follow-up interviews. The Memorial Gates study was undertaken in spring 2019. The Chattri data were collected in spring 2014, which also employed a focus group of stakeholders.

Memorial Gates, London

The Memorial Gates (Figure 9.1) is a monument conceived and driven by select voices within the UK Indian communities. The monument is situated prestigiously in the parkland close to Buckingham Palace and the Wellington Arch on what is now known as Constitution Hill in the centre of busy London. An assemblage of war monuments stands in this area, originating with the Arch, which was erected in 1830 during the reign of

Figure 9.1 Memorial Gates, Constitution Hill, London (photo by the author)

George IV to commemorate Britain's victories in the Napoleonic Wars. The Memorial Gates monument was planned as a Millennium project by the Memorial Gates Trust and funded by the UK's National Lottery, and inaugurated in 2002 by Queen Elizabeth. The aim was to 'maintain in perpetuity':

> for the benefit of the public a memorial in the form of decorative gates to those inhabitants of the Indian sub-continent, the continent of Africa and the Caribbean who served in the armed forces of the Crown, whether by land, sea or in the air, during the World Wars, 1914–18 and 1939–45. (Charity Commission)

The monument was the brainchild of Shreela Flather, a teacher and politician, now the Baroness Flather, first Asian woman to receive a peerage and sit in the House of Lords. She spoke in the House in 2008 about her drive to create the memorial:

> My proudest achievement is building a memorial to the volunteers from the Indian Sub-continent, Africa and the Caribbean in the heart of London. It stands next to Buckingham Palace wall at the top of Constitution Hill.... I would like to be remembered for the fact that when nobody was doing it, I had the courage to stand for mayoralty as an Asian woman in Windsor. I had the courage to fight for a memorial which nearly wrecked my health and indeed altogether accepting the possibility of not being able to do these things.

The Memorial Trust were a group of prominent Indian and non-Indian politicians and businessmen gathered by Flather in 1998 to plan and develop the war monument. Liam O'Connor Architects and Planning Consultants were commissioned to design the site and structures. Construction began in 2001 with the first stone laid by the Queen Mother. The monument comprises four plain stone pillars on both sides of Constitution Way, and an adjacent pavilion which is shaped like an Indian chattri or 'umbrella'. The four stone piers are each topped by a bronze urn, and names of commonwealth countries are inscribed on their sides. The dome of the chattri bears the 74 names of those from these regions who were awarded the Victoria Cross or the George Cross in the two World Wars. There are 23 VC recipients from World War I listed, 12 GC recipients from World War II and 39 VC recipients from World War II. Poet and Booker Prize winner Ben Okri's epigraph is carved into one of the piers: 'Our future is greater than our past'.

The site is now run by the Memorial Gates Council presided over by the Baroness Flather. Their purpose is to hold an annual commemoration and to offer educational services 'to help promote understanding and respect' for the wartime contributions of Indian, African and Caribbean servicemen (memorialgates.org). They note that more than five million people from those regions contributed to all aspects of the allied effort during those conflicts, in troops and auxiliary services.

The Memorial Gates remembrance ceremony is held each year in March, on Commonwealth Day. As an invitation-only event, it attracts about a' hundred to two hundred formal guests to a speech and wreath-placement ceremony. The event is chaired by the Lord Karan Bilimoria and overseen by current chair of the Memorial Gates Council Inderjeet Nijhar, and life president the Baroness Flather, who is the key driver behind the monument construction, but also behind the continued commemorations. The guest list reflects the high-status nature of the activities, where uniforms with medals or formal civilian clothes are the required dress code. The Metropolitan Police provide crowd barriers and security. A large marquee shelters a reception with food and tea service for guests. Said Baroness Flather at the 2018 event:

> It's a very special day for me because every year I get to see my dream in reality and with all the people here, all of you who are here. And that makes it so very, very special and satisfying for me. So thank you, first of all, for coming to this memorial because it's a living – we want it to be a living memorial, not just a pile of stones – and that's why we have a ceremony, and we hope that this ceremony will keep on being done. (12 March 2018)

Chattri Memorial, near Brighton

The Chattri Memorial (Figure 9.2) is a public monument built by the British government in 1921 on an isolated spot on the South Downs near Brighton to honour the more than 1 million soldiers from undivided-India who fought on the Western Front during the First World War. Between 1914 and 1916, 4306 wounded Indians were hospitalised at the Royal Pavilion estate in the city of Brighton (Hyson & Lester, 2012). Fifty-three Sikh and Hindu soldiers died there, and their remains were cremated at the site of the monument. This monument was not part of the broader government programme of Great War memorial construction across Britain after the war. It was, instead, a later British government gesture aimed at India, to portray a good image in its handling of colonial soldiers during and after the war (Hyson & Lester, 2012: 19). The monument was unveiled by the Prince of Wales in a military ceremony on 21 February 1921 in a visually symbolic and well-publicised ceremony demonstrating Britain's worthy intentions towards its colony. The inscription on the

Figure 9.2 The Chattri Memorial near Brighton (photo by the author)

marble base of the Chattri gives a textual indication of the combined fune-real and colonial purpose of the memorial. It reads in Hindi and English:

> To the memory of all the Indian soldiers who gave their lives for their King-Emperor in the Great War, this monument, erected on the site of the funeral pyre where the Hindus and Sikhs who died in hospital at Brighton, passed through the fire, is in grateful admiration and brotherly affection dedicated.

The monument incorporates a chattri in its design, similar to the later Memorial Gates structure; a dome and eight pillars built from white Sicilian marble. This had been indicated by the India Office of the time which ordered 'that where cremation has been resorted to, a simple monument of an oriental character should be erected on the site of the crematorium' (Donovan, 2005: n.p.). The columned dome is encircled by a series of granite platforms and steps including three large slabs that clearly indicate the original cremacry bases. Unlike the busy urban location of the Memorial Gates, the Chattri is situated in a wilderness upland, only accessible by walking trail, overlooking the English Channel in the distance. This siting marks a clear contrast to the atmosphere of the London case study, as the space engenders a profound sense of spirituality – more like a cemetery than a war monument, with the crematory bases marking where bodies were burned at this spot.

The Chattri went through a series of government administrations after 1921, incorporated into an area of manoeuvres during the Second World War and subject to army target practices, but mostly deserted in its isolated location (Donovan, 2005). Then in 1951, 30 years after its opening ceremony, local Second World War veterans began annual memorial ceremonies at the Chattri, aiming to perpetuate remembrance of that war and soldiers' sacrifice, attended by military representatives but, uniquely, also by British-Indian veterans groups. The city of Brighton took over administration of the memorial.

But in 1999 the Legion wished to give up the event, as its members were too old to trek across the fields to the monument. One Brighton resident from the Sikh community, who had never been to the ceremony, was not a veteran, nor had any connection to the dead soldiers, stepped forward to help. The first Indian-led memorial service in 2000 was poorly attended, but through the labour of this volunteer, with some support from a local Black History group, word spread within the Asian communities and through the local media. The Chattri Ceremony became a well-known and well-populated event in June, blending formal and informal rituals in a unique sense of 'occasion' that reinforces the site's extraordinary sense of physical space. Thus, while this historical space was originally associated with colonial memory and empire, grassroots activities at the Chattri led by local Indian residents have now imbued the site with new meaning and value.

Discussion

The goal now is to think about how Indian communities relate to these two 'heritagisation spaces' described above, in ways that are more complex than mere representation and transmission of values. Analysed below are how the publicness and visibility of the formal and informal – material monuments and immaterial activities – demonstrate complex and multiple versions of postcolonial citizenship. Drozdzewski *et al.* (2019) in their important work 'Cultural memory and identity in the context of war: Experiential, place-based and political concerns', inspect how memorialisation works as a spatial concept that reflects this dual material/immaterial approach, experienced through location, events and everyday spacing activities. These parameters were clearly manifest at the Memorial Gates and the Chattri: the symbolic and rhetorical structuring of meaning through tangible forms and rituals, as well as the emergent valuations as enacted by participants during formal ceremonies and as voiced through participants' comments (Fairclough, 2003; Pink, 2013). This enables observation of the colonial framing that constrained the memorials, as well as the Arendtian and Foucauldian processes at work in the public performances in the spaces.

The first point of comparison must be the colonial roots of each. Their very existence reflects colonial aims in relation to Indians positioned as outsiders. The Brighton Chattri is the older memorial, devised as an imperial address with orientalist intentions aimed by the 'Emperor-King' to appease separatist movements in India (Hyson & Lester, 2012). The Memorial Gates came 80 years later, but was also aimed at highlighting India's place as part of the British Empire, and 'those who paid the utmost sacrifice from the Commonwealth those many years ago' (Archbishop of York). Both are marked by their singularity and separateness from mainstream war monuments in the UK. The Chattri sits in a remote location and specifically honours Indian soldiers who were cremated there. The Memorial Gates represents the broader topic of 'Commonwealth' soldiers who died: but the Commonwealth presented here does not include Canada, Australia and other 'white' nations. Instead, this commemoration singles out racialised soldiers who were part of the allied effort under the mantle of the UK.

The physicality of each space works to reveal particular ideas about Indian heritage. On a broad scale, as suggested by Nora (1996), collective memory is attached to *lieux de mémoire* or symbolic elements of a landscape that remind a group of the past. He writes that 'statues or monuments to the dead owe their meaning to their intrinsic existence' as solid and monumental lieux that act as mnemonic markers (Nora, 1996: 23). Within the UK context, typical war monuments were built to channel emotions and set-in-stone a collective national ethos about the legitimacy of war and soldiers' deaths. This ethos was organised visually and physically: as well as occupying central locations in everyday urban spaces, the grand stone aesthetics imparted a sense of higher moral authority (Abousnnouga & Machin, 2011). The Memorial Gates were intentionally sited on Constitution Way to symbolically communicate their significance and authority. On the other hand, the obscurity of the Chattri location near Brighton also communicates its relative lack of significance.

The design sensibility of typical war monuments contrasts with the aesthetic strategies used at the two case studies. Both employ a marble chattri motif, a flowing and 'oriental' style that is recognisable by both white Britons and Indians as representative of a particular Indian flavour, clearly differentiating them from mainstream monument designs. This can be read as condescendingly colonial, but when viewed from below, is also oppositional to the staid British monumental approach. Interestingly, the Memorial Gates incorporated both visual codes in its design: a curved and ornate chattri as well as four tall and austere stone pillars mounted with Greek urns, a possible compromise between 'oriental' and 'British' monumental forms.

Interpreting the visual form implies a lack of 'Britishness' in both monuments, reinforcing the idea that this colony and people of India are separate from the British nation. In her research on the Kashmiri Gates in Delhi, Rajagopalan (2012) writes about the close management of the colonial frames under which ideas of empire, colony and nation are controlled. Those in power own the means of production which generate and manage the aura of authenticity that emerges from the physicality of objects like monuments. This control separates the narrative of what constitutes Britishness and what constitutes Indianness (2012: 97). This separation was echoed at both memorial sites. At the Chattri, participants expressed 'Englishness' as a white trait separate from Indian or Black, unconsciously employing a We–They division in their speech: there is us, and then there are those 'English' people or 'white' people, slipping into phrases like 'We do have some *British* people coming down, they do come to Chattri' or '*English* people come up to me and say what an amazing feeling there is at the Chattri', or according to another participant, 'I'll talk to an *English* family just because I'm proud and I think "Oh, why did they come?"'. At the Gates ceremony an informant talked about 'It wasn't just *British* soldiers that's had to die, or gave their lives trying to fight for our freedom. There's also people of Indian descent, Nepalese, Caribbean' (all italics added by author).

Drozdzewski *et al.* point out that 'public representations of memory should be perceived as an integral part of a nation's story of remembering, commemoration and identity-making' (2019: 269). But as an 'inescapably political' activity, memorialising 'always includes and excludes people, and has always been a powerful means of defining the "other" in national terms (Drozdzewski *et al.*, 2019)'. Clearly, the visual and material forms at both memorial sites cannot be read as intrinsic parts of British or English national heritage. In addition, the official events carried out at each site, the rituals of commemoration, also reveal a continued othering despite efforts by each to align with British norms. The nature of the formal rituals at the Gates and the Chattri did appear to impose specifically British ways of thinking and doing – a regimented form of performance in the laying of wreaths and military dress and playing of the Last Post by a bugler; the voiced reflections in speeches that suggested the benevolence and generosity of British imperial authority, and the superior honour and value of war sacrifice to the British nation. But such actions adhering to British 'norms' of war remembrance can be interpreted not as inclusive in the imagining of nation, but as highly colonial. Rather than intrinsically British, these were cases of Bhabian mimicry in expression rather than inclusively part of a nation's narrative.

Figure 9.3 Dignitaries at the Memorial Gates ceremony (photo by the author)

At the Memorial Gates, the annual commemoration procedures followed the British script presided by the titled dignitaries and Anglican archbishop (Figure 9.3). But by its location and material design, and ritual ceremony on Commonwealth Day rather than ingrained in the UK Remembrance Day, this ritual stands apart from the national heritage. Emphasised on the Memorial Gates website is the idea that the people being honoured were 'members of the Commonwealth family', part of 'a free association of sovereign independent states highly valued by its members'. This positions them as separate from Britain, even though the soldiers served in the British military in the world wars, as part of the empire that was Britain. The majority of participants interviewed at the ceremonies – students, military personnel and onlookers, some descendants and mostly people of colour – were also citizens of the UK born or residing in the country. Thus, this story is a story of the nation, not separate as those Commonwealth countries overseas.

At the Chattri (Figure 9.4), the overall shape of the formal memorial event in June appears to follow British patterns as well, with invited Lords, wreath laying, speeches and military uniforms. In this case, however, these ceremonies were highly hybridised: new activities were added to that re-organised meaning and valuation with little reference to the authorised or normalised discourses. There was a desire to put a new stamp on

Figure 9.4 Chattri ceremony June 2013 (photo by the author)

procedures and space – a Christian priest was replaced by a Hindu religious leader. The bugle was subsumed by an evocative and emotional Indian hymn. The annual ritual exhibited subtle changes to reflect what the new organisers felt was significant and valuable about memorialising there. Familiar tropes of war remembrance were combined these new cultural referents in a classic case of 'almost the same but not quite' (Bhabha, 1994: 85). 'We're creating our own culture' was the comment by one organiser (Interview, 9 Dec 2013). The British-Indian identity of the event chairperson was perceived as 'one of them' by the Indian veterans and audiences thus sharing understandings and responsibility (Focus Group, 23 March 2014).

The formal remembrance rituals at both sites were structured in colonial patterns, and consciously resisted by organisers at the Chattri. But it was also the informal on-site movements and presencing at the ceremonies that allowed observations about how Indian participants understood and used memorialising. This is the moment where 'the ritual and the casual face each other' in gatherings and public spaces, that allow us to observe people when 'a guard has been let down' (O'Shea, 2020). Observation of their embodied performances in public at both memorials allowed assessments of the behaviour of participants and the affective sensibilities of the space and space-making activities. Both case studies involved the annual presencing of individual Indian participants in these spaces – the continuity of their bodily connections with these places reinforced their identification with the past and with each other (Osborne, 2001). An Indian presence indicated a symbolic and ethical investment on their part, for both officials from India and those of Indian descent living in Britain. To return continuously to this specific place, to maintain a bodily public presence and to re-enact specific rituals on each occasion, attests to the strength of their motivations and the significance of these locations. The desire to maintain such connections –materially and abstractly –was a central component of their activities here.

Such actions suggest Lefebvre's concept of lived space (1991), which includes both conceived and perceived spaces without being reducible to either. Beyes and Steyaert (2012) take Lefebvre's ideas further, suggesting the concept of 'spacing' as a non-representational way to think about informal practices like those studied at the Memorial Gates and the Chattri. Spacing describes ongoing material practices of the everyday that are embodied, affective, sensational and with a novelty that expresses a minor politics (2012: 51). Drozdzewski (2019) reinforces the idea that in spaces of memorialisation, 'being there', in an 'authentic' place, coupled with the visceral sensations of pride and honour that are produced there, thickens a site's affective capacity (2019: 258). Thus, it can be seen as more-than-representational (Waterton, 2012), conceiving the world in practical terms in a process of 'perpetual becoming' (Thrift, 2008).

Such conceptualisation of lived spaces can also encompass Arendt's spaces of appearance and Foucault's spaces of surveillance, which both entail people behaving 'in public' in view of others, and their visible 'presencing' in these spaces (Ashley, 2016). Being 'in public' is a condition of being: a formal, imagined place out there that we enter and participate in symbolically and where we make an 'appearance' (Miller et al., 2017). As noted above, Hannah Arendt and Michel Foucault present complementary theories about such visibility and power in spaces. In an Arendtian 'space of appearance', common visibility generates power and the potential for collective action. In a Foucault's 'space of surveillance', visibility facilitates control and adherence to norms. But Marquez importantly points out that 'power generated in spaces of appearance depends on and reproduces horizontal relationships of equality, whereas power in spaces of surveillance depends on and reproduces vertical relationships of inequality' (2012: 7).

These relationships appeared to manifest differently in the two case studies. For example, both ceremonies placed great value on the socialising of the tea services. At the Memorial Gates, a 'patriotic nationalism' was evidenced in people's actions on the ground (Drozdzewski *et al.*, 2019), where appearances reproduced vertical relationships. Observations at the 2019 ceremony noted that participants' presence was by invitation only, cordoned into allotted spaces by security, and adhering to elite forms of dress and manner. The following tea was also a formal affair with titled dignitaries and upper ranks isolated from more ordinary participants. The whole procedure appeared to be managed by how one appeared and acted under the scrutiny of others, and the control of external policing. The Chattri organisers cherished the tea as well, but as observed in 2013 and 2014, carpools transported everyone to a local school. Bikers, war vets and ordinary citizens queued for pastries and shared folding tables with the Marquess, Indian dignitaries and the Queen's representative in a demonstration of horizontal relations. A mixed group of strangers here created a sense of occasion that was a spontaneous experience – a Third Space in Bhabha's terms, or a case of lived space or 'spacing' that organised the world unconsciously in a less hierarchical way.

The sensibility of the 'presencing' or 'appearances' throughout the two events demonstrated differing modes of celebrating Indian heritage, belonging and citizenship. In contrast to the Memorial Gates, the Chattri was an affective experience: a liveliness, a sense of chaos and an openness to unexpected and random cross-cultural encounters. The day began with a journey across farmers' fields, with the 250 participants arriving by foot, by car and motorbike, and others by hired bus from London. Dress code was not specified, but a profusion of suits, saris, turbans and military uniforms were joined by t-shirts and blue jeans. The presence of a military biker group in leather regalia added to the heterogeneous sensibility of the space. Marked by a profusion of skin colour from white to various shades of black, clusters of people mingled. The immediate effect was affective and visceral, as pointed out in conversations with fellow participants.

A playful episode marks and records the annual Chattri ceremony each year, reinforcing the sense of communality and solidarity in the proceedings. Willing participants mass and jostle onto the steps and *ghat* platform for cheerful group photos, bringing the racialised bodies into prominence. There was also a sense that they were tenuously making it up as they went along, they were unsure of correct performance so were able to behave in spontaneous and novel ways. The emotional responses of the closely packed bodies, transmitted electrically through the crowd, imbued the practice with a strong sense of 'importance'.

These actions at the Chattri can be seen as a 'minor politics' (Beyes & Steyaert, 2012: 51) that signified and affirmed an intentional insertion into a British social, political and military milieu in order collectively to achieve solidarity and assert power. Said one interviewee:

> This could have been just a footnote of history but actually, it needs to be celebrated. One, it counteracts all racism immediately, especially in post 9/11 age where people are very quick to lash out against anyone who looks different, whoever they may be.

Many felt the Chattri politics was done on their terms, in a heritage event organised by one of their own, who shaped the event in a way that suited their needs. This was a conscious act that involved the physical process of mutual witnessing and recognition and the transformation of human relationships.

> I feel like it's the only event that celebrates... a little piece of history in our landscape, a very significant piece of history that could very easily been forgotten about, and so I feel a bit of ownership that this is my home and I have that Indian connection as well.

The making of heritage and the making of citizens share characteristics. Both are parts of social imaginaries that underpin personal and collective identities (Anderson, 1983). Both heritage and citizenship are invoked in disputes over membership, identifying who belongs and who does not. So the potential politics of both words is important, and public statements and in-public positionings were made in places of heritage wield power. This coming together at the Chattri memorial was a creative practice of 'world-making' that Arendt saw in spaces of appearance, a kind of productive publicness that lies at the foundation of democratic practice (1958/1989). Through the mutual recognition that occurred here, the memorialising practices enabled the formation of a democratic 'public', a social imaginary based on heritage. Such is the nature of 'acts of citizenship': not state-sponsored acts but active relationships through which individuals and groups enact themselves as citizens, struggling for recognition or other matters of concern, but also interacting purposefully to change the shape of society and making claims about the nature of belonging (Isin, 2008). In the case of the Chattri memorialising activities, a mixed group of participants assembled to re-interpret old rituals in relation to each other, acts of creating new heritage that consciously aimed at changing the shape of their world. And participants could feel that something innovative – and something valuable – was created here.

> It's about humanity, right? Humanity rises above nations, we are all humans. (Focus Group – March 23, 2014)

Conclusion

This chapter demonstrated how memorialising can be seen as a complex combination of objects and practices that organise both meaning and value. It explored the monuments and memorial practices of Indian communities in the UK through two case studies, the Memorial Gates in London and the Chattri Memorial near Brighton. The chapter analysed 'what' aspects of heritage are emphasised through spaces of memorialisation, 'who' expresses and makes knowledge about those aspects and by what processes or 'how' heritage, both official and unofficial, is planned, expressed and experienced through such spaces. The chapter highlighted the colonial nature of the form and process of memorialising in the UK. Remembrance rituals are an accepted duty to nation in the case of most war memorials, whereas those in the Indian communities have a more ambivalent attitude while they sort out their ideas about subjectivity, identity, belonging and heritage.

Heritage can be seen as one part of the 'logic of culture'; the process of working on and transforming the self that arises from the ongoing tension between the unconscious traditions we inherit and the self-conscious efforts we make throughout our lives to strive for individuality (Bennett, 2006: 52). On national, group or individual levels, self-conscious efforts to construct identity might embrace and project a particular version of heritage or tradition. The Memorial Gates was presented here as a more mainstream heritage site with rituals that echoed normalised remembrance practices, and whose participants appeared to fit themselves in to 'English' hierarchical behaviours. Within the visibility and publicness of the Gates ceremonies, a more Foucauldian process shaped colonial and hierarchical forms of behaviour among participants. At the Chattri on the other hand, the public nature of the site and its memorialising interactions created a more hybrid, disruptive and democratising vision of heritage. This was seen as an enactment of a different form of citizen-membership within an Arendtian space of appearance, where new British Indian values were expressed.

While this might be seen as a minor political act, it allows us to think about how such memorials like the Chattri, while not considered central structures in the organising of society, should not be underestimated in the role they play in the organising and legitimation of what is accepted and valued as normal. For these people who tend to be racially marked by society, their conscious demonstrations of the value of heritage can also be seen as acts of citizenship (Isin, 2008) that asserted their belonging within UK society. It is here that the potential politics of heritage becomes important, as a cultural and political space and practice that does work in the present, especially to socially legitimise or to exclude individuals and cultures. Deciding what parts of these unconscious ideas to keep and how to change them becomes an emotional decision about choices, about what to include and exclude in the communal articulation of heritage, and this affects ideas of belonging and citizenship. Argued here is that in seemingly minor spaces and practices of heritagisation, new and transformative ideas about heritage could develop.

Note

(1) 'Indian' is used broadly here in reference to the Indian subcontinent, but activities were undertaken predominantly by those who identify with post-1947 India.

References

Abousnnouga, G. and Machin, D. (2011) The changing spaces of war commemoration: A multimodal analysis of the discourses of British monuments. *Social Semiotics* 21 (2), 175–196.

Anderson, B. (1983) *Imagined Communities: Reflection on the Origin and Spread of Nationalism*. London: Verso.

Arendt, H. (1958) [1989] *The Human Condition* (pp. 22–78). Chicago, IL: University of Chicago Press.

Ashley, S. (2016) Acts of heritage, acts of value: Memorializing at the Chattri Indian Memorial, UK. *International Journal of Heritage Studies* 22 (7), 554–567

Bennett, T. (2006) Exhibition, difference and the logic of culture. In I. Karp and C. Kratz (eds) *Museum Frictions: Public Cultures/Global Transformations* (pp. 46–69). Durham, NC: Duke University Press.

Beyes, T. and Steyaert, C. (2012) Spacing organization: Non-representational theory and performing organizational space. *Organization* 19 (1), 45–61.

Bhabha, H.K. (1994) *The Location of Culture*. London: Routledge.

Bourdieu, P. and Wacquant L. (1992) *An Invitation to Reflexive Sociology*. Chicago: The University of Chicago Press.

Charity Commission for UK and Wales (2020) Memorial Gates Trust. See https://register-of-charities.charitycommission.gov.uk/ (accessed 25 October 2020).

Crang, M. and Tolia-Kelly, P. (2010) Nation, race and affect: Senses and sensibilities at national heritage sites. *Environment and Planning A* 42 (10), 2315–2331.

Dale, K. (2005) Building a social materiality: Spatial and embodied politics in organizational control. *Organization* 12 (5), 649–678.

Donovan, T. (2005) Chattri Memorial Service – a more in depth history. See http://www.chattri.com/index.php?A_More_In_Depth_History:Part_IV (accessed 8 October 2020).

Drozdzewski, D., Waterton, E. and Sumartojo, S. (2019) Cultural memory and identity in the context of war: Experiential, place-based and political concerns. *International Review of the Red Cross* 101 (910), 251–272.

Drozdzewski, D., De Nardi, S. and Waterton, E. (eds) (2016) *Memory, Place and Identity: Commemoration and Remembrance of War and Conflict*. New York: Routledge.

Fairclough, N. (2003) *Analysing Discourse: Text Analysis for Social Research*. London: Routledge.

Flather, Baroness S. (2008) Contribution, House of Lords, 19 June 2008. Hansard: Parliament UK. See https://hansard.parliament.uk/Lords/2008-06-19/debates/08061967000002/details#contribution-08061967000184 (accessed 25 October 2020).

Halbwachs, M. (1992) *On Collective Memory*. Chicago: University of Chicago Press.

Hallam, E. and Hockey, J. (2020) *Death, Memory and Material Culture*. Abingdon: Routledge.

Harvey, D.C. (2017) Critical heritage debates and the commemoration of the First World War: Productive nostalgia and discourses of respectful reverence during the centenary. In *Heritage in Action* (pp. 107–120). Cham: Springer.

Herbert, J. (2012) The British Ugandan Asian diaspora: Multiple and contested belongings. *Global Networks* 12 (3), 296–313.

Hyson, S. and Lester, A. (2012) British India on trial: Brighton military hospitals and the politics of Empire in World War I. *Journal of Historical Geography* 38 (1), 18–34.

Ibarra-Colado, E. (2006) Organization studies and epistemic coloniality in Latin America: Thinking otherness from the margins. *Organization* 13 (4), 463–488.

Institute of Race Relations (2020) Ethnicity and religion statistics. Online. See https://irr.org.uk/research/statistics/ethnicity-and-religion/ (accessed 30 January 2022).

Isin, E.F. (2008) Theorising acts of citizenship. In E.F. Isin and G. Nielsen (eds) *Acts of Citizenship* (pp. 15–43). London: Zed Books.

King, A. (2014) *Memorials of the Great War in Britain: The Symbolism and Politics of Remembrance*. Oxford: Berg.

Lawson, P. (2014) *The East India Company: A History*. New York: Routledge.

Lefebvre, H. (1991) *The Production of Space*. Oxford: Blackwell.

Marquez, X. (2012) Spaces of appearance and spaces of surveillance. *Polity* 44 (1), 6–31.

McIlvenny, P. and Noy, C. (2011) Multimodal discourse in mediated spaces. *Social Semiotics* 21 (2), 147–154.

Miller, E., Little, E. and High, S. (2017) *Going Public: The Art of Participatory Practice*. Vancouver: UBC Press

Ndletyana, M. and Webb, D.A. (2017) Social divisions carved in stone or cenotaphs to a new identity? Policy for memorials, monuments and statues in a democratic South Africa. *International Journal of Heritage Studies* 23 (2), 97–110.

Nora, P. (1989) Between memory and history: les lieux de mémoire. *Representations* 26, 6–25.

Omissi, D. (1994) *The Sepoy and the Raj: The Indian Army, 1860–1940*. Cham: Springer.

O'Shea, T. (2020) *The Light of Day*. Bristol: RRB Photobooks.

Osborne, B.S. (2001) Landscapes, memory, monuments, and commemoration: Putting identity in its place. *Canadian Ethnic Studies* 33 (3), 39–77.

Pink, S. (2013) *Doing Visual Ethnography*. London: Sage.

Rajagopalan, M. (2012) From colonial memorial to national monument: The case of the Kashmiri Gate, Delhi. In M. Rajagopalan and M. Desai (eds) *Colonial Frames, Nationalist Histories: Imperial Legacies, Architecture and Modernity* (pp. 73–101). Farnham. Ashgate Publishing.

Said, E.W. (1978) *Orientalism*. New York: Pantheon Books.

Stevens, Q. (2015) Master planning public memorials: An historical comparison of Washington, Ottawa and Canberra. *Planning Perspectives* 30 (1), 39–66.

Smyth, H. (2019) Identity and memory at First World War British imperial memorials on the Western Front. In F. Jacob and K. Pearl (eds) *War and Memorials* (pp. 157–187). Verlag Ferdinand Schöningh.

Somerville, W. and Dhudwar, A. (2010) Indian migration to the United Kingdom. Working Paper No. 21, National Institute for Economic and Social Research, UK.

Thrift, N. (2008) *Non-Representational Theories*. Abingdon: Routledge.

Uche, C. (2017) The British Government, Idi Amin and The Expulsion of British Asians From Uganda. *Interventions* 19 (6), 818–836.

Visram, R. (1986) *Ayahs, Lascars and Princes: Indians in Britain 1700–1947*. London: Pluto Press.

Waterton, E. (2005) Whose sense of place? Reconciling archaeological perspectives with community values: Cultural landscapes in England. *International Journal of Heritage Studies* 11 (4), 309–325.

Waterton, E. (2012) Landscape and non-representational theories. In P. Howard, I. Thompson and E. Waterton (eds) *The Routledge Companion to Landscape Studies* (pp 66–75). Abingdon: Routledge.

Wilson, R. (2013) *Cultural Heritage of the Great War in Britain*. Farnham: Ashgate Publishing.

10 Tracing the Graphic Heritage of Hackney's Migrant Communities through Food

Alison Barnes

Introduction

The borough of Hackney's position within the East End of London, and its proximity to the docks, means that migrants have been settling there since the 18th century. The borough can be described as 'super-diverse' (Vertovec, 2007) with several well-established, large communities of migrants who settled in Hackney in the 1900s having been joined by many more recent arrivals from across the world. These newer arrivals bring with them not only diversity in terms of their country of origin, but also language, religion, migration channels and immigration status, gender, and socioeconomic status (Vertovec, 2007). This chapter focuses primarily on diversity in relation to country of origin, ethnicity and language and outlines how, as part of the process of negotiating a sense of belonging and identity, food's 'graphic heritage' (Harland & Xu, 2021) plays a critical part in facilitating the navigation of a transnational and 'translocal' space (Brickell & Datta, 2011), connecting migrants with notions of 'home' in the material present and a remembered or imagined sense of 'home' elsewhere in the past.

The term 'graphic heritage' defines any object 'through which people experience and are informed about urban heritage in graphic form' (Harland & Xu, 2021: 19). Such a broad definition can therefore be extended to contexts beyond formally managed and designed heritage sites and to both high and popular culture. Graphic heritage is related to the concept of linguistic landscapes; however, linguistic landscape studies tend to focus primarily on the text used on signs within public and commercial space. Although useful for exploring how language impacts on people's sense of identity and experience of place, this approach does not engage with the diverse modes of visual communication that are regularly used within the urban environment – often incorporating the use of specifically chosen or designed letterforms, colour, images, icons or symbols. This chapter interrogates the design and use of these graphic heritage elements and, in the context of migration research, is therefore able to bring a further nuanced understanding of ways communities reflect their differing heritages in their making of place. In this study, the concept has been applied to the visual language of the streetscape, with a particular focus on food.

Food and the practices surrounding its preparation and consumption are rich in tradition and often inextricably linked to place. Since 2008, under the intangible cultural heritage programme, UNESCO has defined and safeguarded a range of food and food-related practices that are linked to specific countries and regions, connecting to a core culture. Many of these listings – for example Turkish coffee, Qvevri wine from Georgia or Korean kimchi – will be encountered in contexts that incorporate elements of graphic communication. This will include the use of traditional patterns or colours on dishes; packaging, branding and advertising; or signage. Such graphic heritage is clearly part of the experience of this 'consumption', yet graphic design is often overlooked in relation to heritage (Harland *et al.*, 2019: 5).

Food is one of the key ways in which diasporic communities maintain a sense of identity and links with 'home' and differentiate themselves from other communities within the area they have relocated to. In a diverse borough like Hackney, the graphic heritage associated with food from particular communities offers an opportunity to facilitate a broader, more inclusive understanding of heritage that goes beyond the 'Authorised Heritage Discourse' (Smith, 2006). Viewed through a critical heritage studies lens, food's graphic heritage is implicit in the creation of everyday heritage spaces (Muzaini & Minca, 2018) that are very different from the more usually memorialised monumental sites and buildings. Here, heritage is not simply something to be assessed technically by experts and decreed as conforming to a set of assessment criteria; it emerges in place through practice and is fundamental to a sense of identity and belonging.

The research that forms the basis of this chapter was undertaken along the three-mile stretch of the A10, which bisects Hackney. Running from its Southern-most tip to its Northern-most it is home to a large number of food-related establishments. This part of the A10 is made up of several different roads, each passing through a different area of

Hackney: Kingsland Road in Shoreditch, Kingsland High Street in Dalston and the eponymously named Stoke Newington High Street and Stamford Hill. An initial mapping of the commercial premises along the roads revealed over 150 food-related businesses, many of which represented the different migrant communities who have made their home within the borough. Photography was used to gather a body of visual ethnographic material of the exterior signage of these businesses. The visual analysis of this material enabled the identification of a range of multimodal aspects of food's graphic heritage in Hackney – colour, symbol, typography, letterforms and language – which function as visual codes for the local communities.

This chapter highlights examples of these multimodal elements, showing how the visual language of food's graphic heritage offers a way for migrant communities to be seen and 'heard' within the contemporary urban streetscape. However, the transient nature of the high street and planning decisions can impact on this type of graphic heritage. Formal heritage listing processes also focus on criteria that may preclude much of this material being considered as heritage. Such graphic heritage is rarely remembered or treasured and is, therefore, unable to fully engage in the dialogue it might, both within and beyond the wider local communities. Together, these issues impact on the difficulties migrant heritage making practices have in this context; and local councils or visitors will usually just see this as a 'vibrant addition' to an area rather than part of its core heritage.

The London Borough of Hackney

Hackney is situated in the East End of London and, having been vilified in 2006 as the UK's worst place to live by the Channel 4 programme *The Best and Worst Places to Live in Britain* due to the levels of pollution and crime, the borough is now seen as one of the 'coolest' places to live in London. Property prices and rents have risen dramatically, and gentrification continues to sweep through the borough. Disused industrial buildings that once housed artists are being redeveloped as luxury apartments and mainstream brands are moving into spaces previously tenanted by independent shops. Yet, in 2019, Hackney still ranked as one of the top ten deprived authorities within England (Domman, 2019). These polarised narratives of 'worst' or 'coolest' are clearly the product of mainstream, largely white British discourse. They oversimplify Hackney – as they would any place – and the borough remains more complex and diverse than this.

Hackney is home to approximately 280,000 people. The 2011 census reveals the largest ethnic groups as: 36.2% white British; 23.1% black African, Caribbean, or black British; 18.5% other white; 6.4% mixed/ multiple ethnic groups; and, 6.4% Indian, Pakistani or Bangladeshi or British Asian. The borough therefore has a smaller white British population than either London (44.9%) or England as a whole (79.8%). Conversely, it has a larger Black population than both London (13.3%) and England (3.4%) (LB Hackney Policy and Insights Team, 2020: 9). While offering a sense of the population differences in Hackney as compared to elsewhere, categories used for figures such as these have a tendency to hide the borough's more nuanced heterogeneity (Agyemang et al., 2005: 1015) and several diasporic communities well established within Hackney are not obviously visible within these statistics. For example, in the 1920s, the Charedi orthodox Jewish community began arriving in the borough and expanded greatly prior to, and during, the second world war, now forming approximately 7% of the borough's population; a large Turkish community began to emerge in the 1930s with the arrival of commonwealth citizens, expanding further in the 1970s and 1980s following the arrival of economic and political migrants; also, in the late 1980s and early 1990s many Kurds fled persecution in Turkey, Iran and Iraq forming a well-established community (Hackney Council, 2020a). The Caribbean population in Hackney is diverse, and has grown to sizeable numbers since the 1960s and 1970s – now making up 7.8% of the borough's residents, coming from countries such as Antigua, Jamaica, St Lucia, Dominica and, more recently, Monteserrat; the Vietnamese community was established in the mid 1970s through a planned re-settlement scheme; a large African community from countries such as Nigeria, Ghana, Congo, Senegal, Sierra Leone and Uganda forms 11.4% of the borough's population, most of whom migrated in the 1960s and 1980s; and approximately 6.4% of the borough's residents form a large South Asian community, who began arriving in the 1950s and 1960s, the largest groups of which are originally from India and East Pakistan (now Bangladesh). More recently, large communities of those moving to the UK from Eastern Europe to seek work have become established, with the Polish community the largest of these (Hackney Council, 2020b).

Many members of these communities migrated to the UK due to economic hardship, political upheaval, unrest or natural disasters. As part of the process of settling into life in Hackney they have to negotiate their often-complicated relationship with shifting perceptions of 'home' and a sense of belonging (for further reading see Wessendorf, 2010, 2014). The concept of 'home' is often conflated with ideas of safety and security, but for many migrants this unlikely to be the case – their decision to depart may have been traumatic or they may have been uprooted without their consent. For diasporic communities, access to familiar food plays a role in this negotiation; it provides a visible community presence within unfamiliar surroundings and offers a connection to homelands that have been left behind – even if this connection is often complicated by the circumstances of their departure.

Food Practices, Migration, Identity and Belonging

This description of Hackney by Joanna Zawieja captures a sense of the diversity of the borough through the myriad flavours and ingredients available within its shops, restaurants and cafés:

> In a straight line from north to south one smell follows another. Fried chicken, sweet potatoes, saltfish pie, banana cake. Spring rolls, lemon grass, soy sauce, fish sauce. Cumin, ginger, dal, coriander, cinnamon, saffron. Lamb, yoghurt, sesame, mint, hummus, thyme. (Zawieja, 2009: 141)

Our relationship with food is closely linked to our identity and for those who have migrated to a new country, food is central to both maintaining and signifying one's ethnic identity. It enables a connection to others from the same diasporic community (Vallianatos & Raine, 2008: 356) and, conversely, marks out difference between those from other communities (Abbots, 2016: 115). Much has been written about the act of eating and the process of remembering, with food offering an opportunity for an act of remembrance (Sutton, 2001) and providing a conduit to a time and place where, for diasporic communities, their relationship with place – and thus their lives – were not fragmented (Holtzman, 2006: 367).[1] Our food preferences and eating habits are instilled at an early age, with close ties to family, the social dimensions of eating and emotion all interlinked (Lupton, 1996: 37). Food, therefore, has the ability to connect across time and place and, for migrants, is one of the primary ways to maintain a connection to 'home' (Abbots, 2016: 115) and family and friends that have been left behind (Vallianatos & Raine, 2008: 356).

The connection to one's diasporic community and home is not only invoked through the act of eating – the everyday practices of food shopping and visiting cafés and restaurants are also important and one of the inevitable developments in the migration process is the establishment of grocery shops and restaurants (Tuomainen, 2009: 528). These businesses provide further opportunities for the types of connection and differentiation referred to above and create spaces where the global and local flows of people and objects intersect. Such spaces are central to the interrelationship between the material site of 'home' in the present and the remembered and reimagined site of 'home' in the past – they are 'social spaces' in which migrants 'might forge identity and community' (Mankekar, 2002: 88). For future generations these spaces also enable the development of a sense of place for somewhere they have perhaps never visited and have only been told stories about.

For migrants, the process of developing a sense of home, and therefore a sense of belonging, demands a continual readaptation and readjustment to new and changing realities (Marcu, 2014: 327). Thus, not only do grocery stores run by migrants play an important role in offering the relevant diasporic community access to ingredients that are specific to their traditional cuisine, such stores can also reduce the anxiety of migrating to and settling in an unfamiliar place (Vallianatos & Raine, 2008: 365). The experience of shopping in a grocery store is an embodied, multisensorial one that includes the smells and sounds, the visual display of the products, the packaging, branding and advertising of these and the decoration and signage both inside and out. These elements act as 'cultural mnemonics' (Mankekar, 2002: 86), coming together to create a familiarity which essentially transports migrants back 'home' (Abbots, 2016: 119). The memories triggered will be personal to each visitor as the selective remembering and forgetting involved in the construction of the past is inevitably informed by one's particular experience of 'home' and the circumstances in which it was left behind.

Migrants inevitably have to '(re)construct identities that cut across fixed notions of belonging' (Marcu, 2014: 331). Grocery shops and restaurants don't just provide tangible connections to a 'home' that has been left behind, therefore; they also provide an everyday, embodied way of negotiating 'home' in the present, developing a sense of belonging in a new neighbourhood and facilitating a local–local connection (Brickell & Datta, 2011: 5).

Food, Graphic Heritage and Place

In the context of a superdiverse borough like Hackney, the ethnic diversity of the communities is clearly represented within the 'visual signscape' (Hall & Datta, 2010) and in this context, graphic heritage is one of many elements that come together to construct a local narrative that enables the development of a sense of place and belonging. In urban contexts all over the world, such graphic heritage is a familiar sight, more often than not, evidencing both transnational and translocal connections. For example, sociologist Amanda Wise describes the main shopping street in Ashfield, Sydney, as having changed dramatically through the area's growing community of mainland Chinese people who have arrived since the mid 1990s and now own or run 85% of the businesses along the street. A large proportion of the premises feature 'Chinese language and shopping aesthetics' and have 'significantly reconfigured the aesthetic and material character of Ashfield's urban landscape' (Wise, 2011: 93–94). It is clear that these place-making practices are 'creating and reproducing translocal neighbourhoods' that tie Ashfield and Shanghai (and, more broadly, China) together (Wise, 2011: 95). Wise cites this as visual evidence that the diasporic community have been able to flourish within Ashfield (Wise, 2011: 96) and have been empowered to use this signage as part of their 'homebuilding practices' (Hage, 1997). However, as we will see below in relation to Walthamstow in East London, local planning laws may mean that this is not always the case. Wise also notes that such signage is contentious and can cause 'localised displacements' for the white Anglo-Saxon residents who have lived in Ashfield for many decades (Wise, 2011: 96). Unlike Ashfield, in which the businesses in the main street are run predominantly by one migrant community, the section of the A10 that runs through Hackney reveals its multiplicitous translocal connections via the diversity of the graphic heritage evident within the streetscape. Thus, the polarisation of 'us' and 'them' is perhaps not so evident, and the shops along the stretch of the road reflect a 'complex intermingling of a multitude of local worlds' (Hall & Datta, 2010: 71).

Graphic heritage and the construction of place

External shop signs that relate to a particular language community, like those in Ashfield, are part of the 'linguistic landscape' of a place and define and delineate the 'territorial limits' of language groups (Landry & Bourhis, 1997: 25). They are also part of the 'semiotic landscape' of the city – a public space that incorporates 'visible inscription made through deliberate human intervention and meaning making' (Jaworski & Thurlow, 2010: 2). Therefore, the cumulative effect of the multitude of such signs imbues a place with specific social meanings (Papen, 2015: 5) and constructs a visual identity within a place (Patch, 2004: 174) through the use of graphic heritage elements. Adopting a multimodal approach to the discussion of graphic heritage enables the inclusion of elements beyond language, such as colour, symbols, lettering and typography, that play a role in the construction of cultural and symbolic meaning.

Graphic heritage plays a role in the 'discursive construction of place' (Jaworski & Thurlow, 2010: 1) and many disciplines have encountered a 'spatial turn' in recent years (Hubbard & Kitchin, 2011: 2), with place central to discussions of heritage, identity and belonging. Place can be defined in three fundamental, interlinked ways: location; locale – which differs from location in that it relates not to coordinates, but to the material, visual form of a place; and a 'sense of place' – an understanding that every place is unique (Agnew, 2005). A sense of place connects to ideas of belonging and participation (Agnew, 2005: 89) and it further confirms the idea that people and place are reciprocally constructed and inextricably linked. However, this contemporary understanding of a sense of place should not be confused with the idea that it is possible to define a unique spirit of place, or 'genius loci'. Place is inevitably experienced in different ways by different people. Assuming a 'universal subjectivity' in place, therefore, ultimately leads to a defining meta narrative, which, in turn, results in the voice of more marginalised communities being overlooked and a lack of critical engagement with the inequalities relating to class or ethnicity, for example, that are often evident within place (Holloway & Hubbard, 2001: 112–3).

Following the development of a global economy, discussions of place focused on the global connections between places rather than their differences (Castree, 2003: 158–9) and this led some academics to suggest that 'non-places' (Augé, 1995) were becoming prevalent and that 'placelessness' was a danger of this homogenisation (Relph, 1976). However, Doreen Massey's conception of place enables us to connect the local and global, allowing us to view place as both interconnected and unique (Massey, 1994: 51). It is the way the global networks and flows intersect and interact locally that results in the particularity of place. As we will see below, food's graphic heritage evident within Hackney is clearly representative of this view of place and paints a picture that is familiar across many cities in the world today.

Tracing the Graphic Heritage of Migrant Communities in Hackney through Food

The following sections discuss the key elements identified within food's graphic heritage in Hackney. Individually, and often collectively, these elements speak to the relevant migrant communities. Not restricted to the single mode of language, they incorporate multiple communicative modes that include colour, symbol, typography and letterforms.

Colours and symbols

The exterior of a shop is the first point of contact with a customer and can not only be used to convey information about what might be sold inside and define the business' visual identity, it can also be used symbolically to connect to a shared heritage and mediate one's identity in relation to place (Xu, 2019). Many of the colours being used on businesses along the road reflect a transnational connection that often relates to national flags. For example, Andu Ethiopian Café uses the green, yellow and red of the Ethiopian flag in the three-dimensional letters they have used to create their fascia (see Figure 10.1). The colours follow left to right, in the same order that the flag uses them from top to bottom – VEGAN is green, ETHIOPIAN is yellow and FOOD is red. The words ANDU CAFE sit above this with the colours matching the letterforms below – AND is green, U and C, yellow and AFE, red. From a design perspective this arguably causes some readability issues as the different colours give some words and letters more contrast than others and the name of the café is effectively 'broken' into different sections. However, the design of this sign has not solely been developed with readability in mind, its symbolic meaning is also important. Similarly, many of the Chinese takeaways feature the red and yellow of the Chinese national flag (see Figure 10.1). Not conforming to this pattern are many of the Vietnamese restaurants at the southern end of the road. A large number of these feature various shades of the colours green and yellow – for example, Hanoi Café and Sông Quê (see Figure 10.1). Given the Vietnamese flag is red and yellow there is clearly not an obvious transnational connection here with colour but it positions the businesses as visually distinct from the red and yellow of the Chinese takeaways along the road. It seems to have been adopted as something of an unofficial local branding strategy with which to give this stretch of the road a 'place identity' (Xu, 2019: 613) and differentiate and recognise the Vietnamese heritage that is prevalent here.

Transnational connections are also evidenced with national flags featuring regularly on fascias, signs and window graphics. For example, Andu café has a small sign facing oncoming pedestrians featuring the Ethiopian flag; a Polish store includes the red and white national coat of arms that is more often seen on the national flag when it's used abroad; and this freestanding pavement sign for a grocery store specialising in Portuguese and Brazilian products features the relevant flags (see Figure 10.1). The meaning of such symbols is culturally learned, so for some, the Ethiopian flag will be a powerful symbol of belonging, for others it may well be confused with other flags using the same three colours. Other

Figure 10.1 Use of colour and symbols on shop fronts in Hackney (images author's own)

culturally important symbols can also be found along the street, for example, the Roti Stop shop fascia includes the crest of the West Indies cricket team which depicts a palm tree and set of stumps on an 'island' and the sun (see Figure 10.1). This is a symbol that speaks to a particular audience that, although beyond the borders of a single nation, reflects a sporting heritage key to many whose roots are in the Caribbean islands.

'Badges' that link particular food production and preparation procedures to religious traditions are also evident. The halal symbol is one example present on high streets up and down the UK, but more particular to Hackney's heritage are the badges found on some of the shops in Stamford Hill that serve the orthodox Charedi Jewish community (see Figure 10.1). Such symbols will be recognised as confirming the food has been deemed Kosher by the Kashrut authority that confirms the application of dietary laws relating to food preparation. In a similar way that access to familiar products reduces the anxiety of recently arrived migrant (Vallianatos & Raine, 2008: 365), this badge offers reassurance to a more established community that their cultural practices are recognised as part of place. Finally, logos relating to specific brands and products are also used on fascia and window graphics to connect customers with foodstuffs that connect to a sense of 'home' for them. For example, the fascia that uses the Jumbo logomark connects customers with a stock cube brand launched in Africa over 40 years ago – with the tagline of 'Proudly African' – that is a popular ingredient in home cooking (see Figure 10.1).

Typography, letterforms and language

Grocery stores, cafés and restaurants inevitably use written language in their signage. This might encompass anything from the name of the premises, information relating to products, or opening and closing times. The signs themselves may also vary from those professionally designed and produced to those of a 'DIY' nature. However, one thing remains consistent; written signs all feature typography of some sort. Typography gives visual form to language and in doing so, renders the text a 'semiotic object, rather than a mere physical entity' (Mermoz, 2002: 287; see also Van Leeuwen, 2006: 144). Thus, the typographic text is not only a vehicle for the delivery of information, it also provides further opportunities for the making of meaning at a more symbolic level and the forging of trans-national connections. In the examples that follow this happens in two different ways. Firstly, the use of a particular non-English language and/or non-Latin script is likely to include some letterforms that are specific to that language and therefore simultaneously mark out similarity and difference between those who can read this language and those who can't. This is important as seeing one's own language represented within the urban environment is also likely to impact positively on one's sense of belonging and social identity (Landry & Bourhis, 1997: 27). Secondly, specific typefaces can be chosen to evoke a particular time, place or identity for potential customers.

Along the A10, a variety of examples of the first category are evident. The two Turkish and Polish examples shown here incorporate letterforms that use a specific set of diacritics that are not used within the English alphabet (see Figure 10.2). Examples of different scripts include Hebrew, which is prevalent in the Stamford Hill stretch of the road and seen here in the badge that confirm products are Kosher, and the Amharic script used in the hand-made sign for the sale of chat at Andu Café (see Figure 10.2). With this sign, it is not only the letterforms that speak to a specific community. Khat, or chat as it is written in English here, is an evergreen tree that grows in Ethiopia, Somalia and Yemen. It has grown

Figure 10.2 Language, lettering and naming on shop fronts in Hackney (images author's own)

and chewed for hundreds of years 'due to its psychostimulant effects' (Silva *et al.*, 2022: 1). At Andu, the leaves have been shipped from East Africa so lose some of their potency during the journey. However, there were still several men within a space at the rear of the café chewing chat. Its use has become a deeply rooted social tradition in East African countries (Silva *et al.*, 2022: 2) and this tradition has been carried forward in London but comes with a series of well reported issues linking to crime, domestic violence and anti-social behaviour, for example (see Anderson & Carrier, 2011).

The second category is less prevalent, perhaps because the various languages used may already be visually different to the English alphabet. However, one example is Bobby Jo's bar, which, in the word fáilte – which in Gaelic means welcome – not only has a diacritic over the 'a' but is also set in a typeface that evokes the Insular script of the 7th century (see Figure 10.2). A second example are the several Ghanaian shops and cafés just off Kingsland High Street in Ridley Road market which use hand painted signs (see Figure 10.2). Much like the green used by the Vietnamese restaurants, this style creates a particular vernacular style of typography that cumulatively comes to reflect a shared heritage.

Finally, language can also be important when it comes to naming and can connect not only transnationally, but also translocally. For example, Yerushalmi – the name of a now closed takeaway in Stamford Hill – means person from Jerusalem; Miên Tây on Kingsland Road is named after the Western region in Southern Vietnam where the family who own the business are from (Welcome to Mien Tay Restaurants, no date); and Tây Dô – also on Kingsland Road – is named after the city (now known as Cân Thó) where the family are from in Southern Vietnam (About us, no date) (see Figure 10.2). All of the above uses of colour, symbols, typography, lettering and language are examples of business owners exercising 'visual capital' and are therefore a 'carefully crafted negotiation between the structure and agency of everyday livelihoods' (Hall & Datta, 2010: 71). They are also acts of 'communication and interpretation' through which diasporic communities are able to undertake a 'translocal practice of translating' who they are and where they are and of understanding 'who else is here' (Hall & Datta, 2010: 73). Such graphic heritage 'indexes' these communities and allows them to claim places as their own and 'make the foreign and distant, familiar and present' (Jaworski & Thurlow, 2010: 8). Thus, the development of graphic heritage in this context is a key part of a diasporic community's place-making activity. However, as we will see in the next sections, the precarious nature of running a small business and local planning activity can both affect the way in which graphic heritage might impact upon the diasporic community, the broader community within the local neighbourhood, and the wider heritage landscape.

Recognising and Preserving The Graphic Heritage of Migrant Communities

Place is often described as palimpsestuous in nature, with the continual process of change producing a visible material and temporal 'collage' (Edensor, 2012: 448) and the city functioning as an archive 'of the way things used to be' (Dittmer, 2014: 482). Formal heritage sites are recognised and constructed to celebrate and commemorate the past – from war memorials and cemeteries to blue plaques celebrating the famous occupant of a house. However, such interventions inevitably 'fix' meaning in a way that is likely to reflect a particular ideology which effectively erases the 'ambiguity and multiplicity' of the past (Edensor, 2005: 830–1). As heritage and history are inextricably linked, often, the past that is celebrated tends not to be the recent past; therefore, what might traditionally be considered the 'core heritage' of a place usually reflects a time period prior to the arrival of most diasporic communities. When it comes to food in particular, migrant communities are often framed as adding 'vibrancy' to an area, with unfamiliar tastes literally being positioned as adding 'a spice, a seasoning that can liven up the dull dish that is mainstream, white culture' (hooks, 1992: 181). Although this perspective has since been criticised (for example Karaosmanoglu, 2014) – and in a superdiverse borough like Hackney this critique is understandable – in heritage terms, this idea of merely *contributing* to a place rather than *constituting* its core heritage is a small but significant semantic distinction.

Establishing a small, independent food business in the current climate is not easy, and the industry could be described as transient at best, thus aligning with Tim Edensor's (2012) description of place as palimpsest. However, when it comes to graphic heritage, traces of contemporary businesses are often completely erased from the landscape unlike a palimpsest on which visible traces of prior inscriptions remain. One example of this can be seen at 41 Kingsland High Street. Originally opened in 1910, the premises were home to F. Cooke's pie and mash and jellied eel shop – both pie and mash and jellied eels are traditional working-class East end dishes.

The shop was heritage listed in 1991 and it features a range of eel-related elements in the ceramic tiles and brass fittings in the interior and in the mosaic tiled entrance way (see Figure 10.3). In 1996, F. Cooke's ceased trading and Shanghai – a Chinese restaurant with karaoke in the rear dining room – opened in its place (see Figure 10.3). In 2019,

Figure 10.3 Interiors and exteriors of 41 Kingsland High Street (images author's own)

Shanghai closed and Draughts – a board game and cocktails restaurant opened. They not only have pie and mash available on the menu (albeit with gravy, not the traditional liquor), they have also installed a replica of the original F. Cooke shop sign with its ornate gold lettering and green surround (see Figure 10.3). Here, both the heritage listing process and the recent takeover have enabled the continued visual representation of East end traditions and in doing so perhaps reinforced the notion of a core cultural heritage within Hackney. Any trace of Shanghai has simply been erased.[2] One could perhaps argue that the more ephemeral nature of many of the materials or styles used in shopfitting these days inevitably results in a desire to replace rather than preserve. However, there are examples of ephemeral commercial material that are not only valued, but in Hackney's case have been locally listed. Two Victorian 'ghost signs' advertising pianos and fountain pens have achieved this status following a project called 'Love Local Landmarks' run by the Hackney Society and funded by a grant from English Heritage. Painted high up on the flank walls of buildings, these signs are ephemeral in nature, but their position has led to their endurance and continuing visibility. That they have remained in place for so long has led to them being cast as 'history'. They also reference a particular design aesthetic from a particular period that could be said to conform to a Euro centric design canon. Both have been recognised for their 'artistic or aesthetic merit' and their 'historical significance' – two of the criteria required to be met by Hackney Council.

For something to be listed in Hackney it must meet one or more of the criteria which, in addition to 'artistic or aesthetic merit' and 'historical significance', also include 'architectural interest' and 'environmental significance'. That half of these criteria relate to the visual or material form of a listing perhaps leads to a particular canon of design being applied to decisions. Indeed, the Hackney Society who describe their organisation as campaigning locally for the protection of 'Hackney's unique heritage' also promote what they describe as 'the highest standards in design' (The Hackney Society, no date). The obvious questions to be asked here are whose heritage and whose standards? A perspective on whose heritage can be offered by analysing the entries for all locally listed buildings in Hackney in relation to age and type. Of the 492 catalogued entries as of January 3, 2020, 58 were Georgian; 346 Victorian; 27 Edwardian; 36 interwar; 21 post war; 3 post-modern; and 1 mid 1980s (Hackney Council, 2020b). Only three items within this extensive list have a clear connection to Hackney's migrant heritage: Masjid Ramadan, commonly known as Shacklewell Lane Turkish Mosque, which inhabits the former Stoke Newington Synagogue built in 1903; Azizye Turkish Mosque occupying the former Astra cinema built in 1914; and the mural on Dalston Lane that depicts the 1983 Hackney Peace Carnival held after the 1981 race riots and features images of a multicultural carnival procession and references to anti-racism, alongside anti-nuclear, the Campaign for Nuclear Disarmament (CND), anti-war, green, feminist and pro-tolerance references. It is also clear that the overwhelming majority of the listings are from a period in history when most of Hackney's diasporic communities had not yet arrived. Furthermore, the criteria involved in the listing process and the periods in history that are representative of core heritage within Hackney reinforce the 'Authorised Heritage Discourse' (AHD) (Smith, 2006). It seems unlikely that hand painted signs on shops within Ridley Road market will be listed, no matter how meaningful they might be to many residents or the fact that they clearly constitute and demonstrate an aspect of the borough's heritage.

Graphic Heritage, Placemaking and Urban Regeneration

Signage such as Andu's and those in Ridley Road market also face a threat from council-led place-making activities which often look to utilise aspects of graphic heritage such as colour and typography within design schemes that are part of wider regeneration activities. The following example – from Walthamstow, in the borough bordering Hackney to the East – shows how the specific elements used in the scheme focus on a particular era and once again reflect the AHD, thus missing the opportunity to construct a graphic heritage that symbolically communicates to a more diverse audience.

The St James' area was the main gateway into Walthamstow High Street in the late 1800s. By the early 1900s the rapidly expanding shopping street included large stores such as Woolworths, the Co-operative, Marks & Spencer and Sainsbury's as well as a plethora of smaller, independent businesses. The western section of the High St in the St James' area was designated a conservation area in 2002 and in 2017 was the recipient of a £2.9m Townscape Heritage Regeneration Scheme, of which £1.46m was provided by a Heritage Lottery Fund grant. The scheme's focus was to 'preserve and enhance the historic character' and 'restore the fine historic architecture' of the area (Heritage Fund, 2015). According to Zoe Sellers, Head of Area Regeneration (Central) for the London borough of Waltham Forest, alongside works such as repairing and restoring historic architectural features, traffic calming and the installation of bespoke street furniture and public art, a design scheme was developed to 'bring some unity and calm' to the streetscape through 'straightforward and consistent shopfront signage' (Sellers, 2020). To this end, the shop fronts all use the same minimal sans serif typeface and are painted in a range of muted tones (see Figure 10.4). Robin Lee, the scheme architect, confirmed that 'heritage colours' were chosen that 'related to the late Victorian/early Edwardian period'. These reflected a set of 'generally deep muted colours' that were then matched as closely as possible with existing colours from the Farrow and Ball range (see Figure 10.4). The idea was for the selected

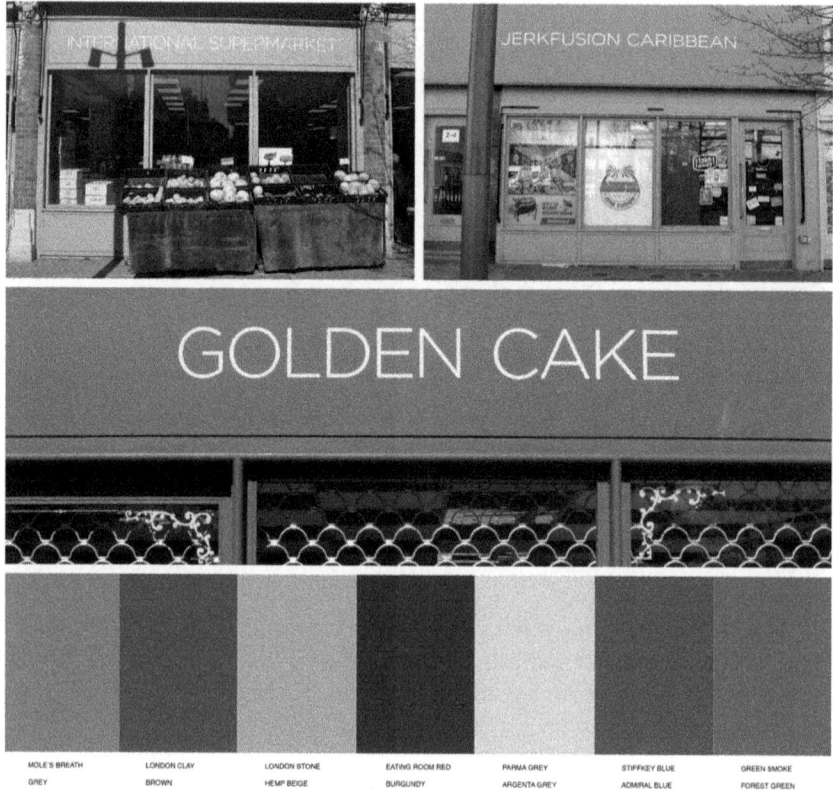

Figure 10.4 Colours and typography used in Walthamstow Heritage Regeneration scheme (images author's own)

complementary colours to 'create a coherent local identity, but one with variation to reflect the range of businesses' (Lee, 2020).

The typeface used is *Gotham*, designed by Tobias Frere-Jones in 2000 for *GQ* magazine and released for public use in 2002. It was inspired by 20th-century architectural signage in New York City and presents a direct, straightforward, 'no frills' visual approach (Hawley, 2019). This minimalist, sans serif typographic style has become ubiquitous in the last decade used for everything from the Obama 'Hope' poster, designed by Shepard Fairey, to the music streaming service Spotify. It was chosen for the scheme as the architects felt it evoked a 'democratic or egalitarian spirit', characteristics which were deemed 'appropriate to the St James Street end of Walthamstow' (Lee, 2020). For Lee, the scheme is not a 'dogmatic' heritage approach as it 'introduces a contemporary flavour through the Farrow and Ball selections' and 'offers something other than a heritage character' through the choice of typography (Lee, 2020). However, once again one might ask the question as to whose dogma? The muted heritage tones of Farrow and Ball and the on-trend sans serif typography are choices that seem to connect most closely with the young, largely white, middle-class population whose numbers are rapidly growing in an area that has an increasing number of pockets of gentrification. They also reflect an era when the vast majority of Walthamstow's diasporic communities were not resident in the borough. So, although the scheme gives the area a sense of unified order, in doing so it removes a sense of identity and individuality for shops and, in some cases, may remove a visual connection with a particular cultural heritage.

Guy Julier's term 'urban designscape' frames how place-identity is produced through material artefacts and designed objects within cities and discusses how regeneration strategies and place-branding activities construct particular narratives and a specific 'aesthetic outlook' within place (Julier, 2005: 871). The regeneration scheme in Walthamstow discussed above has resulted in the construction of an urban designscape. Julier's discussion is largely focused on 'top down' regeneration schemes in which professional designers and architects are seen at the fore – there is no recognition of the type of less 'formal' design interventions discussed prior to this section. The notion of 'scapes' was originally proposed by Arjun Appadurai (1990) to describe how the five dimensions of cultural flow move through the world carrying people, ideas, information, capital and technology. There is a connection here to Massey's (1994) ideas that the particularity of place is formed through the ways such global flows interact in the local context. However, the scheme in Walthamstow ignores the global flows of people through the borough that continue to make it what it is today. In evoking the heyday of the British Empire through its Victorian inspired colour scheme, an attempt is made to construct a 'genius loci' that privileges a particular meta-narrative, invoking notions of a regressive, bounded sense of place (Massey, 1991: 168). In discussing the gentrification of Berlin, Uta Papen notes that there is an impact on the linguistic landscape as a result (Papen, 2012) and, while there was some community engagement with the Walthamstow scheme and business owners were not forced to take part, making meaning through establishing a graphic heritage that makes place translocally involves questions of power (Wise, 2011: 96). A reduction of diversity within the types of graphic heritage represented within the semiotic or linguistic landscape of the neighbourhood implies other cultures are not valued and have less status within the area (Landry

& Bourhis, 1997: 28), and, given this scheme was undertaken by the council, it also suggests that they have less political capital (Landry & Bourhis, 1997: 32).

Conclusion

'Ethnic cuisine' is often 'invoked as an indicator of multicultural society' (Frost, 2011: 231), yet this can gloss over the reality of more complex, fractured or non-existent relationships within communities in areas such as Hackney. Often, these 'vibrant' additions to the high street draw 'food adventurers' (Heldke, 2003) or the 'cultural classes' (May, 1996: 59) who continually seek out the 'exotic' and the 'authentic',[3] often in areas that are in the throes of gentrification. This practice has been described as a type of 'cultural food colonialism' (Heldke, 2003: xv) and 'cultural voyeurism' (May, 1996: 206) and very much positions newer culinary arrivals as 'the other' and as external to the core cultural heritage of a place. However, David Lammy, MP for Tottenham, an area north of Hackney, has suggested that 'food can and should be a crucial resource' that can help to 'build shared cultural experiences and promote intercultural understanding' and be utilised in 'wider strategies for promoting social inclusion' (2002: 42).

Recognising the role graphic heritage plays in this context could help. In an urban context, food is predominantly purchased or consumed within environments that are dense in graphic communication. Food has a capacity to act as a site of memory and meaning and therefore, not only provides us with essential nourishment but plays a central role in the construction of our identity and our relationship with place. These connections can be triggered by food's 'graphic heritage', which functions as a symbolic resource. Yet, currently, formal heritage listings in this context are almost entirely from an era prior to the arrival of many diasporic communities. This, coupled with the transient nature of small businesses and formal place-making activities that 'design out' the varied voices of the superdiverse city, suggests that the agency diasporic communities have to wield their 'visual capital' (Hall & Datta, 2010: 71) is inevitably limited through economic conditions and definitions as to what might be considered 'historically important' or 'aesthetically pleasing'. Adopting a critical heritage approach to the contemporary urban streetscape would facilitate a more progressive sense of place; one that is outward looking, recognising the global and local flows which come together to construct our experience of place. Engaging with the diversity of local communities would enable the range of food's graphic heritage to be recognised as in, and part of, place rather than out of place. This, in turn, would be reflected in a richer urban designscape, one that acknowledges a broader visual language through the use of colours, symbols, lettering and typography that resonate with local residents and enable the graphic heritage of migrant communities to be both seen and heard.

Notes

(1) It should be noted that 'home' is not always a simple binary construction between a single homeland elsewhere and home (in this case) in London. Some migrants will have encountered multiple 'homes' in their lifetime or within their family history. Thus, not only are the trajectories of migrants superdiverse, their food heritages may also be complex.
(2) The shop sign from Shanghai, and some associated ephemera such as menus, are held in the local Hackney Museum. However, no items are on display or can be accessed virtually. So, although someone has thought to preserve this graphic heritage, it is possibly not thought of as interesting or important enough to be made accessible to the public.
(3) Clearly, authenticity is a problematic concept where food in particular is concerned, as cuisines will almost certainly change over time, particularly in contexts where there is or has been some form of intercultural encounter.

References

Abbots, E.-J. (2016) Approaches to food and migration: Rootedness, being and belonging. In J. Klein and J. Watson (eds) *The Handbook of Food and Anthropology* (pp. 115–132). London: Bloomsbury.

About us (no date) http://taydo.co.uk/about-us/ (accessed May 2023).

Agnew, J. (2005) Space: Place. In P. Cloke and R. Johnston (eds) *Spaces of Geographical Thought: Deconstructing Human Geography's Binaries* (pp. 81–96). London: Sage.

Agyemang, C., Bhopal, R. and Bruijnzeels, M. (2005) Negro, Black, Black African, African Caribbean, African American or what? Labelling African origin populations in the health arena in the 21st century. *Journal of Epidemiolgy and Community Health* 59, 1014–118.

Anderson, D.M. and Carrier, N.C.M. (2011) Khat: Social harms and legislation A literature review. *Home Office*, July: Occasional Paper 95.

Appadurai, A. (1990) Disjuncture and difference in the global culture economy. *Theory Culture Society* 7, 295–310.

Augé, M. (1995) *Non-Place: Introduction to an Anthropology of Supermodernity.* London: Verso.

Brickell, K. and Datta, A. (2011) *Translocal Geographies: Spaces, Places, Connections.* Farnham: Ashgate.

Castree, N. (2003) Place connections and boundaries in an interdependent world. In S.L. Holloway, S.P. Rice and G. Valentine (eds) *Key Concepts in Geography* (pp. 252–282). London: Sage.

Dittmer, J. (2014) Geopolitical assemblages and complexity. *Progress in Human Geography* 38 (3), 385–401.

Domman, A-M. (2019) Indices of deprivation 2019: A London Councils member's briefing, London Councils. See https://www.londoncouncils.gov.uk/members-area/member-briefings/local-government-finance/indices-deprivation-2019#:~:text=In%20London%2C%20Hackney%20has%20the,Chelsea%20(ranked%2091st) (accessed November 2020).

Edensor, T. (2005) The ghosts of industrial ruins: Ordering and disordering memory in excessive space. *Environment and Planning D: Society and Space* 23, 829–849.

Edensor, T. (2012) Vital urban materiality and its multiple absences: The building stone of central Manchester. *Cultural Geographies* 20 (4), 447–465.

Frost, N. (2011) Green Curry. *Food, Culture & Society* 14 (2), 225–242.

Hackney Council (2020a) The History of Hackney's Diverse Communities. See https://hackney.gov.uk/hackney-diversity (accessed October 2020).

Hackney Council (2020b) *Hackney's Local List*. See https://drive.google.com/file/d/148kIHdEN0yik2-7jg0KkPY4FYxdcbAzE/view (accessed November 2020).

Hage, G. (1997) At home in the entrails of the west: Multiculturalism, ethnic food and migrant home-building. In J. Langsworth, H. Grace, M. Symonds, G. Hage and L. Johnson (eds) Home/world: space, community and marginality in Sydney's west, 99–153. Sydney: Pluto Press.

Hall, S. and Datta, A. (2010) The translocal street: Shop signs and local multi-culture along the Walworth Road, South London. *City, Culture and Society* 1 (2), 69–77.

Harland, R.G., Du, Q., Xu, J. and Zhang, X. (2019) Defining urban graphic heritage for economic development in the UK and China. *International Association of Societies of Design Research Conference* (Manchester, 2–5 September). See https://iasdr2019.org/uploads/files/Proceedings/li-f-1368-Har-R.pdf (accessed November 2020).

Harland, R.G. and Xu, J. (2021) *Repositioning Graphic Heritage* (online version). Loughborough University. Report. https://doi.org/10.17028/rd.lboro.14273105.v1

Hawley, R. (2019) How this one font took over the world. See https://theoutline.com/post/7356/gotham-font-is-everywhere?zd=1&zi=nrbgxi5i (accessed November 2020).

Heldke, L. (2003) *Exotic Appetites: Ruminations of a Food Adventurer*. London: Routledge.

Heritage Fund (2015) St James Street set for regeneration. See https://www.heritagefund.org.uk/news/st-james-street-set-regeneration (accessed November 2020).

Holloway, L. and Hubbard, P. (2001) *People and Place: The Extraordinary Geographies of Everyday Life*. Harlow: Pearson Education.

Holtzman, J.D. (2006) Food and memory, *Annual Review of Anthropology* 35, 361–378.

hooks, b. (1992) Eating the other. In R. Scapp and B. Seitz (1998) (eds) *Eating Culture* (pp. 181–200). Albany: State University of New York Press.

Hubbard, P. and Kitchin, R. (2011) Introduction: Why key thinkers? In P. Hubbard and R. Kitchin (eds) *Key Thinkers on Space and Place* (2nd edn) (pp. 1–17). London: Sage.

Jaworski, A. and Thurlow, C. (2010) Introducing semiotic landscapes. In A. Jaworski and C. Thurlow (eds) *Semiotic Landscapes: Language, Image, Space* (pp. 1–40). London: Continuum.

Julier, G. (2005) Urban designscapes and the production of aesthetic consent. *Urban Studies* 22 (5/6), 869–887.

Karaosmanoglu, D. (2014) Authenticated spaces: Blogging sensual experiences in Turkish grill restaurants in London. *Space and Culture* 17 (3), 224–238.

Lammy, D. (2002) The spice of life? In J. Holden, L. Howland and D. Stedman Jones (eds) *Foodstuff: Living in an Age of Feast and Famine* (pp. 37–43). London: Demos.

LB Hackney Policy and Insights Team (2020) *A Profile of Hackney, its People and the Place.* See https://drive.google.com/file/d/1JZLZFzNUSO40l7-vCA_dy9Dk08e6jXa_/view (accessed November 2020).

Landry, R. and Bourhis, R.Y. (1997) Linguistic landscape and ethnolinguistic vitality: An empirical study. *Journal of Language and Social Psychology* 16 (1), 23–49.

Lee, R. (2020) Email correspondence, 17 July.

Lupton, D. (1996) *Food, The Body and The Self.* London: Sage.

Mankekar, P. (2002) 'India Shopping': Indian grocery stores and transnational configurations of belonging. *Ethnos* 67 (1), 75–97.

Marcu, S. (2014) Geography of belonging: Nostalgic attachment, transnational home and global mobility among Romanian immigrants in Spain. *Journal of Cultural Geography* 31 (3), 326–345.

Massey, D. (1991) A global sense of place. *Marxism Today*, June, 24–29.

Massey, D. (1994) *Space, Place and Gender.* Minneapolis: University of Minnesota Press.

May, J. (1996) 'A little taste of something more exotic': The imaginative geographies of everyday life. *Geography* 81 (1), 57–64.

Mermoz, G. (2002) On typographic signification…, *Mind the Map: Third International Conference on Design History & Design Studies*, Istanbul, Turkey, 9–12 July, pp. 287–290.

Muzaini, H. and Minca, C. (2018) Rethinking heritage, but 'from below'. In H. Muzaini and C. Minca (eds) *After Heritage: Critical Perspectives on Heritage from Below* (pp. 1–21). Cheltenham: Edward Elgar Publishing.

Papen, U. (2012) Commercial discourses, gentrification and citizens' protest: The linguistic landscape of Prenzlauer Berg, Berlin. *Journal of Sociolinguistics* 16 (1), 56–81.

Papen, U. (2015) Signs in cities: The discursive production and commodification of urban spaces. *Sociolinguistic Studies* 9 (1), 1–26.

Patch, J. (2004) The embedded landscape of gentrification. *Visual Studies* 19 (2), 169–186.

Relph, E. (1976) *Place and Placelessness.* London: Pion.

Sellers, Z. (2020) Email correspondence, 21 July.

Silva, B., Soares, J., Rocha-Pereira, C., Mlad'enka, P. and Remião, F. on behalf of The OEMONOM Researchers (2022) Khat, a Cultural Chewing Drug: A Toxicokinetic and Toxicodynamic Summary. *Toxins* 14, 71. https://doi.org/10.3390/ toxins14020071

Smith, L. (2006) *Uses of Heritage.* Abingdon: Routledge.

Sutton, D. (2001) *Remembrance of Repasts: An Anthropology of Food and Memory.* London: Berg.

The Hackney Society (no date) *The Hackney Society.* See http://www.hackneysociety. org/ (accessed November 2020).

Tuomainen, H.M. (2009) Ethnic identity, (post)colonialism and foodways. *Food, Culture & Society* 12 (4), 525–554.

Vallianatos, H. and Raine, K. (2008) Consuming food and constructing identities among Arabic and South Asian immigrant women. *Food, Culture & Society* 11 (3), 355–373.

Van Leeuwen, T. (2006) Towards a semiotics of typography. *Information Design Journal* 14 (2), 139–155.

Vertovec, S. (2007) Super-diversity and its implications. *Ethnic and Racial Studies* 30 (6), 1024–1054.

Welcome to Mien Tay Restaurants (no date) See https://mientay.co.uk/ (accessed May 2023).

Wessendorf, S. (2010) Commonplace diversity: Social interactions in a super-diverse context. *MMG Working Paper* (pp. 10–11). See https://pure.mpg.de/rest/items/item_1126645/component/file_2057868/content (accessed December 2021).

Wessendorf, S. (2014) 'Being open, but sometimes closed'. Conviviality in a super-diverse London neighbourhood. *European Journal of Cultural Studies* 17 (4), 392–405.

Wise, A. (2011) 'You wouldn't know what's in there would you?' Homeliness and 'Foreign' Signs in Ashfield, Sydney. In K. Brickell and A. Datta (eds) *Translocal Geographies: Spaces, Places, Connections* (pp. 93–108). Farnham: Ashgate.

Xu, J. (2019) Colour in urban places: A case study of Leicester City Football Club blue. *Colour Research and Application* 44, 613–621.

Zawieja, J. (2009) Imagine a house: Transcript. In D. Naik and T. Oldfield (eds) *Critical Cities: Ideas, Knowledge and Agitation from Emerging Urbanists: Volume 1* (pp. 138–145). London: Myrdle Court Press.

11 Contesting Everyday (Food) Heritage in London's Chinatown

Xiao Ma

Introduction

London's Chinatown is not an officially designated World Heritage Site or a UK national heritage site, but it is a place to which many London residents, irrespective of their ethnicity, age, socioeconomic status and personal histories, are symbolically attached through their everyday bodily interactions with the urban space. Informed by the notion of 'everyday heritage' (Mosler, 2019), this study conceptualises London's Chinatown as a 'lived everyday heritage space'. This chapter aims to highlight individual agency in the making of Chinatown as a meaningful space, demonstrate the place's cultural complexities and challenge the homogenising portrait of Chinatown as a bounded place defined by fixed ethnic difference.

In critical heritage studies, the concept of heritage has been re-theorised as a social and cultural practice of meaning-making rather than a thing frozen in material form (Harvey, 2001; Smith, 2006; Urry, 1995). Many scholars argue that the idea of human agency is central to understanding how heritage is used by individuals or groups to address their needs and concerns of the present (Harvey, 2001; Macdonald, 2013; Smith, 2020). While three scales of the practice of heritage-making have been recognised, namely international and national institution-led, sub-national collective-led and individual-led (Smith, 2020), this research focuses on the heritage-making actions taken by individuals, particularly through everyday activities, in relation to London's Chinatown, in order to examine how it is symbolically experienced by different inhabitants of London in diverse ways.

Lefebvre's (1991) idea of the production of social space as perceived space (enduring materials in space), conceived space (thoughts about space) and lived space (symbolically lived realities), has often been used to examine the politics of contested urban spaces in the context of negotiating plural heritages/meanings. Lefebvre (1991) argues that the three spatial facets are not separate; rather, they produce a simultaneous space through dialectical interrelations. Urban spaces, such as London's Chinatown, are not simply locations where people 'do things', but rather they are always being constituted, re-constituted and contested by the actions taken by people in everyday life. Mosler (2019) has examined the 'everyday' character of urban experience, what Lefebvre (1991) calls 'lived space', from the perspective of heritage. Highlighting the nature of urban heritage as a lived experience, Mosler (2019) conceptualises the idea of 'everyday heritage' to differentiate the officially designated heritage, for example, in the form of a UNESCO World Heritage Site, and the 'personal heritage' (Pendlebury, 2009) that exists as part of the urban landscapes of everyday life. Giombini (2020: 54) further argues that this concept signifies 'the complex sum of practices, activities, and meanings by which communities quotidianly use all types of local heritage to strengthen their connection to particular places and each other'.

Drawing upon the ideas discussed above, this research studies London's Chinatown as a 'lived everyday heritage space', continuously created and recreated by London's inhabitants. Informed by criticism of the problematic 'ethnicity-centred epistemology' applied in migration studies (Dahinden, 2016) and the recent anti-essentialist conceptualisation of Chinatown (Anderson et al., 2019), I will explore the embodied acts of everyday heritage-making in Chinatown beyond the simplistic dichotomies of 'Chinese' and 'non-Chinese', 'sameness' and 'difference', 'authenticity' and 'inauthenticity'. Instead of selectively focusing on self-identified Chinese people and Chinese businesses only, this study ethnographically examines how business operators and visitors of diverse backgrounds use and symbolically experience London's Chinatown and reveals both the commonalities and the differences of Londoners' lived experiences of this neighbourhood. Three types of everyday heritage-making practices shaped by London residents' different connections to the area are identified: *everyday operation as heritage, everyday connection as heritage* and *everyday encounter as (non-)heritage*. These personal heritages interact and negotiate with each other in the making of London's Chinatown as an open, plural, hybrid and contested 'everyday heritage space'. At the same time, different layers of time and identities incorporated in the space (Massey, 2005) are being authenticated by different individuals on the ground, engaging and contesting with the 'official' representation of Chinatown conceived by the area's powerful actors.

In the following sections, I will first offer a historical account of the social production of London's Chinatown and present the popularised narratives about the area. I will then introduce my 12-month ethnographic fieldwork in London's Chinatown and discuss the research methods employed. I will subsequently use the life stories of interviewees to structure my analysis of the three categories of everyday heritage-making practices in Chinatown, referred to above, in order to demonstrate the diversity of people's lived experiences. The chapter concludes by arguing that viewing London's Chinatown as a 'lived everyday heritage space' reveals the anti-essentialist, decentred, plural and hybrid narratives about Chinatown, which make it possible to acknowledge the cultural complexities of this central London space.

The Making of Chinatown in London's Soho

London's Chinatown is socially produced by both Chinese and non-Chinese actors in the Soho district but the Chinatown transformation was associated with exotification and self-exotification practices. It is critical to examine the development of Chinatown in the context of Soho's long history of ethnic, cultural and social diversity.

Soho, a central urban space in London, has been a centre of immigrant life since the second half of the 19th century when it became both the residential and business home for many European diasporas (Walkowitz, 2012). The next 50 years saw the cosmopolitan transformation of Soho from 'a dingy, foreign, proletarian quarter into a commodified centre of cultural tourism' (Walkowitz, 2012: 9). During the interwar period, Soho became famous for offering 'restaurants of all nations', including Italian, Greek, Hungarian, Chinese, Spanish and Japanese, and the multi-ethnic entrepreneurs adapted their businesses to accommodate British palates and to meet their travel fantasies (Walkowitz, 2012). After the Second World War, Gerrard Street and its surrounding area in the southern part of Soho were developed into a place dominated by sex businesses and foreign businesses including Italian restaurants, Jewish bakeries and Indian curry houses, etc.

Also after the Second World War, large scale Chinese migration to the UK occurred. In the 1950s, the low commercial rents of Gerrard Street and its surrounding area attracted Chinese immigrants to establish restaurants there (Benton & Gomez, 2008). The majority of the new Chinese entrepreneurs in the area migrated from the New Territories of Hong

Kong, which was one of the greatest sources of Chinese immigration to the UK between the 1950s and the 1970s (Benton & Gomez, 2008). These Cantonese-speaking, former agricultural workers mostly worked in the Chinese catering sector in the UK and this employment pattern was driven by four main factors: the booming Chinese catering trade due to the Chinese culinary gap in the market, low levels of education limiting Chinese immigrants' employment options, their deliberate actions in minimising direct competition with white British people in the mainstream economy, and the Commonwealth Immigrants Act 1962 (Benton & Gomez, 2008; Parker, 1998). This law required prospective entrants to present a British employment voucher when entering Britain. As a result, the law channelled most Chinese immigrants into catering work as it was the most viable employment they could secure at that time.

Between the 1950s and the 1970s, Gerrard Street and its surrounding area witnessed the rapid growth of restaurants and services run by Chinese people alongside other migrant businesses. By the late 1970s, around 40 Chinese businesses, including restaurants, cinemas, bookshops, traditional Chinese medicine shops, barbershops and travel agencies were operating in the area, though the area was not exclusively Chinese (The Making of Chinatown, 2019). Many Chinese people commonly referred to the district simply as 'Soho' in English or '*wong sing* 皇 城' (royal city) in Cantonese as it is close to Buckingham Palace (The Making of Chinatown, 2019). Calling the place 'Chinatown' became more popular among Chinese people from the 1980s. This shift was directly linked to the official designation of the area as 'Chinatown' in 1985, a project developed through a cooperation, for mutual benefits, between Westminster City Council and local Chinese entrepreneurs, represented by the London Chinatown Chinese Association (Christiansen, 2003).

As a 'conceived space' (Lefebvre, 1991), 'Chinatown' was imagined as a place of ethnic difference. The 'Chinatown' makeover, exoticising and self-exoticising the area with the primary aim of attracting tourists (Christiansen, 2003), included building three interpretations of Chinese-style gates,[1] constructing a pavilion, installing a pair of stone lions, putting up bilingual street signs (in English and Chinese) and planting ginkgo trees, etc. In later years, the bilingual name of 'Chinatown' has also appeared in several maps and signs installed in central London to direct visitors to the area (Figure 11.1).[2] The institutionalisation of Chinatown has been seen as 'part of a multicultural agenda which promotes the celebration of difference as a tool of urban regeneration and the management of ethnic relations' (Sales *et al.*, 2011: 227). Barabantseva (2016) argues that the Chinatown-making projects across Britain in the 1980s were

Figure 11.1 An on-street signage map located on Wardour Street that shows London's Chinatown (photo by Xiao Ma, 2022)

based on an essentialised understanding of Chinese ethnicity and culture developed by the British planning system of that time. The development of an area into a Chinatown has also involved silencing other shared histories and identities associated with the place (Barabantseva, 2016).

Today, both the local authority and the corporate world have been continually capitalising on the Chinatown brand and the area has been 'marketed and packaged for consumption through different branding strategies that focus on its cultural representation' (Dang, 2021: 13). Two of the Chinatown association leaders, Christine Yau and Chu-Ting Tang, claimed that Chinatown can showcase 'all the distinctive characteristics of Chinese culture' while Westminster City Council has described it as 'an integral part of what makes this [London] a world class city' (City of Westminster, 2003: 1–3). The area's majority landlord, Shaftesbury Capital PLC (formerly known as Shaftesbury PLC), sells it as a place offering 'the authentic East Asian cuisines' (Chinatown London, no date). Chinatown was described as 'a strong beacon for the Chinese community in the United Kingdom' (Chinese Embassy in the UK, 2019) by former UK Prime Minister, Theresa May. Former Chinese Ambassador to the UK,

Liu Xiaoming, praised the new Chinese-style gate in Chinatown as 'a symbol of China-UK friendship' (Chinese Embassy in the UK, 2016). These claims, whether perceived from 'inside' or 'outside', declare Chinatown's association with the so-called real Chinese culture, the Chinese community, the authentic East Asian food, and the genuine connection to the nation-state, China. These popularised narratives about London's Chinatown convey a sense of cultural authenticity that is not only considered standard, but generally deemed 'culturally sensitive'. However, this normalisation invisibilises the underlying problematics at play. These ideas related to London's Chinatown are constructed by selectively amplifying some layers of time and identity incorporated into the urban space while silencing others, and largely shaped by an essentialised understanding of place, ethnicity, culture and identity.

Today's Chinatown is primarily a commercial district, which is open for people to come to work and visit (Dang, 2021). There are over 150 businesses operating in the designated Chinatown area and the vast majority are in the catering industry.[3] In terms of the cultural background claimed by food businesses themselves through individual brand positioning, around 70% are Chinese (differentiating regional cuisines) and the remaining 30% are other East Asian, Southeast Asian and European cuisines.[4] Workers in the area are ethnically, culturally, linguistically and socially diverse. The majority of Chinatown workers have ancestral ties to China, but they are not a homogeneous group. They or their parents migrated to the UK at different periods of time, for various reasons, and from a wide range of geographical locations, including Hong Kong, Malaysia, Singapore, Vietnam, the Caribbean, India and mainland China. There are also a great number of other racially minoritised people and white (both British and non-British) people working in the Chinatown area. Today's Chinatown is in addition one of the most popular tourist attractions in London, welcoming over 50 million visitors from all backgrounds annually (Shaftesbury PLC, 2019). In Chinatown, 'commonplace diversity' (Wessendorf, 2013) is part of people's everyday encounters.

Unpacking the Cultural Complexities of London's Chinatown through a Heritage Lens

It is not possible for me to explain my ethnographic curiosity in London's Chinatown without talking about my work experience and my location in my own history, ethnicity, culture and identity. I was born and grew up in mainland China and moved to the UK in 2012 to study. Having lived in

London since 2013 and having worked for China Exchange, a Chinatown-based independent charity, since 2016, I am one of the many Londoners who have developed an emotional attachment to Chinatown through everyday encounters. As a Chinatown heritage practitioner, I have witnessed that different histories and identities in the area interact and contrast with each other, which has led me to start conducting doctoral research on London's Chinatown in 2020 to develop a better understanding of this contested space. My liminal position, in-between Chinese Londoner, heritage practitioner, and researcher, has impacted on me in different and complex ways in studying the cultural complexities of London's Chinatown.

This article is based on findings from fieldwork that I carried out as a doctoral researcher over a 12-month period in 2021–2022 in London's Chinatown. My fieldwork included overt observation of two workshops organised by China Exchange as part of the *London Chinatown Food Heritage Trail* project (LCFHT) in 2021, which sparked my interest in researching the 'everyday heritage' of London's Chinatown. The LCFHT project aimed to 'explore the area's food heritage highlighting parts of the neighbourhood that show traditional techniques, contemporary tastes, and ways of expressing ourselves through food and flavours' (China Exchange, 2022). The project involved nine volunteers from diverse backgrounds, who were trained by a food anthropologist to work on documenting, developing and selecting materials for a printed *London Chinatown Food Heritage Trail* map based on their interviews with chefs and entrepreneurs in Chinatown. I was not involved in organising the LCFHT project and the workshops. I observed the two workshops as a PhD researcher after obtaining consent from the workshop leaders and participants. My original plan was to observe the collective heritage-making practices conducted by the volunteer group during the two workshops, but I quickly realised that there was something else shared in the workshops that deserved serious examination – individuals' meaning-making actions in an everyday context. I was struck by the diversity of the volunteers' personal connections to Chinatown and the richness of emotions that these connections evoked during the workshops. It was through the everyday embodied activities in Chinatown, for example, walking, looking, listening, smelling, eating, shopping and meeting friends, that they generated emotional bonds and invested everyday significance to the place. This observation inspired me to explore an under-researched area, namely, what Chinatown is and means to Londoners who work in or visit Chinatown on an everyday basis, and their personal heritage-making activities in relation to food, which became the focus of the research presented in this chapter.

After deciding on the focus of my fieldwork, I conducted data collection by using three interrelated methods, including documentary analysis, participant observation and semi-structured life-story interviews. In total, I formally recruited 15 research participants[5] for this study through my local networks in London's Chinatown and 'snowballing'. The criteria for sampling interview candidates were: diversity in terms of ethnicity, gender, age and migration history, and willingness to share their thoughts and feelings. The research participants include six business operators, six regular visitors and three occasional visitors. These interrelated methods enabled me to capture the embodied, performative, experiential, verbalised and discursive aspects of the meaning-making process through materialised practices.

As a result, this research has identified three different but interrelated types of everyday heritage-making practices shaped by Londoners' different ways of using Chinatown and the different depths of their connections to the area, namely: *everyday operation as heritage*, by which I refer to the materialised practices of meaning-making by business operators in Chinatown that occur in their everyday restaurant operations; *everyday connection as heritage*, by which I refer to the embodied acts of meaning-making that take place during regular visitors' everyday interactions with Chinatown, when their connections to Chinatown are strengthened and new connections may be created; and *everyday encounter as (non-)heritage*, by which I refer to the actions of creating or not creating place attachment by occasional visitors through their everyday encounters in Chinatown. A few encounters in the area may or may not lead to the purposeful investment of symbolic meanings in the space of Chinatown about their identities. In the following sections, I will introduce each of the three everyday heritage-making practices, respectively, to demonstrate how different Londoners symbolically experience London's Chinatown in diverse ways.

Everyday Operation as Heritage

To business operators in London's Chinatown, the area is their workplace and a source of employment. The experiences of business operators demonstrate 'how people and things interact on different scales and in various contexts in the making of "migrant worlds"' (Wang, 2016: 4). Chinatown is a source for them to meet not only economic, but also social and personal needs. They invest personal meanings into their everyday business operating activities, through which they make sense of their migrant, cultural, or social worlds, their place within them and tactically assert their personal voices in the history. In this section, I will use the life stories of five of the six business operators, Eva, Wen, Yue, Yin and Dylan, to discuss the first category of everyday heritage-making practice, *everyday operation as heritage*. I will firstly introduce the different personal and business goals envisioned by different individuals that are shaped by multiple factors including ethnicity, age, socioeconomic status, migration trajectories in family and personal histories, etc. I will then follow this with some discussion. The strongest theme that emerged from the interview data is 'authenticity', although none of my interview questions included the word 'authenticity'. In this section, I will also discuss how different business operators adopted diverse recipe and menu development strategies to achieve personal and business goals, contesting the essentialist idea of Chinatown as an authentic place of ethnic difference constructed by the area's powerful actors.

Different dreams

In 1986, Eva, then in her early 20s, came to London from Malaysia. Her original plan was to study accounting in the UK, but she started working in a restaurant in Chinatown the next year. She describes herself as a gastronome. Feeling homesick for the tastes of Malaysia and her favourite street food, laksa (a spicy noodle soup, available in different variations), she ate at every existing Malaysian restaurant in London at that time but could not find a bowl of laksa to her liking. The disappointment was turned into a business idea. Eva and her husband, who had migrated from Hong Kong, opened a family-run restaurant in Chinatown in the 1990s, offering big and bold flavours hand-picked by Eva:

> Eva: I think, in the UK, if you are hard-working and talented, you can achieve what we want to achieve. Because I think it is full of opportunities here… but if I stayed in Malaysia, I wouldn't be working in the catering industry. There seems to be an unwritten hierarchy of professions in Malaysia. People who received little education would choose restaurant jobs. People who are literate, like me, would be doing white-collar work in offices… Here in the UK, I opened a restaurant because most Chinese people worked in the catering industry at that time.

Listening to Eva, there seems to be a contradiction between her perception of 'opportunities' and the fact that Chinese people concentrated in one industry as a result of a lack of opportunities in other industries. In fact, the Home Affairs Committee estimated that, in 1986, around 90% of Chinese people in Britain worked in the catering industry (Dummett & Lo, 1986).

Wen and Yue, from Fujian province and the northeast of mainland China respectively, arrived in the UK in the late 1990s and found restaurant jobs in London's Chinatown around 2000. Both came to Britain for job opportunities but they had different 'dreams'. For Wen, Chinatown was a source of employment that would enable her to provide for her family; for Yue, Chinatown was the starting point for his future multinational food business:

> Wen: At that time I didn't have a choice. Back in my hometown, because of overpopulation, it was hard to make money. I needed money to pay for my children's education, so we went abroad to earn money in a comparably quicker way. I did it for my children.

> Yue: I think our company's goal is different from many other Chinatown businesses'. Many of them only have one restaurant in Chinatown and their aim perhaps is to make profit for 20 to 30 years. In contrast, we want to become a stock exchange–listed company one day and we aim to open hundreds or thousands of restaurants around the world.

Yin was born in Guangdong province of mainland China and grew up in three countries. She came to the UK to study before launching her 'passion project' in 2017 as an architect–designer–restaurateur, combining her love for food and design. In 2019, Yin opened her second restaurant in London's Chinatown. Reflecting on the changes in the neighbourhood's restaurant landscape, Yin thinks there is a big difference between the older and the younger generations of restaurateurs. Informed by her experiences of living in several white-majority societies over the past two decades, she believes that most early Chinese immigrants established food businesses mainly for survival and created accessible flavours for the majority groups. In contrast, with a financially comfortable background, she feels very privileged to be able to open a restaurant as 'a hobby'. Her determination to reverse the power relations between the ethnic minority food business and the ethnic majority diners shaped her approach to running the start-up:

> Yin: I believe, in Chinatown, a lot of the second-generation business owners or younger-generation business owners, like me, are trying to reinvent Chinese food. It's kind of like a movement…Whatever has been displayed in the design or in the experience that we created, or the food that is on the table, is probably a pure passion project. It's about how I want you to eat my food. It's not about how you think my food should be.

Dylan grew up in Wales and in 2001 he moved to London, 'the best place' in his own words, to look for more career opportunities. Different from Eva, Wen, Yue and Yin, he did not need to cross an international border to come to London and he would tick the box of 'white' when taking part in the national census: 'To be British from my generation is to be multicultural…When I first came to London, I had a meal in Chinatown, everybody does', he recalled, not without a touch of nostalgia. When we met, Dylan had been the manager of a self-branded 'Dutch' pub inside today's Chinatown for nearly 10 years. The pub was established in the late 19th century, predating the history of Chinatown in Soho. As part of the job package, he was provided with a flat to live above the pub. Chinatown is therefore both his workplace and home, but he feels that he is an 'outsider':

> Dylan: I feel like we are part of Chinatown, but we also stand alone, this pub…We celebrate Chinese New Year. It's great. We invite people in, grab some drinks and stuff. You know, we were always right in the thick of it, but we never get invited to any planning meetings…They [London Chinatown Chinese Association] don't really involve us in anything to do with Chinatown. But why would they?

Dylan revealed that he would be interested in getting more involved in Chinatown-related activities if there was an opportunity: 'Pubs are great for communities and they have always been a place where people get together'. However, he is also aware that, as a 'Dutch' pub run by white people, it will be a challenge for them to be seen as part of Chinatown in a meaningful way as it does not fit in with the 'branding strategies' envisioned by the area's more powerful actors, which focus on the cultural representation of Chinese and other East Asian ethnic groups. In the process of 'ethnic boundary management' (Christiansen, 2003) in relation to maintaining the area's branding image as an authentic place of ethnic difference, the 'outside' has been created as part of what constitutes the 'inside'.

These Chinatown business operators shared personal stories of a gastronome (Eva), a parent (Wen), an entrepreneur (Yue), a re-inventor (Yin) and a domestic migrant (Dylan) and how they achieve their different personal goals through capitalising and creating the area's cosmopolitan assets. These business operators' lived experiences and their meaning-making processes in Chinatown cannot be assumed to simply belong to a particular culture defined along ethnic lines alone.

Negotiating authenticity: Adaptation, diversification and innovation

Previous research has shown that the idea of authenticity is at the centre of any discussion related to Chinatowns around the world (Wu et al., 2020). Cohen (1988) argues that the notion of authenticity is socially constructed and negotiated. In his view, authenticity is a projection of opinions, ideologies, contexts and imaginations rather than an innate quality possessed in an object. In the literature on heritage tourism, there has been a shift away from the conceptual investigation into 'authenticity' to a focus on the contested authentication process in recent years (Cohen & Cohen, 2012). However, previous studies have shown that for tourists and heritage users, objective authenticity remains a common reference point as many people prefer the 'true-false continuum' (Chhabra, 2021). 'Authenticity' is a buzzword that sells well in Chinatown, one of the most popular tourist attractions in global London. It is common to see the word 'authentic' in marketing materials created by Chinatown's majority land-lord, Shaftesbury Capital PLC and Chinatown's restaurants (Figure 11.2), including some of the businesses I interviewed. However, it is clear that all the business operators I spoke with have developed different strategies behind the scenes to attract, accommodate and influence customers

Figure 11.2 A restaurant with a sign 'Authentic Chinese' on Gerrard Street, London's Chinatown (photo by Xiao Ma, 2022)

beyond the dichotomy of 'authentic' and 'inauthentic'. They take actions to adapt, diversify and innovate in relation to recipe and menu development and this is shaped by their personal and business aims.

When it comes to creating menus, Eva explained that her menu is a selection of personal favourite dishes with some adaptations in the recipes for practical reasons. Like most business owners in Chinatown, Eva faces the challenge of rapidly increasing operating costs and her every decision in adapting recipes is aimed at sustaining the future of her small restaurant:

> Eva: All the dishes have been simplified, for example, Nasi Lemak. In Malaysia, we sometimes eat Nasi Lemak wrapped in a banana leaf as breakfast, but we won't add in curry sauce. Nasi Lemak usually comes with fried chicken or fish. When we first opened our restaurant, our kitchen was very small, so there was no space for us to fry food. As a solution, we added a dish, Curry Chicken with Steamed Rice, to our menu because we could also use the chicken curry in Nasi Lemak as a substitute.

Twenty years later, Eva's version of Nasi Lemak still comes with chicken curry and it remains popular. She also pointed out that a few dishes on her menu were particularly designed for people who might be less familiar with the flavours popular in Malaysia. It is common for restaurant operators in Chinatown to adapt their recipes and menus by making them more accessible in order to attract and accommodate a broad spectrum of customers. Wen, a senior waitress working for a self-branded 'Cantonese' restaurant, told me that they have two versions of the menu. One menu focuses on some flavour profiles that have proven popular in the UK, for example, sweet and sour, salt and pepper, and black bean sauce. The other menu offers a wider range of flavour profiles, which, in Wen's own words, are more often enjoyed by 'Chinese people'. Indeed the restaurant operators I interviewed often referred to the dichotomy between 'Chinese customers' and 'non-Chinese customers' as shorthand to describe the diversity of their diners in relation to their adaptation strategy; however, they also acknowledged that whether a person likes a certain dish or flavour is not essentially related to the person's ethnicity.

Similar to Eva and Wen, Dylan also applied the strategy of adaptation in the everyday operations of his 'Dutch' pub. Dylan told me that the pub was first run by a Dutch manager in the early 20th century and during the Second World War Dutch resistance exiles frequently met at this pub. Today it is run by a team of Londoners, welcoming diverse visitors to the Chinatown area. Dylan developed his strategy to present the pub's Dutch connection and promote its business in a competitive commercial district:

> Dylan: we serve Dutch and Belgium beers, and British pub food. When there is a big sports event from Holland, we will show them on our screens...A lot of people have asked me, are you from Holland? I think over the last 130 years, maybe there have been only two Dutch managers, but people expect that you are from Holland because it is a Dutch pub. Well, it is a pub with a lot of Dutch history...We recruit people based on their skills rather than their ethnicity.

Different from Eva, Wen and Dylan, Yue's personal and business ambitions go beyond Chinatown. Often referring to the global corporations created by Elon Musk and Jack Ma, Yue passionately explained his international business plans for his 'Sichuan' restaurant group, which is funded by mainland Chinese investors. As a highly motivated entrepreneur, Yue aims to succeed in the commercial world through leading the diversification of Chinese regional cuisines across the UK and the whole world:

> Yue: In Britain, Cantonese cuisine has been dominating the Chinese catering industry for at least 50 years. For many diners, Chinese food means Cantonese food only. We want to enrich their understanding... Our restaurant group wants to be the game changer, we want the UK and the whole world to learn more about Chinese food culture through us.

The numbing spiciness is often surprising to diners who are new to Sichuan cuisine. Yue initiated a free refund and exchange policy to encourage diners to explore the new taste sensation in his restaurants. Behind this policy is Yue's commercial ambition and the company's financial strength, which cannot be matched by many small businesses in Chinatown. When describing the brand positioning of his restaurants, Yue stressed: 'we offer creative Sichuan cuisine rather than the traditional one... the idea is that we can cook in the way we like as long as the food is delicious'.

One of the newest Chinatown restaurateurs, Yin, also puts creativity and innovation at the heart of her business: 'We are never trying to make anything traditional or authentic', Yin said confidently, going on to add 'in my opinion and my own upbringing, Chinese food is borderless'. The restaurant project was described as 'a blank canvas' where she collages personally selected 'fragments' from different cultures. The foundations of most flavour profiles and dishes are based on traditions that she experienced in China and in her family, but she builds on and changes them. However, when she first launched a collection of unconventional steamed buns, the restaurant received many negative reviews from Chinese customers who claimed the way Yin makes buns is 'wrong'. Using the barbecue pork bun as an example, Yin explained that she reinvented the classic bun in order to 'improve' the meat texture, flavour and sauce to her personal liking:

> Yin: We fixed the sauce into something less sweet and it harmonises rather than covering the meat. We sourced one of the best meats. There is a mixture of fatty and lean cuts of pork. One of the biggest changes we did was putting lardo, an Italian cured bacon, into our pork buns. A lot of cured meats really bring out the meaty flavour... We didn't use any gelatin, instead there is actually sweet potato paste in our pork filling.

Yin believed in her taste buds and ignored the attack on 'authenticity', and one month later, she started seeing more positive feedback coming in. 'Authenticity also means original, like means what I've created, what is unique is also authentic, right?' Yin suggested. She has created an authentic Yin style of food combining nostalgia and modernity as a product of confident expressions of her transnational experiences in an increasingly globalised and hybridised world. The pork bun was the top seller at Yin's restaurant when we met.

The different migratory journeys and experiences of Eva, Wen, Yue, Yin and Dylan are embodied in the diverse culinary experiences curated by them. Among the five business operators, Dylan and his 'Dutch' pub have been largely excluded from most people's imagination of Chinatown. However, as business operators working in one of the most expensive and competitive commercial districts in global London, they all actively negotiate the idea of authenticity and their identities through everyday decisions in their business operations and in the sensory experiences they have created for diverse customers. They have used recipe and menu development strategies of adaptation, diversification and innovation to attract, accommodate and influence diners from different backgrounds, unsettling the essentialist idea of Chinatown as an authentic place of fixed ethnic difference.

Everyday Connection as Heritage

For the London-based regular visitors to Chinatown, the neighbourhood is part of the everyday urban landscape of their city. They keep on revisiting Chinatown because this place matters to them. They have developed diverse and multi-layered personal connections to the area through their frequent visits over the years. Place is a product of routes encompassing multiple layers of time (Massey, 2005) and Chinatown is embedded with multiple histories and identities. Regular visitors continually create and recreate connections to the area through their bodily interactions with Chinatown's built environment, in relation to certain moments/fragments of the urban space that they recognise from specific angles shaped by their socio–cultural–historical locations. In this section, I will use the life stories of six regular visitors, Jing-Mei, Yuk Fung, Cynthia, Ella, Sean and Hannah, who visit London's Chinatown a few times per month, to discuss the second category of everyday heritage-making practice, *everyday connection as heritage*. I will firstly introduce their different personal connections to London's Chinatown and explore how the emotional bonds have been shaped by their migration trajectories, sociocultural backgrounds, personal histories and current social needs. I will then discuss how they act as the 'authenticating agents' (Cohen & Cohen, 2012) of their own lived experiences and have been continually negotiating and making sense of 'my taste', 'my community' and 'my own culture' through their sensory, emotional and bodily interactions with Chinatown, challenging the essentialist ideas of authenticity, community and culture that have shaped the dominant narratives of London's Chinatown. For brevity, of the six regular visitors, I will selectively use the most illustrative life stories in the following discussion.

Different senses of place

The six regular visitors work in diverse sectors including education, healthcare, government and the creative industry. They often visit Chinatown for the culinary experience. Food was described by them as a way to stay close to other people or navigate different cultures, but it did not appear to be the focus of what they wanted to talk about in relation to Chinatown. Food as a topic seemed to serve as an opener to conversations related to their complex experiences and feelings about their personal journeys, which had been intertwined with the physical space of Chinatown. It is through their banal embodied actions of visiting, walking, looking, talking, listening, smelling, eating, shopping and meeting people, etc., that they have generated emotional bonds to, and invested everyday significance in, Chinatown as reflected in their specific 'collections of stories' (Massey, 2005) about the place. Smith (2006: 75) argues that heritage is about 'a sense of place':

> Heritage, particularly in its material representations, provides not only a physical anchor or geographical sense of belonging, but also allows us to negotiate a sense of social 'place' or class/community identity, and a cultural place or sense of belonging.

When talking about Chinatown, what most of them said reflected 'a sense of place' in different ways. To them, Chinatown is a significant place that not only represents but also evokes personal or family memories. During our interviews, which took place in Chinatown restaurants or on Chinatown streets, the six regular visitors often shared stories with me immediately after seeing, smelling, tasting, hearing or touching something in the physical space.

In 1973, four-year-old Jing-Mei left her hometown, a small village in Hong Kong, and got on a plane with her mother and siblings to reunite with her father in England. During the 1970s–1980s, like many Hong Kong families of that time who were determined to pursue better lives in Britain, Jing-Mei's parents worked in Chinese restaurants in different places, including what is now called London's Chinatown. For this reason, the area is special for Jing-Mei:

> Jing-Mei: I have 'grown up' in the area [Chinatown] … with family members working here, eating here … It's a regular place of visits even though I live miles away…I don't know how to describe it, this is my local.

'I am Cantonese, but I only speak English'. She said this like a scripted statement she carries heavily around with her. Jing-Mei's children are half Chinese and half Jamaican and did not learn Cantonese, so food has become a way of communicating among the three generations whenever language becomes a barrier. Visiting Chinatown for a family gathering over a meal is like practising a shared family 'language'.

Yuk Fung worked in an NHS hospital located in the Chinatown area in the 1980s. She is among many Chinese Malaysians who were recruited by the UK government to be trained as nurses. She described her reason for leaving Malaysia as 'running away from racial discrimination'. 'Chinese people in Malaysia were classified as second-class citizens', she explained frustratedly. However, she did not entirely escape discrimination. Yuk Fung told me that, as a racially minoritised person, she faced bullying and a glass ceiling within the NHS. Yuk Fung has been actively looking for a place or a community to which she can feel she belongs.

> Yuk Fung: Oh, Chinatown means a lot to me. It helps me to identify with my culture, my food, my past and my present too, and yeah, it's lovely. I feel comfortable coming here.

During the early 2000s, Cynthia went to a Chinese school near Chinatown. As a young child, she explored Chinatown through the gaze of her parents who were well-connected in the area, knowing many restaurateurs and being given special treatment. This place and its changes often evoke her childhood nostalgia. Cynthia described herself as a British-born Chinese who has experienced 'the blending of English or British culture with Chinese culture' in everyday life through languages and tastes. Watching people walking past us on the crowded Gerrard Street, Cynthia recalled a trip to Beijing when she was a teenager, which made her think that Chinatown is a 'British Chinese place':

> Cynthia: I felt it [Chinatown] was a representative space of my being, of my identity. It's like, we shared that same thing – we were born to be Chinese, but in a London, British context.

Ella moved from southwest England to London for career opportunities in 2019. She described herself as a white British German with Irish heritage. Growing up in different cultures makes it easier for her to bond with people who have shared experiences. The fact she has studied and worked in mainland China has shaped her connection to this central London space. Ella explained:

> Ella: I kind of felt a bit of a sense of belonging (in London), but for me more so in Chinatown than in other bits of London...I'd go and walk around in Chinatown during my lunch break and think, okay, these are familiar smells, familiar sounds, this is quite nice. So it's that sense of I was still in touch with China and my friends... but then again, you look at some of the colours and things. They're quite similar, but only really to a lot of the touristy areas in China...You don't see the gates everywhere in China, that's not on your general normal street, so it's kind of exaggerated, isn't it?

Sean left home, a small town near the border between Malaysia and Thailand, in 2016. A sense of not belonging there made him come to the UK. Visiting community organisations in Chinatown and making new friends there have been part of his journey of making London his new home. Sean stressed that the very word 'Chinatown' perhaps has influenced how he used to see the place, which left him with conflicted feelings:

> Sean: The word Chinatown has deep meanings, it's powerful. The word makes you automatically separate non-Chinese businesses in Chinatown from the rest in your mind...Chinatown is an important part of the history of overseas Chinese, but Chinatown's history is not entirely about Chinese people.

Jing-Mei, Yuk Fung, Cynthia, Ella and Sean invested personal attachment into this urban space in diverse ways shaped by their migration histories, personal experiences and current social needs. I have felt rich and different emotions carried in these stories: joyful, hopeful, nostalgic, confused, frustrated, uncertain, angry, a sense of belonging or not belonging. Cynthia and Ella have addressed the nuances about the cultural representation associated with Chinatown, but it is beyond a simplistic binary of thinking of Chinatown as being 'Chinese' or 'non-Chinese'. No matter if it is 'my local', 'a representative space of my being', 'my past and present' or 'a place to belong', they have created genuine emotional bonds to the area through their mundane and symbolic interactions with Chinatown.

Performing authentication: 'my taste', 'my community' and 'my own culture'

Much like most of the restaurant operators, the six regular visitors I interviewed actively brought up the topic of authenticity when describing their experience about and beyond food in different contexts. However, they appeared not keen to judge their notions of authenticity against a set of measurable criteria; instead, their reflections showed how they had been actively seeking to make sense of and authenticate their different lived experiences, which may or may not directly associate with London's Chinatown.

Yuk Fung recalled her early memories of dining in Chinatown, which was dominated by Cantonese-style restaurants at that time. Although there was a lack of diversity in the food landscape at that time – for example, Malaysian restaurants were rare – she gradually adapted her tastes and found the unfamiliar food available tasty. In this way, these flavours have become authentic to her:

> Yuk Fung: I remember when I went home to Malaysia and came back in the 1980s I couldn't eat the food there [in Chinatown] because it was just so different. But then after a while, I was like, oh yummy! Because you don't have anything else to compare (laughs)... If you want to have authentic Chinese food, you have to go to Chinatown!

In British public, political and media discourses, London's Chinatown is often described alongside the term 'community'. The word actually refers to different groups in different contexts, ranging from Chinatown workers (see e.g. Hui, 2020) to the whole Chinese population in London (see, for example, Sales *et al.*, 2011). Among the six regular visitors, there are also different ideas about who counts as 'the Chinatown community'. 'No one can take a claim over Chinatown because Chinatown belongs to so many people', Cynthia passionately argued. Instead of a singular and homogenous community, she thinks there are many different communities associated with Chinatown. Hannah, who previously studied in mainland China and Taiwan, visits Chinatown regularly. She found it challenging to define 'community' in the context of London's Chinatown, which 'many people have a sense of belonging towards, but they don't live in the area'. Hannah grew up in London and described herself as white British. She felt, however, that she is part of 'the community' of Chinatown in a symbolic way through her weekly visits. In contrast, Sean revealed that taking on a part-time waiter job in Chinatown had changed how he views this area.

> Sean: Of course everyone can belong to this so-called 'Chinatown community', but I feel community in this sense is not community enough...To me, the ideal group should be the people who work here.

The temporary change in his connection to Chinatown from a visitor to waiter makes him see Chinatown from the perspective of restaurant workers. 'They are under-represented, although they make up the majority of the workforce in Chinatown', Sean said. Physically involved in the everyday business operations and emotionally invested in his personal connections to co-workers, Sean wants to advocate for them by authenticating them as the 'ideal group' who should be called 'the Chinatown community', which he is part of.

Cynthia often referred to the politics of cultural representation when talking about Chinatown. She studied fashion and explored the idea of 'Chineseness' in many of her designs. Cynthia had decided to take a career break, as she explained:

> Cynthia: I was thinking about how much of it [Chineseness] was performed, and how much of it is my actual culture and my heritage, and how much of it is what I've read through the eyes of Western people... Especially walking through Chinatown is actually, like, told back to me from a Western point of view. And how much of it is my heritage that I've experienced with my family? Which bit of it is authentic? But then I was like, this is what I've lived, that's my lived experience, it should be authentic, because you've lived through it. And that's your own culture that you kind of created and that you live with every day.

Walking through Chinatown and seeing the exoticised Chinese symbols evoked conflicted emotions within Cynthia: 'The *difference* between cultures becomes what defines a culture from the view of the majority', she reflected, 'those differences become the bank of reference representing Chinese culture'. She wants to reverse the power relations and change people's perception of Chinatown, which sees Chinatown as a natural symbol of Chinese culture. Reclaiming Chinatown without neglecting the contested past of the area is important to her. It is a process for her to make sense of her authentic lived experience in the making of her own culture.

Performing as the 'authenticating agents' (Cohen & Cohen, 2012) of their own lived experiences, Yuk Fung, Hannah, Sean and Cynthia have been continually negotiating and making sense of their taste, their community, and their own culture, challenging the essentialist ideas of authenticity, community and culture that have shaped the popular narratives of London's Chinatown.

Everyday Encounter as (Non-)Heritage

Chinatown is a place where people can visit, spend time in or walk through (Figure 11.3). Quotidian use of the place does not always strengthen the connection between Chinatown and visitors, as the embodied actions of investing everyday significance in Chinatown are actively rather than passively taken by people. It is open for the visitors themselves to assess and interpret whether this place matters to them. In this section, I will use the life stories of three occasional visitors, Jade, Lei and Jie, who visit London's Chinatown a few times per year, to discuss the third category of everyday heritage-making practice, *everyday encounter as (non-) heritage*. I will firstly introduce their different types of visit to Chinatown. I will then examine their individual agency in transforming London's

Figure 11.3 Visitors on Newport Court, London's Chinatown (photo by Xiao Ma, 2022)

Chinatown into a 'lived everyday (non-)heritage space', contesting the racialised idea of Chinatown as a Chinese space.

Different types of visiting

Jade is a London-based Mandarin teacher in a secondary school. Reflecting on her life in this diverse city over the past ten years, she said: 'I have a multicultural identity'. Growing up in a middle-class family in the central part of mainland China, Jade first came to the UK to study, then decided to settle down out of her love for London. She visits Chinatown a few times each year; for her it is a place for social gatherings and for her students' school trips. In early 2022, Jade brought 20 students to Chinatown for a visit as part of their Mandarin course:

> Jade: I think Chinatown is a stepping stone for my students to learn different cultures while they can still stay in their comfort zone, because in Chinatown they can speak English to communicate, and they can see English architecture, people of different cultures and ethnicities. When I brought them to Beijing, the situation was different. They asked me, Miss, why is everyone here Chinese? (laughs)

Before the Covid-19 pandemic, Jade organised a few school trips to mainland China for the young Mandarin learners. She prefers, however, to take her students to London's Chinatown first, to prepare them before flying them to mainland China: 'Chinatown is a combination of London, English, Western culture and Chinese culture', she said. Jade utilises Chinatown as a 'bridge' and a 'transitional zone' for her students to explore 'some elements of Chinese culture' without feeling completely overwhelmed by 'cultural shock'.

In London's Chinatown, many businesses have stressed the importance of international students from China for their trade (The Making of Chinatown, 2019). Between 2020–2021, there were about 144,000 students from China studying at UK universities, making up 32% of all non-EU students (The Higher Education Statistics Agency, 2022). However, there is a lack of meaningful ties between these students and the early Chinese immigrants who came under different socioeconomic circumstances. Both Lei and Jie moved to the UK to study in 2019 and currently live in London. Chinatown is a place, which they would walk through as part of the London urban landscape, rather than paying a special visit. Jie grew up in a major city in Guangdong province, to which most early immigrants from Hong Kong have ancestral ties. Jie finds it thought-provoking when encountering Chinese people who migrated to the UK a few decades before her:

Jie: I noticed a group of older Chinese women in the area [Liverpool Street] and their fashion style and make-up style are from the 1980s or the 1990s! It was unforgettable. They reminded me of *Taohuayuan ji* (Tale of Peach Blossom Land), in the sense that they are frozen in a period of time…I have met more people like them in Chinatown. They have kept certain habits from the time just before they came to the UK. You can imagine that there will be a gap in cultural continuity.

Jie felt that the cultural differences between her and the group of people she described are shaped by not only the generation gap but also their different migration trajectories.

Lei grew up in a few places in mainland China and wants to find a job in the creative industry in London after graduation. When asked about his first impression of Chinatown, he said:

Lei: Chinatown is very much like China from the foreign gaze, emphasising elements like lanterns, traditional architectures and so on.

Lei used examples of stereotypical depictions of China and Chinese people in early Hollywood films to elaborate his point about 'the foreign gaze', and criticised them. Chinatown is a place he would like to walk past quickly; he did so when we met. With little bodily engagement with the physical surroundings, his body language sent one clear message – 'I don't want to be here'.

(Not) my Chinatown

Jade shared that her students were already interested in Chinatown before the visit because joining the school trip was on a voluntary basis. Jade recalled two memorable moments during the tour when some of her students engaged with the urban space at a personal level. An Urdu-speaking student had a brief encounter with a Chinese souvenir store owner of South Asian ethnicity. They chatted in Urdu, which became a special memory of that student's visit to Chinatown. Another student who had lived in mainland China for several years took his classmates into a Chinese supermarket and passionately showed them his favourite snacks. The teenager encouraged his friends to try new flavours, such as matcha and red bean: 'These snacks remind me of my childhood', he told Jade and she replied: 'they are my childhood too'! The connections between not only the people and the place but also among people themselves were strengthened to some extent, through the embodied acts of meaning-making.

Topics related to food and drink are important parts of the Mandarin curriculum. Jade is keen to find engaging ways for her students to learn new vocabulary. During their visit, the group went to a Chinese bakery: 'They were so excited to see pastries with different fillings and in different shapes', Jade recalled with a big smile, 'this is a great way to link to what they learnt in school'. As a Mandarin teacher, Jade's connection to Chinatown, as 'a stepping stone for my students', is strengthened during every positive learning moment facilitated by her students' bodily interactions with the place. The visit confirmed her existing understanding of Chinatown as a 'bridge' for her students.

In contrast, Jie and Lei came across as much less interested in Chinatown. Unlike Jade's Mandarin students, Jie and Lei, who grew up in mainland China, are not interested in having a 'cultural experience' in Chinatown for educational purposes; unlike Jing-Mei (regular visitor), Jie and Lei cannot directly draw on personal or family memories of the migration stories represented by Chinatown; unlike Cynthia (regular visitor), Jie and Lei showed little interest in reclaiming Chinatown as a more nuanced cultural representation, apart from simply stating that Chinatown is associated with the stereotypical depictions of Chinese people and culture. When talking about what Chinatown means to them, acts of reinforcing their existing beliefs related to Chinatown occurred:

> Jie: My view on Chinatown hasn't really changed since I first visited it in 2012 during my summer camp in London. It's a street for food. People come here to eat and I wouldn't think about anything else about this place. Or perhaps it's also about the stereotypes of us created by others...

> Lei: I don't think they're worth being called heritage. To me, most of the food I tried in Chinatown are not even good to my personal liking... If these restaurants were in Chengdu (capital city of Sichuan, mainland China), they wouldn't survive for more than two months.

There were 'heritage moments' (Smith, 2006) when Jie and Lei engaged with their ideas of Chinatown – 'a street for food' or 'China from the foreign gaze' – to make sense of their own cultural, social and migrant worlds, but Chinatown had no place in these worlds.

Conclusion

The physical space of London's Chinatown does not possess an innate quality as heritage; instead, Chinatown can be transformed into a 'lived everyday (non-)heritage space' by individuals to address their different contemporary needs and concerns. This ethnographic study has revealed that London's Chinatown is associated with diverse experiences, contested meanings and conflicting views that cannot be contained within the imagined ethnic and cultural confines, unsettling the essentialist ideas of Chinatown, ethnicity, culture and identity. The popular narratives about Chinatown as a conceived space emphasising fixed ethnic and cultural differences disconnect from how London's inhabitants work in, visit and symbolically experience the neighbourhood in relation to their complex connections to the past and to other places.

This research has identified three different but interrelated types of everyday heritage-making practices shaped by Londoners' different ways of using Chinatown and the different depths of their connections to Chinatown, namely: *everyday operation as heritage*; *everyday connection as heritage*; and *everyday encounter as (non-)heritage*. The three categories have revealed the diversification of meaning-making processes in Chinatown as a lived space and how the plural everyday heritage meanings are shaped by the intersection and interaction of multiple factors, including ethnicity, age, socioeconomic status, migration trajectories in family, personal histories and contemporary needs and concerns.

In the Chinatown branding strategies conceived by the area's different main stakeholders, the notion of Chinatown is constructed by amplifying some layers of time and identities incorporated in the urban space while silencing others. In contrast, this research has shown that Londoners continually engage with, negotiate and make sense of the multiple historical and contemporary trajectories and meanings associated with this central London space. More specifically, everyday heritage-making practices in Chinatown are intertwined with the dynamic social processes of authentication (Cohen & Cohen, 2012) undertaken by different individuals. Through their ongoing sensory, emotional and bodily interactions with the material surface of this contested neighbourhood, people's different lived experiences, embodied in the form of recipes and flavours, views of and feelings about Chinatown, or practices of (not) belonging and identification, become (temporarily) authentic to themselves. These authentic lived experiences may be in concordance with, in opposition to or without reference to the branded or popularised identity ascribed to Chinatown.

Places are produced out of social interactions within and beyond themselves (Massey, 2005). Cresswell points out that place is not about being but about becoming, and 'place in this sense becomes an event rather than a secure ontological thing rooted in notions of the authentic' (2004: 39). London's Chinatown is not a place where 'Chineseness' resides, but it is an ongoing event being produced out of ever-changing social relations associated with Chinese migration, which includes inter-ethnic relations, urban regeneration, anti-racism activism and international, national and local politics, etc. Place is not simply an end product of social processes but it is a process itself (Cresswell, 2004). Chinatown, as an event, in return acts as a tool for making, maintaining and transforming these relations in an increasingly globalised and hybridised world. As part of their everyday urban landscapes, Londoners continuously re/create and re/negotiate meanings related to Chinatown, in reference to certain fragments/moments of the urban space that they recognise from specific angles shaped by their socio-cultural-historical locations. Therefore, London's Chinatown cannot only be seen from one single angle. Homogeneous narratives about the area authenticated by a few 'representatives' or 'representative organisations', as are often found in media reports, 'official' marketing materials or government documents, need to be replaced with anti-essentialist, decentred, plural, complex and multi-layered narratives, which can do justice to the cultural complexities of Chinatown.

Notes

(1) These three gates (two on Gerrard Street and one on Macclesfield Street) were both designed and funded by Westminster City Council. However, Richard Swain of Westminster City Council's planning department, the designer of the gates has no Chinese cultural background. Richard Swain told a local newspaper, A&J, in 1984 that the gate design was the result of 'research at the V&A into authentic Chinese design'. According to an interview conducted by the Chinese Mental Health Association between 2012–2014 as part of the London Chinatown Oral History Project, Harry Lee, the then Chairman of the London Chinatown Chinese Association, proposed to build Chinese-style gates and gave visual examples to Westminster City Council for consideration. However, the council told him that they could not make them and the council used Richard Swain's gate design instead. As a result, an interpretation of Chinese-style gates was created and made into three iron gates between 1985 and 1986.

(2) 'Chinatown 倫敦華埠' can be seen on the street map shown in Figure 11.1. 倫敦 means 'London' in Chinese. 華埠 (Cantonese: Waa Fau 華埠, Mandarin: Huabu 华埠) is one of the three most common terms that Chinese speakers use to refer to the area. The other two terms are Tong Jan Gaai 唐人街 in Cantonese or Tangren Jie 唐人街 in Mandarin, and Zung Gwok Sing 中國城 in Cantonese or Zhongguo Cheng 中国城 in Mandarin.

(3) About Chinatown London, https://chinatownmarketing.co.uk/ (accessed 15 March 2022).

(4) Chinatown Directory, https://chinatown.co.uk/en/directory/ (accessed 15 March 2022).

(5) All interviewees' names are pseudonyms, and some non-sensitive personal information has been replaced with similar but unrelated information. All quotations from interview data recorded in Chinese have been translated into English by Xiao Ma.

References

Anderson, K., Ang, I., Del Bono, A., McNeill, D. and Wong, A. (2019) *Chinatown Unbound: Trans-Asian Urbanism in the Age of China.* London: Rowman & Littlefield International.

Barabantseva, E. (2016) Seeing beyond an 'ethnic enclave': The time/space of Manchester Chinatown. *Identities* 23 (1), 99–115.

Benton, G. and Gomez, E.T. (2008) *The Chinese in Britain, 1800-Present: Economy, Transnationalism, Identity.* Basingstoke: Palgrave Macmillan.

Chhabra, D. (ed.) (2021) *Authenticity and Authentication of Heritage.* Abingdon: Routledge.

China Exchange (2022) Chinatown Food Heritage Trail. *China Exchange.* Available from https://chinaexchange.uk/chinatown-food-heritage-trail/ (accessed 3 April 2022).

Chinatown London (no date) Chinatown London: Discover the real taste of East Asia. *Chinatown London.* Available from https://chinatown.co.uk/en/ (accessed 3 April 2022).

Chinese Embassy in the UK (2016) H.E. Ambassador Liu Xiaoming Attends the Ceremony to Celebrate the Completion of the New Chinese Gate in London Chinatown. *Embassy of the People's Republic of China in the UK.* Available from http://www.chinese-embassy.org.uk/eng/ambassador/dshd/2016ambevents/t1390754.htm (accessed 15 April 2021).

Chinese Embassy in the UK (2019) Ambassador Liu Xiaoming Attends Chinese New Year Celebration at Trafalgar Square. *Embassy of the People's Republic of China in the UK.* Available from http://www.chinese-embassy.org.uk/eng/EmbassyNews/t1640809.htm (accessed 15 April 2021).

Christiansen, F. (2003) *Chinatown, Europe: An Exploration of Overseas Chinese Identity in the 1990s.* London and New York: Routledge Curzon.

City of Westminster (2003) *Chinatown Action Plan: Consulting on the Future of Chinatown.* London: City of Westminster.

Cohen, E. (1988) Authenticity and commoditization in tourism. *Annals of Tourism Research* [Online] 15 (3), 371–386.

Cohen, E. and Cohen, S.A. (2012) Authentication: Hot and cool. *Annals of Tourism Research* 39 (3), 1295–1314.

Cresswell, T. (2004) *Place: A Short Introduction.* Malden, MA: Blackwell Pub.

Dahinden, J. (2016) A Plea for the 'De-migranticization' of Research on Migration and Integration. *Ethnic and Racial Studies* 39 (13), 2207–2225.

Dang, Q.D. (2021) Branding Chinatown and the opposition between national and local politics in the United Kingdom. *Observatoire de la société britannique* (26), 13–33.

Dummett, A. and Lo, J. (eds) (1986) *The Chinese Community in Britain: The Home Affairs Committee Report in Context.* London: The Runnymede Trust.

Giombini, L. (2020) Everyday heritage and place-making. *ESPES* 9 (2), 50–61.

Harvey, D.C. (2001) Heritage pasts and heritage presents: Temporality, meaning and the scope of heritage studies. *International Journal of Heritage Studies* 7 (4), 319–338.

Hui, A. (2020) London no longer has one Chinatown. It has many. *Resy.* Available from https://blog.resy.com/2020/08/london-no-longer-has-one-chinatown-it-has-many/ (accessed 10 December 2021).

Lefebvre, H. (1991) *The Production of Space.* Oxford: Blackwell Publishers.

Macdonald, S. (2013) *Memorylands: Heritage and Identity in Europe Today.* Abingdon: Routledge.

Massey, D. (2005) *For Space*. London: Sage.

Mosler, S. (2019) Everyday heritage concept as an approach to place-making process in the urban landscape. *Journal of Urban Design* 24 (5), 778–793.

Parker, D. (1998) Chinese people in Britain: Histories, futures and identities In G. Benton and F. Pieke (eds) *The Chinese in Europe* (pp. 67–95). Great Britain: Macmillan Press Ltd.

Pendlebury, J. (2009) *Conservation in the Age of Consensus*. Abingdon: Routledge.

Sales, R., Hatziprokopiou, P., Christiansen, F., D'Angelo, A., Liang, X., Lin, X. and Montagna, N. (2011) London's Chinatown: Diaspora, identity and belonging. *International Journal of Business and Globalisation* 7, 195–231. 10.1504/IJBG.2011.041832.

Shaftesbury PLC (2019) *Shaftesbury Annual Report 2019*. London: Shaftesbury PLC.

Smith, L. (2006) *Uses of Heritage*. London: Routledge.

Smith, L. (2020) *Emotional Heritage: Visitor Engagement at Museums and Heritage Sites*. London: Routledge.

The Higher Education Statistics Agency (2022) Higher Education Student Statistics: UK, 2020/21 – Where students come from and go to study. *The Higher Education Statistics Agency*. Available from https://www.hesa.ac.uk/news/25-01-2022/sb262-higher-education-student-statistics/location (accessed 1 March 2022).

The Making of Chinatown (2019) [Exhibition] China Exchange, London. 14 June 2019–30 August 2019.

Urry, J. (1995) How societies remember the past. *The Sociological Review* 43 (1), 45–65.

Walkowitz, J.R. (2012) *Nights Out: Life in Cosmopolitan London*. New Haven: Yale University Press.

Wang, C. (2016) Introduction: The 'material turn' in migration studies. *Modern Languages Open* p. None. https://doi.org/10.3828/mlo.v0i0.88

Wessendorf, S. (2013) Commonplace diversity and the 'ethos of mixing': Perceptions of difference in a London neighbourhood. *Identities (Yverdon, Switzerland)* [Online] 20 (4), 407–422.

Wu, H., Techasan, S. and Huebner, T. (2020) A new Chinatown? Authenticity and conflicting discourses on Pracha Rat Bamphen Road. *Journal of Multilingual and Multicultural Development* 41 (9), 794–812.

12 A Museum for Me: Place and Memory Making with Mujer Diáspora

Ailsa Peate and Lucia Brandi

Introduction

This chapter focuses on Colombian women migrants in London who are part of the autonomous network *Mujer Diáspora* (Diaspora Woman) and their engagement with *A Museum for Me* (*Un Museo Para Mí*), a project in which users create and curate miniature museums to tell their own stories.[1] These miniature museums are constructed from specially designed cardboard kits, part of a range of physical and digital resources the project has developed to facilitate memory- and place-making practices and self-directed representation and which fall under the umbrella of *A Museum of Me*'s product line (such as a make-your-own theatre, a timeline and a calendar). One of several outputs arising from AHRC-funded research *Memory, Victims and Representation of the Colombian Conflict* (2018–2021, MVR), the project created the activity *A Museum for Me* after identifying a lack of resources for women's representation in the Museo Nacional de Colombia (National Museum of Colombia, MNC), with whom the University of Liverpool worked to develop the resource in the form of the miniature museum activity. The kits provide an accessible tool that allows victims to curate personal memories and, moreover, to intervene directly in representations of the Colombian conflict. The aim is to make visible those victims who are too often excluded or misrepresented in public space. *A Museum for Me* supports work on memory and representation among community groups and networks of women victims in Colombia but also engages with Colombian migrant women in London, bringing stories from the diaspora into narratives of the conflict.

In this work, we analyse interactions between Mujer Diáspora and *A Museum for Me*, focusing on the function of museum-making kits in the performance and representation of individual and shared stories embodied by Colombian migrant women in London; in communicating the multi-layered, gendered identities and globalised yet localised experiences of diasporic victims of the Colombian conflict. We provide context by first introducing the Colombian conflict and issues of concern around historical memory practices regarding the visibility of women. Following a brief overview of the Colombian diaspora in London, we reflect on the identity of *Mujer Diáspora* as a social actor and cultural network of displaced women before moving on to consider four of Mujer Diáspora's interactions with the miniature museum kits. First, we discuss the Being Human Festival of 2019, when women piloted the kits at Latin America House in Kilburn, London. Next, we turn to the display of miniature museums created in the aforementioned workshop as part of an 'intrusive' exhibition at the MNC in Bogotá, Colombia, in February 2020. We then consider the women's involvement in co-creating a virtual museum in response to COVID lockdown, which showcases their own work and the creative testimony of a wider Colombian diaspora in London and beyond. Finally, we analyse the group's co-creation of *A Museum for Me* workshop and exhibition at the British Library in London for the 2021 Being Human Festival. We consider how these four interactions reinforce and nuance the gendered experiences of conflict and migration among Colombian women in London, and we situate these acts within a wider movement that uses innovative, creative forms to visibilise the stories of women victims. We note how the women of Mujer Diáspora in London prioritise self-representation, concluding that *A Museum for Me* contributes to memory- and place-making processes among women migrants. Furthermore, we argue the kits provide a mechanism for re-imagining the 'traditional' form and function of museums, empowering women in challenging the perspectives of patriarchal, Eurocentric museum spaces in London, Bogotá and beyond.

The Colombian Conflict

The Colombian conflict is one of the world's longest-running armed conflicts, with an estimated 220,000 deaths between 1958 and 2013 (see Grupo de Memoria Histórica, 2013) and approximately 60,000 forced disappearances (Centro Nacional de Memoria Histórica, 2016: 14). In 2018, the UN Refugee Agency estimated the number of displaced peoples at 7,671,124 (UNHCR, 2022). Currently, the total number of victims of all forms of violence associated with the conflict who are registered in the Registro Único de Víctimas stands at 9,250,453 (Unidad Víctimas, 2022). In June 2022, the Colombian Truth Commission presented its interim report, noting that 'If we had to observe one minute of silence for each victim of the armed conflict in Colombia, we would have to keep silent for 17 years' (de Roux quoted in Le Monde, 2022).[2] In rural Colombia in the 1960s and 1970s, guerrilla groups such as the FARC-EP (*Fuerzas Armadas Revolucionarias de Colombia—Ejército del Pueblo* [Revolutionary Armed Forces of Colombia – People's Army]) and the ELN (*Ejército de Liberación Nacional* [National Liberation Army]) set themselves against State-sponsored paramilitary groups intent on eliminating communist threats to the country. From the 1980s onwards, violent conflict continued because of the prosperity of drug lords, trafficking and state corruption. The conflict only officially ended in 2016, when the Peace Agreement brought a definitive ceasefire and the decommissioning of weapons on both sides of the political spectrum.

The conflict affected, and continues to affect, all aspects of Colombian society and political life, but it is important to note its disproportionate effect on women: this social group is more likely to be long-term affected by deaths and disappearances of male members of their families, leaving rural women destitute, displaced, and in poverty (Arnoso-Martínez *et al.*, 2017). Yet, women's experiences have, until very recently, been overlooked in narratives of the conflict (Arnoso-Martínez *et al.*, 2014 and 2017: 2; Delgado Rojas, 2017). We thus consider post-conflict identities from the perspective of the diaspora, taking into account the validity and purposes of symbolic reparations, which have been central in Colombia's discourse. Greeley *et al.* (2020) present symbolic reparations as:

> [...] a common juridical measure used to address human rights violations in the context of international law. Broadly distinguished from material and monetary measures, symbolic reparations are generally defined as non-pecuniary and can take many forms. They may be tangible, such as monuments, commemorative sites, memory museums and re/naming public spaces. Or they may involve more performative or ephemeral gestures of recognition and atonement, such as public apologies, annual ceremonies and rituals or performances. (2020: 166)

Symbolic reparations have been a significant feature of Colombia's move away from conflict, which has seen popular participation in the construction of historical memory. As a result, stories of women victims of the conflict are gradually becoming more visible. We consider this trend before turning to the Colombian diaspora in London and placing interactions between Mujer Diáspora and *A Museum for Me* into this context.

We argue that trends for greater agency among women victims and representation of their experiences find an echo and, moreover, reinforcement, in the memory practices of Colombian migrant women in London. Mujer Diáspora raise the profile of all Colombian women victims, and migrant women, staking their claim to recognition and representation. They clarify how victimising acts of the armed conflict – often unacknowledged – have pushed Colombian women into migration, which in turn constitutes another oft-unacknowledged, victimising act with long-term implications. By securing the participation of Colombian women in London and beyond and reinforcing the visibility of women victims, so Mujer Diáspora clarify and expand both narratives of the Colombian conflict and ongoing processes of transitional justice from the migrant perspective.

Conflict Narratives: Invisible Women

Colombia stands out as different to other transitional justice contexts in Latin America since its efforts towards symbolic reparations are linked to a very recent past, not one more distant as in Argentina or Chile. The push towards transitional justice was enshrined in the 2011 Victims and Land Restitution Law (Law 1448). Law 1448 delineates victims' rights to damages, rights to access to legal proceedings and, significantly, the foundations for symbolic reparations, which are presented in Article 141 of Law 1448 as being 'any provision made on behalf of victims or the community at large which serves to ensure the preservation of historical memory, the non-repetition of victimising events, public acceptance of the facts, the seeking of public forgiveness, and the restoration of the dignity of victims' (2011). Colombia's interactions with historical and traumatic memory do not point to the past but rather to the construction of a present and future: Article 142 of Law 1448 stipulates a National Day of Memory and Solidarity with Victims, and Article 143 outlines the state's responsibility to ensure civil society organisations advances in memory construction. Provision for the documentation of testimonies, participatory activities, exhibitions and performances, the creation of a National Centre for Historical Memory (Article 144, purposes Article 147) and the creation of a Memory Museum (Article 148) all demonstrate how Law 1448 highlights the construction of present and future. However, the immediacy of this approach has been interpreted as 'transitional justice without transition' (Weber, 2018: 89), given that the Peace Accords between the FARC-EP and the Colombian State were only signed in 2016.

Colombia's memory practices are thus taking place within a contested present, with little to separate it from a violent past; as Claire Taylor (forthcoming) observes, this push for symbolic reparations and the specificities of Law 1448 (2011) have led to a 'memory boom' in the country (Riaño-Alcalá, 2015: 286; Rios Oyola, 2015, both referenced by Taylor). Indeed, the 2016 Peace Agreement stipulated that three artworks be commissioned to commemorate the end of the conflict; one of these, *Fragmentos*, was created by and for women victims and is discussed below.[3] At times, top-down memory practices and monuments in Colombia feel unsettling, a form of state-sanctioned heritagisation of a bloody conflict whose scars are still very fresh. Yet, bottom-up approaches and practices are also multiplying, evidenced by 'thousands of local initiatives of memorialisation led by grassroots victims' associations' across the country (Rios Oyola, 2015: 11). This civil society momentum is meaningful for victims around the country and as well as in the diaspora: it contextualises the initiatives of women migrants in London who, as we will see, memorialise their experiences themselves and write their own narratives.

The Colombian Diaspora in London

Approximately 16,000 Colombians were living in the UK in 2021, primarily in London, according to the Office for National Statistics, although informal sources estimate almost double this number (McIlwaine, 2012: 4–5). The London diaspora is a particularly varied social group comprising elites, refugees, students, workers, and the motivations of Colombian migrants are fluid and nuanced. Historically, Colombian migration was predominantly to neighbouring Venezuela and to the US (Bermúdez & Cubreros-Gallardo, 2021: 187); however, during the last two decades of the 20th century, a shift occurred in favour of Europe. Earlier, as of the late 1970s, Colombians arriving in London mostly found employment in hospitality and cleaning (McIlwaine, 2014: 420) or other 'low-skilled, low-paid elementary jobs' (2014: 423), which McIlwaine attributes to newer migrants' lack of language skills. Migrants arriving in the 1980s were predominantly escaping heightened violence in Colombia in the wake of increasingly powerful cartels (McIlwaine, 2012: 4); in the 1990s, migration was more commonly documented as a direct consequence of the armed conflict (2012: 9).

During this same period, factors said to pull migrants towards the UK were its then 'strong' currency (McIlwaine, 2012: 10) and opportunities in London for English-language learning before subsequent government cuts to ESOL provision (Patiño-Santos & Márquez Reiter, 2019: 229). Earlier waves of migration also meant that family connections already existed in

London (McIlwaine, 2012: 9) and, at the time, obtaining a UK visa was perceived as feasible.[4] Thus, London was perceived as a place of working and learning opportunities and intangible cultural interest (McIlwaine, 2012), becoming a preferred destination for Colombian migrants, particularly the (more affordable) London borough of Southwark (Patiño-Santos & Márquez Reiter, 2019: 229). Indeed, the 1990s and early 2000s were a particularly bloody period for Colombia due to the expansion of paramilitaries to quell violence by left-wing guerrilla groups, notably in rural areas (Centro Nacional de Memoria Histórica, 2013: 156). McIlwaine (2014: 420) points to urban violence in Colombia as the primary factor driving up migration to London during this period (2014: 420), but acknowledges the consequences of armed conflict, which have affected the everyday lives of Colombian women. For example, the death of male family members in the context of an armed conflict can often lead to physical displacement, disruption or destruction of family networks and incomes and is significant in the motivations of women who, as single parents, seek stability and opportunities abroad (McIlwaine, 2012: 8). The subsequent siting of Colombian government Commissions in London is an acknowledgement of both the scale of migration towards London and the significance of the armed conflict in driving transnational displacement.

Mujer Diáspora and the Truth, Memory and Reconciliation Commission of Colombian Women in the Diaspora: Migrant Women in London as Agents for Change

Mujer Diáspora is an activist group of women of the Colombian diaspora, set up in London in 2014. The group has since forged relationships with the diaspora in the wider UK and Ireland and spread to Spain, Sweden, Belgium and Colombia for women returning home. Despite diverse backgrounds and motivations, group members are united by the shared experience as women escaping conflict, and the group's primary objective is to heal personal trauma and loss (Mujer Diáspora, 2018).

The size of Colombia's diaspora, like the number of victims of its conflict, is significant, and the Colombian Truth Commission is the first in history to include testimony from victims outside national boundaries.[5] The country's Peace Accords have recognised that the process of restoring peace to the country means all victims – wherever they may be located – should be recognised and included in symbolic reparations. For example, the Consolidation of the Truth Commission in the UK was set up as an extension of the Truth Commission in Colombia to specifically incorporate the migrant experience into its findings, thus expanding and clarifying its narrative of the conflict (Rodeemos el Diálogo, 2020). Similarly, London-based Mujer Diáspora operates as the lead hub for the Truth, Memory and Reconciliation Commission of Colombian Women in the Diaspora (TMRC). An international network of Colombian women, its aims are to 'empower women in the diaspora to become agents of change in the Colombian peace process and in their host countries' (Conciliation Resources, no date). Mujer Diáspora is therefore contextualised by the 2016 Peace Agreement, the Truth Commission's remit to reach out to the diaspora, and the Colombian State's moves towards symbolic reparations.

However, it would be misleading to characterise Mujer Diáspora as merely reactive to initiatives by the Colombian state: rather, the group was founded autonomously in the wake of events in Colombia and has been instrumental in creating demand from women in the diaspora for inclusion and acknowledgment. It has worked independently from, as well as in collaboration with, the Colombian Truth Commission, forging relationships with state and non-state actors in the UK and Colombia, including the academic community, to make visible Colombian women migrants as a community, and communicate experiences of the conflict from this perspective. In their own words, Mujer Diáspora are peace-builders and agents of social transformation, seeking to 'create a process as women that allows us to participate and position ourselves as agents of peace and social transformation' (Mujer Diáspora, 2018). The group's stated objectives include:

- Healing traumas caused by the conflict.
- Documenting experiences of the war and migration to contribute to ongoing truth, memory, and reconciliation processes in Colombia.
- Facilitating the integration process in the host country.
- Identifying skills and contributing tools towards the empowerment of women. (Mujer Diáspora, 2018) (our translation)[6]

Their language highlights how imperative agency is to their cause, in active participation in meaning-making, and in healing traumas resulting from the conflict. The group's interactions give credence to the women's own experiences, communicating that these are not forgotten. Moreover, they affirm how Colombian migrant women in London can – and do – contribute to the truth narrative, not least by clarifying that migration is not simply a victim's exit from conflict but another victimising experience to negotiate.[7]

Membership of Mujer Diáspora, therefore, intersects with the TMRC, who also positions women migrants as agents of change. The TMRC considers women to have specific perspectives and skills that can shape social history and restorative justice, invoking their lived experiences as 'sources of knowledge in a process of empowerment of the participants' (Conciliation Resources, no date) and arguing that the experience of migration has 'equipped the diaspora with skills and a certain worldview that can become fundamental assets in the quest of building a more peaceful, democratic and inclusive society' (Conciliation Resources, no date). The contribution of women in the diaspora is thus vital to creating historical, collective memory, and symbolic reparations that 'address the violent past' (Conciliation Resources, no date). This community, doubly implicated as both women and migrants, has nonetheless been crucially discounted. As a result, the TMRC has 'specifically focused our efforts on empowering women as agents of change, with the understanding that women experience conflict and migration differently to men and have therefore had a different set of skills and expertise that too often remain unnoticed' (Conciliation Resources, no date). Detail concerning these skills is not given, but their character is fleshed out in wider literature: Arnoso-Martínez *et al.* (2014, 2017) posit women's ability for coping strategies, for dealing with lower incomes, raising families alone and for maintaining more frequent contact with home as specific abilities ascribable to women experiencing conflict. They also note that even if women are more often secondary, rather than primary, victims of the conflict, they are more likely to pursue justice in the framework of symbolic reparations.

Mujer Diáspora are thus closely bonded to issues of individual and collective memory, trauma, healing and empowerment from a gendered, diasporic perspective. Their actions in London are contextualised by the wider impetus for post-conflict narrative construction, symbolic reparations and transitional justice: Their group identity, like that of the TMRC network, is bound up with events in Colombia. However, a defining characteristic is a focus on personal agency and capacity for transforming their context as migrant women in London. These themes are revisited as we discuss Mujer Diáspora's interventions on self-representation and interactions with *A Museum for Me.*

Women Curating Memory and Identity in Colombia and the UK

A range of cultural and creative forms have been instrumentalised by Colombian migrant women in London to perform their specific identities and illustrate why they should 'claim a voice' (Conciliation Resources, 2017) within the peace process. For example, in 2017, the TMRC participated in the Women and War Festival by showing a short film *Breaking the Silence*, that features members of the TMRC and Mujer Diáspora.[8]

This was accompanied by poetry readings, the photography exhibition *Imagine Peace* and a monologue by Colombian actor Alejandra Borrero about the experience of one TMRC member who had been kidnapped by armed traffickers before her escape to the UK. Thus, through film, photography, poetry and performance, migrant women in London organise creatively to underline the importance of stories and voices from the Colombian diaspora.

So, too, women creatively perform and address the contested and contesting identities of the diaspora: *Lilophilia* is the pseudonym of Liliana A. Romero, a Colombian migrant in London and graphic and visual artist whose artistic work demonstrates a clear preoccupation with visibility, agency and intersectional experience as a lesbian Afro-Colombian woman. Romero amplifies a voice seldom heard in Colombia; yet, rather than becoming further peripheralised by the migration experience, Romero outlines how her diasporic identity affords her visibility that was previously unattainable in Colombia:

> London's pluricultural pool led me to refine and reconsider aspects of my identity that I thought were essential to my personality. But as this notion of challenging the boundaries for identity grows, so does nostalgia for roots, for provenance, as well as an urgency of representation in the face of this tremendous city. London has allowed me to be more authentic in my work without abandoning the awareness of who I am: a Black, indigenous Colombian woman. (Romero, 2021)

The artist here highlights that it is precisely her migrant experience in London that has encouraged her self-expression and her self-identification, which is only truly possible outside her home country. The very existence of Romero's output within the London diasporic scene, as well as its character, signifies a certain visibility and power that was not previously accessible to her. She states, 'in a country like Colombia, making the decision to be an artist is both a privilege and a risk' (Romero, 2021), thereby implicitly acknowledging how migration to the UK has afforded certain opportunities, a space where the arena of politics and conversations around social issues are not so dangerously contested as in Colombia.[9] Romero's work thus communicates diverse identities and experiences, forms of resistance, and indeed, it demonstrates how the Colombian diaspora in London is multi-layered and interlinked. Romero has drawn portraits of individual members of Mujer Diáspora, highlighting their stories as migrant women, and released these portraits on her Instagram page to celebrate International Women's Day 2022; this formed part of initiatives by and for Latin American Women's Aid, a UK and European NGO that supports Latin American women of 'any cultural context, ethnicity, social class, religion, and sexuality' (Latin American Women's Aid, no date) who are fleeing sex-based violence. Such initiatives exemplify how Mujer Diáspora engages with a wide circle of agents in London and diverse media to pursue their psycho-social and political objectives.

This creative agency among the London diaspora feeds into and from a small but growing movement among women in Colombia, increasingly claiming visibility and representation and engaging with cultural and artistic memory practices to narrate conflict and peace from their own perspective. In fact, women's actions both at home and as part of the diaspora have directly echoed and reinforced one another. For example, mini-museums created in London using *A Museum for Me* kits by Mujer Diáspora have been exhibited alongside those of women victims in Colombia, and women have formed personal connections across the divide (discussed in the section 'Going home'). In Colombia, notable memorialisation projects and artworks by women include the award-winning *Tapices de Mampuján*, a series of tapestries created collaboratively between women members of the group *Mujeres Tejiendo Sabores y Sueños de Paz* (2006–present).[10] These textiles tell the story of the incursion of paramilitaries in the Afro-Colombian region of Montés de María and ensuing displacements and massacres of the early 2000s, and have been brought to the UK and Ireland. *Desenterrando Memorias* (2013–14) are pencil drawings of the conflict by Inty Maleywa, an artist who was embedded with the FARC-EP guerrilla and whose work forms a century-long overview of violence in Colombia. Meanwhile, the artist Erika Diettes has toured extensively and internationally with her large-scale multi-media installations that commemorate victims of the conflict, for example, *Sudarios* (2011), a series of huge shrouds featuring the faces of women victims from Antioquia. While *Sudarios* was displayed at Liverpool's Anglican cathedral in 2019, Diettes worked directly with local refugees and artists to co-create a response to this work.[11]

In terms of the representation of women victims on the national stage and Colombia's push for symbolic reparations, probably the most visible and lauded work has been Doris Salcedo's (2018a) artwork/art space, *Fragmentos*. The first state-sanctioned monument to the conflict commissioned in response to the 2016 Peace Agreement, the work is constituted of 37 tonnes of molten, decommissioned ex-FARC-EP weaponry, cast into floor tiles that cover a vast area and thus create the *Fragmentos Art and Memory Space*.[12] It was accomplished through the involvement of 20 women from the Colombian NGO *La Red de Mujeres Profesionales y Víctimas* (Network of Women Professionals and Victims, La Red), who had experienced sexual violence during the conflict. As women hammered matrix tiles into moulds for the molten gunmetal, they symbolically and physically hammered the pain and trauma of sexual violence into the tiles, leaving disfiguring traces on them, intended as a metonym for the conflict. Thus, women's collective action converted decommissioned weaponry into both artwork and arts space. For the next 50 years – the approximate length of the conflict – *Fragmentos Art and Memory Space* will house artworks and exhibitions on the conflict. Significantly, Salcedo's explanations of *Fragmentos* reference her rejection of conventional ideas of monumentalisation, born from the violent, colonial past:

> I preferred not to construct a monument because, as its name indicates, a monument is monumental; it hierarchically structures and presents a triumphant vision of a nation's warring past. Its principal function is to make us small as individuals against a grandiose, totalising version of the past. (Salcedo in Esferapublica.com, 2018b) (our translation)

Salcedo's interpretation of the counter-monument is significant as it suggests that the violent, colonial past is the place from which the concept of monumentalisation is borne: The lack of conventional monumentalisation in *Fragmentos* and its collaborative involvement of a grassroots group of women victims (La Red) are deliberate acts that challenge such a discourse, an example of what Hite and Collins (2009) have termed 'counter-memorial mobilising', or deliberate acts that challenge conventional discourse.

A Museum for Me: Women Reimagining the Museum

Colombian migrant women's engagement in London with *A Museum for Me* speaks to the same representative practices as *Fragmentos;* first, however, we must recall that 'museum', like 'monument', is also contested and problematic, not least because of the centrality of elites in museum spaces, and the erasure or peripheralisation of non-elite social classes. Of equal concern is the conceptual association between 'museum' and 'colonisation': Decolonial Theory and New Museology are growing research fields continually deconstructing how museums perpetuate state-sponsored narratives to the benefit of elites (see, for example, Chipangura, 2020; Lonetree, 2012; Matherne & Quaintance, 2019; McCall & Gray, 2014), while obfuscating the person and experiences of non-elites. Chipangura (2020) has termed the museum a 'product of Western modernity which deployed ethnocentric approaches in knowledge production' (2020: 432); in other words, it typically functions to disseminate narratives akin to the values of (white, male) elite social classes. If *Fragmentos* – state-commissioned and curated – is both monu-ment and 'counter-monument', so too, we argue, *A Museum for Me* is both 'museum' and 'counter-museum', a vehicle for women in Colombia and London to reimagine an important site of contestation.

Colombia's premier museum space is the MNC, located in a former penitentiary in Bogotá's business district. Since 2018, anticipating its 200th anniversary in 2023, the MNC has employed a new mission state-ment that includes a focus on inclusivity: 'We recognise that the National Museum's mission is to be a meeting place where citizens of Colombia come into contact with the world and our heritages, so they can dialogue, celebrate, recognise and reflect on what we were, what we are, and what we will be' (Museo Nacional, 2021 [our translation]). This statement was taken as the starting point for fieldwork at the Museum in 2019 by MVR, during which time Peate was Research Associate on the AHRC-funded grant and undertook research at the MNC that was both quantitative (documentation of all objects and displays) and qualitative (interviews with staff from different departments and career stages) with the view to define missing narratives and offer ways forward for visibilisation of women victims and activity creation for self-representation considering the Museum's holdings.[13] The MNC study problematised the disjoint between curatorial intent and output at the museum, interrogating how, if at all, accounts of marginalised groups had been developed and pre-sented in the space in relation to the Colombian conflict. Having identified the lack of visibility of women victims, despite their frequently affected status (given that women are more likely to both be direct victims of the conflict as well as indirect victims, having to deal with its consequences [Arnoso-Martínez, 2017]), MVR responded by working with two wom-en's NGOs in Colombia to develop a means of improving women's visibil-ity at the MNC, and in other memory spaces. These groups were contacted directly by the project's PI, and relationships were built with online and in-person meetings throughout the lifespan of the AHRC-funded project and its ongoing legacy activities.

During a series of workshops, women victims of the conflict from the NGOs *La Ruta Pacífica de las Mujeres* (a national organisation) and *Corporación Zoscua* (an organisation based in the Boyacá region) created their own miniature museums that would go on display at the MNC, using the kit specially designed between the University of Liverpool and the MNC.[14] The kit comprises three large printed sheets of cardboard with images and outlines to be cut, glued, coloured and fashioned into a mini-museum, furnishing women with a space in which to tell their own stories. Their use encourages creation and self-curation, siting agency in the hands of the user, and a mechanism of participatory visibility via the miniature museum to the wider museum space. Thus, in the very location where the invisibility of women victims of the conflict had been identified, women's mini-museums became the mainstay of an 'intrusive' exhibition. A simple, expandable display module in bright yellow began gradually occupying increased space in one of the MNC's exhibition halls, as these first creations were supplemented by others made by visitors using the *A Museum for Me* kits, with the 'intrusion' eventually spreading to walls, porticos and columns. The MNC exhibition would eventually close in 2022, but similar workshops and exhibitions are continuing at smaller, community-curated museums and memorial sites around Colombia using *A Museum for Me* kits.[15]

We will return to the discussion of this intervention at the MNC when we consider Mujer Diáspora's own creations, but to begin, it is worth noting some key characteristics of this experience that are definitive of interactions with *A Museum for Me*. Firstly, from the perspective of women victims, the process itself of participating in museum-making workshops is as valuable as any final product. Secondly, the activity offers a mechanism for mediating the differing perspectives of museum institutions, NGOs and the general public. Indeed, it speaks to what Antón *et al.* (2018: 1407) consider as adding value, such as the knowledge the creator/curator has on entering museum space or after they leave, that they are engaged in 'value creation' focused on themselves as beneficiary (2018: 1409). Finally, the activity's dynamic character challenges what Hite and Collins (2009) term the 'deadening' effect of traditional museum displays since it grows and changes as visitors participate and creations intrude on any available space. *A Museum for Me* opens up performative spaces within museums and galleries for interrogating curatorial control; in both Bogotá and London, when traditional gatekeepers loosen – or lose – their grip over the curation of memory, unforeseen consequences follow, and the character of the practice become yet more dynamic. We trace these characteristics now as we discuss interactions between Mujer Diáspora and *A Museum for Me*, starting in London in 2019, reaching out to the MNC in early 2020, expanding into digital space later the same year, and returning to London in 2021.

A Museum for Me and Mujer Diáspora: Four Instances of Engagement

Starting out: Mujer Diáspora at Being Human 2019

Having been piloted in Colombia with members of Corporación Zoscua and La Ruta Pacífica de las Mujeres, *A Museum for Me* kits were first introduced in the UK at the *Casa Latina* in London for the 2019 Being Human Festival. Workshops were held with children at the centre learning or reinforcing Spanish as a heritage language and a closed group for members of Mujer Diáspora.[16] Mujer Diáspora's strong group identity and capacity mean it can readily engage participants in activities that speak to their aims, i.e. to engage with symbolic reparations and healing for women victims of the Colombian conflict. Consequently, group members arrived for the *A Museum for Me* workshop already motivated towards the topic, and most had brought with them personal objects, photos or other memorabilia to display inside the mini-museums they would create. As participants spent several hours cutting, colouring, drawing and arranging items, working simultaneously but individually, so their primary focus was on the activity in hand rather than one another. These characteristics of the activity allow participants to work at their own pace, to choose what they articulate, and to voice memories and feelings as quiet 'asides' with a neighbour or as comments shared with the whole group. *A Museum for Me*, therefore, assumes a level of sensitivity and consciousness around memory practice on the part of the focus group facilitator, the participants, or the workshop facilitator.

Included is an example of a museum created in the workshop,[17] accompanied by the words in English and Spanish of its creator, Martha Elsesser.[18] Martha names her museum 'Apoyo / Support' to commemorate the support she enjoys from Mujer Diáspora and narrates its contents and process of creation. The main space recreates a living room: on one wall are drawings or objects that communicate recurring 'mysteries and contradictions' in her migrant journey, such as 'time/untimely, roots/uproots [...] sunshine/darkness, loneliness' (Elsesser, 2022); on another wall is a two pence coin, a drawing of a red London phone box, and a sketch of a smartphone, illustrating the theme of communication (as in Figure 12.1).

> Twopence coins, diligently saved in a heavy purse, hundreds of coins with enough value to mutter just simple words – I love you; I miss you – before the cruel sound of the telephone reminds you that the conversation was over, it is time to hang up, cutting with cruelty the umbilical cord that connects me with what was familiar for me, leaving me like an orphan.
>
> The truth now is that I don't need the twopence coins anymore; I have WhatsApp! What I don't have is the loved ones that I had to leave behind. (Elsesser, 2022)

In this way, the quintessentially British telephone box becomes a symbol of difference, localisation, migration, and distance, of the necessary reconstruction of identity in a new, highly specific context, at once

Figure 12.1 'Apoyo/Support', Martha Elsesser (photo courtesy of amuseumforme.org)

highlighting how Martha reacts to place and engages in place-making. A simple coin placed inside a paper structure has become a profound memory object infused with experiences that are uniquely individual, emotions that are often shared, and a narrative that speaks eloquently to anyone who listens. Such creatively communicated narrative, we argue, is a testament to the power of counter-memorial mobilisation: in this 'counter-museum' – a diminutive (literally and metaphorically) museum space, an 'amateur' work of art, a home-spun memorial – is embedded a narrative that spans time, nations, lives, identities, technologies. It amplifies a seldom-heard voice above the monumental noise of a capital city.

Going home: Mujer Diáspora at the Museo Nacional de Colombia

Following the *Casa Latina* workshop, Mujer Diáspora's mini-museums were briefly seen at Tate Liverpool in a one-day workshop in December 2019 before travelling in February 2020 to the MNC.[19] In Bogotá, they joined the museums made by women victims in Colombia to form part of an 'intrusive exhibition' at the MNC (see Figure 12.2), which remained in place for over a year.

This exhibition at the MNC was significant for the London group for two reasons in particular: first, Mujer Diáspora consider artistic articulation to be central to their work and symbolic reparations, stating 'the

Figure 12.2 The opening of the exhibition 'A Museum for Me' at the National Museum of Colombia (photo courtesy of amuseumforme.org)

transformation of testimony into a piece of art is a symbolic form of recognition and of thanks to the women who share their story' (Mujer Diáspora, 2018). At the MNC, the group's participatory art practice was placed centre-stage in the largest, most-frequented museum in Colombia. Second, *A Museum for Me* workshops encourage conceptual and interpersonal connections between participants; this is visually reinforced by placing miniature museums made by women in the diaspora alongside those made by women in Colombia. Messages of resilience, peace, mourning, loss and healing are clearly echoed and reinforced across the range of creations, regardless of where their creators are located.

On this question of location, despite being at a considerable distance of place, Mujer Diáspora have been visibilised at Colombia's National Museum: *A Museum for Me* creations by women victims in the diaspora are physically situated alongside all women victims. The diaspora's centrality within this highly contested space – that of Colombia's National Museum and the country's official narrative of the conflict – is evident; the testimony of migrant women, expressed within miniature museums, is carried from London to a country to which some will never return, in an act of immense symbolism and tangible expression. Life stories that might otherwise remain hidden in the periphery of the Colombian diaspora are centralised and visibilised. Migrated, London identities are communicated to a Colombian public, to the Colombian state and to other victims; the inherent tensions of the migratory experience for Colombian women victims are articulated, always living with one foot in each place. Thus, the exhibition in Colombia of mini-museums created by migrant women in London, alongside those of (under-represented) women victims of conflict in Colombia, represents a symbolic and physical act of place-making and place-taking across borders.

For these reasons, we argue that the presentation of women's mini-museums and micronarratives at the MNC in 2020 chimes with 'counter-memorial mobilising' (Hite & Collins, 2009), seen in, for example, 'counter-memorial collective actions' which the authors regard as rejecting and challenging the 'staid, sedentary and deadening character of conventional monuments and memorials by inviting dynamic, provocative, public interaction' (2009: 383). The participation of Mujer Diáspora in the exhibition challenges traditional museum practice, not only because it places front and centre a social group more commonly erased from view but because of the evocative nature of its metonymy. Those missing – migrated – women whose personal, self-curated experiences are nevertheless on display become an indexical referent for a wider existential condition, i.e. women victims of the conflict living as migrants in London. Visitors see how the women's lives are marked by absence through this presence of their creative traces, echoing the effect of traces left by women in *Fragmentos*. Mujer Diáspora's place and belonging within the exhibition and museum space is not questioned; rather, their identity as victims and survivors of the Colombian conflict is reinforced through this empowering act of metonymic self-display.

Reaching out: Mujer Diáspora co-creating a virtual museum

Soon after the original exhibition launch, COVID forced the MNC to close its doors; nevertheless, the MNC quickly expanded its online offer, showing the exhibition online and re-designing *A Museum for Me* kits as downloads. *A Museum for Me* in the UK acted in the same vein, offering downloadable kits free to school teachers and later to the general public via the BBC 'Get Creative' website.[20] In fact, the move to virtual working encouraged *A Museum for Me* to re-imagine yet again the form and function of museum: lockdown had arrived just as *A Museum for Me* and

Mujer Diáspora were working with the UK & Ireland Representative to the Colombian Truth Commission planning workshops and social events outside London to reach the wider diaspora. The final deadline for submitting victim testimony to the Commission was fast approaching, so there was an urgent need to raise awareness of the support available within the UK for sharing victim testimony. Therefore, Mujer Diáspora joined with *A Museum for Me* in co-creating a virtual museum that would function as a digital platform for outreach during COVID and was launched in May 2020 during the University of Liverpool's *Culture Unconfined* festival. It was never intended to replace the kits, workshops or physical exhibitions but as an additional forum and mechanism of engagement with the diaspora. The virtual museum highlights work in Colombia by community organisations who collaborate with the university's MVR research project and, importantly, by Mujer Diáspora in the UK; for example, testimonial, psycho-social, artistic and cultural activities that the group undertakes with civil society partners, such as the TMRC, and the UK & Ireland Hub in Support of the Colombian Truth Commission.[21] Accordingly, Mujer Diáspora reached out to its members, partners and extensive diasporic network to source new and existing digital material for the virtual museum; a relationship of co-production between Mujer Diáspora and *A Museum for Me* intensified, which would lead later to still further collaborations.

In this iteration as a virtual museum, *A Museum for Me* continues its focus on memory, victims and representations of the Colombian conflict, the impetus behind the original kits. The digital museum challenges identity-blind representations and memorialisations of violence and instead highlights memorials, testimony, artistic production and performance, human rights advocacy, and documentation by women and women-led groups, such as Colombian women migrants in London are visibilised alongside their counterparts in Colombia. Thus, in echoes of the MNC exhibition, women in-country and in-diaspora are conceptually and digitally co-located, both as victims of conflict and as agents of social change. Other parallels lie in the underlying vision informing the original kits and exhibition, i.e. participation, co-creation, self-representation and the enterprise of co-curating a virtual museum with a dynamically changing, ever-expanding form.

Importantly, both these processes reflect and reinforce a transnational, cultural momentum for women's visibility as victims and as transformers of the Colombian armed conflict. Stories of resistance, repression and migration are communicated in the virtual museum through myriad forms such as poetry, music, spoken word, dance, photographic essays, and visual and textile arts.[22] This testimonial and vindicatory content tell uniquely individual stories while speaking for and to a wider community of over-looked victims and peacemakers. It testifies to the acuity of the arts in communicating difficult truths and the real-world meaning of cultural production with a social purpose. Perhaps the London Colombian diaspora, and Mujer Diáspora particularly, might even be characterised by the presence of such cultural activists / activist-artists; at least, the earlier-mentioned 'memory boom' in Colombia appears to be as energetically creative in the diaspora. That said, it is important to note, as Elston (2020) does, that the new wave of official, institutional memory initiatives in Colombia exists in tension, and sometimes direct contention, with 'grassroots, non-official memory initiatives led by human rights groups, peace activists, victims of state crimes, relatives of the disappeared and those displaced by the conflict' (2020: 4). In this respect, the virtual museum performs the important function of visibilising bottom-up initiatives that, moreover, do not represent creative articulations of memory as mere spectacle or artefact.

In any performative space that memorialises narratives of conflict, tensions between production and reception will exist. Even when memory practices transgress and transform emblematic spaces – as with the 'intrusive' exhibition at the MNC – there are inherent risks and contradictions. The same is true in terms of the virtual museum: for example, its potential for greater reach and inclusivity than a single in-person event must be set against the exclusionary, socially divisive character of a high-tech medium; the socio-political risks of exposure in unregulated cyberspace must be set against the creative autonomy and visibility it offers to contributors. Some tensions we may struggle to reconcile, but others we should accept: the museum houses grave and stark testimony, yet perhaps there is no contradiction in characterising the museum as uplifting creative practice and content: the grief of personal memory and testimony, and the life-affirming energy of human solidarity and cultural creativity, co-exist in this space, as they do in the everyday lives and activities of victim and migrant groups. One truth does not obliterate another; each truth is true and claims its own space. In *A Museum for Me*, Mujer Diáspora articulate both the injustices and joys that have brought them together as women, migrants, victims of conflict and agents of change.

Claiming space in global London: (Per)forming identities at the British Library

In shaping the virtual museum, Mujer Diáspora's agency is clear: its engagement in place-making and in the construction of localised (or glocalised) identities as Colombian women in global London is enhanced by and enhances continued engagement with museum-making and reinvention. This disposition and capacity were reinforced in a second event by *A Museum for Me* for the 'Being Human' festival, *Museum Reinvented,* co-created with Mujer Diáspora, the UK & Ireland Hub, and the Latin American Women's Rights Service (LAWRS).[23] Hosted at the British Library in 2021, this iconic space with a global profile lent an intensity to the ongoing interrogation of narratives of conflict and representations of victims, displacement and migration, being undertaken by women migrants in London with *A Museum for Me.*

Mujer Diáspora thus utilised public-facing space in the British Library for communication and consciousness-raising with the public, the migrant groups present and between members. For example, a self-curated display of personal memory objects functioned to attract public interest and communicate stories of home, exile, conflict, women's networking and peace-building; videos, talks and materials were shared among the participant groups, and Zoom calls conducted with *A Museum for Me* in Colombia; kits were used to memorialise the migration experiences of young Londoners of Colombian heritage; and importantly, Mujer Diáspora members worked with the 'Timeline' (Figure 12.3) to help them recall key moments and persons in the group's history. The 'Timeline' is another *A Museum for Me* tool, a folded, printed sheet that opens out concertina-style to reveal a timeline with questions prompting users to write, draw or build a collage that traces their past, present or future. It encourages reflection on the passing of time, external forces and the accumulative impact of everyday experiences and decisions. Moreover, it functions as a bridging tool to introduce reflection considering personal stories with those represented by museums and public memorials; in other words, it is a simple device to foster critical interaction with 'official' narratives, engage in the self-curation of memories, and reimagine museums as polyphonic, co-created spaces.

Of significance and relevance to these ongoing critiques and interventions, the event was instrumentalised by Mujer Diáspora and the UK & Ireland Hub to make formal, public submissions of their own narratives. Four publications were received by the Curator of Printed Collections of the British Library Americas Collections.[24] These communicate experiences of the Colombian conflict from the migrant perspective and embody their stories and sentiments. As she submitted Mujer Diáspora's own book *Poetic Memories* (2019), Marta Hinestroza, an activist with Mujer Diáspora and the UK & Ireland Hub and participant in both Being Human events with *A Museum for Me*, commented: 'We have been working to include testimonies, stories [...] they reflect, they depict the reality

Figure 12.3 'Timeline', part of the suite of A Museum for Me activities (photo courtesy of amuseumforme.org)

of what we have lived through during the armed conflict […] our pain but also our resilience […] so that they form part of the history of Colombia'. With these words, the intentionality of the act is made clear: Colombian women in London consciously, publicly, actively curate, memorialise and document their memories and (gendered) experiences as victims, as migrants and as survivors.

Characterising the relationship of Mujer Diáspora and *A Museum for Me* in this way is not to gloss over the trauma that women have memorialised in miniature museums and timelines and other cultural co-production; rather, the intention is to recall the power of memory practices as devices that impede and obstruct, or facilitate and foster, women's agency as writers of their own narratives, and the narratives of war, conflict and peace.

Conclusion

Just as shared experiences of victimising acts do not collapse women's identities to a single identity as a victim, neither does migration reframe a woman's identity to only that of 'migrant'. Rather, women – like everyone – inhabit multiple identities at different moments, or indeed all at the same time. In this series of engagements between *Mujer Diáspora* and the *A Museum for Me* kits, we can see how acts of cultural custodianship, co-production and curation of memory reveal the women's many-layered identities. The interactions demonstrate a clear drive for place- and memory-making on the part of women in London's Colombian diáspora; creating these miniature museums has encouraged reflection on their current geographical and emotional status in London and an incorporation of earlier migrant experiences in the capital into their construction of contemporary migrant identities in a global London. Various Mujer Diáspora members have participated on more than one occasion in London-based events and taken on significant roles, such as introducing the activity to other members of their own organisation, to members of other Latin American diaspora groups, or to the public. This demonstrates a degree of empowerment and visibility for women in the London Colombian diaspora and affirms both a need for and disposition towards place-making activities among migrant women. Furthermore, it demonstrates how migrant women in London have exercised their right to complete, clarify and modify institutional depictions of the conflict from which they have fled. Their interventions – creating miniature museums for public exhibition, documenting their collective timeline, populating a virtual museum with content, publishing narrative from the migrant perspective – do more than supplement existing narrative; rather, they introduce counter-narrative and use Hite and Collins' (2009) terminology again, constitute acts of counter-memorial mobilising. The women's agency within and beyond their interactions with *A Museum for Me* also signals how institutional bodies (e.g. the British Library; the University of Liverpool; the Colombian Truth Commission; the MNC) and grassroots agents (Mujer Diáspora; the UK & Ireland Hub; TMRC) can move past unidirectional encounters, and closer towards genuine exchange and legacy. Of course, none of the interactions with any of the women's NGOs in Colombia or the UK would have been possible without support from the AHRC, nor the fieldwork at the MNC, which led directly to the creation of the miniature museum kits. We must thus recognise that the features of Eurocentric academia sit in the background of these activities as well as in their very design and construction. However, we would also argue that the NGOs involved have benefitted from enhanced visibility in their involvement with the project, which has also equipped the groups with networking and pedagogical skills as the NGOs have themselves begun to run their own workshops on *A Museum for Me* in their own communities, with participants like

Martha of Mujer Diáspora taking an active role speaking at events aimed at the general public, introducing her museum and widening knowledge about Colombian women in the UK.

Placing personal stories within miniature museums unites a group of women migrants in London; the display of these works at the National Museum of Colombia, alongside those created in situ, unites women victims across time and space and highlights their indelible identity as Colombian women. The exposition of personal stories in iconic spaces such as the MNC and the British Library also speaks to the benefits of the performative display, a step on the path to healing and justice in the context of symbolic reparations. Women in both the diaspora and 'at home' demonstrate a disposition to engage with participatory, artistic and curatorial practices, and become both subject and object of reflection. Within and beyond *A Museum for Me*, Mujer Diáspora have slowly considered and rapidly activated their multi-layered identities in London. Their acts of place-making with *A Museum for Me* acknowledge national borders but also transgress them; so too, they transgress expectations of museum space and curation of memory. At the same time, *A Museum for Me* speaks to the women's existing practice: it places gendered, migrated identities centre-stage; it gives an exposition and clarification of truths that help others *and* wider society to recognise and understand the migratory experience as a victimising act of the Colombian conflict. In sum, it monopolises on their capacity for participatory, creative, transformative actions and reveals their identity as agents of social change.

Mujer Diáspora are continually seeking opportunities for visibility and symbolic reparations within the context of the Colombian conflict. *A Museum for Me* reinforces and is reinforced by this creative energy and commitment among Colombian migrant women in London to curate and represent their past and to determine the shape of their present and future.

Notes

(1) All quotes, newspaper reports, etc., cited in this chapter have been translated into English by the author(s) or given in the original source and noted in-text.

(2) Postponed by COVID, the interim report was eventually released on 28th June 2022, just days after the election of Colombia's current president, Gustavo Petro, a former guerrilla fighter who is seen to represent a potential new start for the war-torn nation.

(3) One of these monuments was to be placed at the headquarters of the United Nations in New York and another in Cuba. The artist Mario Opazo was selected to create the second monument, *Kusikawsay*, which was inaugurated on the sculpture patio of the UN in August 2019. Nothing is currently known about the status of the monument in Cuba.

(4) As of October 2022, visa requirements for Colombian nationals entering the UK have been lifted.

(5) At the end of the 2000s, it was estimated that 1 in 10 Colombians were living abroad (McIlwaine & Bermudez, 2011)

(6) Where translations have been contributed by the authors, this appears with '(our translation)' immediately afterwards.

(7) Public communication by Mujer Diáspora at the inaugural performance of 'La Lancha de la Poesía', a poetic homage to victims of the Colombian conflict, October 2022, Colombian Consulate, London.

(8) This film, directed in London in 2016 by Ingrid Guyón, is now one of Mujer Diáspora's exhibits in its virtual museum; see https://www.amuseumforme.org/performance-space-for-me/

(9) Between 2016 and 2016, 120 social leaders were assassinated in the country. See: https://www.eltiempo.com/colombia/otras-ciudades/el-mapa-de-los-lideres-sociales-asesinados-en-colombia-184408.

(10) See https://fundacioncompartir.org/noticias/mujeres-tejiendo-suenos-sabores-de-paz for images of the textiles (Spanish only).

(11) Work by Erika Diettes is also featured in the virtual museum co-created between Mujer Diáspora and *A Museum for Me*. See https://www.amuseumforme.org/exhibition-space-for-me/

(12) The work raised anger from some ex-FARC-EP combatants, who interpreted the use of only FARC-EP weaponry as overlooking the Colombian State's own involvement in the bloodshed (Cortés, 2018).

(13) See https://www.liverpool.ac.uk/languages-cultures-and-film/Memory-Victims-and-Representation-of-the-Colombian-Conflict/.

(14) The Ruta Pacífica de las Mujeres is a nationwide feminist NGO which works towards transitional justice through the visibilisation of the effects of the war on women; Corporación Zoscua is an organisation based in the Boyacá region of Colombia, focused on social justice and human rights for victims of the conflict in the region, with a strong membership and leadership of women.

(15) See https://www.liverpool.ac.uk/languages-cultures-and-film/Memory-Victims-and-Representation-of-the-Colombian-Conflict/Memory/Grassroots-Museums-and-Memorials/

(16) *Casa Latina*, or Latin American House London, is an NGO and community centre for migrants, founded in the 1980s, and now permanently based in Kilburn. See https://casalatina.org.uk/.

(17) This miniature museum has been selected for inclusion as its owner, Martha Elsesser, has been involved in events featuring *A Museum for Me* since this first activity in the UK, and has spoken about her museum at most of the interventions laid out in this chapter. The authors thus have a good understanding of the aims and meanings of this museum.

(18) Martha Elsesser's museum can be viewed at https://www.amuseumforme.org/a-museum-for-me/

(19) The first UK-based *A Museum for Me* workshop was held at Tate Liverpool and took place during 'Tearing Up the Past', a Tate Exchange residency, 10–15 December 2019, on conflict and artistic resistance in Latin America, and curated by Dr Jordana Blejmar: https://www.tate.org.uk/whats-on/tate-liverpool/tearing-past.

(20) BBC 'Get Creative at Home' website https://www.bbc.co.uk/programmes/p0778tx6

(21) The UK & Ireland Representative to the Colombian Truth Commission, Peter Drury, provides formal liaison between the Colombian entity and the UK diaspora; the UK

and Ireland Hub in Support of the Colombian Truth Commission ('the UK & Ireland Hub') is an independent group within a network, comprising volunteers specifically trained to interview and support migrated victims in submitting identified or anonymous testimony to the Truth Commission; see https://comisionverdadcol-eu.org/en/commission-in-europe/; the virtual museum can be accessed via https://www.amuseumforme.org/ or http://unmuseoparami.org/.

(22) For example, London-based artists' ensemble *Hada Candelaria* performs a multimedia re-creation of Angelica Quintero's poem #MeSalvé, which communicates the true story of Rosita (Rosa Gómez), seriously wounded in a targeted attack in Colombia, but who continues her human rights work in London to the present day.

(23) The young women's group 'Sin Fronteras', coordinated by LAWRS, undertook a virtual *Museum for Me* workshop during the lockdown in 2020 and took this opportunity in 2021 to engage in person.

(24) These are *Una maleta colombiana* (2021), a collection of diasporic testimonial prose, edited by Carlos Beristain, a Colombian Truth Commissioner; de Isusi (2020) *Transparentes: Historias del exilio colombiano*, that narrates testimony in comic form; Grupo Internodal de Género 2020 work *Mujeres*, a 'Declaration of Feelings and Intentions' by the gender caucus of the European network of hubs in support of the Commission; and Mujer Diáspora (2019) *Poetic Memories*, an illustrated collection of poetry, prose and narratives by the group, edited and illustrated by Maria Victoria Cristancho, and published by UK-based NGO Conciliation Resources.

References

Antón, C., Camarero, C. and Garrido, M.J. (2018) Exploring the experience value of museum visitors as a co-creation process. *Current Issues in Tourism* 21 (12), 1406–1425.

Arnoso-Martínez, M., Beristain, C.M. and González-Hidalgo, E. (2014) Collective memory and human rights violations in the western Sahara: Impact, coping, and demands for reparation. *Peace and Conflict: Journal of Peace Psychology* 20 (4), 552–73.

Arnoso-Martínez, M., Cárdenas Castro, M., Beristain, C. M. and Afonso, C. (2017) Armed Conflict, Psychosocial Impact and Reparation in Colombia: Women's Voice. *Universitas Psychologica* 16 (3), 1–12.

Beristain, C.M. (2021) *Una Maleta Colombiana: La experiencia del exilio colombiano y la Comisión de la Verdad*. Bogotá: Verdad Sin Fronteras.

Bermúdez, A. and Cuberos-Gallardo, F.J. (2021) Colombian-Spanish migrants in London since the great recession: Political participation and attitudes amid (dis)integration processes. *Migraciones* 51, 181–205.

Breaking the Silence/Rompiendo el silencio (2016) Dir. Ingrid Guyón, London.

Centro Nacional de Memoria Histórica (2016) *Hasta encontrarlos: el drama de la desaparición forzada en Colombia*. Bogotá: Centro Nacional de Memoria Histórica.

Chipangura, N. (2020) Co-curation and new museology in reorganizing the Beit Gallery at the Mutare Museum, Eastern Zimbabwe. *Curator: The Museum Journal* 63 (3), 431–446.

Comisión de la Verdad (2020) *Declaración de sentimientos e intenciones: Grupo Internodal de Género*. Berlin: Comisión de la Verdad.

Conciliation Resources (2017) *Colombian Women Take Centre Stage at UK Festival*. See www.c-r.org/news-and-insight/colombian-women-take-centre-stage-uk-festival (accessed March 2022).

Conciliation Resources (No date) *Truth, Memory and Reconciliation Commission of Colombian Women in the Diaspora*. See www.c-r.org/our-work-in-action/truth-memory-and-reconciliation-commission-colombian-women-diaspora (accessed March 2022).

Congress of the Republic of Colombia (2011) 'Law 1448 of 2011'. See: https://www.unidadvictimas.gov.co/sites/default/files/documentosbiblioteca/ley-1448-de-2011.pdf (accessed March 2022).

Cortés, J. (2018) *Rabia entre los exguerrilleros de las FARC por el monumento de Doris Salcedo*. See https://www.las2orillas.co/rabia-entre-los-exguerrilleros-de-las-farc-por-el-monumento-de-doris-salcedo/ (accessed June 2022).

Diaspora Woman and Cristancho, M.V. (eds) (2019) *Poetic Memories of Colombian Women in the Diáspora*. London: Conciliation Resources.

Diettes, E. (2011) *Sudarios*. See https://www.erikadiettes.com/sudarios (accessed June 2022).

De Isusi, J. (2020) *Transparentes: Historias del exilio colombiano*. Bogotá: Comisión de la Verdad de Colombia.

El Tiempo (2022) *El mapa de la vergüenza*. See https://www.eltiempo.com/colombia/otras-ciudades/el-mapa-de-los-lideres-sociales-asesinados-en-colombia-184408 (accessed June 2022).

Elston, C. (2020) Open wounds: Commemorating the Colombian Conflict. In C. Gilbert, K. McLoughlin and N. Munro (eds) *On Commemoration: Global Reflections Upon Remembering War*. Oxford: Peter Lang.

Elsesser, M. (2022) *Un Museo Para Mí*. See: https://www.amuseumforme.org/a-museum-for-me/ (accessed June 2022).

Greeley R.A., Orwicz, M.R., Falconi, J.L., Reyes, A.M., Rosenberg, F.J. and Laplante, L.J. (2020) Repairing symbolic reparations: Assessing the effectiveness of memorialization in the inter-American system of human rights. *International Journal of Transitional Justice* 14 (1), 165–192.

Grupo de Memoria Histórica (2013) ¡*Basta ya! Colombia: memoria de guerra y dignidad*. Bogotá: Imprenta Nacional.

Hite, K. and Collins, C. (2009) Memorial fragments, monumental silences and reawakenings in 21st-century Chile. *Millennium: Journal of International Studies* 38 (2), 379–400.

Latin American Women's Aid (No date). Homepage. See https://lawadv.org.uk/en/ (accessed April 2022).

Le Monde (2022) Colombia truth commission delivers interim report on decades of armed conflict. See https://www.lemonde.fr/en/international/article/2022/06/30/colombia-truth-commission-delivers-interim-report-on-decades-of-armed-conflict_5988494_4.html (accessed June 2022).

Lonetree, A. (2012) *Decolonizing Museums: Representing Native America in National and Tribal Museums*. Chapel Hill: University of North Carolina Press.

Matherne, N. and Quaintance, H. (2019) Meaningful donations and shared governance: Growing the Philippine heritage collection through co-curation at the field museum. *Museum Anthropology* 42 (1), 14–27.

McCall, V. and Gray, C. (2014) Museums and the 'new museology': Theory, practice and organisational change. *Museum Management and Curatorship* 29 (1), 19–35.

McIlwaine, C. and Bermudez, A. (2011) The gendering of political and civic participation among Colombian migrants in London. *Environment and Planning A* 43, 1499–1513.

McIlwaine, C. (2012) The Colombian Community in London. See https://www.qmul. ac.uk/geog/media/geography/docs/research/latinamerican/McIlwaine-Report-on-Colombians-in-London.pdf (accessed February 2022).

McIlwaine, C. (2014) Everyday urban violence and transnational displacement of Colombian urban migrants to London, UK. *Environment & Urbanization* 26 (2), 417–426.

Mujer Diáspora (2018) Quienes somos. See www.mujerdiaspora.com/nosotras (accessed April 2022).

Mujeres Tejiendo Sabores y Sueños de Paz (2006-present) *Tapices de Mampuján.* See: https://fundacioncompartir.org/noticias/mujeres-tejiendo-suenos-sabores-de-paz (accessed November 2022).

Museo Nacional (2021) Quiénes somos – Misión. See www.museonacional.gov.co/el-museo/quienes-somos/Paginas/Quienes_somos.aspx (accessed March 2022).

Office for National Statistics (2021) Population of the UK by Country of Birth and Nationality. See https://www.ons.gov.uk/peoplepopulationandcommunity/populationandmigration/internationalmigration/datasets/populationoftheunitedkingdombycountryofbirthandnationality (accessed October 2022).

Onciul, B. (2015) *Museums, Heritage and Indigenous Voice: Decolonising Engagement.* New York: Routledge.

Patiño-Santos, A. and Márquez Reiter, R. (2019) Banal interculturalism: Latin Americans in Elephant and Castle, London. *Language and Intercultural Communication* 19 (3), 227–224.

Riaño-Alcalá, P. (2015) Emplaced witnessing: Commemorative practices among the Wayuu in the Upper Guajira. *Memory Studies* 8 (3), 282–297.

Ríos Oyola, S.M. (2015) *Religion, Social Memory and Conflict: The Massacre of Bojayá in Colombia.* London: Palgrave Macmillan.

Rodeemos el Diálogo (2020) *The Consolidation of The Truth Commission in the United Kingdom* (web editorial). See https://uk.rodeemoseldialogo.org/2020/04/tc-10/ (accessed October 2022).

Romero, L.A. (2021) My art is a cry for help, a call to action. See https://amlatina.contemporaryand.com/editorial/conversation-liliana-a-romero-lilophilia/ (accessed March 2022).

Romero, L.A. *Lilophilia.* https://www.instagram.com/lilophilia/ (accessed March 2022).

Salcedo, D. (2018a) *Fragmentos.* Bogotá: Espacio de Arte y Memoria.

Salcedo, D. (2018b) Doris Salcedo: Este contramonumento será un museo de arte contemporáneo y memoria. See https://esferapublica.org/nfblog/doris-salcedo-este-contra-monumento-sera-un-museo-de-arte-contemporaneo-y-memoria/ (accessed June 2022).

Taylor, C. (forthcoming) Memory practices 'from below': Mnemonic solidarity, affect, and counter-monuments in the practices of Zoscua, Colombia. *Memory Studies.* https://doi.org/10.1177/17506980231170350

UNHCR (2022) Colombia. See www.unhcr.org/uk/colombia.html (accessed March 2022).

Weber, S. (2018) From victims and mothers to citizens: Gender-just transformative reparations and the need for public and private transitions. *International Journal of Transitional Justice* 12, 88–107.

Index

Milton Keynes UK
Ingram Content Group UK Ltd.
UKHW021441040124
435476UK00036B/233